The other day, while I was waiting in line for the register at a bookstore, there was a junior-high school student holding a JUMP magazine standing behind me.

A while later, I recognized a familiar drawing of Ryoma...

It was the first time I'd seen anyone purchase my manga. I felt quite happy for the rest of the day.

To those of you who buy it, thank you very much.

Takeshi Konomi

About Takeshi Konomi

Takeshi Konomi exploded onto the manga scene with the incredible **THE PRINCE OF TENNIS**. His refined art style and sleek character designs proved popular with **Weekly Shonen Jump** readers, and **THE PRINCE OF TENNIS** became the No. 1 sports manga in Japan almost overnight. Its cast of fascinating male tennis players attracted legions of female readers, even though it was originally intended to be a boys' comic. The manga continues to be a success in Japan. A hit anime series was created, as well as several video games and mountains of merchandise.

THE PRINCE OF TENNIS
VOL 6
The SHONEN JUMP Graphic Novel

STORY AND ART BY
TAKESHI KONOMI

English Adaptation/Gerard Jones
Translation/Joe Yamazaki
Touch-up Art & Lettering/Andy Ristaino
Graphics & Cover Design/Sean Lee
Interior Design/Terry Bennett
Editor/Michelle Pangilinan

Managing Editor/Elizabeth Kawasaki
Director of Production/Noboru Watanabe
Editorial Director/Alvin Lu
Executive Vice President & Editor in Chief/Hyoe Narita
Sr. Director of Acquisitions/Rika Inouye
Vice President of Sales & Marketing/Liza Coppola
Vice President of Strategic Development/Yumi Hoashi
Publisher/Seiji Horibuchi

Printed in the U.S.A.

Published by VIZ, LLC
P.O. Box 77010
San Francisco, CA 94107

SHONEN JUMP Graphic Novel Edition
10 9 8 7 6 5 4 3 2 1
First printing, February 2005

www.viz.com

THE WORLD'S
MOST POPULAR MANGA

SHONEN JUMP

GRAPHIC NOVEL

www.shonenjump.com

Shonen Jump Graphic Novel

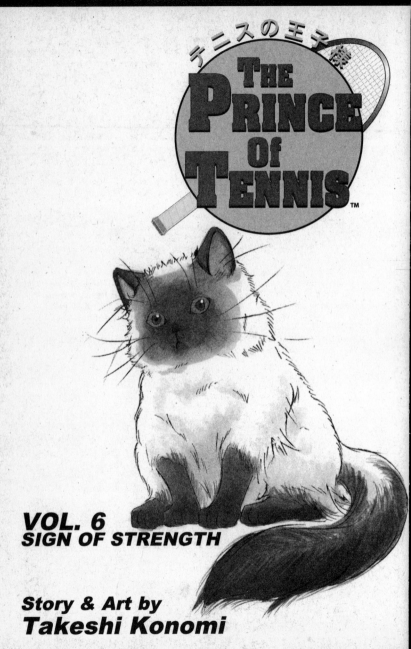

テニスの王子様

THE PRINCE OF TENNIS™

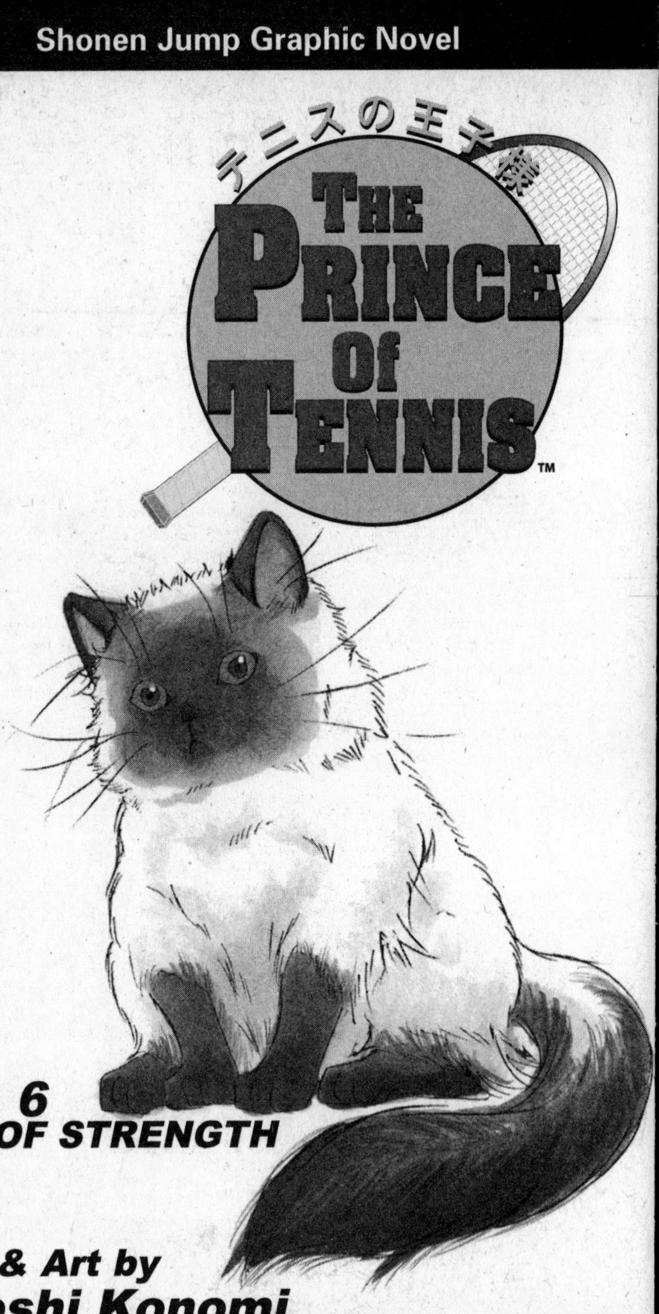

VOL. 6
SIGN OF STRENGTH

Story & Art by
Takeshi Konomi

THE PRINCE OF TENNIS

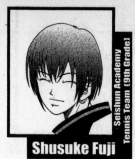

Shusuke Fuji
Seishun Academy Tennis Team [9th Grade]

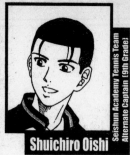

Shuichiro Oishi
Seishun Academy Tennis Team Alternate Captain [9th Grade]

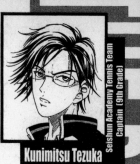

Kunimitsu Tezuka
Seishun Academy Tennis Team Captain [9th Grade]

STORY & CHARACTERS

VOLUME 1 ▶ 6

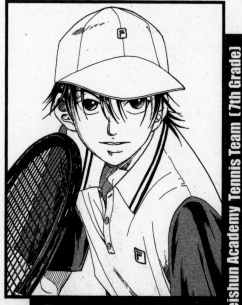

Ryoma Echizen
Seishun Academy Tennis Team [7th Grade]

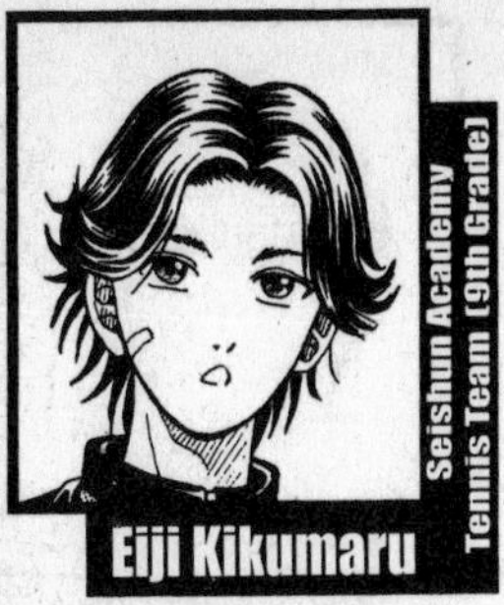
Eiji Kikumaru
Seishun Academy Tennis Team (9th Grade)
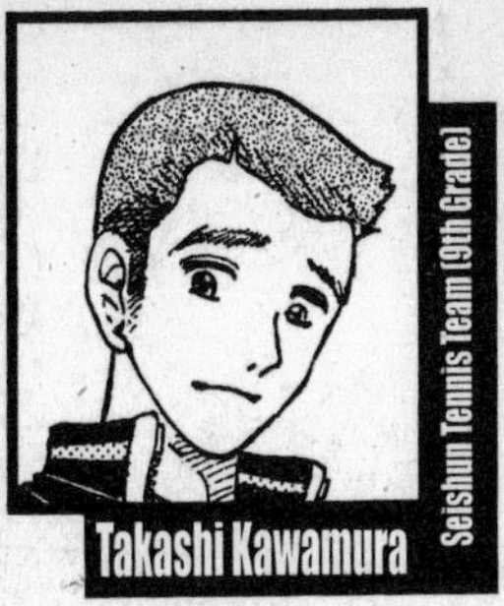
Takashi Kawamura
Seishun Tennis Team (9th Grade)
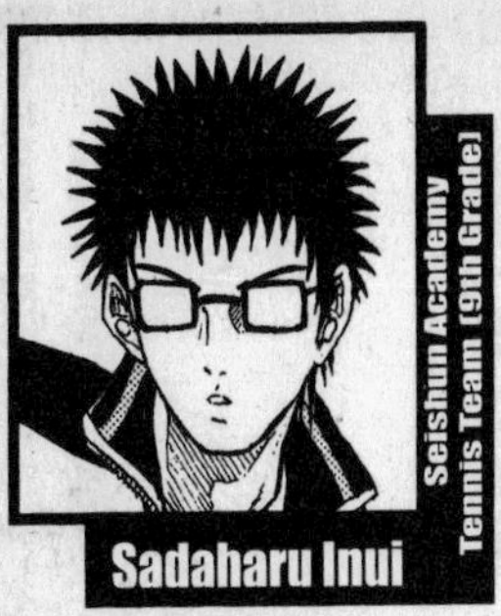
Sadaharu Inui
Seishun Academy Tennis Team (9th Grade)
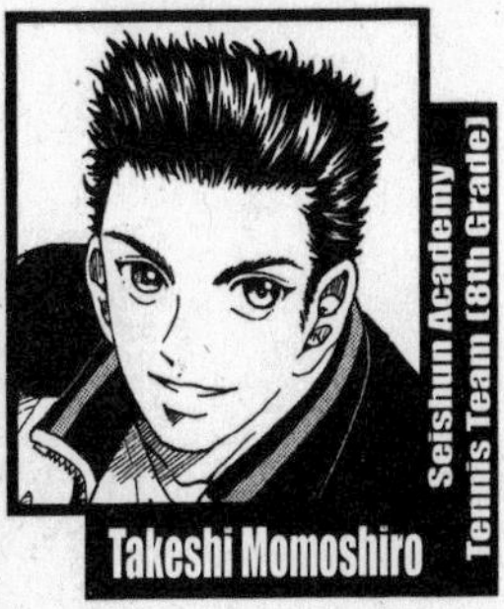
Takeshi Momoshiro
Seishun Academy Tennis Team (8th Grade)
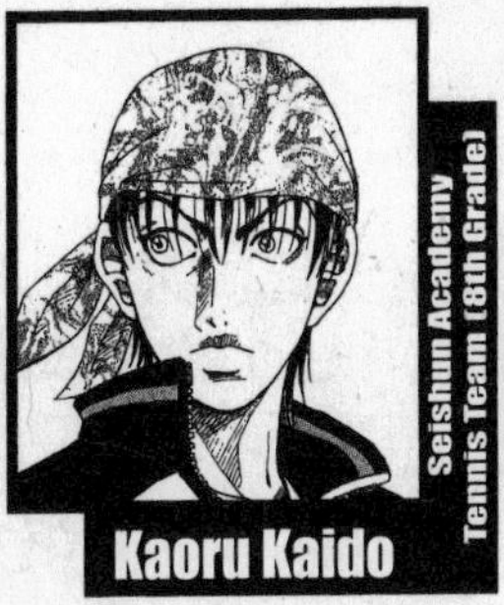
Kaoru Kaido
Seishun Academy Tennis Team (8th Grade)
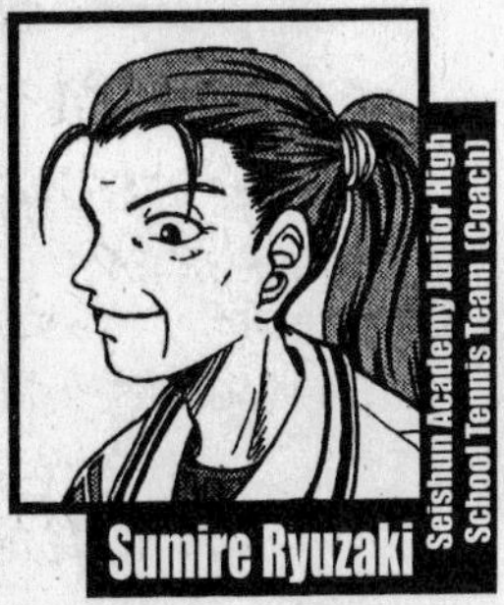
Sumire Ryuzaki
Seishun Academy Junior High School Tennis Team (Coach)

Ryoma Echizen, a tennis prodigy and winner of four consecutive US Junior tournaments, has returned to Japan and enrolled at Seishun Academy Junior High. To everyone's astonishment, he becomes a starter in the District Preliminaries while still in 7th grade, and helps his team advance easily to the finals against Fudomine Junior High.

Ryoma plays his match with a cool head until he suffers a cut eyelid from an accident involving his own racket. Yet through his brilliant play he still wins and hands Seishun the coveted District championship! Next up is the City Tournament...!!

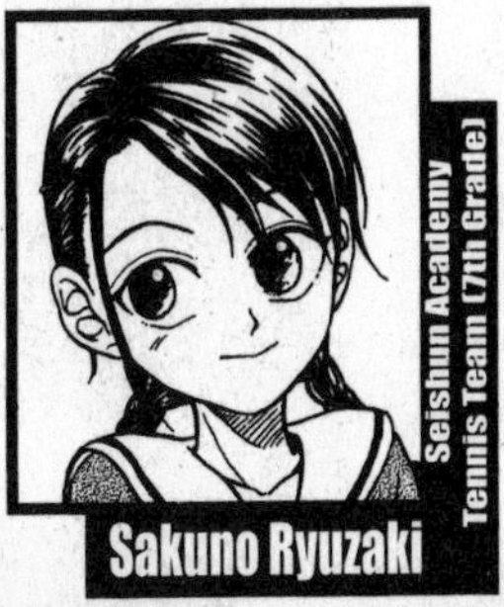
Sakuno Ryuzaki
Seishun Academy Tennis Team (7th Grade)
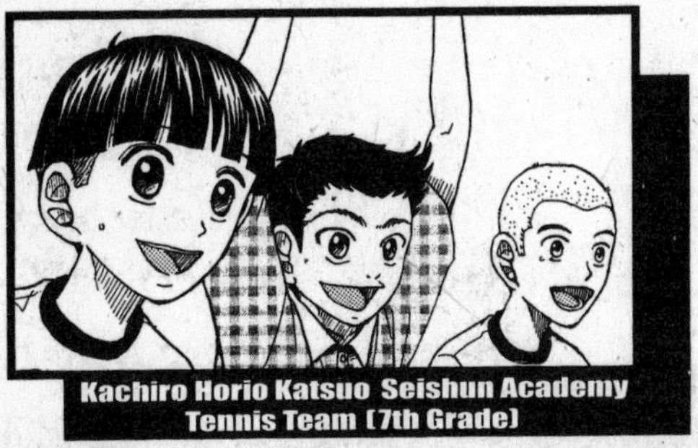
Kachiro Horio Katsuo Seishun Academy Tennis Team (7th Grade)

Contents

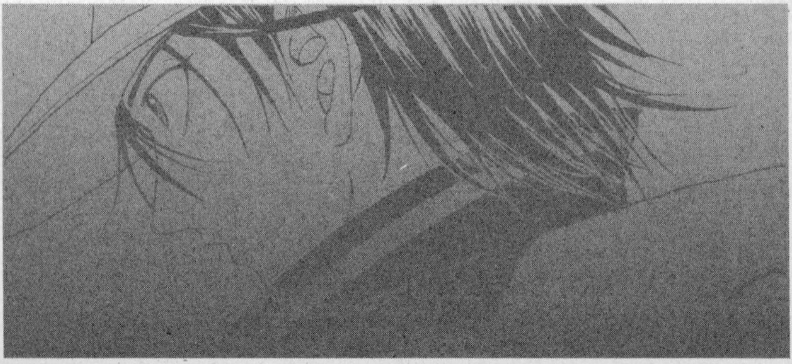

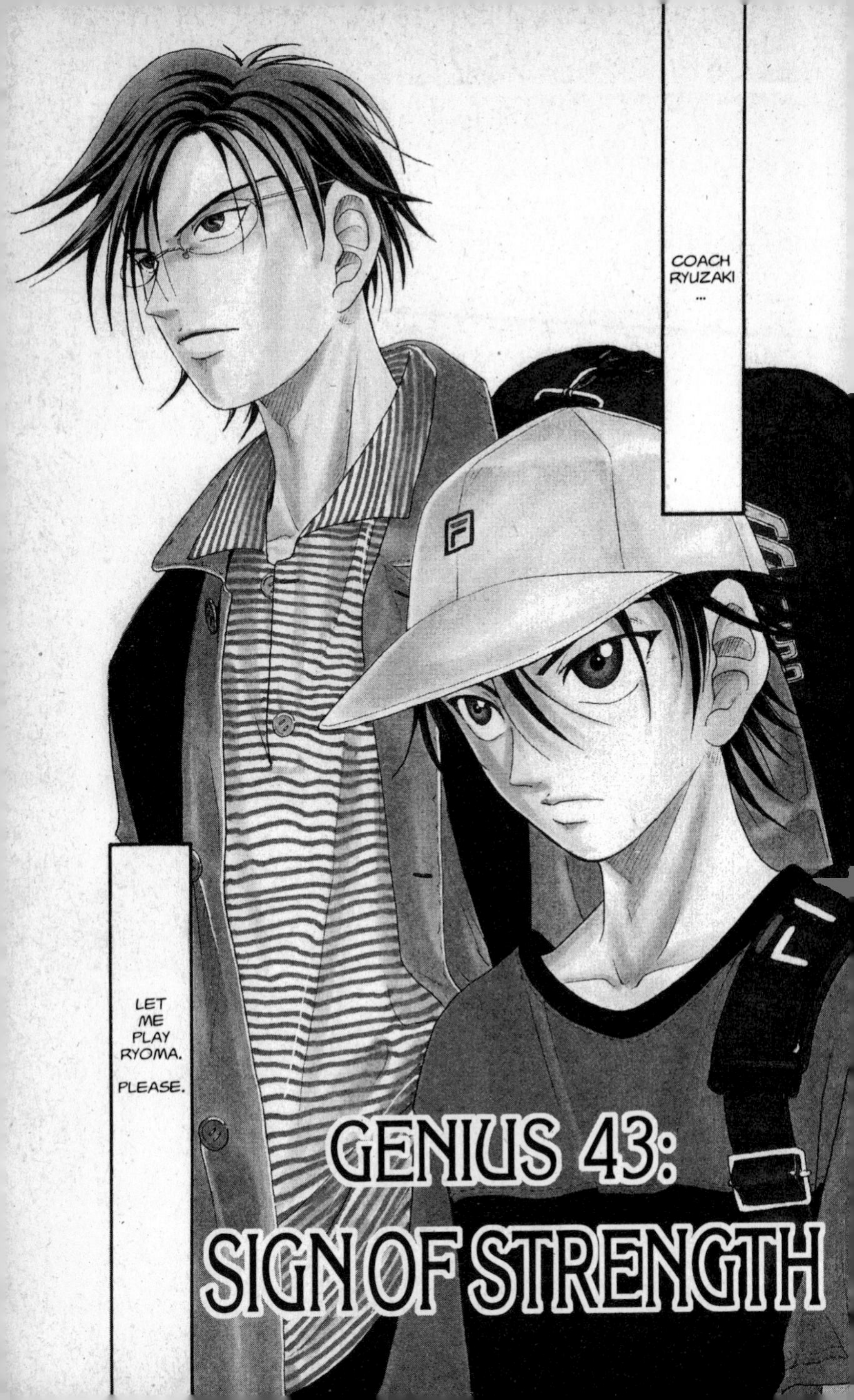
COACH RYUZAKI ...
LET ME PLAY RYOMA.
PLEASE.
GENIUS 43:
SIGN OF STRENGTH

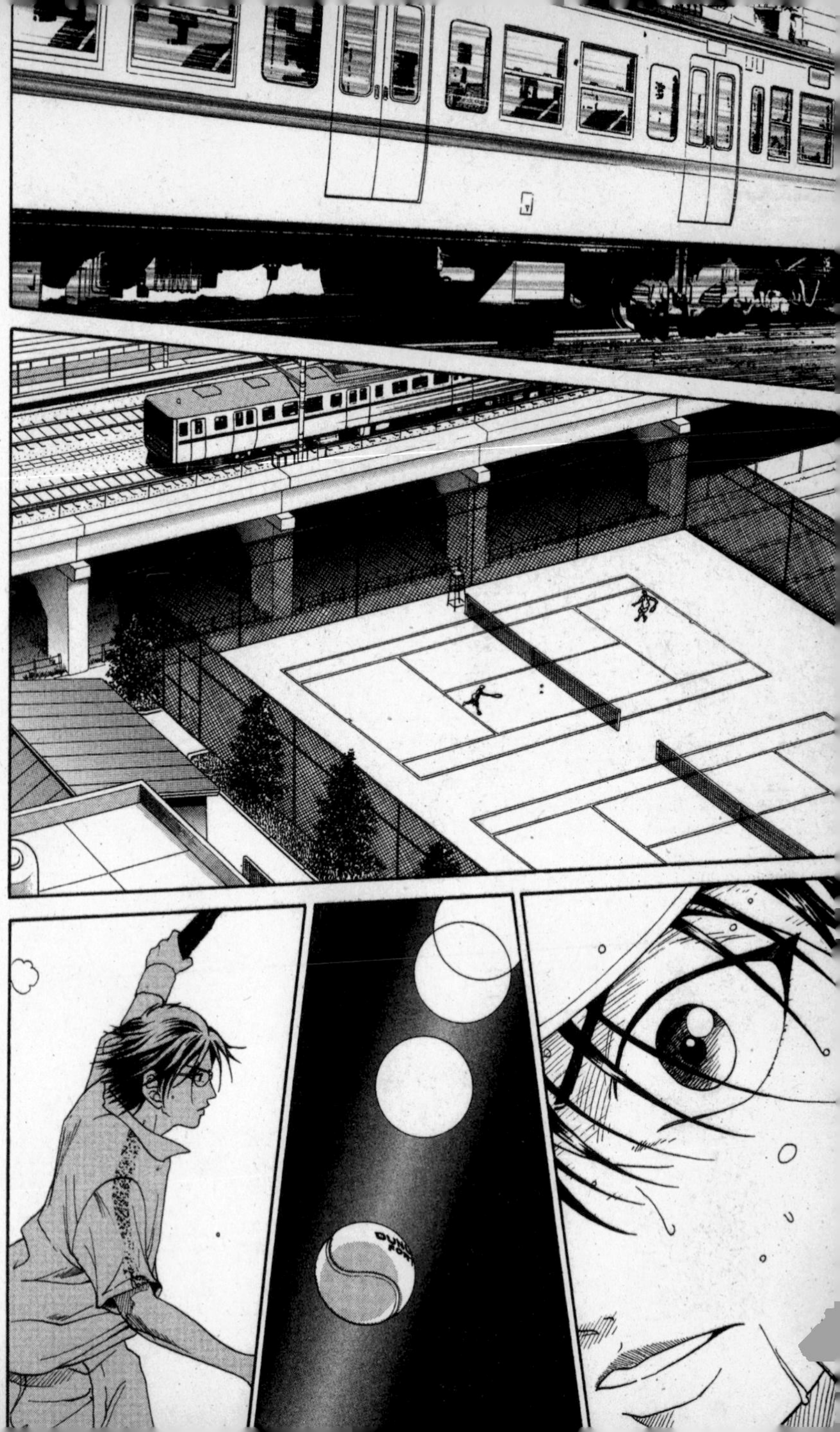

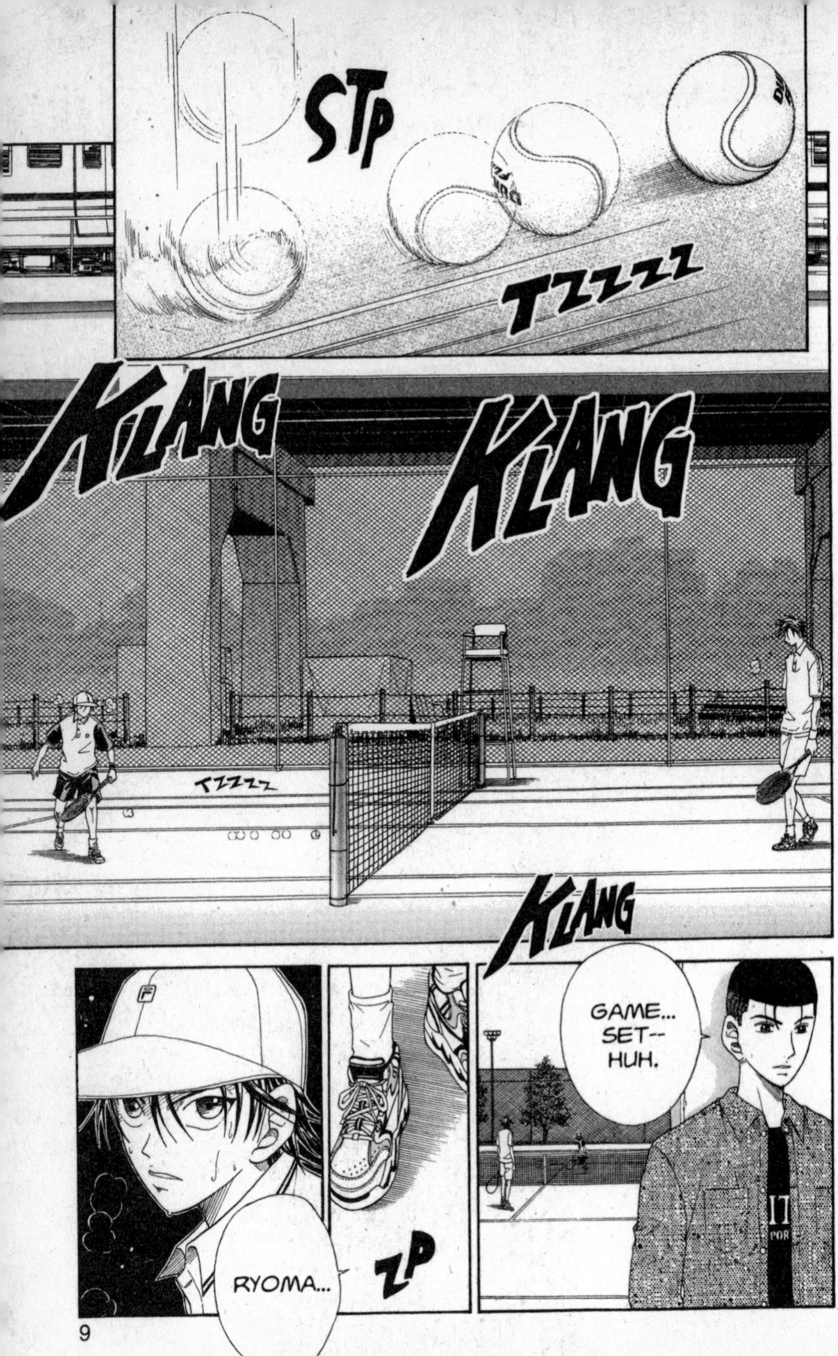
STP
TZZZZZ
KLANG
KLANG
TZZZZ
KLANG
GAME... SET-- HUH.
ZP
RYOMA...

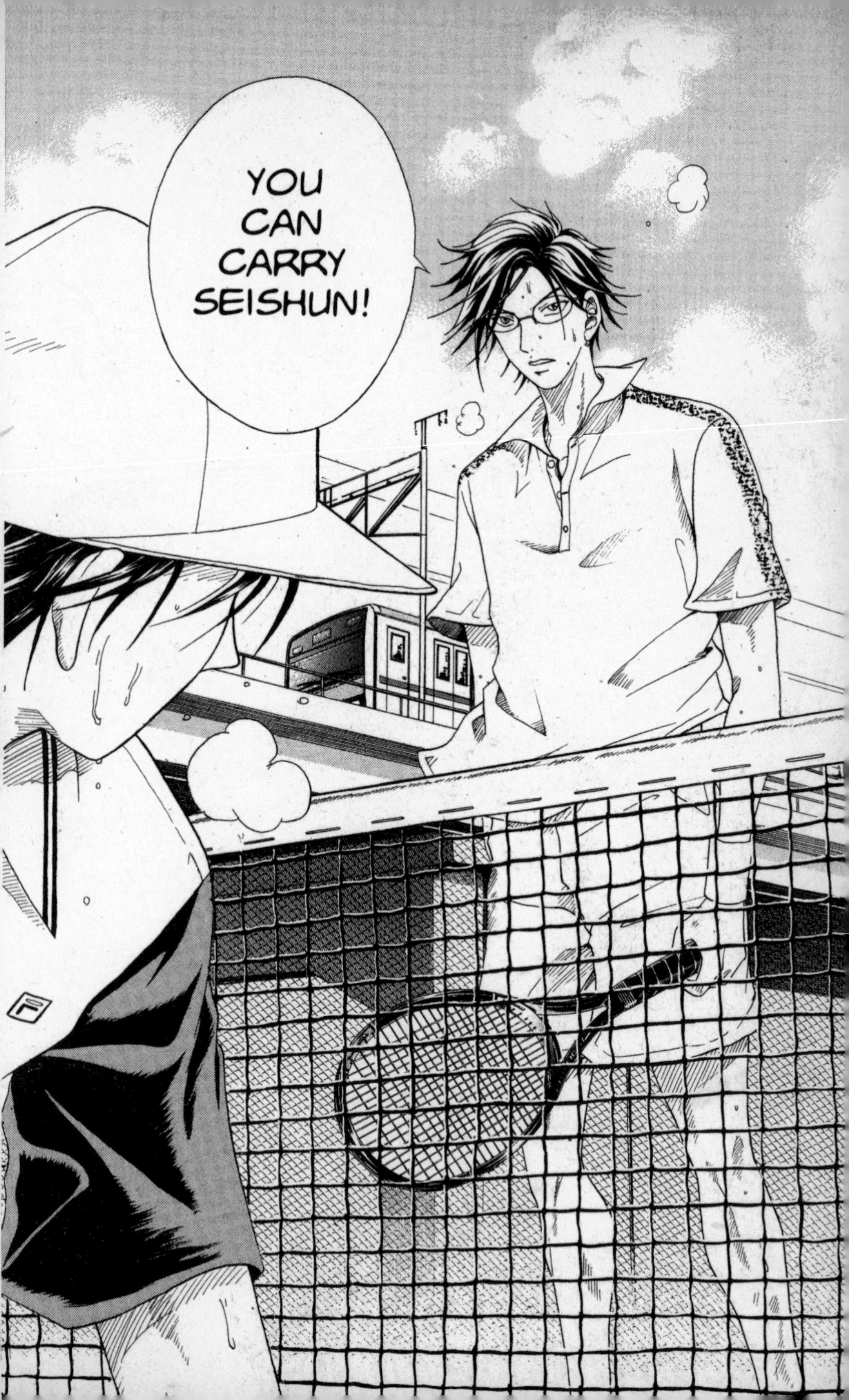
YOU CAN CARRY SEISHUN!

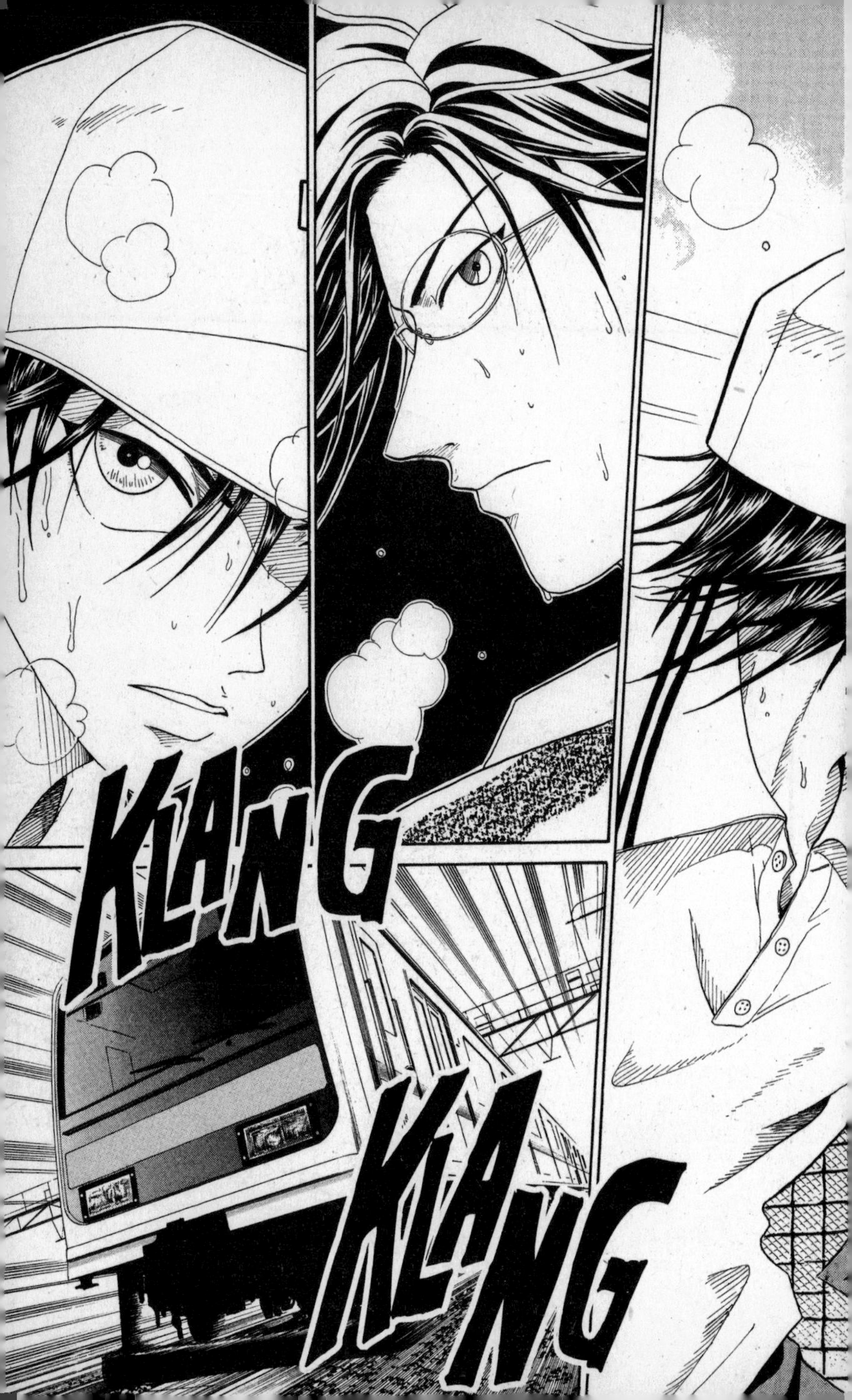
KLANG
KLANG

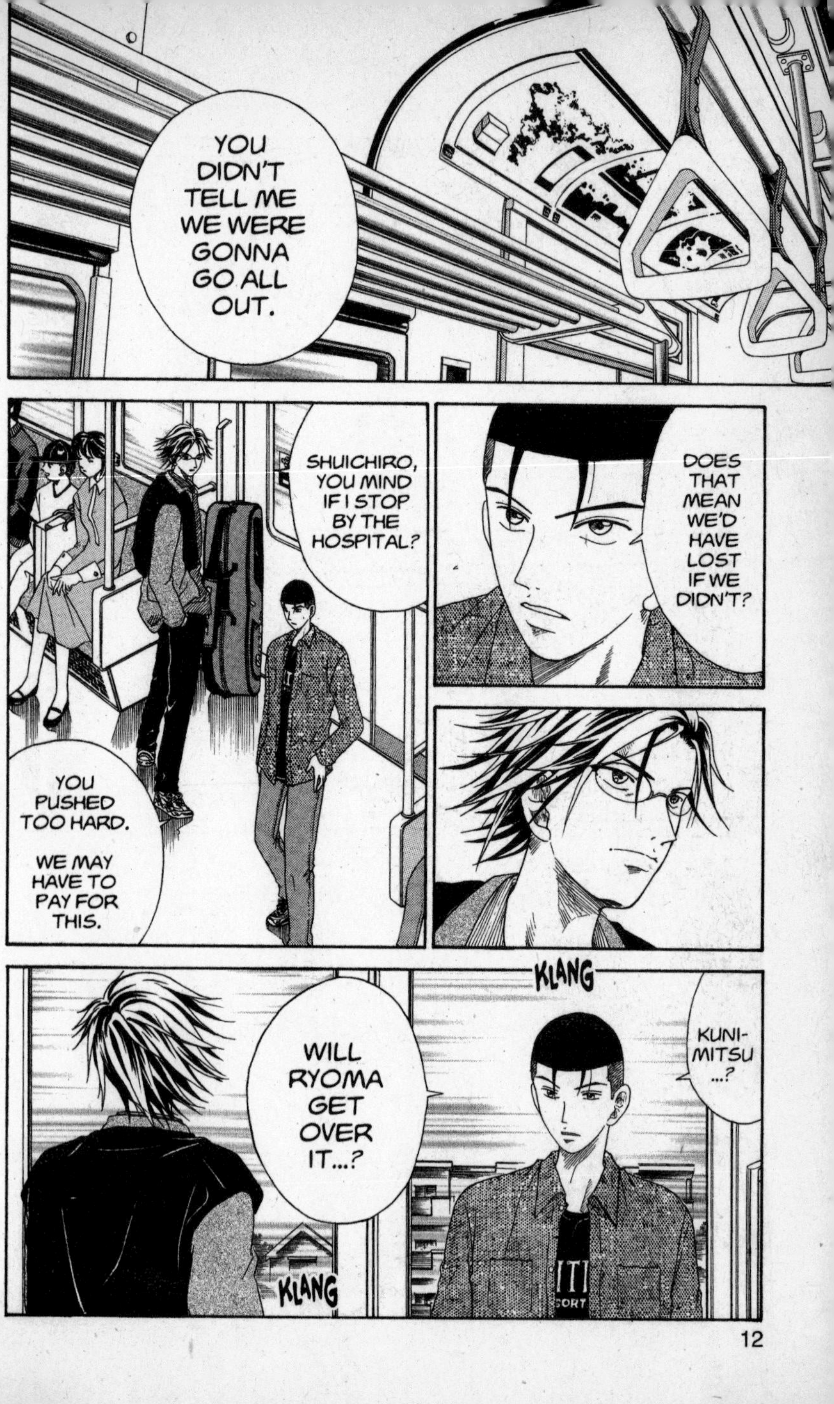

YOU DIDN'T TELL ME WE WERE GONNA GO ALL OUT.
DOES THAT MEAN WE'D HAVE LOST IF WE DIDN'T?
SHUICHIRO, YOU MIND IF I STOP BY THE HOSPITAL?
YOU PUSHED TOO HARD.
WE MAY HAVE TO PAY FOR THIS.
KLANG
KUNI-MITSU ...?
WILL RYOMA GET OVER IT...?
KLANG

READ THIS WAY

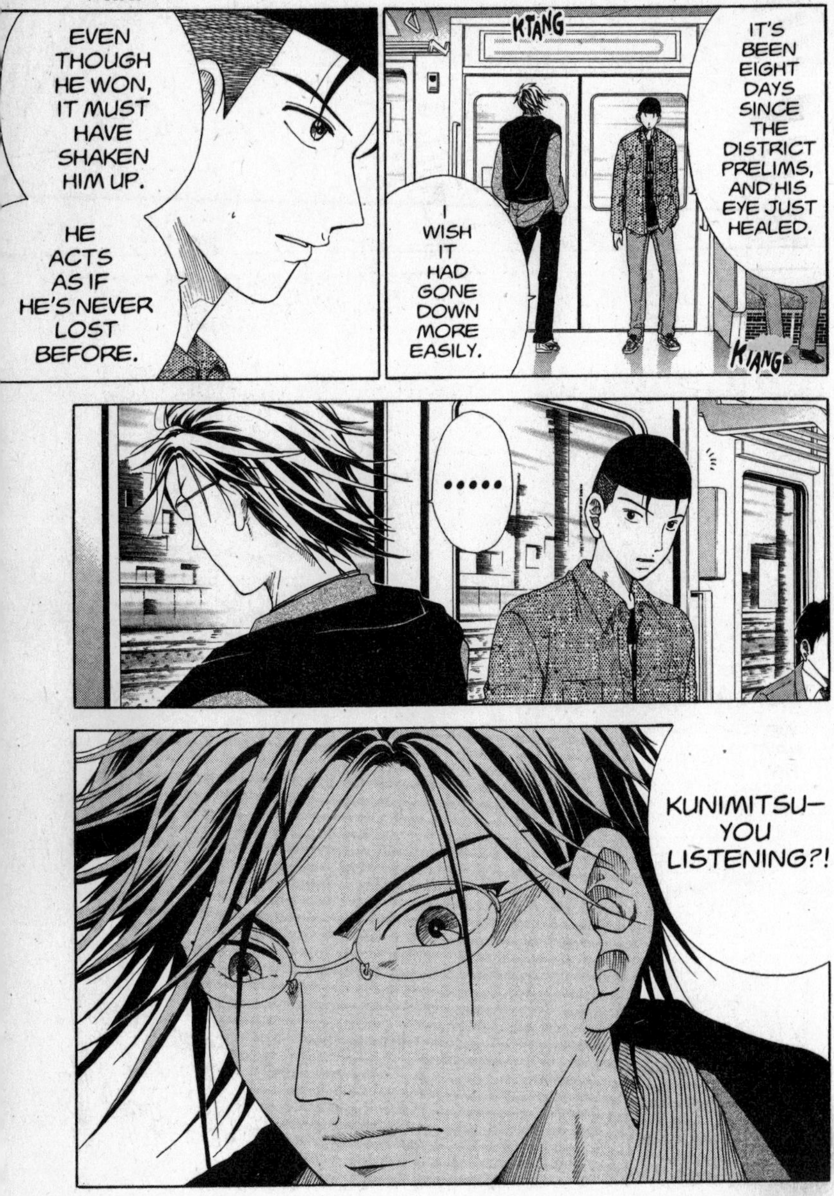
KTANG
IT'S BEEN EIGHT DAYS SINCE THE DISTRICT PRELIMS, AND HIS EYE JUST HEALED.
I WISH IT HAD GONE DOWN MORE EASILY.
KIANG
EVEN THOUGH HE WON, IT MUST HAVE SHAKEN HIM UP.
HE ACTS AS IF HE'S NEVER LOST BEFORE.
.....
KUNIMITSU— YOU LISTENING?!

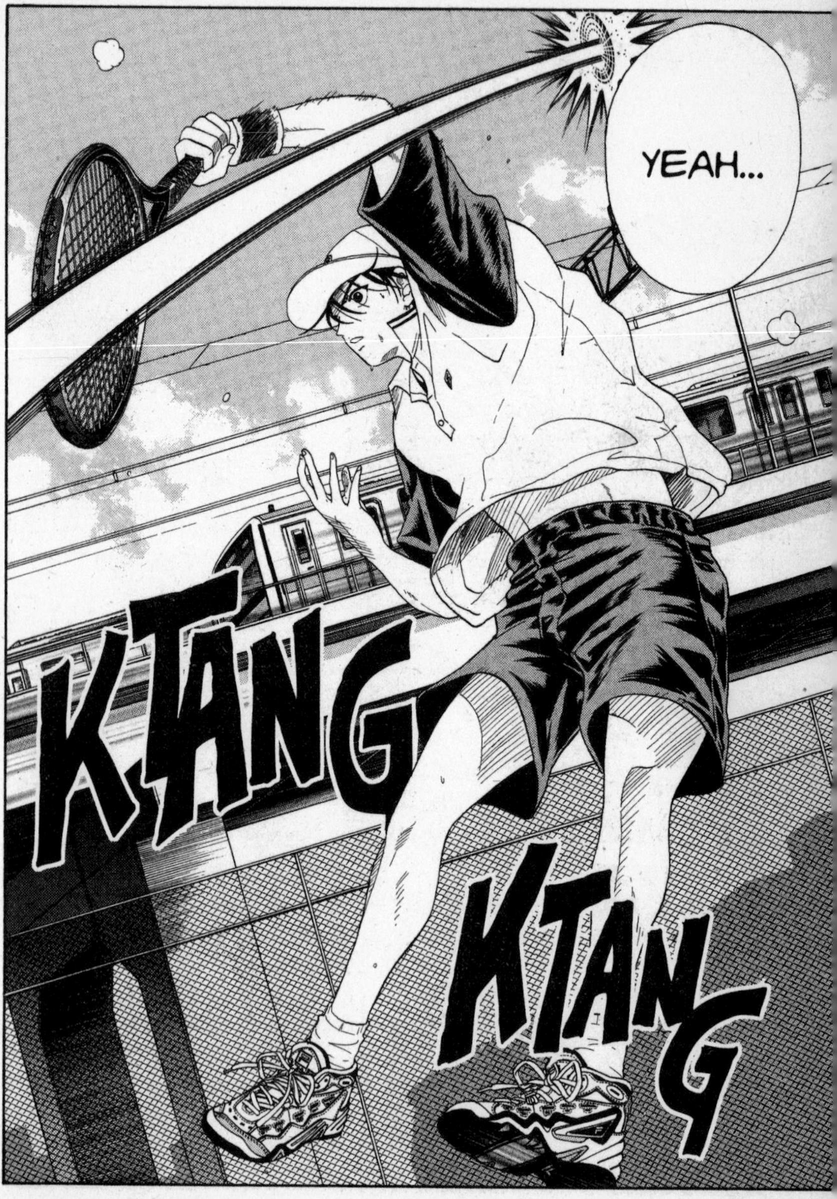
YEAH...
KTANG
KTANG

READ THIS WAY

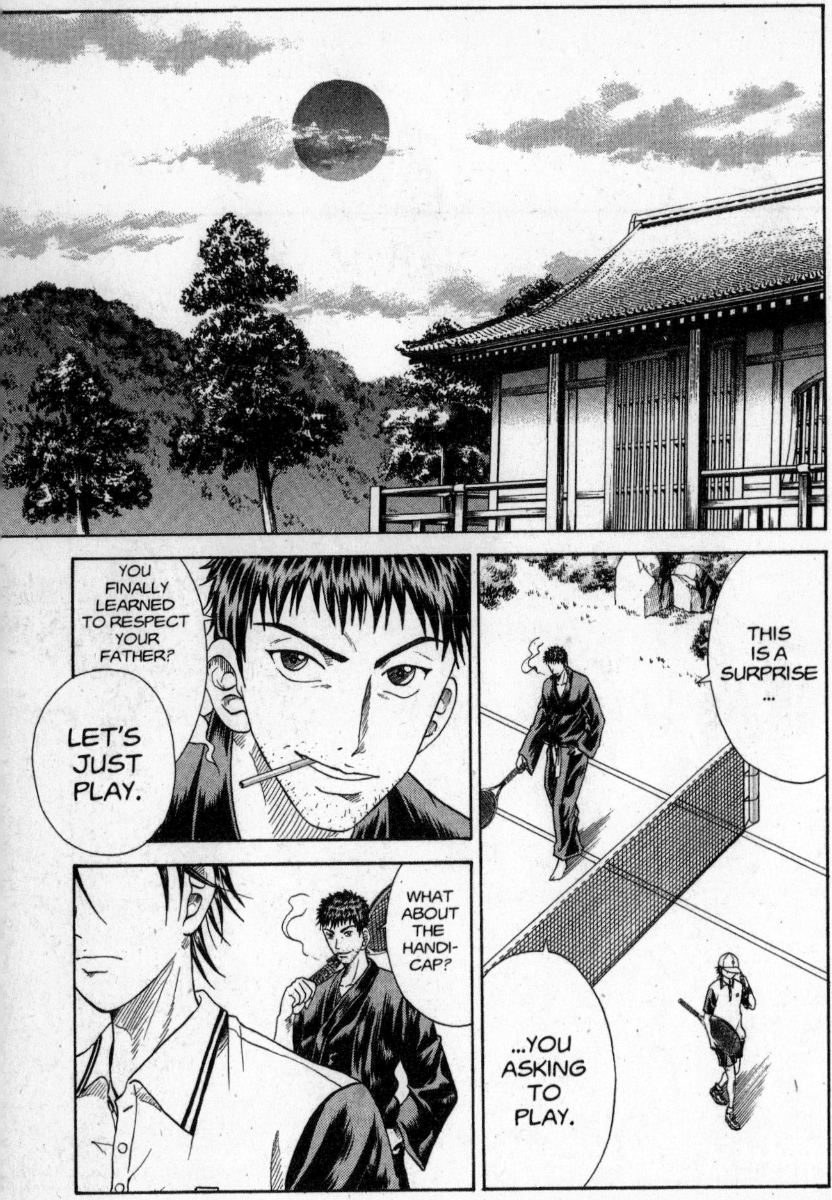
THIS IS A SURPRISE ...
...YOU ASKING TO PLAY.
YOU FINALLY LEARNED TO RESPECT YOUR FATHER?
LET'S JUST PLAY.
WHAT ABOUT THE HANDI-CAP?

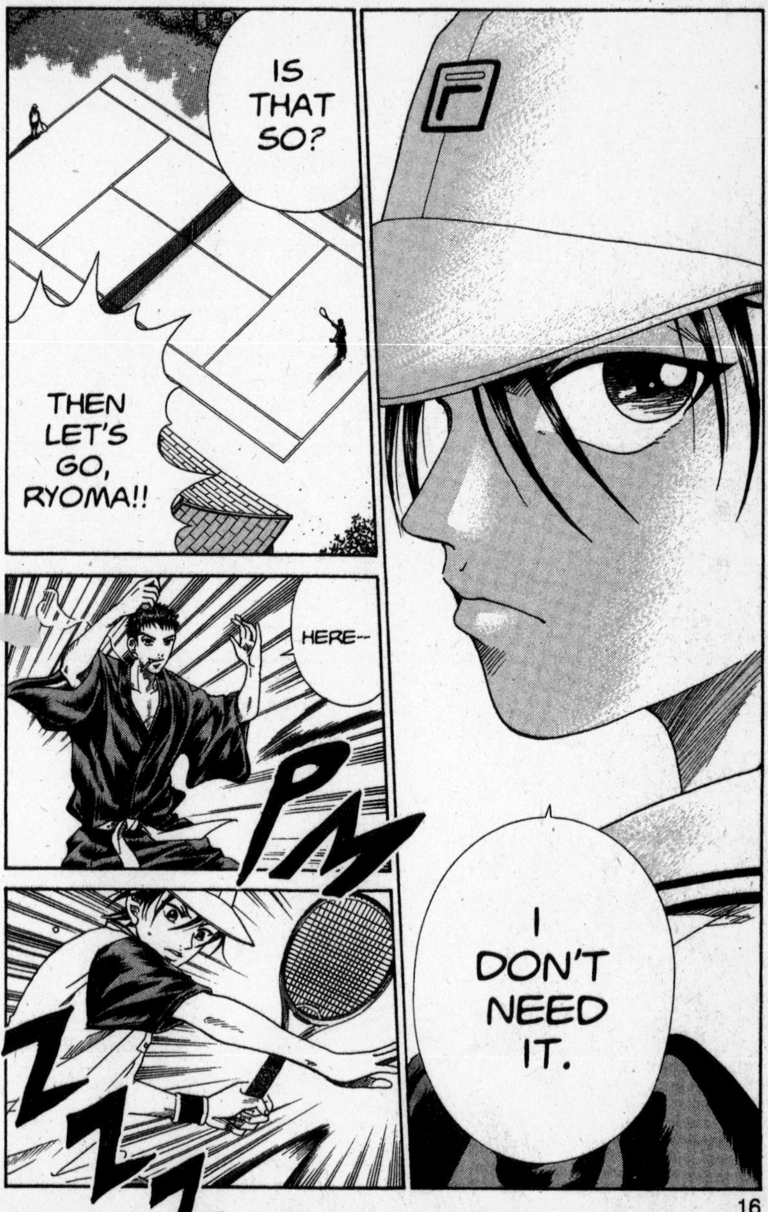
I DON'T NEED IT.
IS THAT SO?
THEN LET'S GO, RYOMA!!
HERE--
PM
ZZZZ

READ THIS WAY

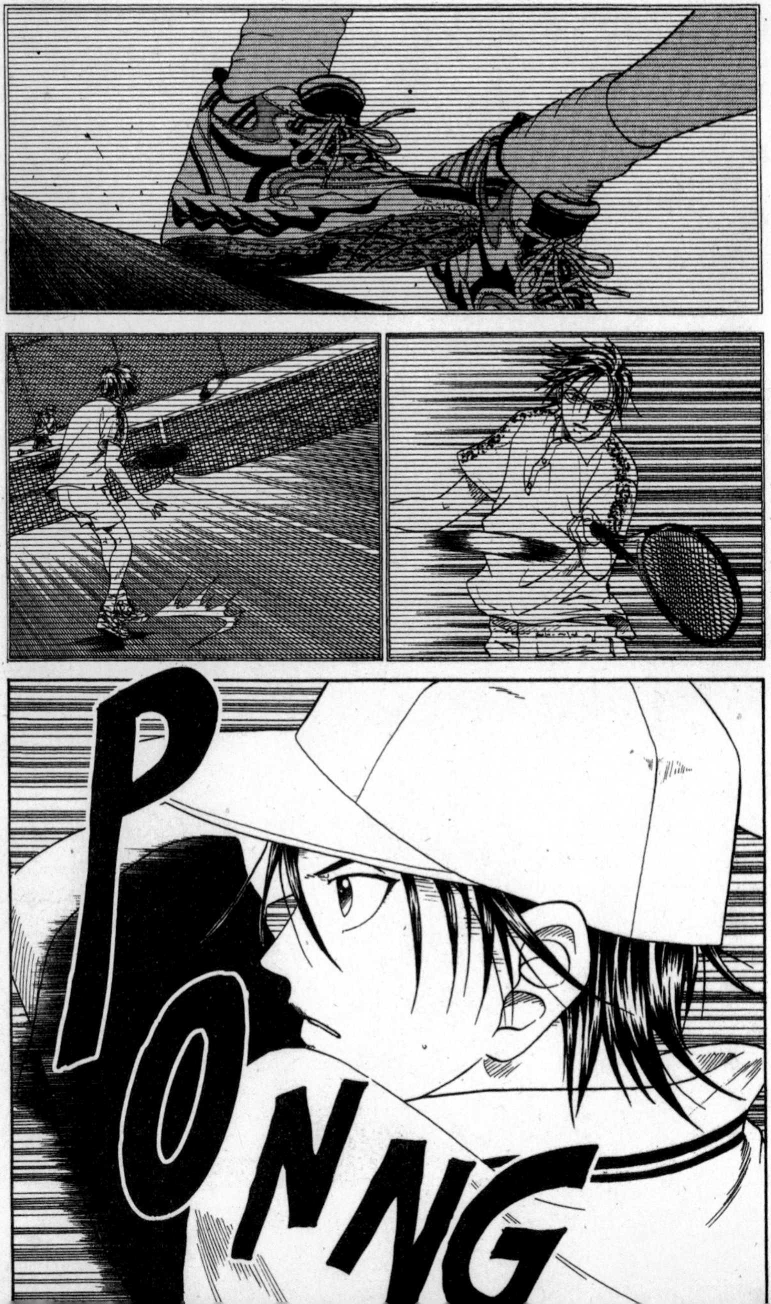
PONNG

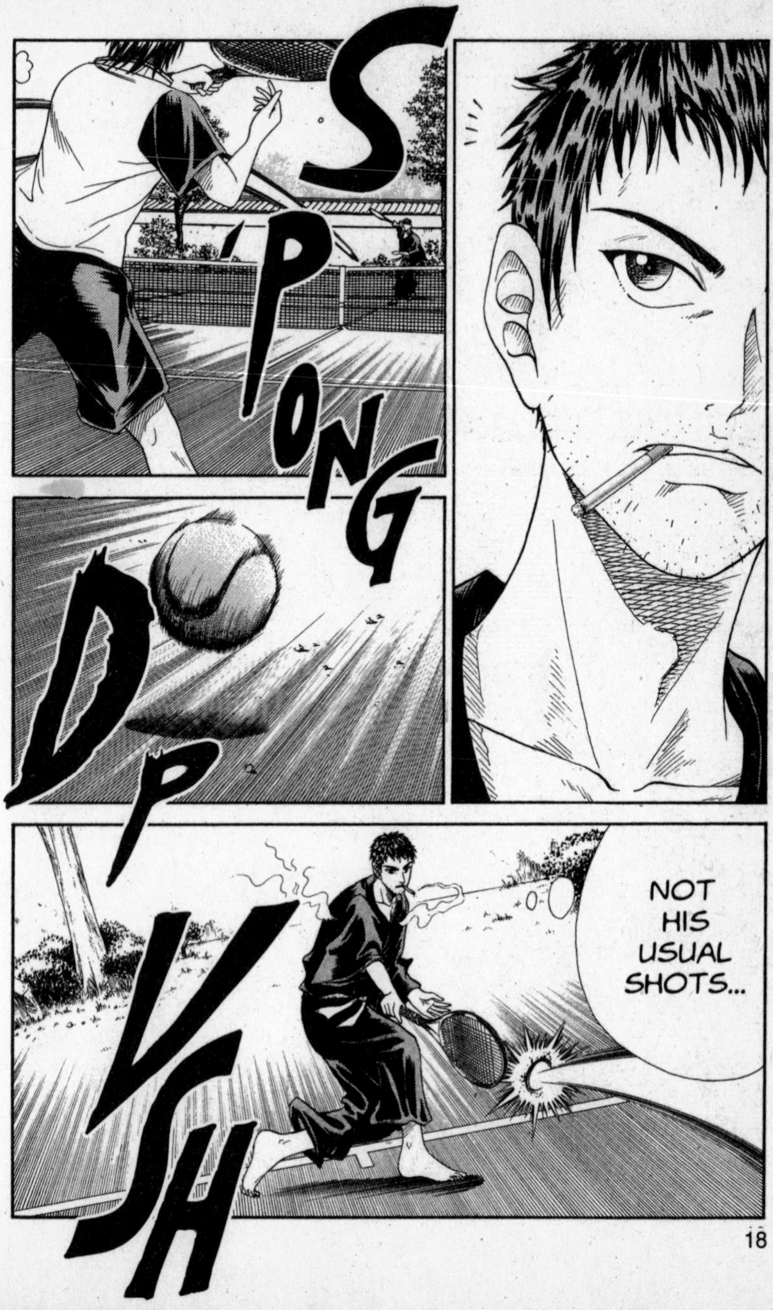
SPONG
DP
VSH
NOT HIS USUAL SHOTS...

READ THIS WAY

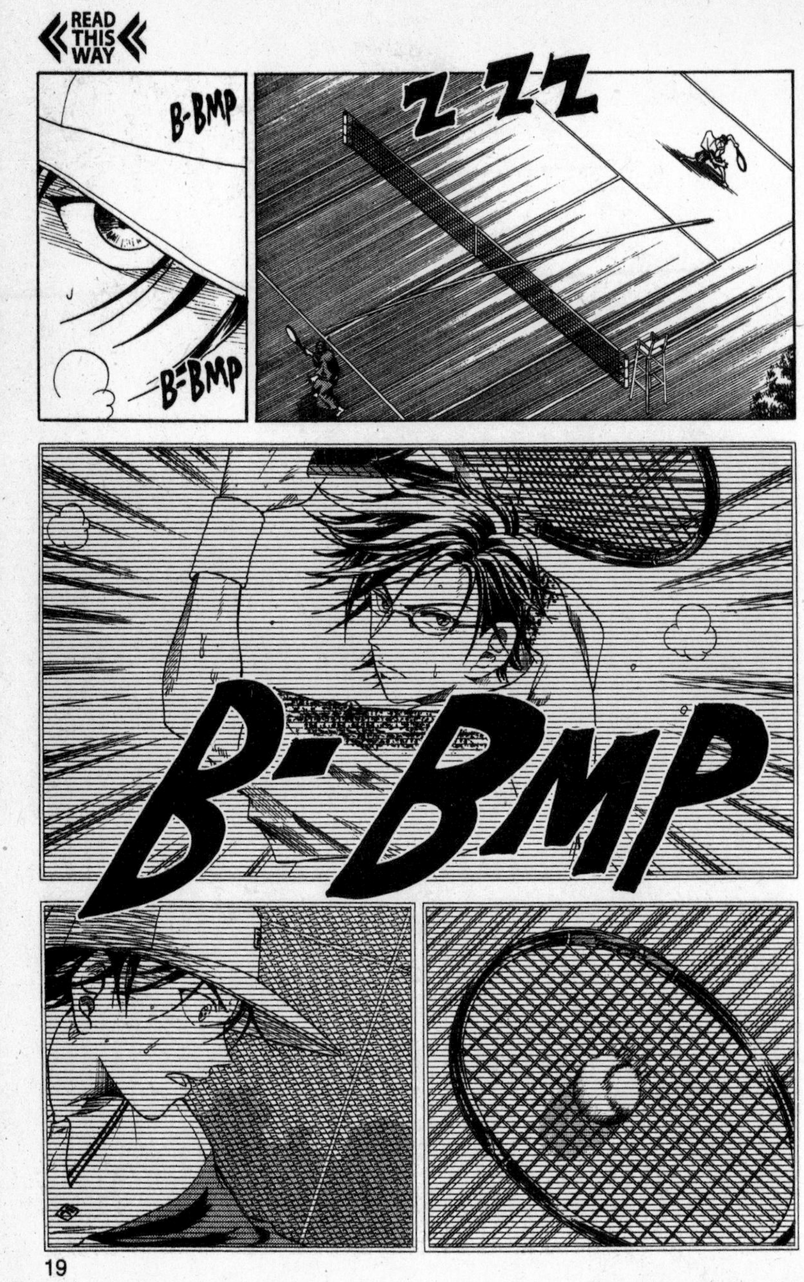
ZZZ
B-BMP
B-BMP
B-BMP

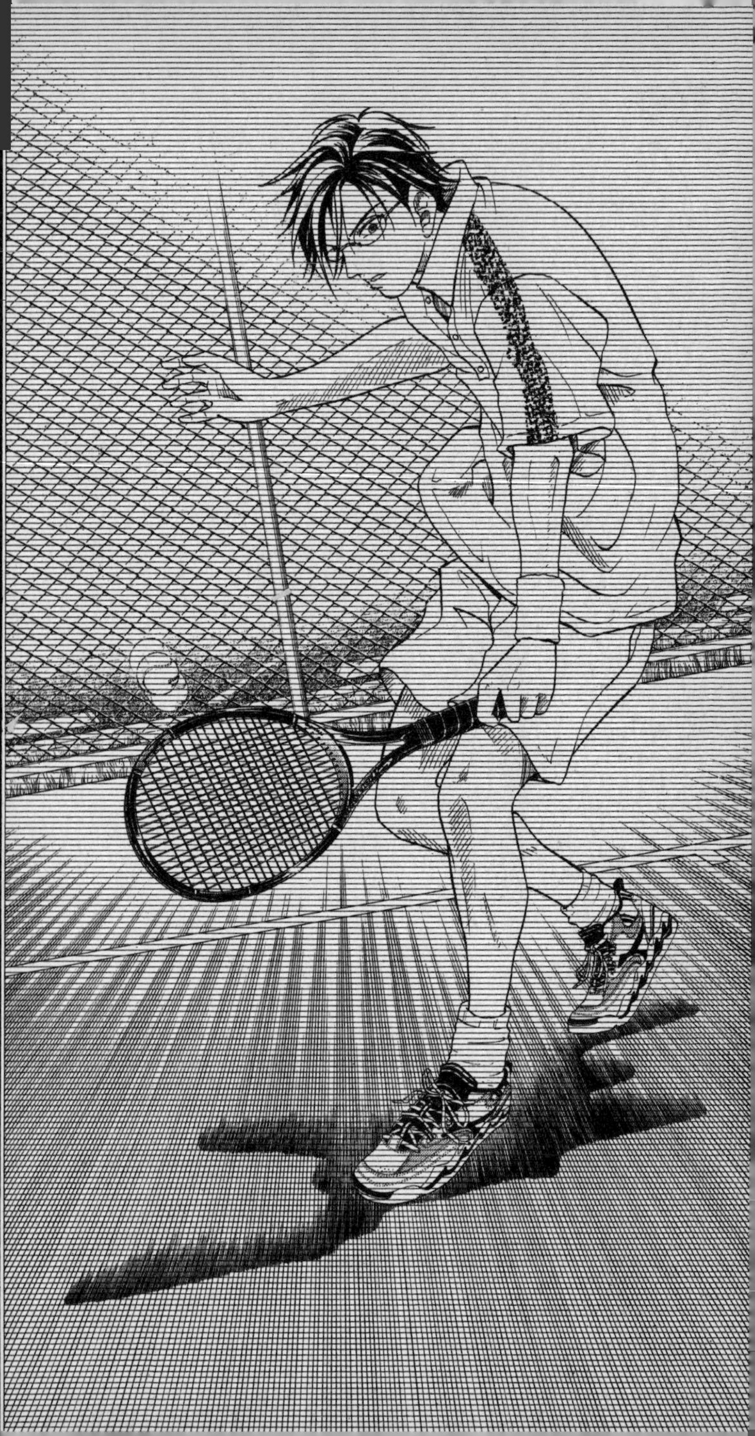

READ THIS WAY

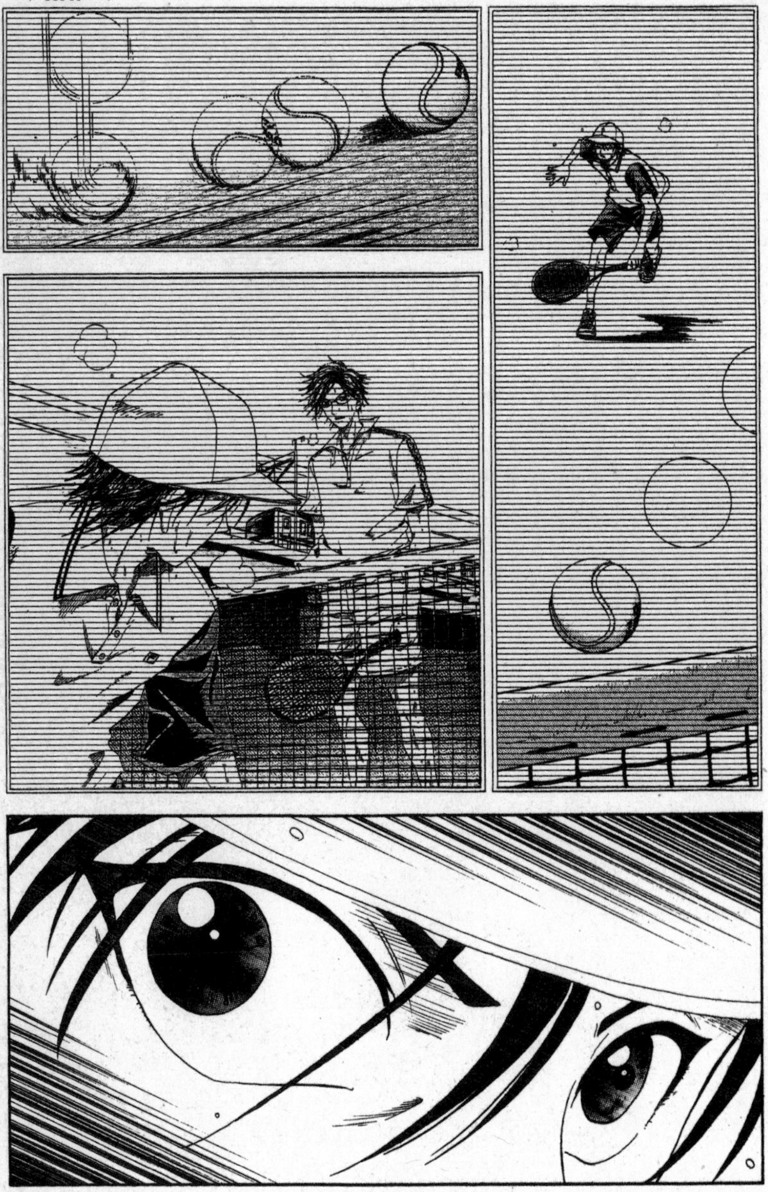

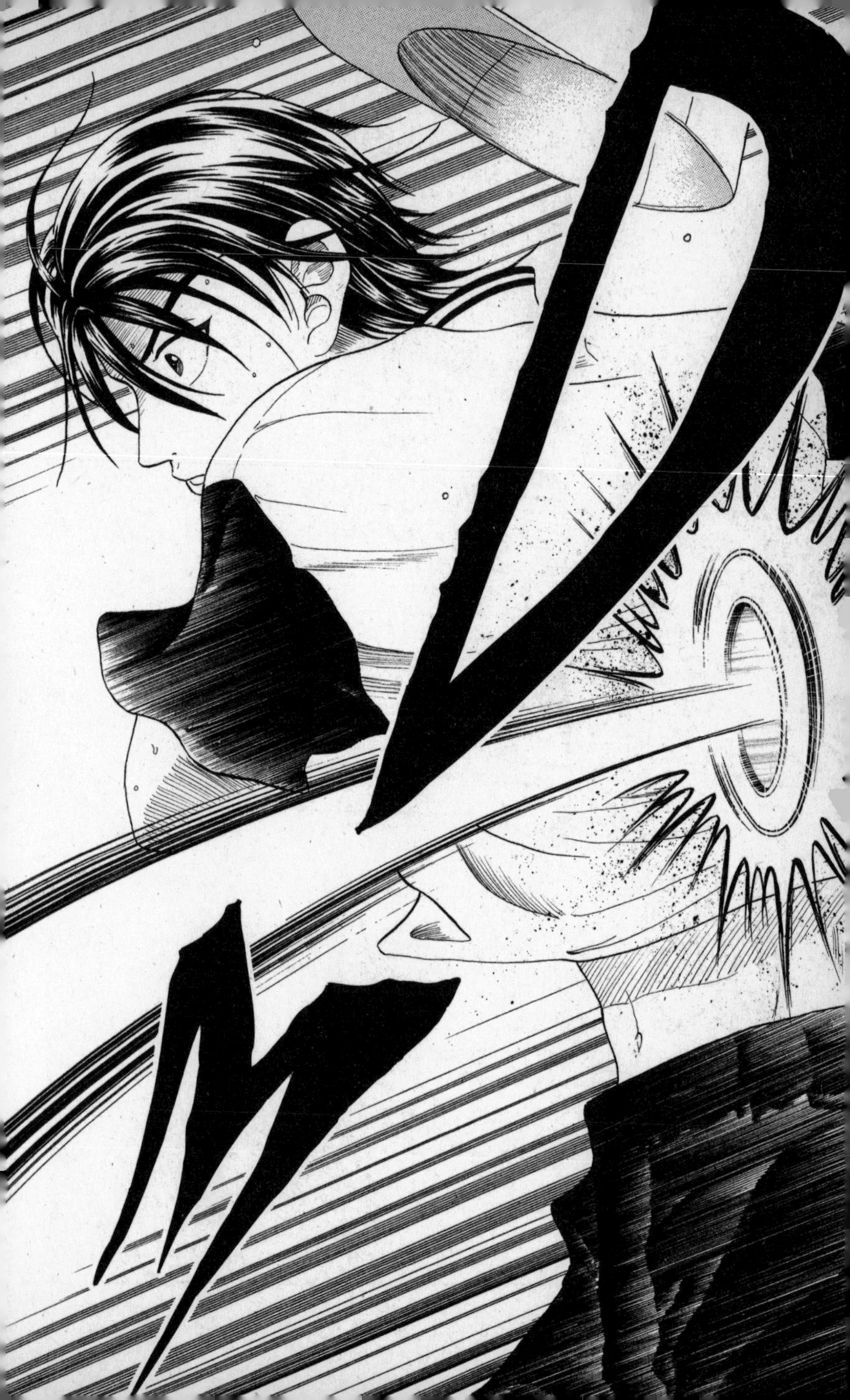

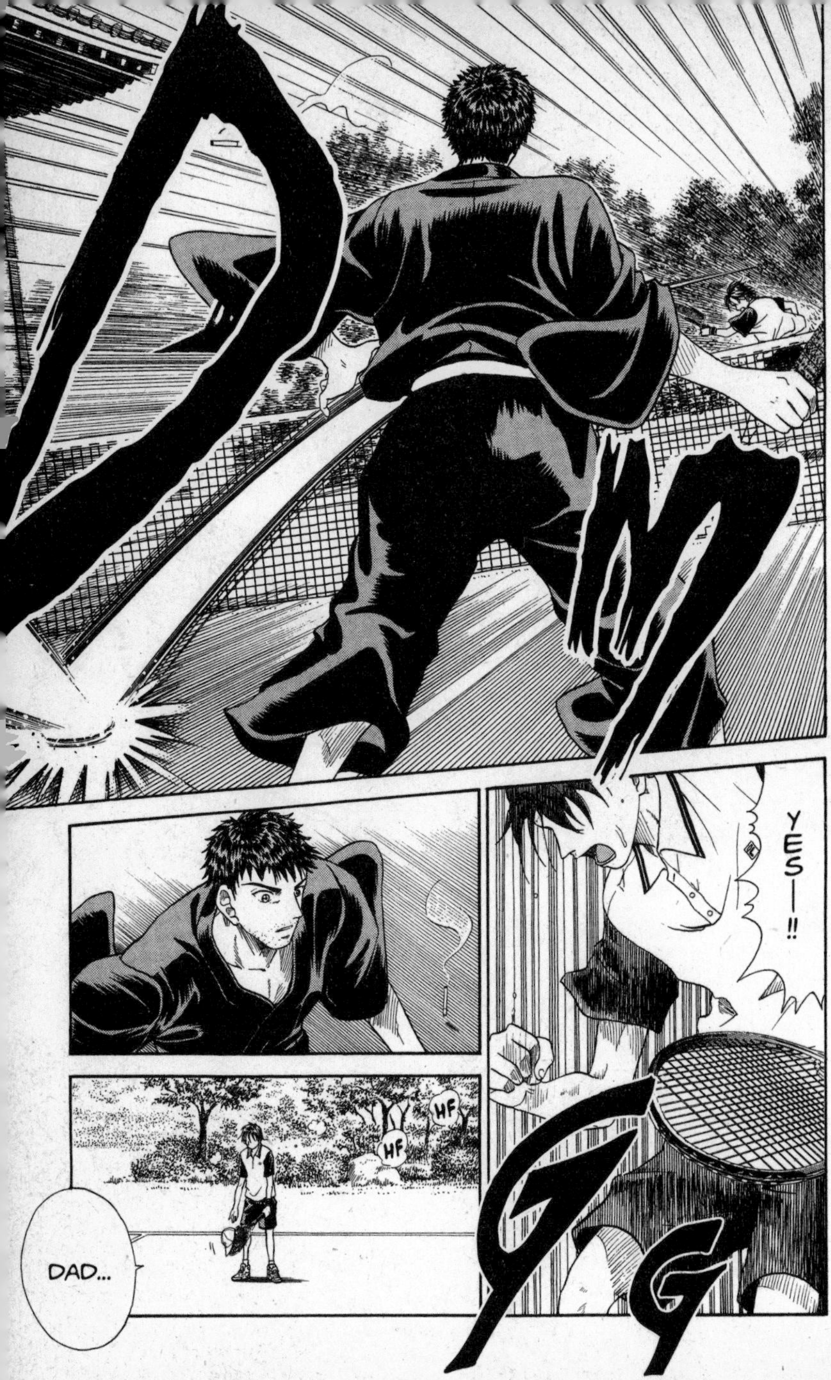
YES—!!
G
G
HF
HF
DAD...

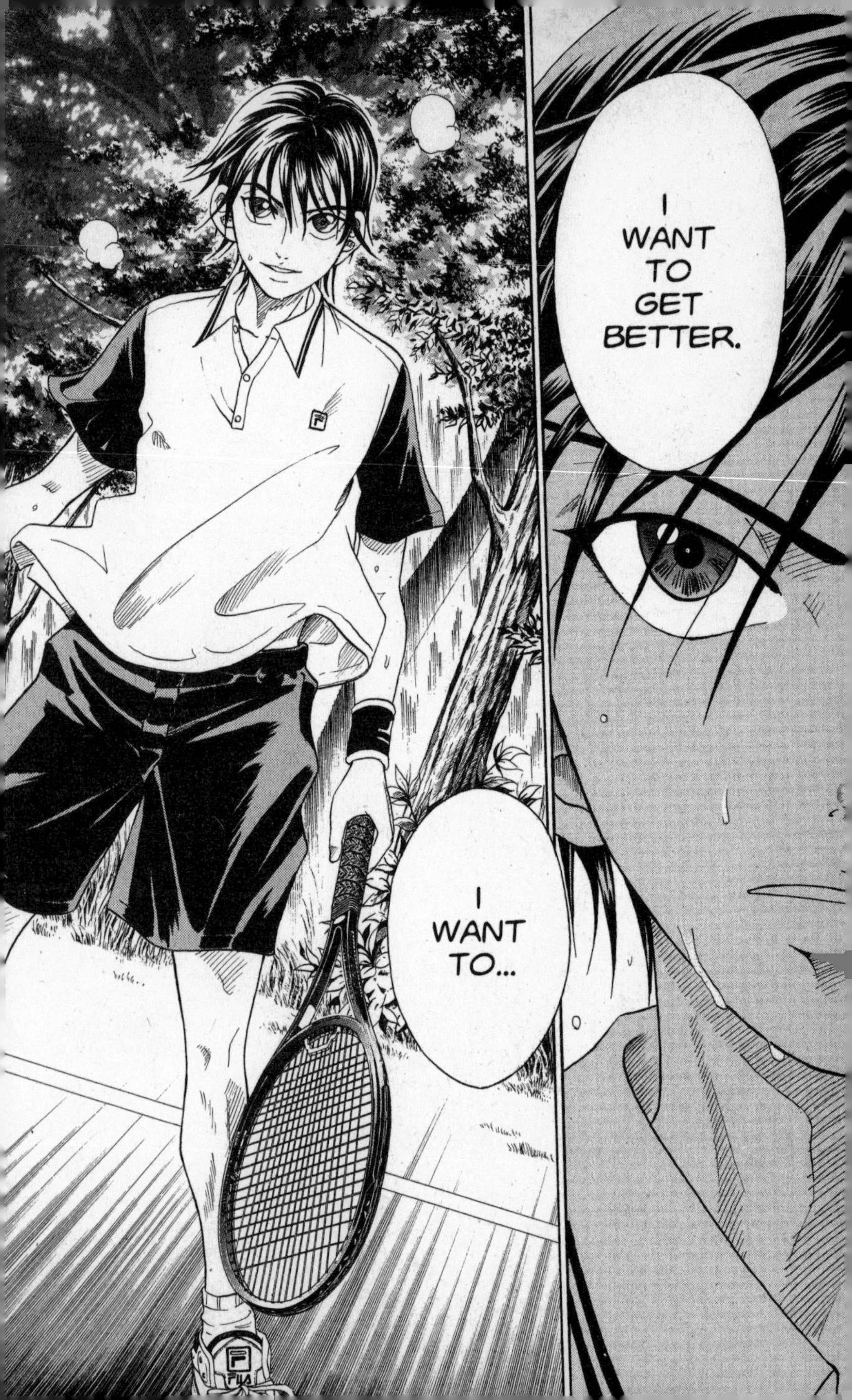
I WANT TO GET BETTER.
I WANT TO...

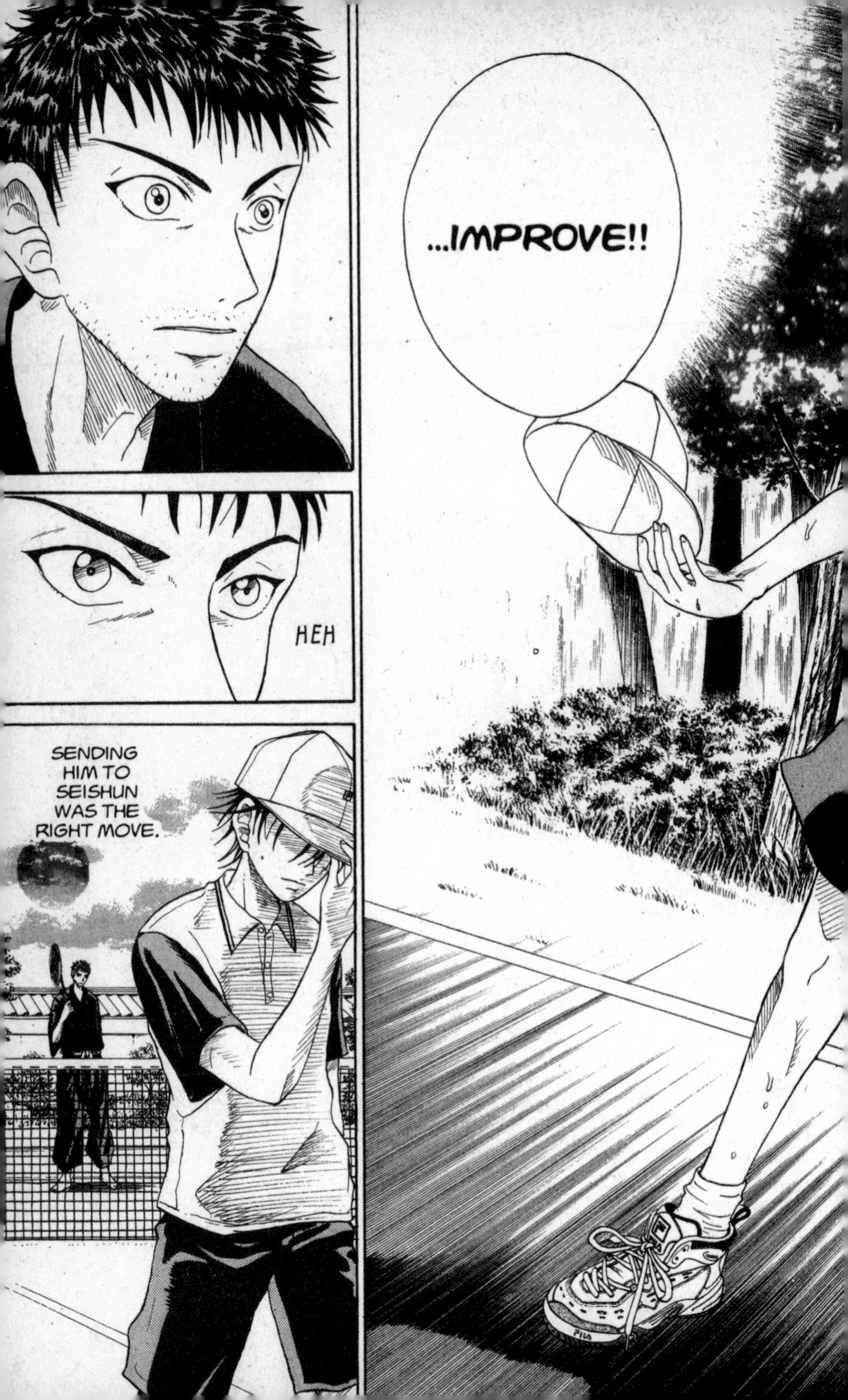
...IMPROVE!!
HEH
SENDING HIM TO SEISHUN WAS THE RIGHT MOVE.

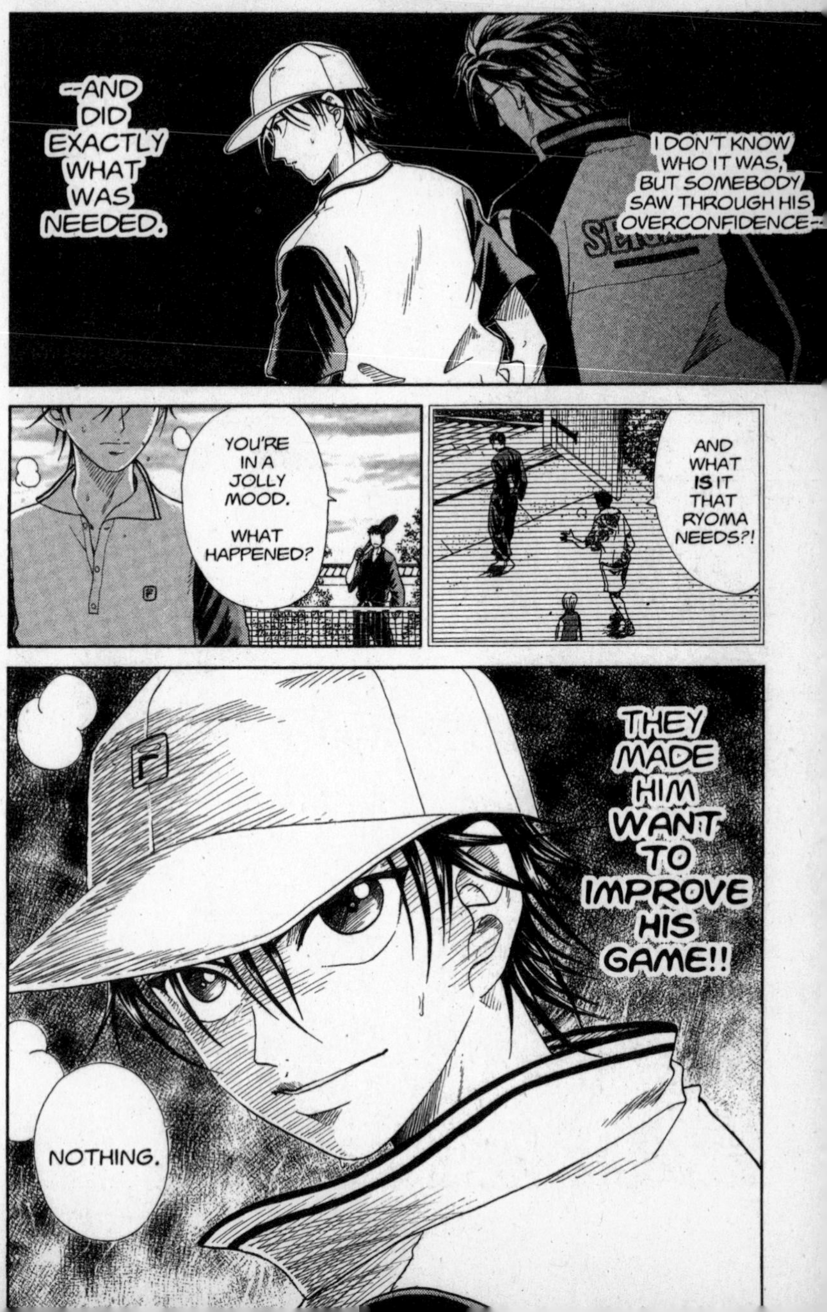
I DON'T KNOW WHO IT WAS, BUT SOMEBODY SAW THROUGH HIS OVERCONFIDENCE--
--AND DID EXACTLY WHAT WAS NEEDED.
AND WHAT IS IT THAT RYOMA NEEDS?!
YOU'RE IN A JOLLY MOOD. WHAT HAPPENED?
THEY MADE HIM WANT TO IMPROVE HIS GAME!!
NOTHING.

READ THIS WAY

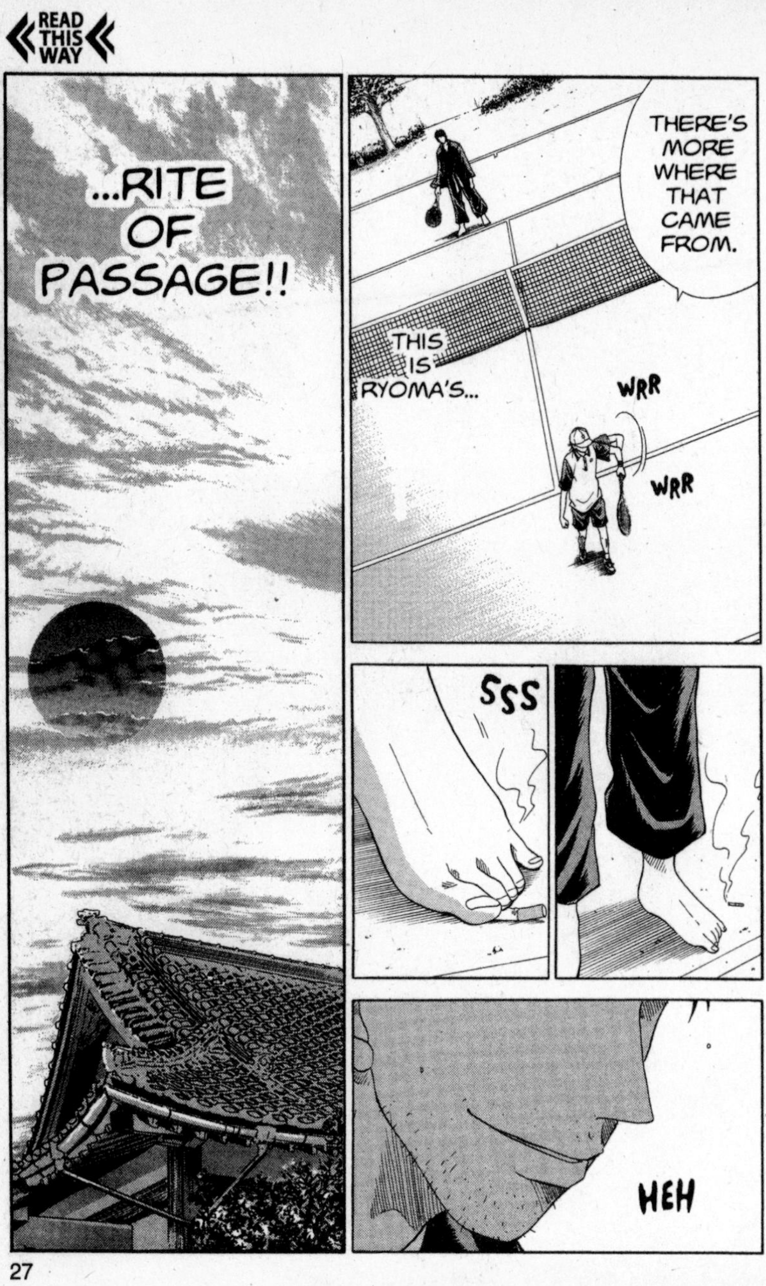
THERE'S MORE WHERE THAT CAME FROM.
THIS IS RYOMA'S...
WRR
WRR
SSS
HEH
...RITE OF PASSAGE!!

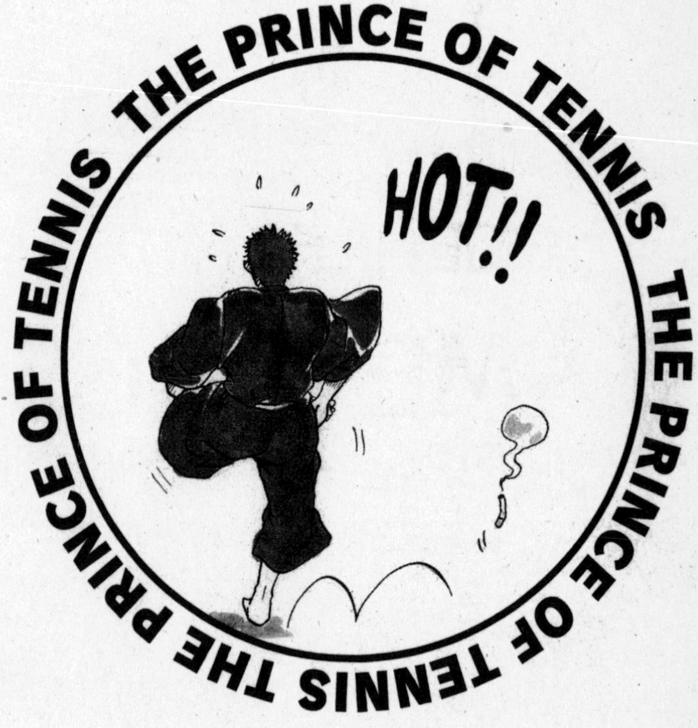
THE PRINCE OF TENNIS THE PRINCE OF TENNIS THE PRINCE OF TENNIS
HOT!!

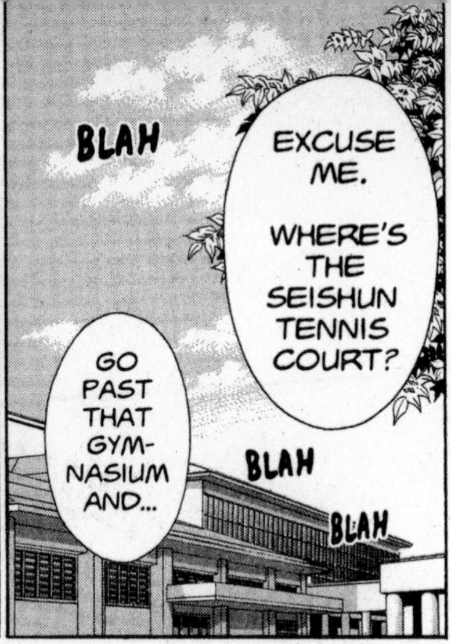
BLAH
EXCUSE ME. WHERE'S THE SEISHUN TENNIS COURT?
GO PAST THAT GYM- NASIUM AND...
BLAH
BLAH

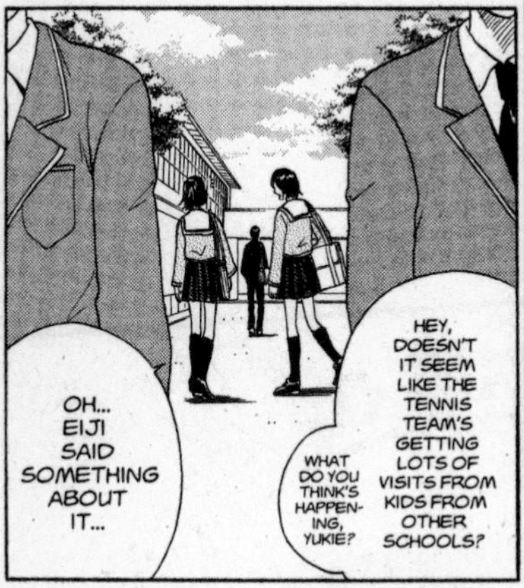
HEY, DOESN'T IT SEEM LIKE THE TENNIS TEAM'S GETTING LOTS OF VISITS FROM KIDS FROM OTHER SCHOOLS?
WHAT DO YOU THINK'S HAPPEN- ING, YUKIE?
OH... EIJI SAID SOMETHING ABOUT IT...

GENIUS 44:

GAME FACES

(TWO WEEKS BEFORE THE TOURNAMENT)

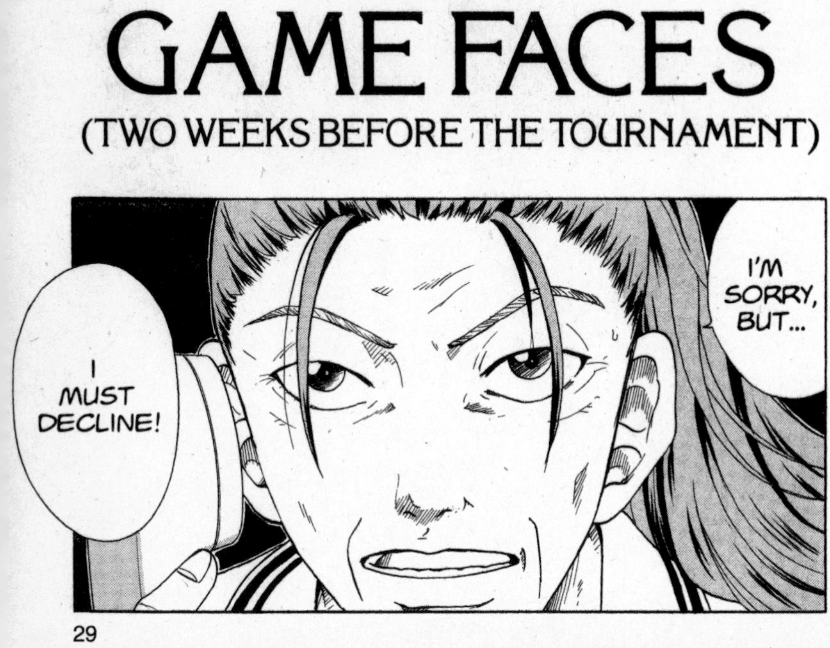
I'M SORRY, BUT...
I MUST DECLINE!

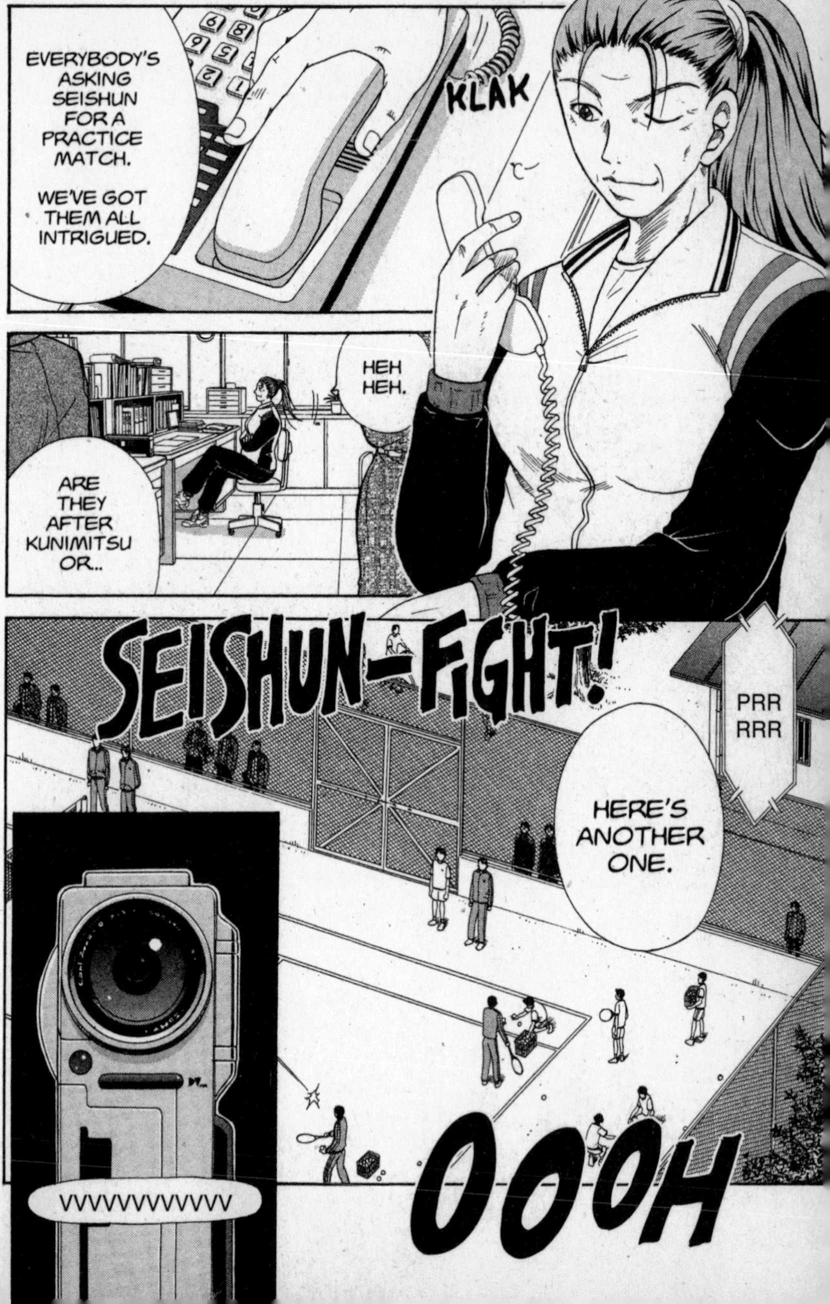
KLAK
EVERYBODY'S ASKING SEISHUN FOR A PRACTICE MATCH.
WE'VE GOT THEM ALL INTRIGUED.
HEH HEH.
ARE THEY AFTER KUNIMITSU OR...
PRR RRR
HERE'S ANOTHER ONE.
SEISHUN-FIGHT!
VVVVVVVVVVVV
OOOH

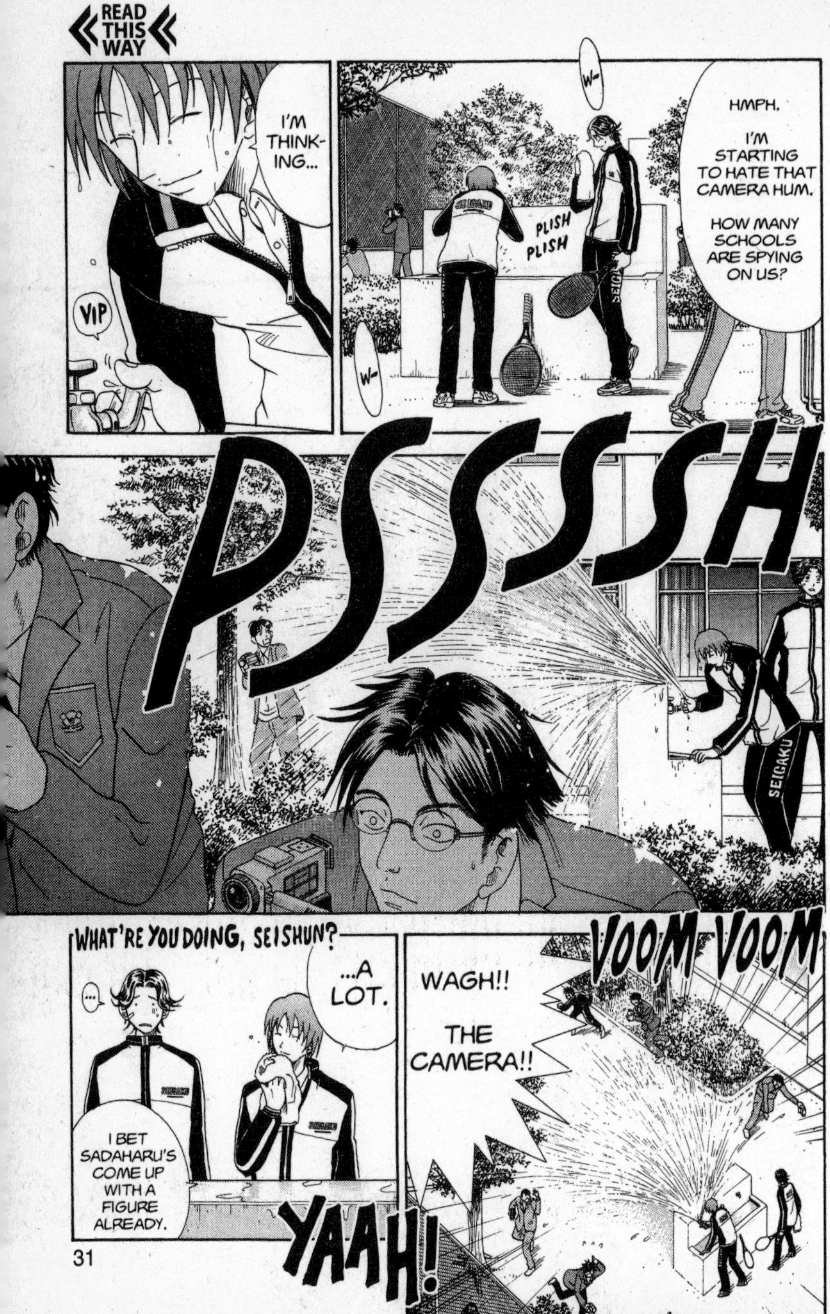
READ THIS WAY
W-
HMPH.
I'M STARTING TO HATE THAT CAMERA HUM.
HOW MANY SCHOOLS ARE SPYING ON US?
PLISH PLISH
W-
I'M THINKING-ING...
VIP
PSSSSH
VOOM VOOM
WAGH!!
THE CAMERA!!
YAAH!
WHAT'RE YOU DOING, SEISHUN?
...A LOT.
...
I BET SADAHARU'S COME UP WITH A FIGURE ALREADY.

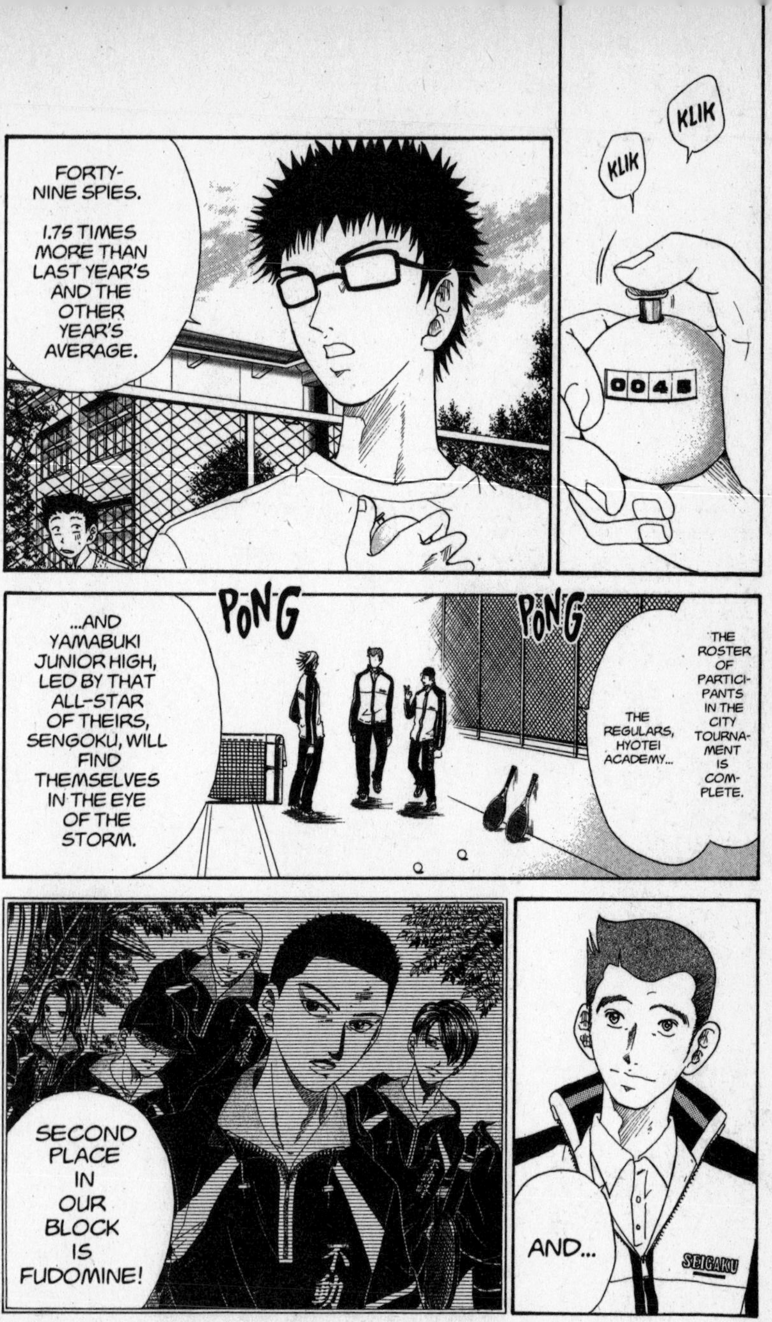
KLIK
KLIK
0045
FORTY-NINE SPIES.
1.75 TIMES MORE THAN LAST YEAR'S AND THE OTHER YEAR'S AVERAGE.
THE ROSTER OF PARTICIPANTS IN THE CITY TOURNAMENT IS COMPLETE.
THE REGULARS, HYOTEI ACADEMY...
PONG
PONG
...AND YAMABUKI JUNIOR HIGH, LED BY THAT ALL-STAR OF THEIRS, SENGOKU, WILL FIND THEMSELVES IN THE EYE OF THE STORM.
AND...
SEIGAKU
SECOND PLACE IN OUR BLOCK IS FUDOMINE!

READ THIS WAY

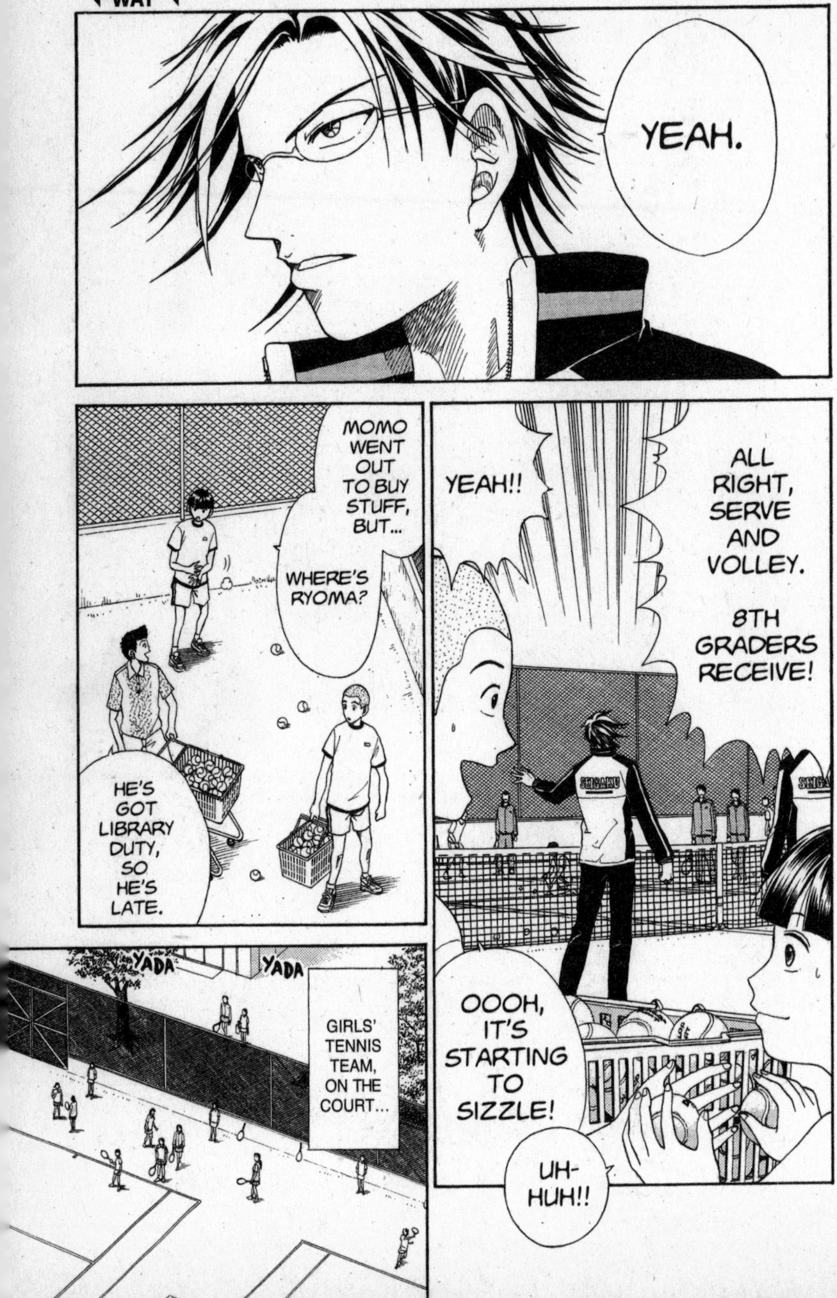
YEAH.
ALL RIGHT, SERVE AND VOLLEY.
8TH GRADERS RECEIVE!
YEAH!!
OOOH, IT'S STARTING TO SIZZLE!
UH-HUH!!
MOMO WENT OUT TO BUY STUFF, BUT...
WHERE'S RYOMA?
HE'S GOT LIBRARY DUTY, SO HE'S LATE.
YADA
YADA
GIRLS' TENNIS TEAM, ON THE COURT...

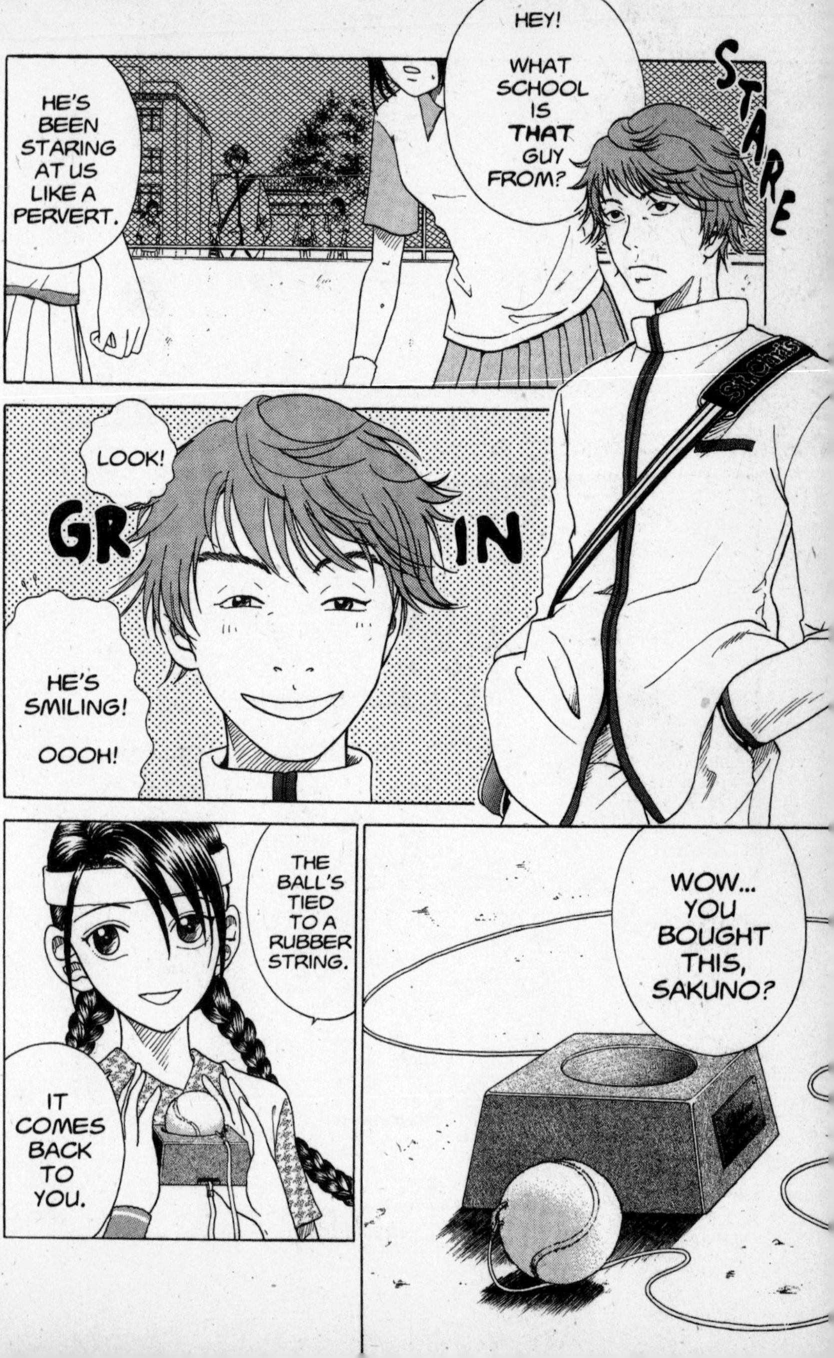
HEY! WHAT SCHOOL IS THAT GUY FROM?
STARE
HE'S BEEN STARING AT US LIKE A PERVERT.
LOOK!
GRIN
HE'S SMILING! OOOH!
WOW... YOU BOUGHT THIS, SAKUNO?
THE BALL'S TIED TO A RUBBER STRING.
IT COMES BACK TO YOU.

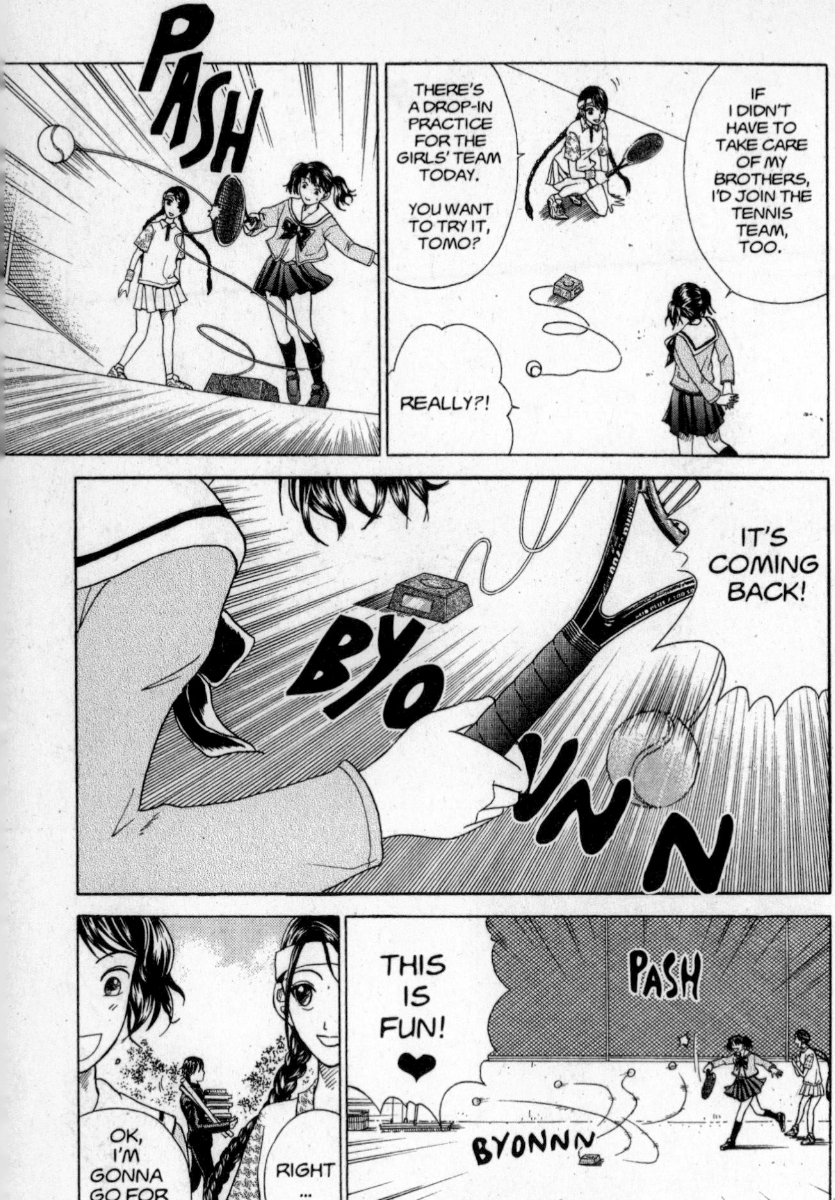
IF I DIDN'T HAVE TO TAKE CARE OF MY BROTHERS, I'D JOIN THE TENNIS TEAM, TOO.
THERE'S A DROP-IN PRACTICE FOR THE GIRLS' TEAM TODAY.
YOU WANT TO TRY IT, TOMO?
REALLY?!
PASH
IT'S COMING BACK!
BYOINNN
THIS IS FUN!
PASH
BYONNN
HA-HA-HA-HA-HA
OK, I'M GONNA GO FOR FIVE!
RIGHT ...

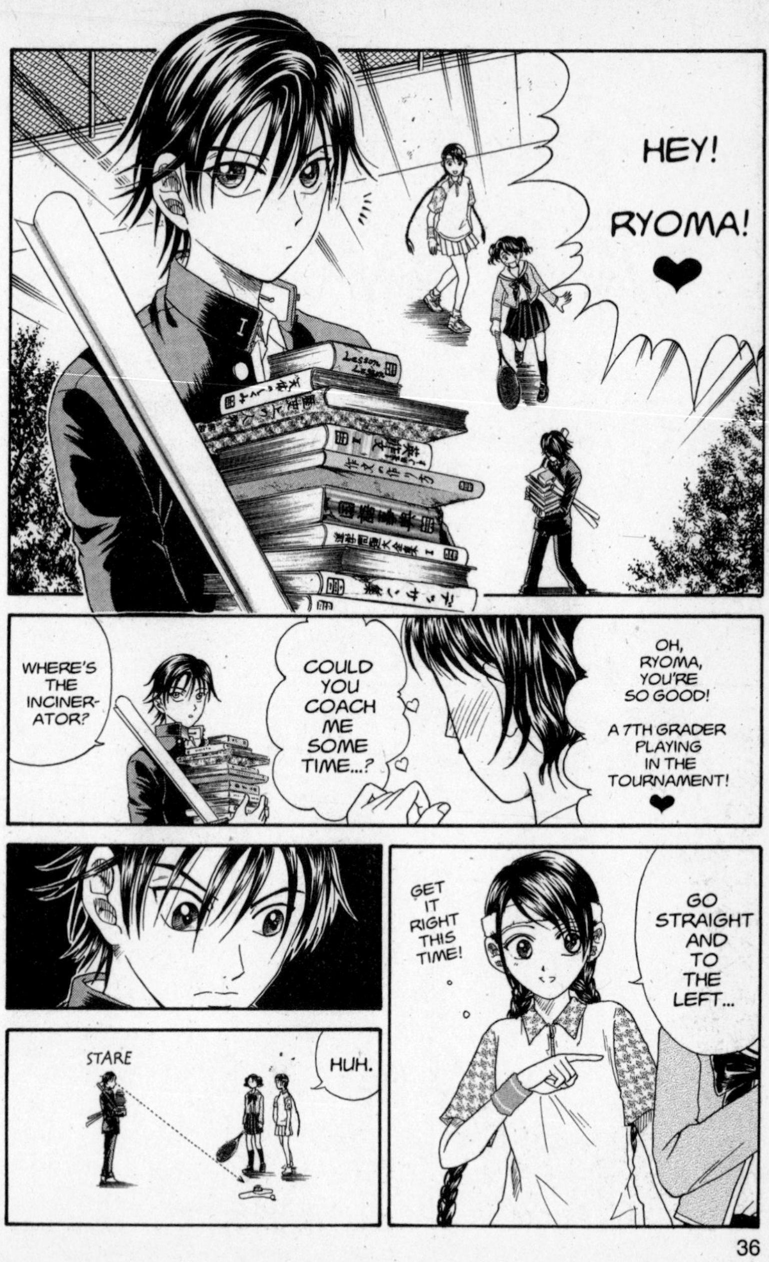
HEY!
RYOMA! ❤
OH, RYOMA, YOU'RE SO GOOD!
A 7TH GRADER PLAYING IN THE TOURNAMENT! ❤
COULD YOU COACH ME SOME TIME...?
WHERE'S THE INCINER-ATOR?
GO STRAIGHT AND TO THE LEFT...
GET IT RIGHT THIS TIME!
HUH.
STARE

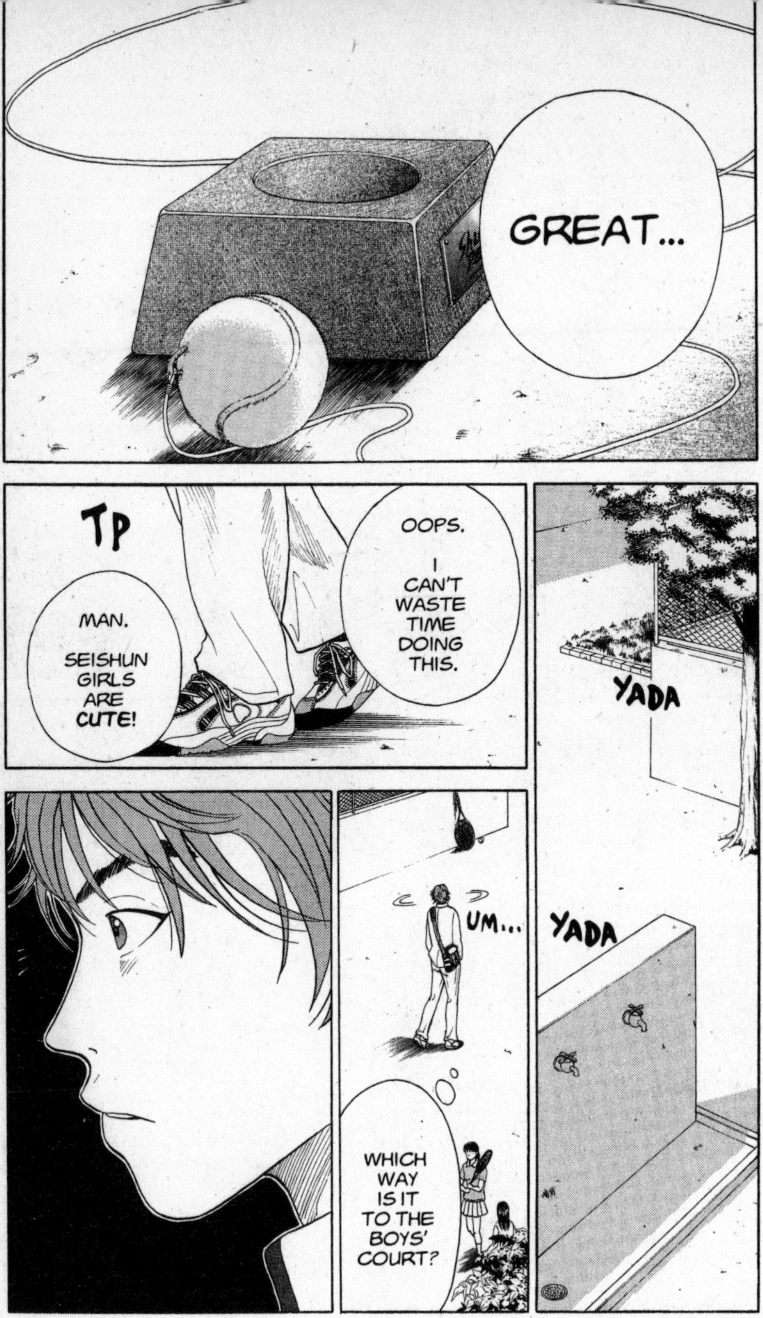
GREAT...
YADA
YADA
OOPS. I CAN'T WASTE TIME DOING THIS.
TP
MAN. SEISHUN GIRLS ARE CUTE!
UM...
WHICH WAY IS IT TO THE BOYS' COURT?

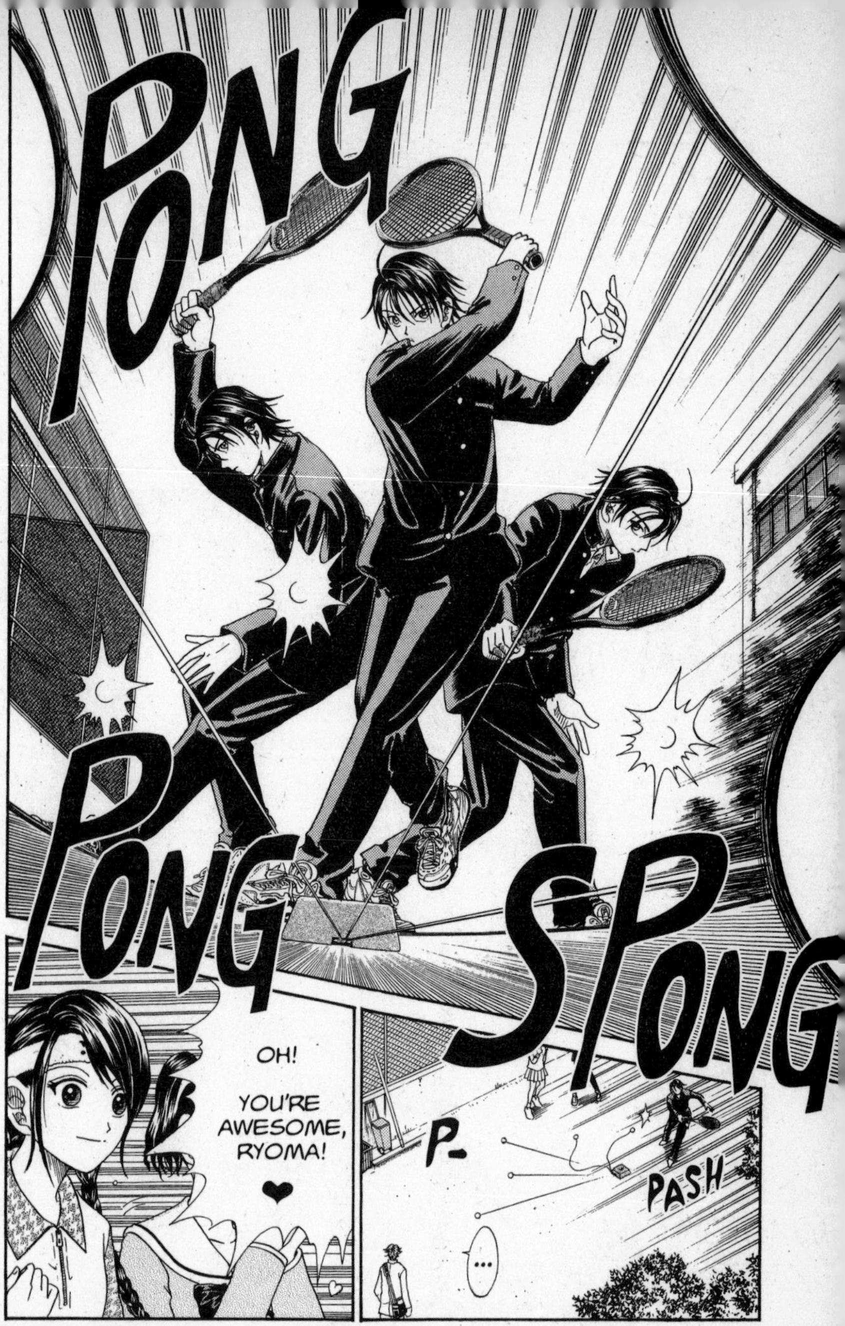
PONG
PONG
SPONG
P-
PASH
...
OH!
YOU'RE AWESOME, RYOMA!

READ THIS WAY

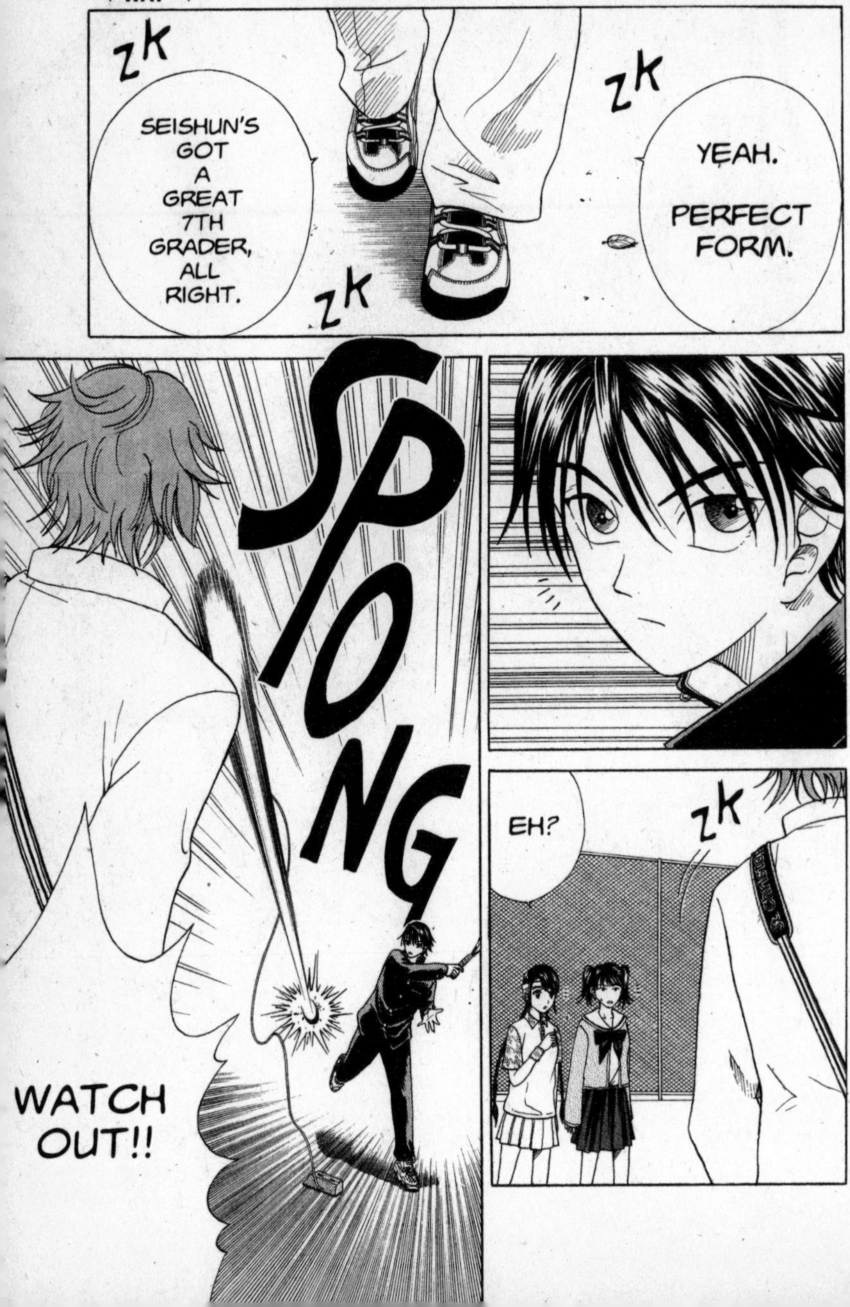
zk
YEAH. PERFECT FORM.
zk
SEISHUN'S GOT A GREAT 7TH GRADER, ALL RIGHT.
zk
zk
EH?
SPONG
WATCH OUT!!

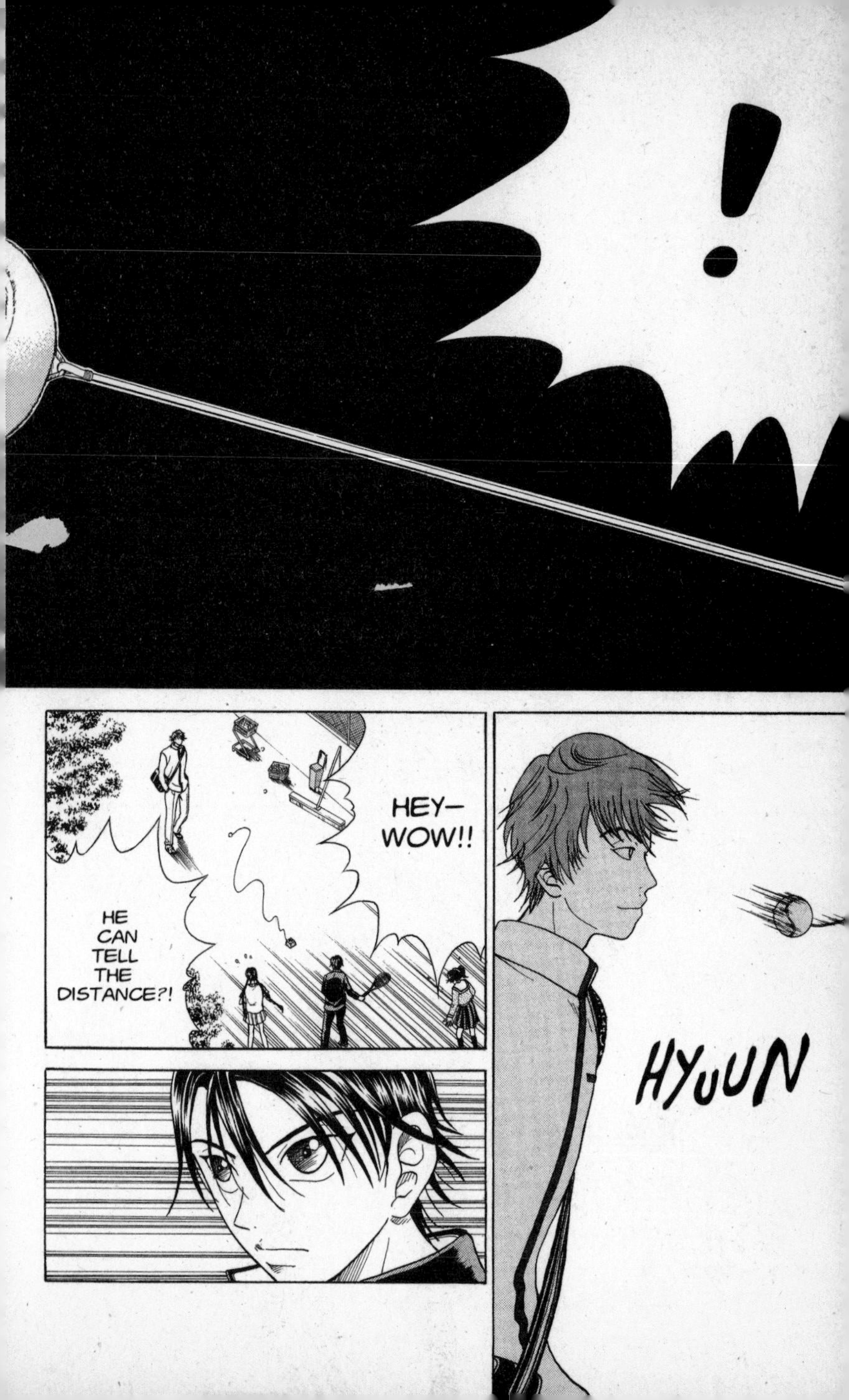
!
HYUUN
HEY—
WOW!!
HE CAN TELL THE DISTANCE?!

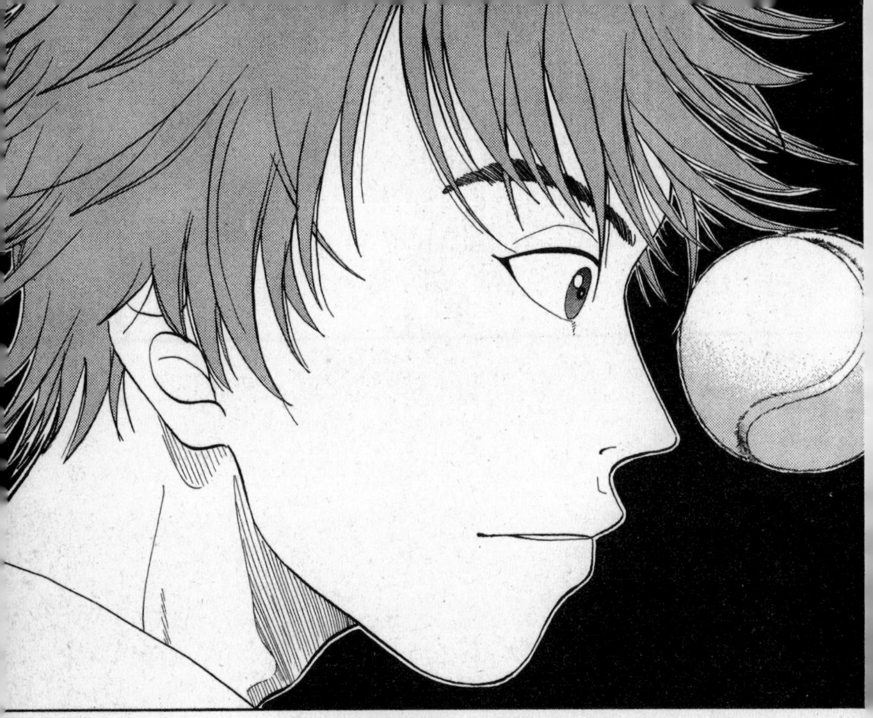

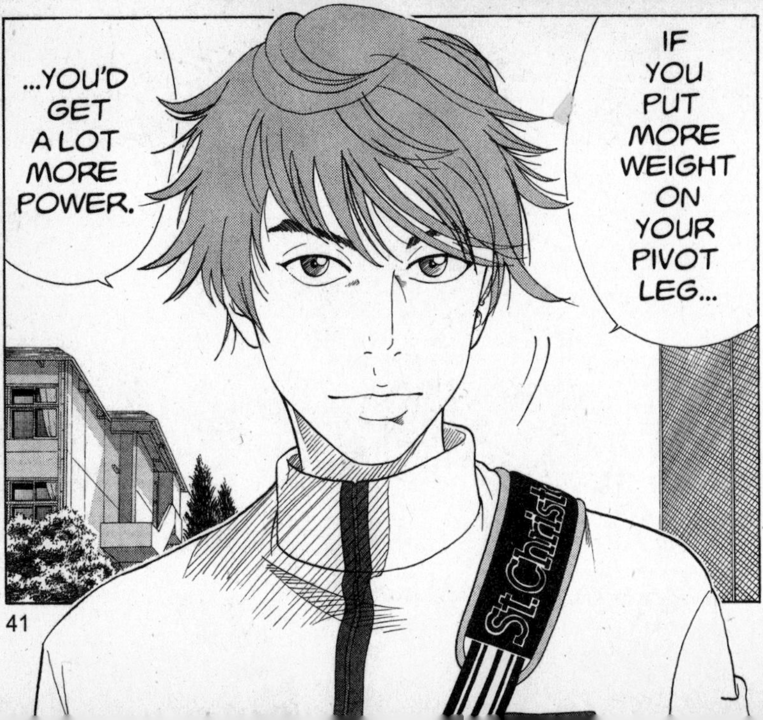
IF YOU PUT MORE WEIGHT ON YOUR PIVOT LEG...
...YOU'D GET A LOT MORE POWER.
St.Christ

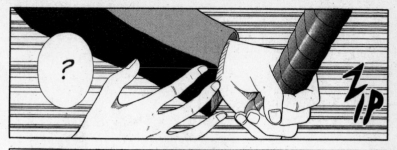

ZIP

WELL, THANKS.

LEFT-HANDED. INTERESTING...

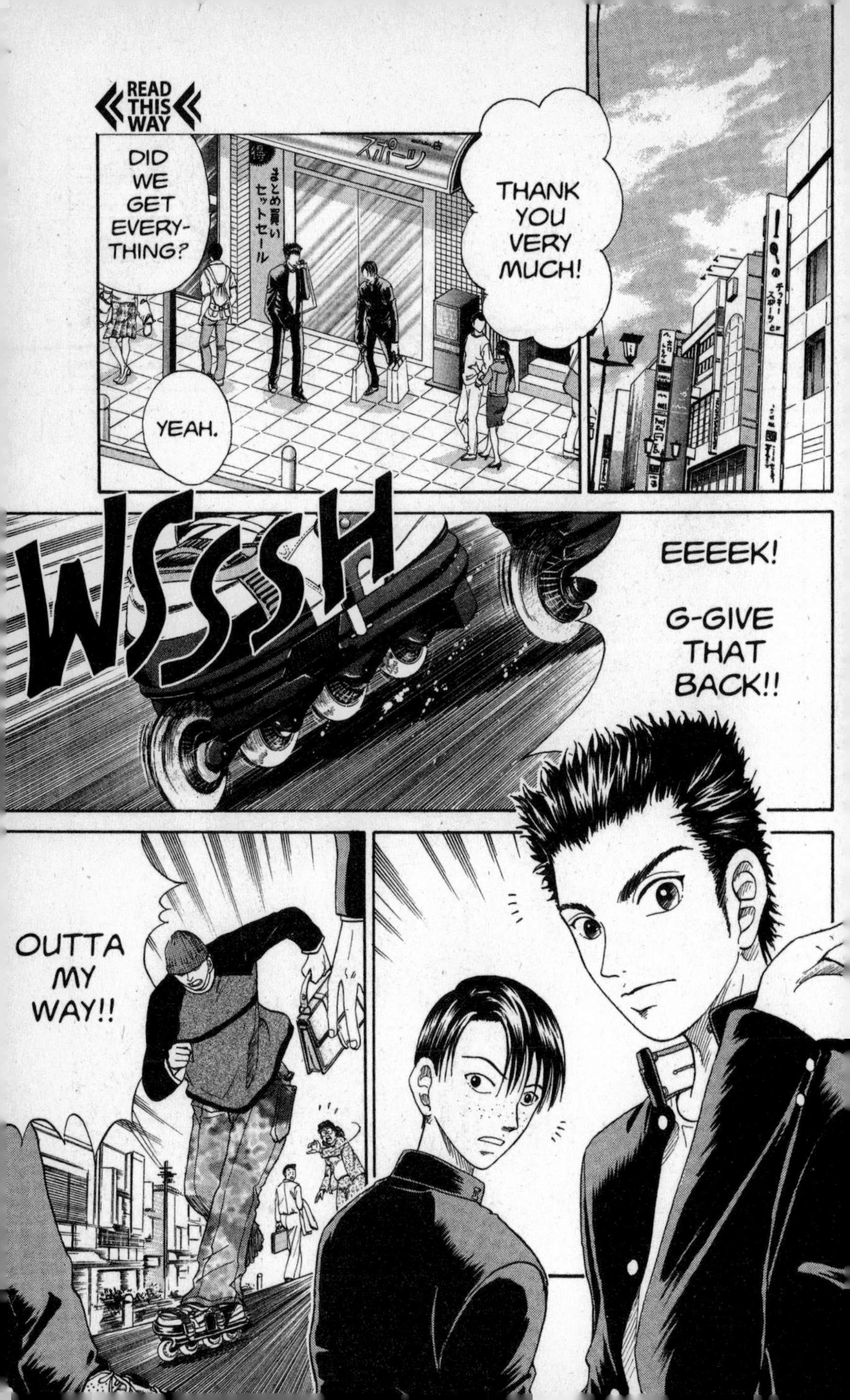
READ THIS WAY
THANK YOU VERY MUCH!
スポーツ
まとめ買い セットセール
DID WE GET EVERY-THING?
YEAH.
EEEEK!
G-GIVE THAT BACK!!
WSSSH
OUTTA MY WAY!!

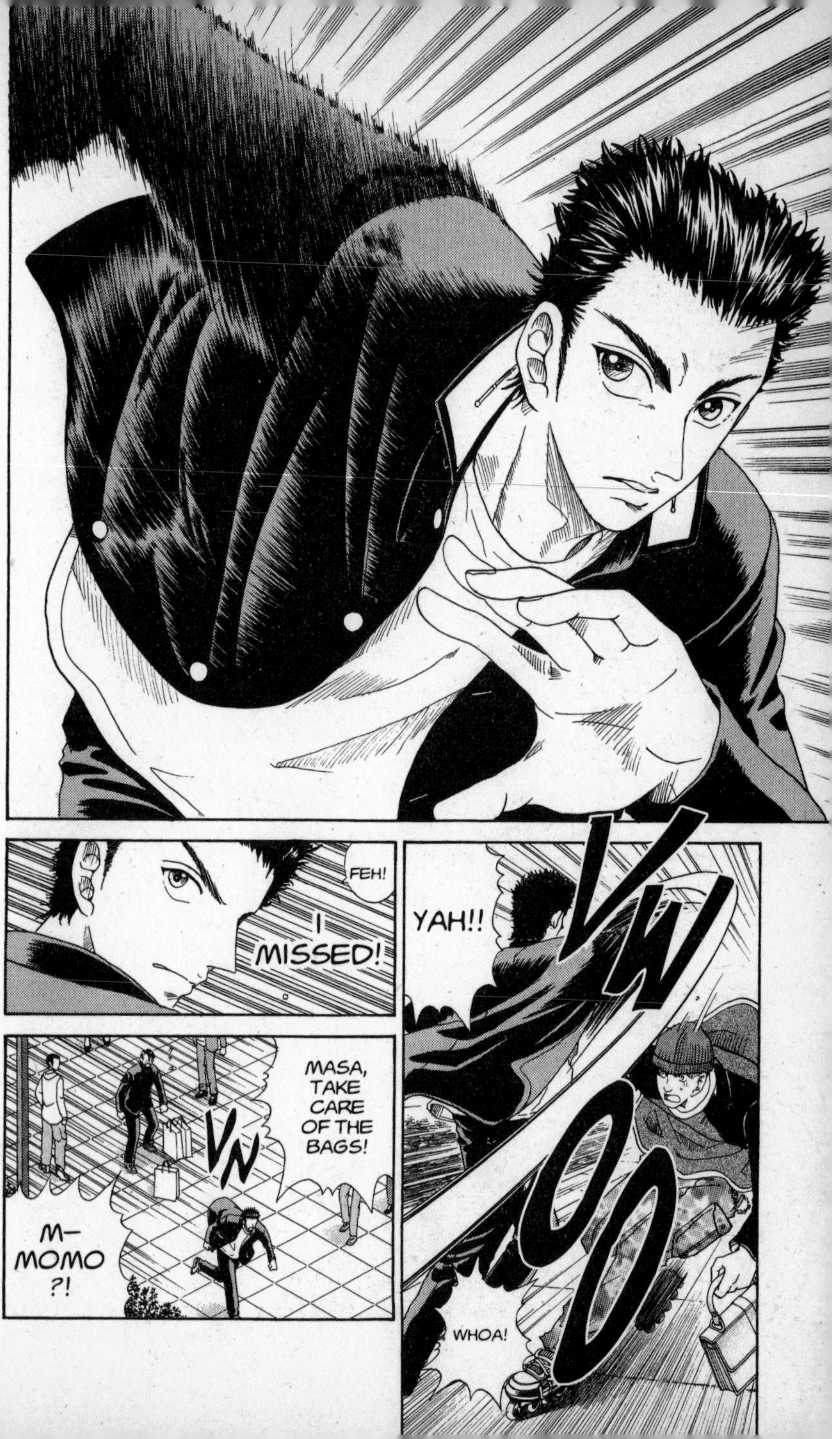
YAH!!
VW
WHOA!
FEH!
I MISSED!
MASA, TAKE CARE OF THE BAGS!
VN
M— MOMO ?!

READ THIS WAY

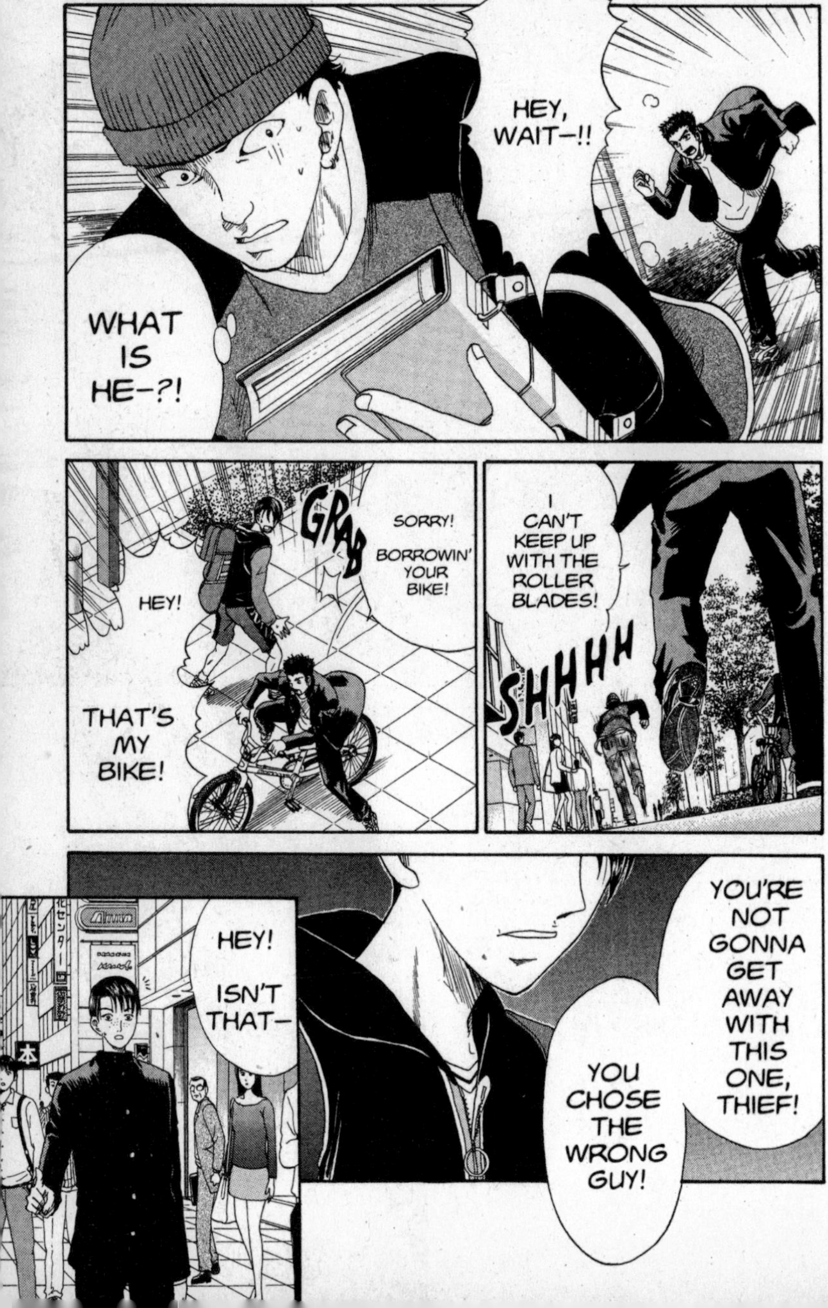
HEY, WAIT—!!
WHAT IS HE—?!
I CAN'T KEEP UP WITH THE ROLLER BLADES!
SHHHH
GRAB
SORRY! BORROWIN' YOUR BIKE!
HEY!
THAT'S MY BIKE!
YOU'RE NOT GONNA GET AWAY WITH THIS ONE, THIEF!
YOU CHOSE THE WRONG GUY!
HEY! ISN'T THAT—

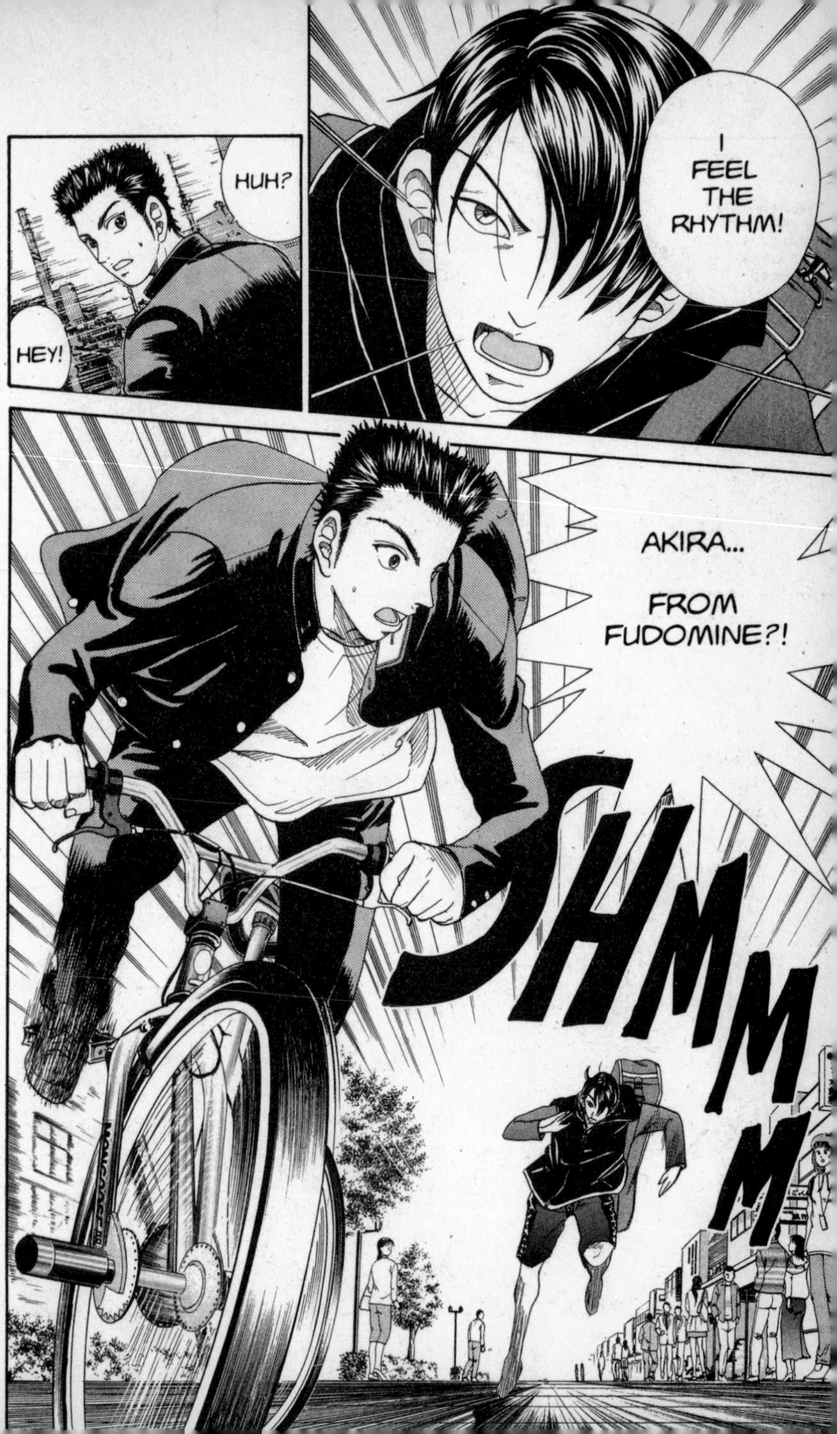
I FEEL THE RHYTHM!
HUH?
HEY!
AKIRA... FROM FUDOMINE?!
SHMMMM

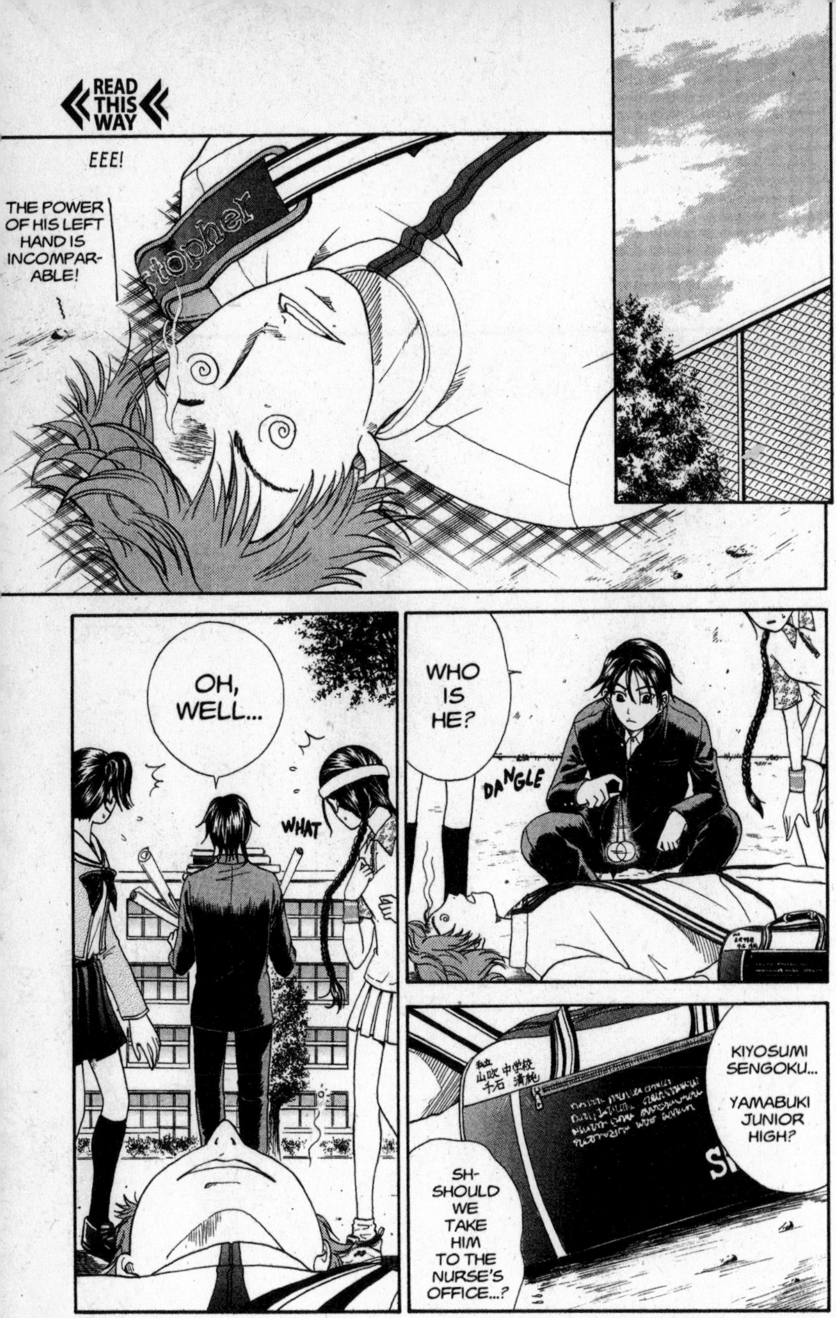
READ THIS WAY
EEE!
THE POWER OF HIS LEFT HAND IS INCOMPAR-ABLE!
WHO IS HE?
DANGLE
KIYOSUMI SENGOKU... YAMABUKI JUNIOR HIGH?
SH-SHOULD WE TAKE HIM TO THE NURSE'S OFFICE...?
OH, WELL...
WHAT

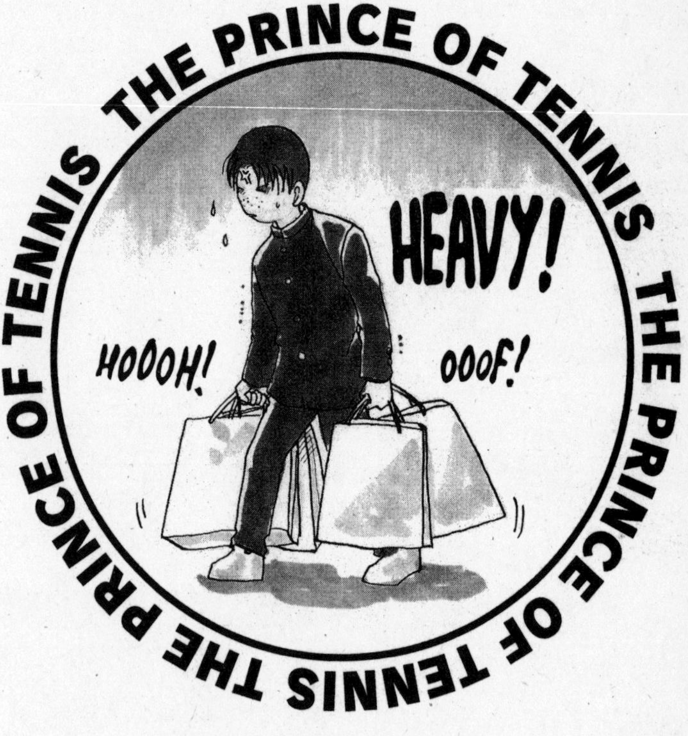
THE PRINCE OF TENNIS THE PRINCE OF TENNIS THE PRINCE OF TENNIS
HEAVY!
HOOOH!
OOOF!

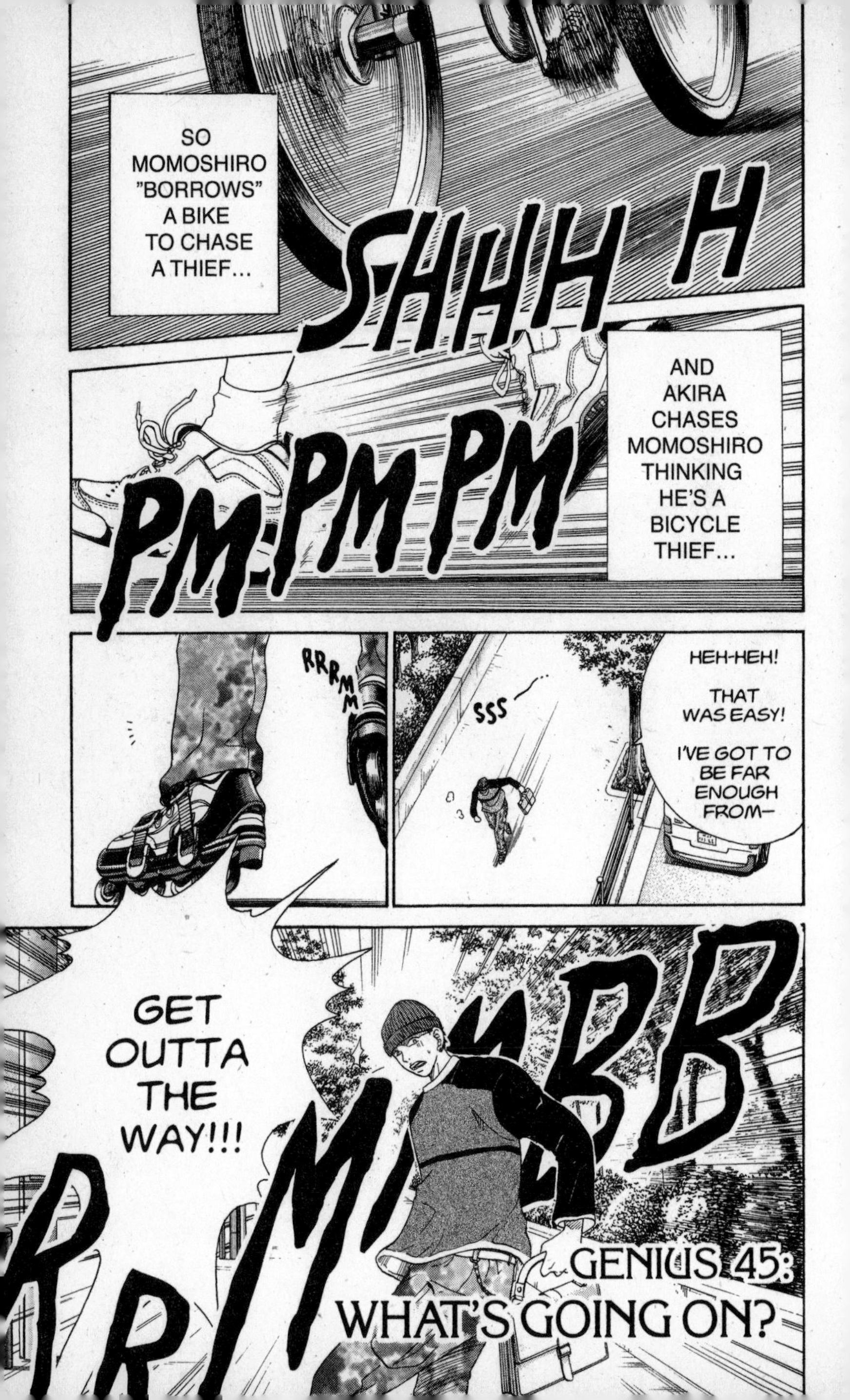
SO MOMOSHIRO "BORROWS" A BIKE TO CHASE A THIEF...
SHHHH H
AND AKIRA CHASES MOMOSHIRO THINKING HE'S A BICYCLE THIEF...
PM-PM-PM
HEH-HEH! THAT WAS EASY! I'VE GOT TO BE FAR ENOUGH FROM–
SSS
RRRMM
GET OUTTA THE WAY!!!
GENIUS 45: WHAT'S GOING ON?

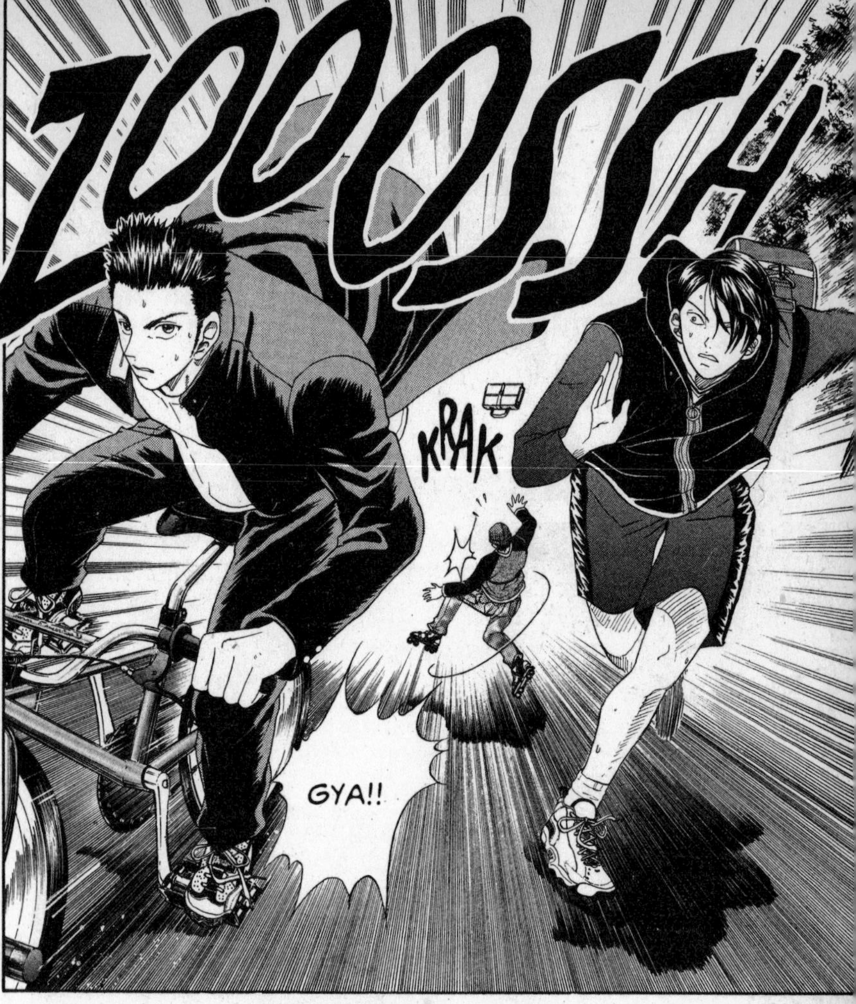
ZOOOSH
KRAK
GYA!!

GENIUS 45:

WHAT'S GOING ON?

READ THIS WAY

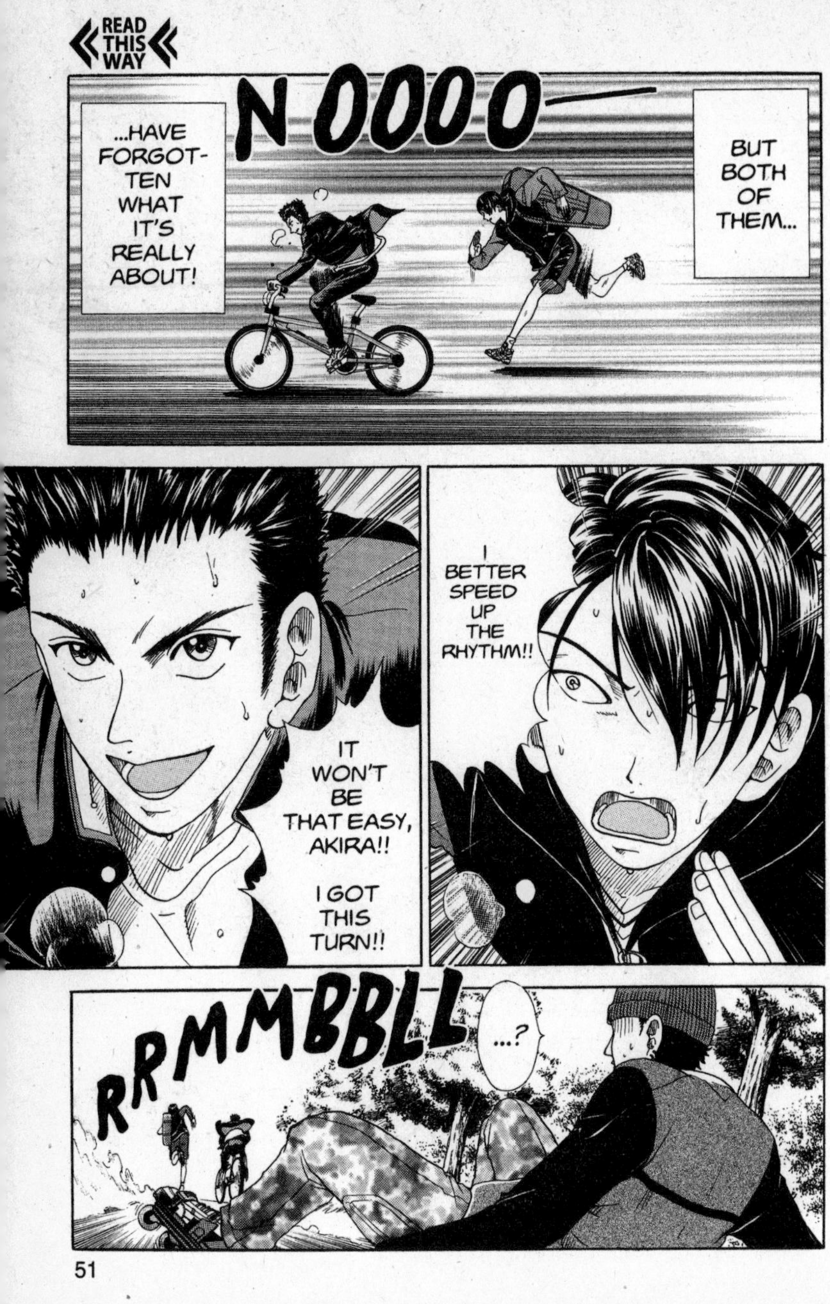
BUT BOTH OF THEM...
N OOOO—
...HAVE FORGOTTEN WHAT IT'S REALLY ABOUT!
I BETTER SPEED UP THE RHYTHM!!
IT WON'T BE THAT EASY, AKIRA!!
I GOT THIS TURN!!
...?
RRMMBBLL

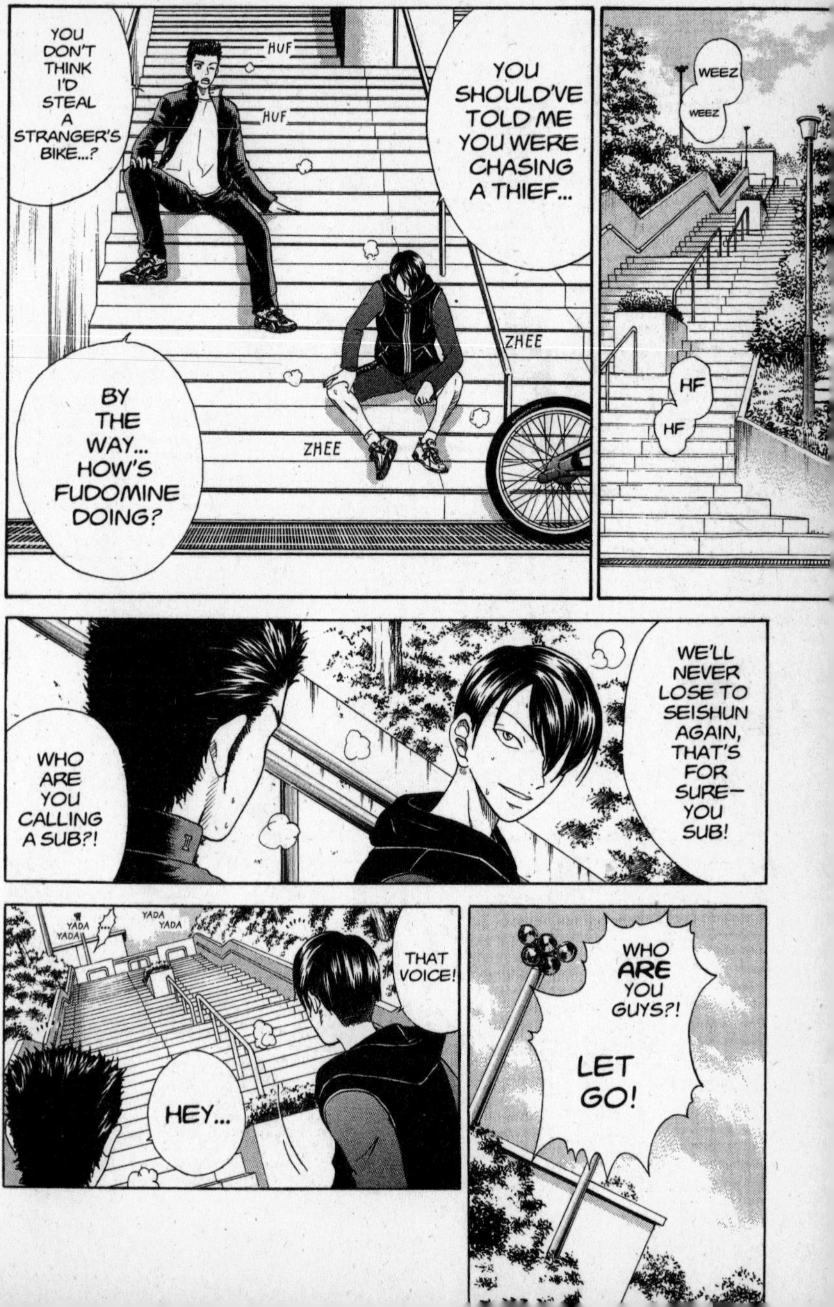
WEEZ
WEEZ
HF
HF
YOU SHOULD'VE TOLD ME YOU WERE CHASING A THIEF...
HUF
HUF
ZHEE
ZHEE
YOU DON'T THINK I'D STEAL A STRANGER'S BIKE...?
BY THE WAY... HOW'S FUDOMINE DOING?
WE'LL NEVER LOSE TO SEISHUN AGAIN, THAT'S FOR SURE— YOU SUB!
WHO ARE YOU CALLING A SUB?!
WHO ARE YOU GUYS?!
LET GO!
THAT VOICE!
YADA YADA
YADA YADA
HEY...

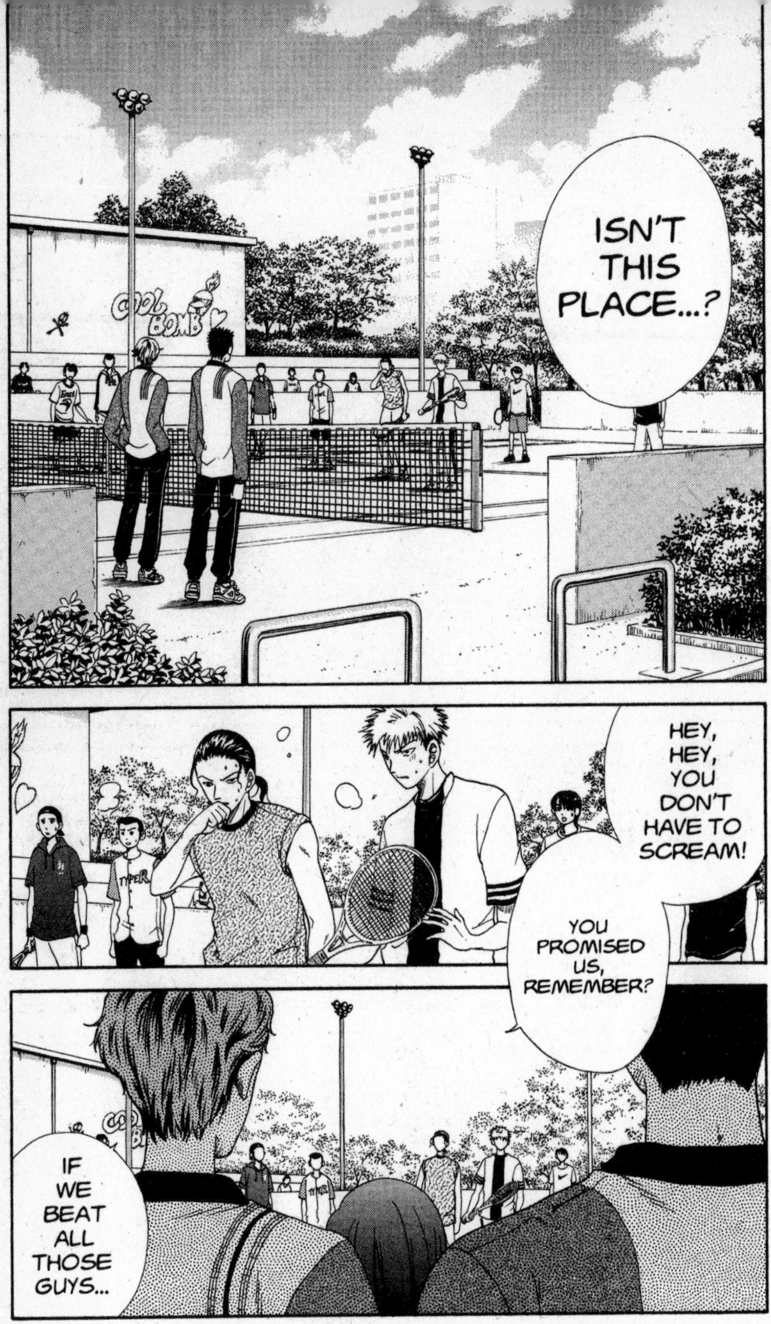
ISN'T THIS PLACE...?
HEY, HEY, YOU DON'T HAVE TO SCREAM!
YOU PROMISED US, REMEMBER?
IF WE BEAT ALL THOSE GUYS...

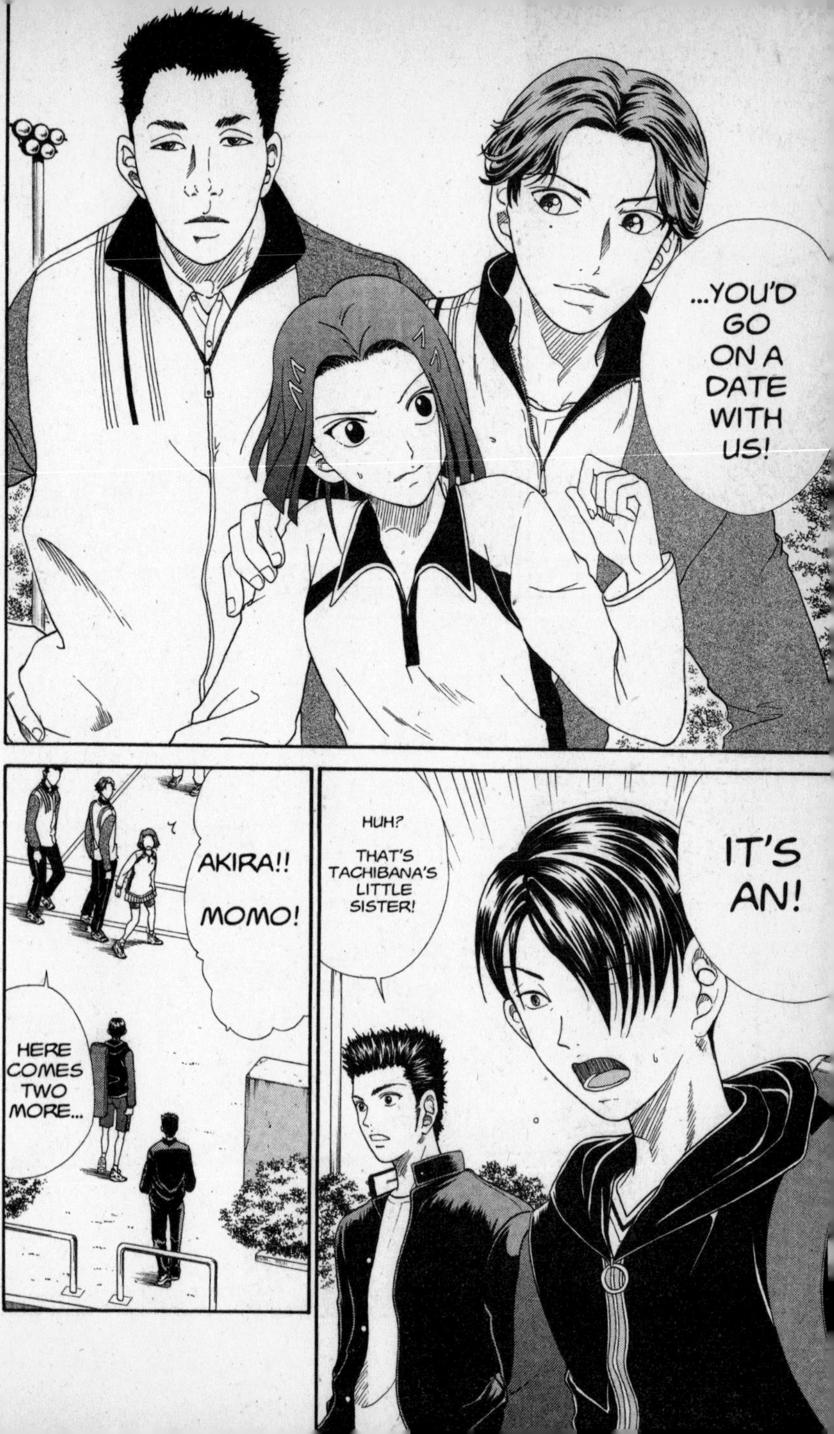
...YOU'D GO ON A DATE WITH US!
IT'S AN!
HUH? THAT'S TACHIBANA'S LITTLE SISTER!
AKIRA!! MOMO!
HERE COMES TWO MORE...

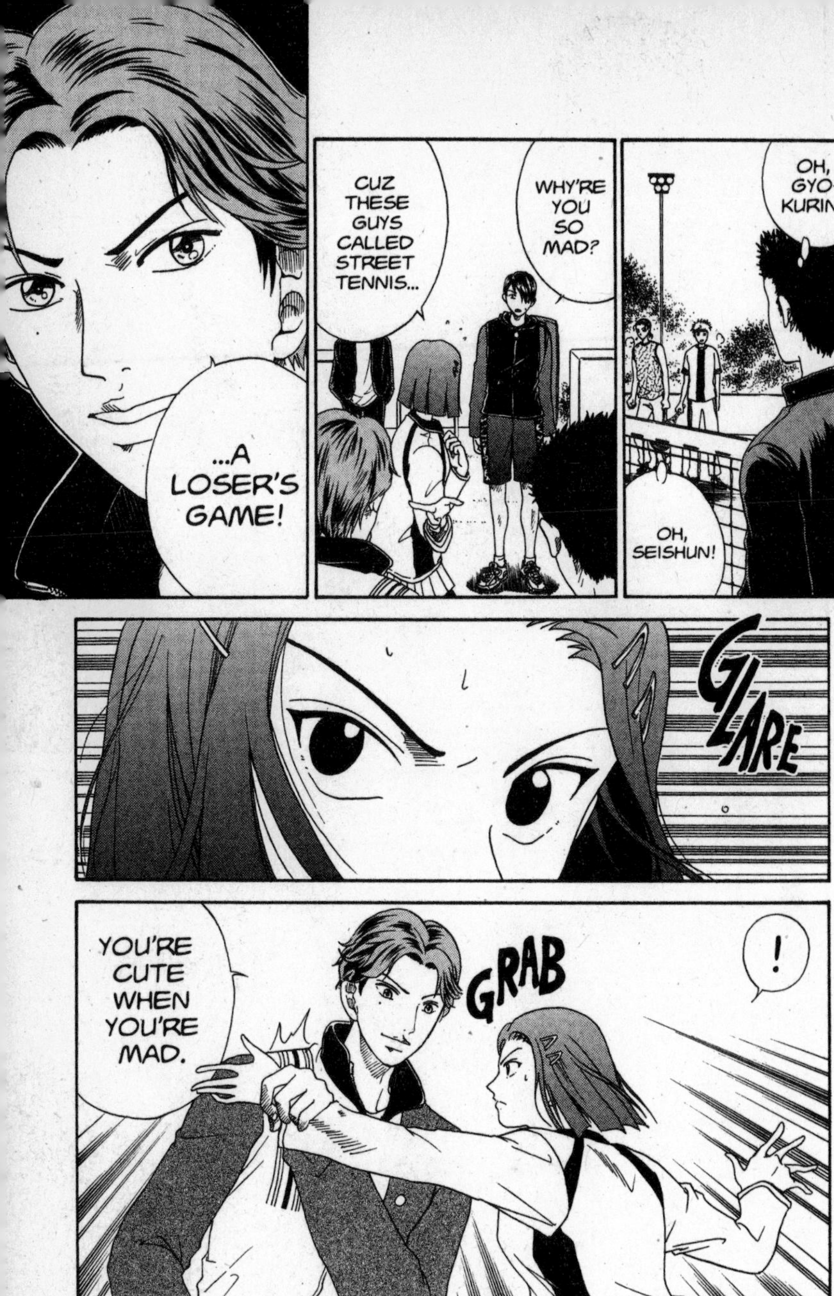
OH, GYO-KURIN!
OH, SEISHUN!
WHY'RE YOU SO MAD?
CUZ THESE GUYS CALLED STREET TENNIS...
...A LOSER'S GAME!
GLARE
!
GRAB
YOU'RE CUTE WHEN YOU'RE MAD.

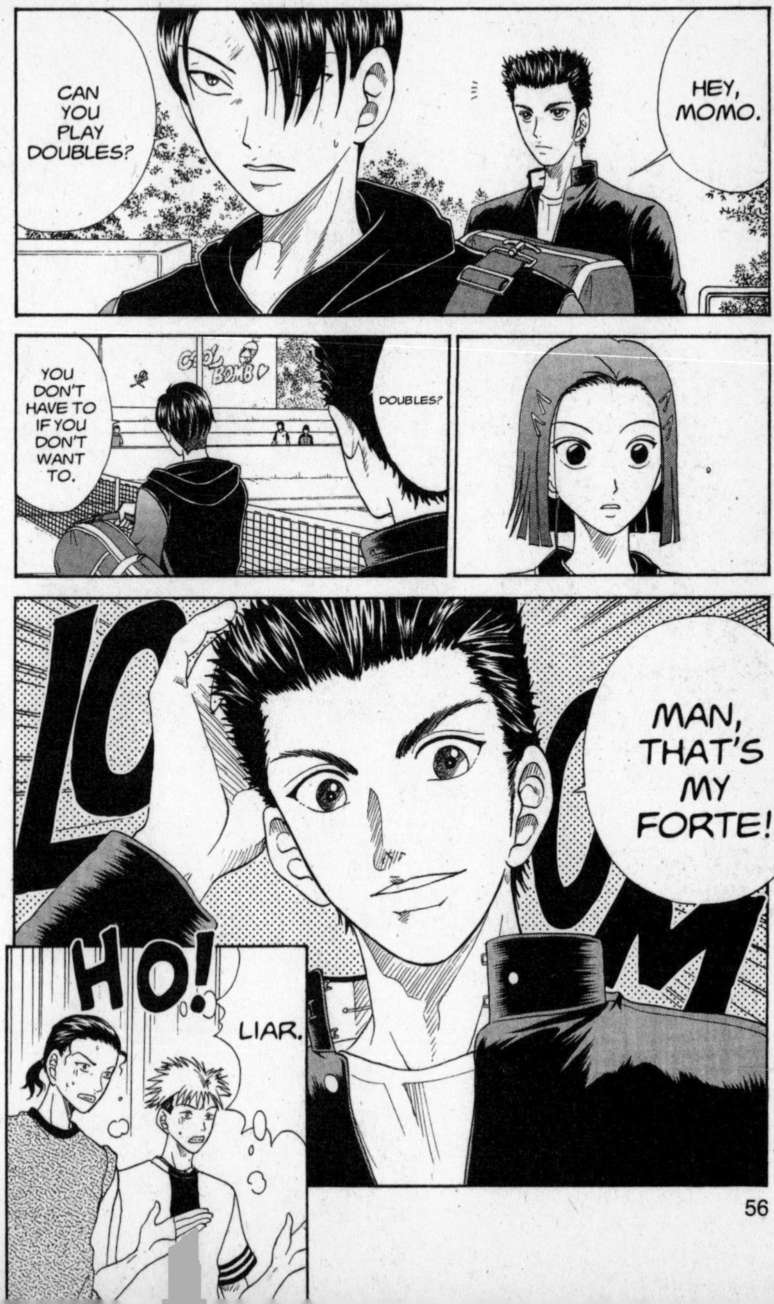
HEY, MOMO.
CAN YOU PLAY DOUBLES?
DOUBLES?
YOU DON'T HAVE TO IF YOU DON'T WANT TO.
MAN, THAT'S MY FORTE!
HO!
LIAR.

READ THIS WAY

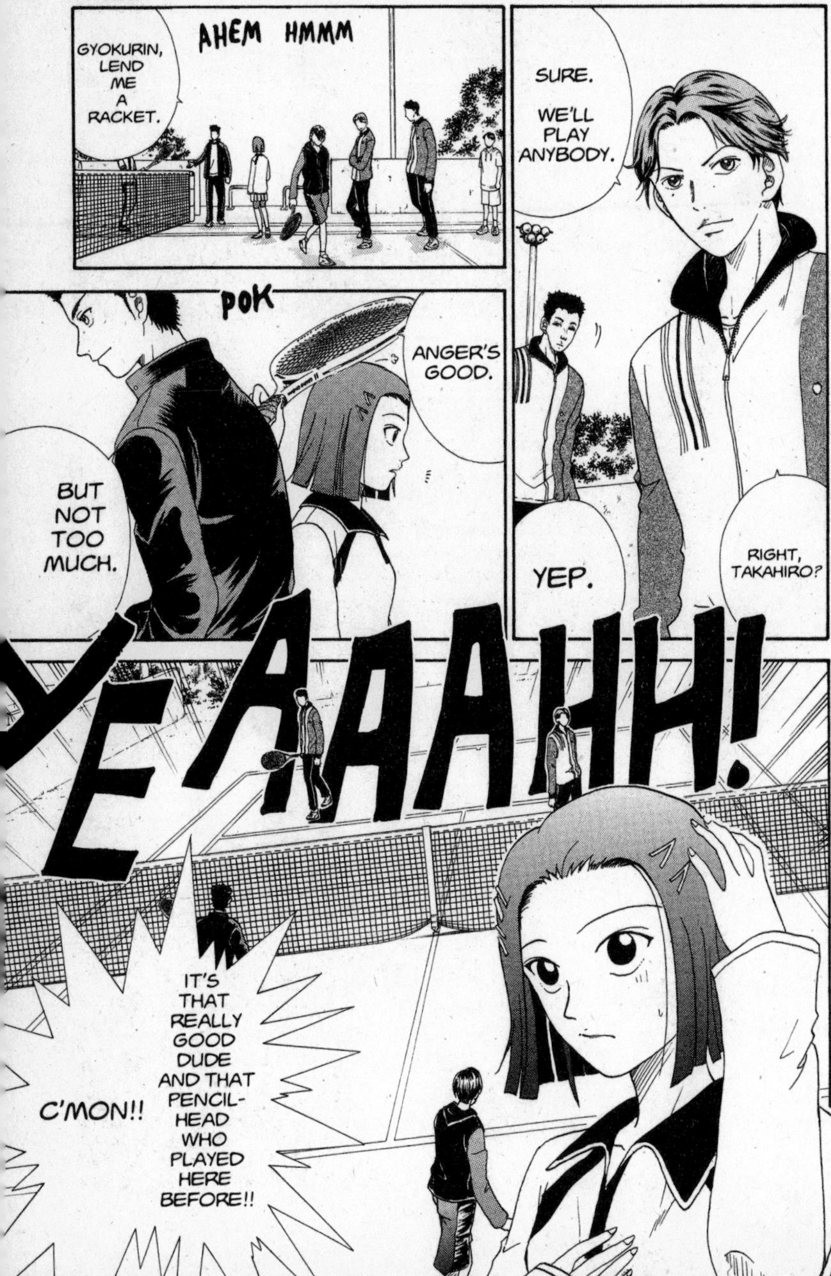
SURE.
WE'LL PLAY ANYBODY.
RIGHT, TAKAHIRO?
YEP.
AHEM HMMM
GYOKURIN, LEND ME A RACKET.
POK
ANGER'S GOOD.
BUT NOT TOO MUCH.
YEAAAHH!
IT'S THAT REALLY GOOD DUDE AND THAT PENCIL-HEAD WHO PLAYED HERE BEFORE!!
C'MON!!

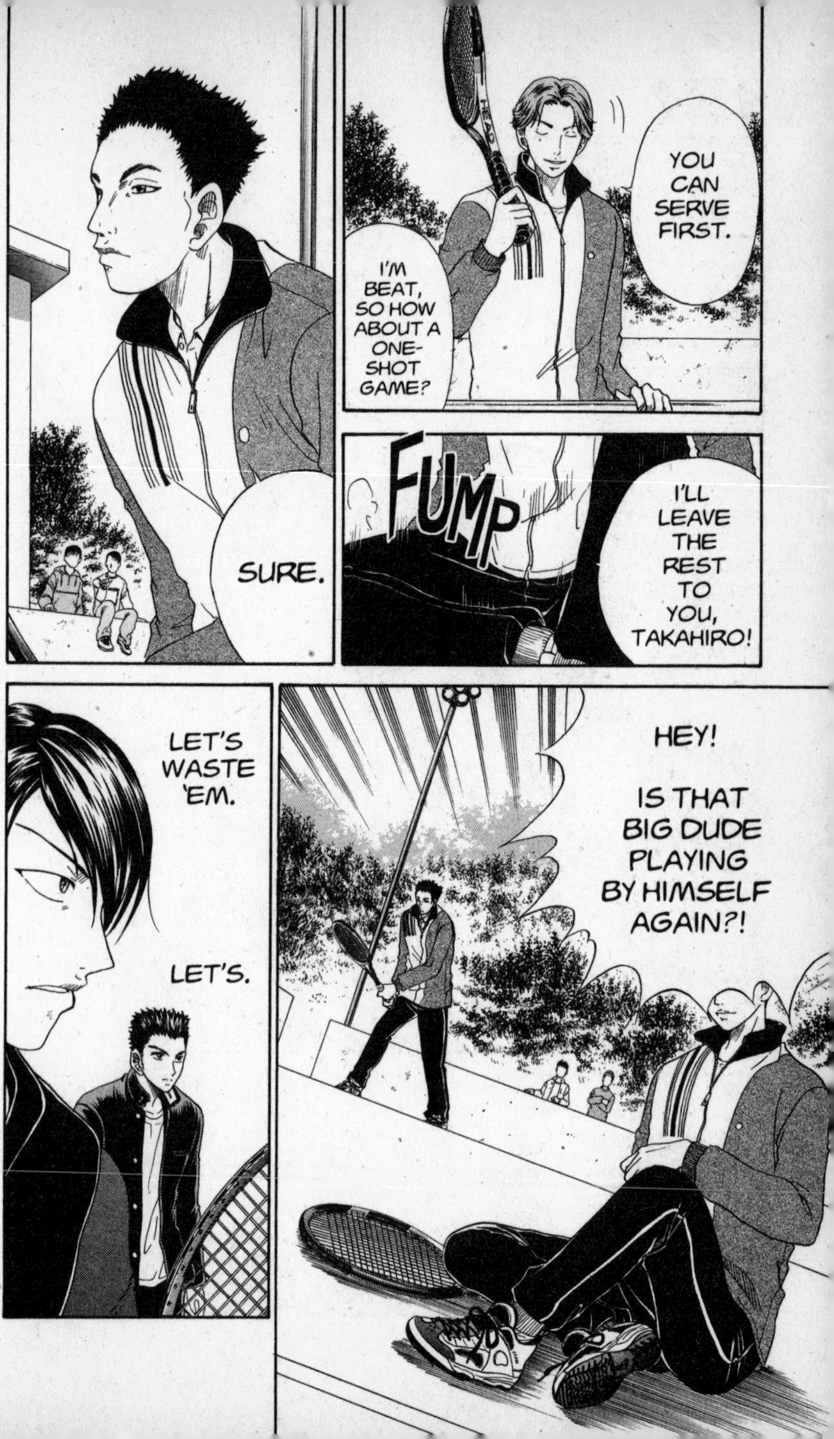
YOU CAN SERVE FIRST.
I'M BEAT, SO HOW ABOUT A ONE-SHOT GAME?
FUMP
I'LL LEAVE THE REST TO YOU, TAKAHIRO!
SURE.
HEY!
IS THAT BIG DUDE PLAYING BY HIMSELF AGAIN?!
LET'S WASTE 'EM.
LET'S.

READ THIS WAY

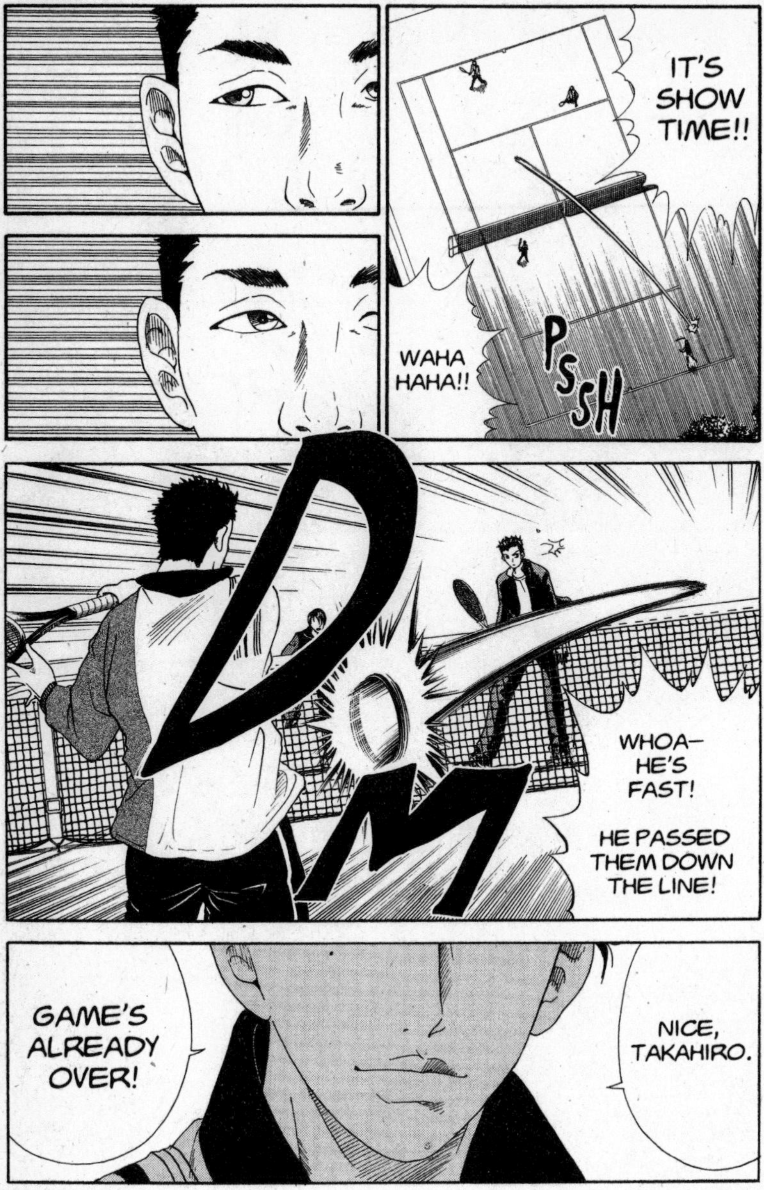
IT'S SHOW TIME!!
WAHA HAHA!!
PSSH
DOM
WHOA— HE'S FAST!
HE PASSED THEM DOWN THE LINE!
NICE, TAKAHIRO.
GAME'S ALREADY OVER!

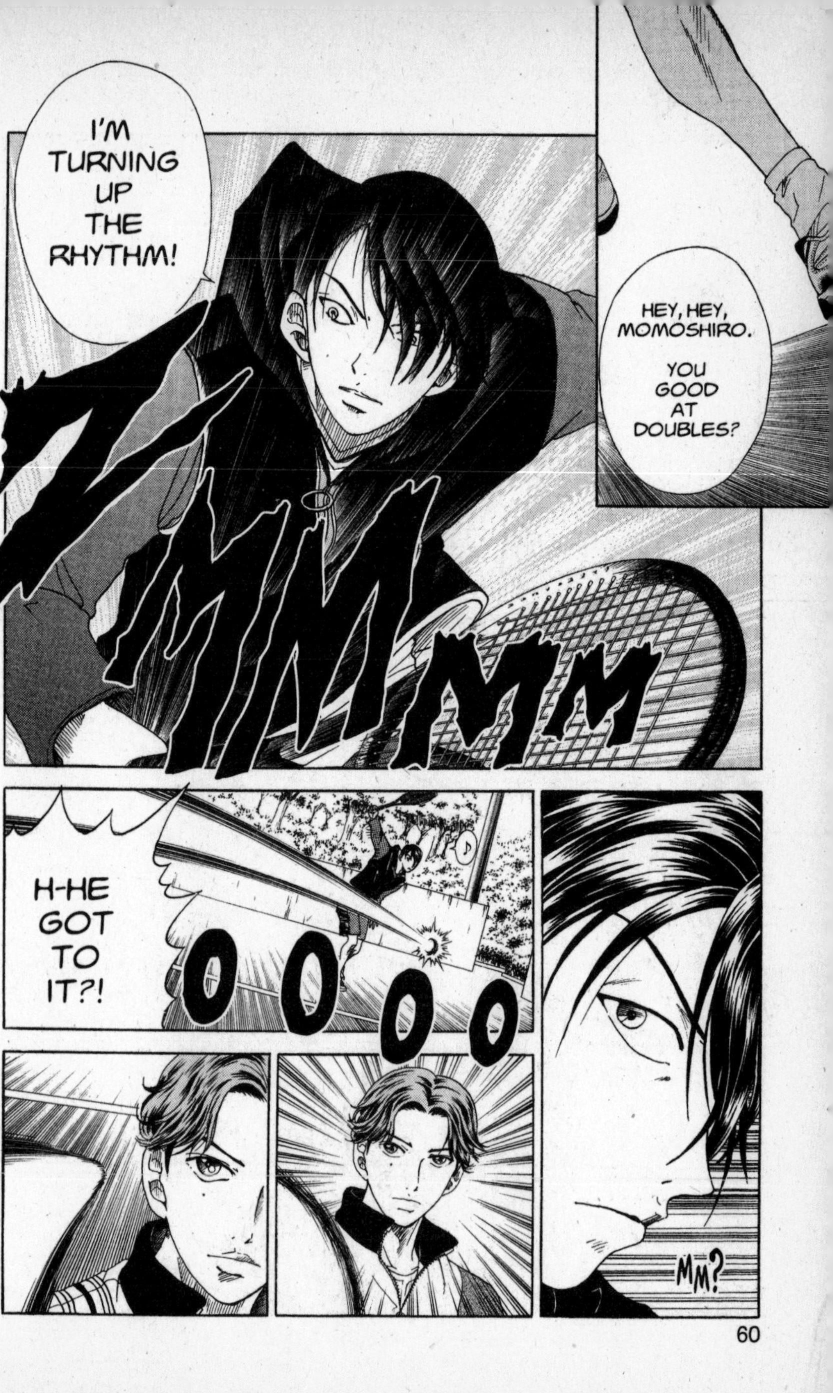
HEY, HEY, MOMOSHIRO. YOU GOOD AT DOUBLES?
I'M TURNING UP THE RHYTHM!
ZMMMMM
MM?
H-HE GOT TO IT?!
OOOOO

READ THIS WAY

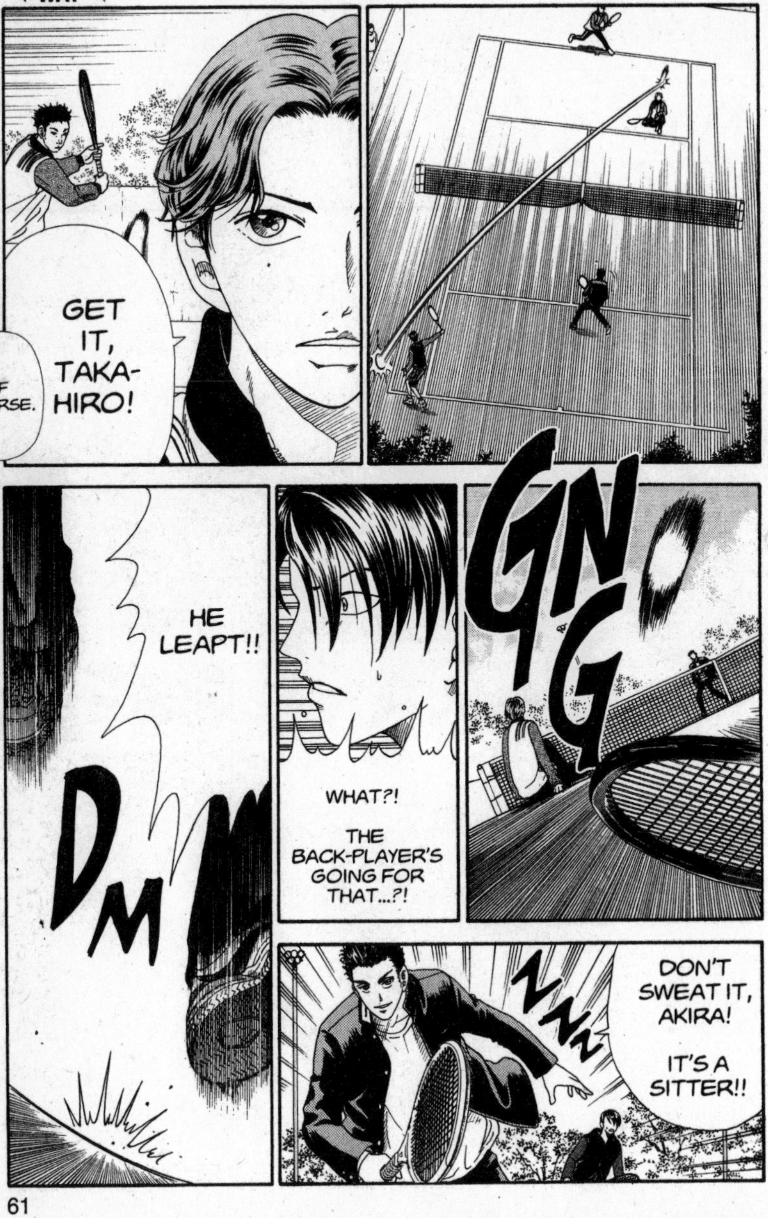
GET IT, TAKA-HIRO!
OF COURSE.
GNG
WHAT?!
THE BACK-PLAYER'S GOING FOR THAT...?!
DON'T SWEAT IT, AKIRA!
IT'S A SITTER!!
NNN
HE LEAPT!!
DM

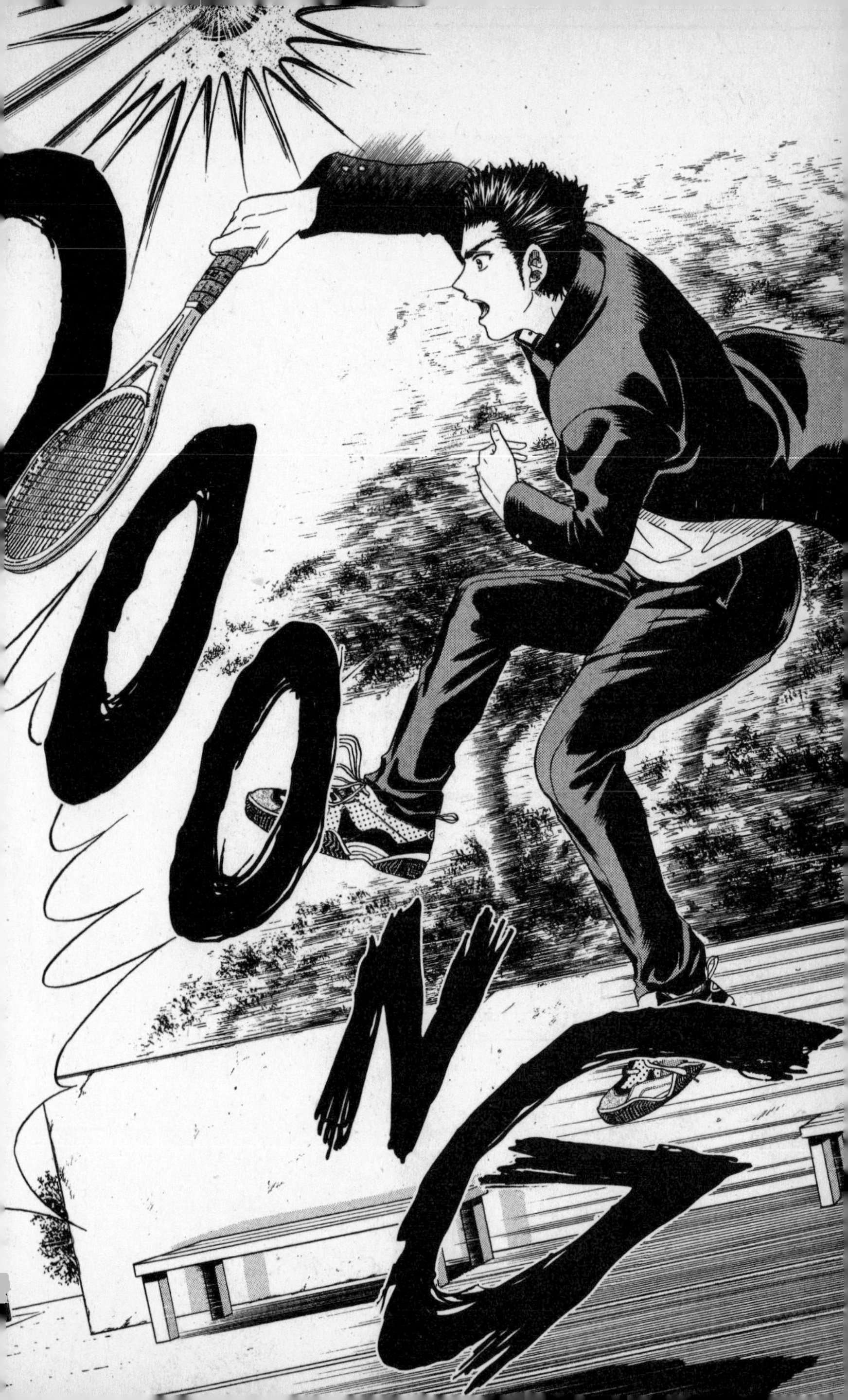
DOONG

READ THIS WAY

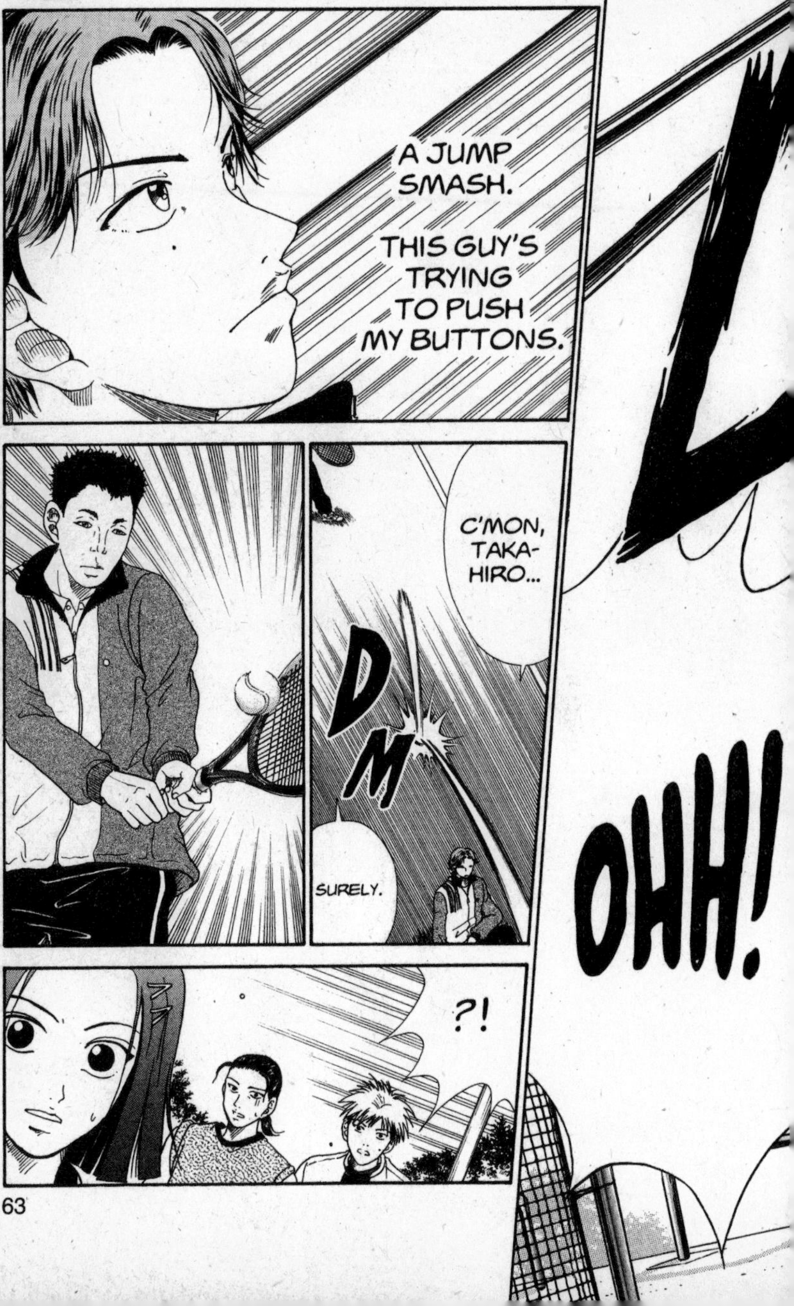
OHH!
A JUMP SMASH.
THIS GUY'S TRYING TO PUSH MY BUTTONS.
C'MON, TAKA-HIRO...
DM
SURELY.
?!

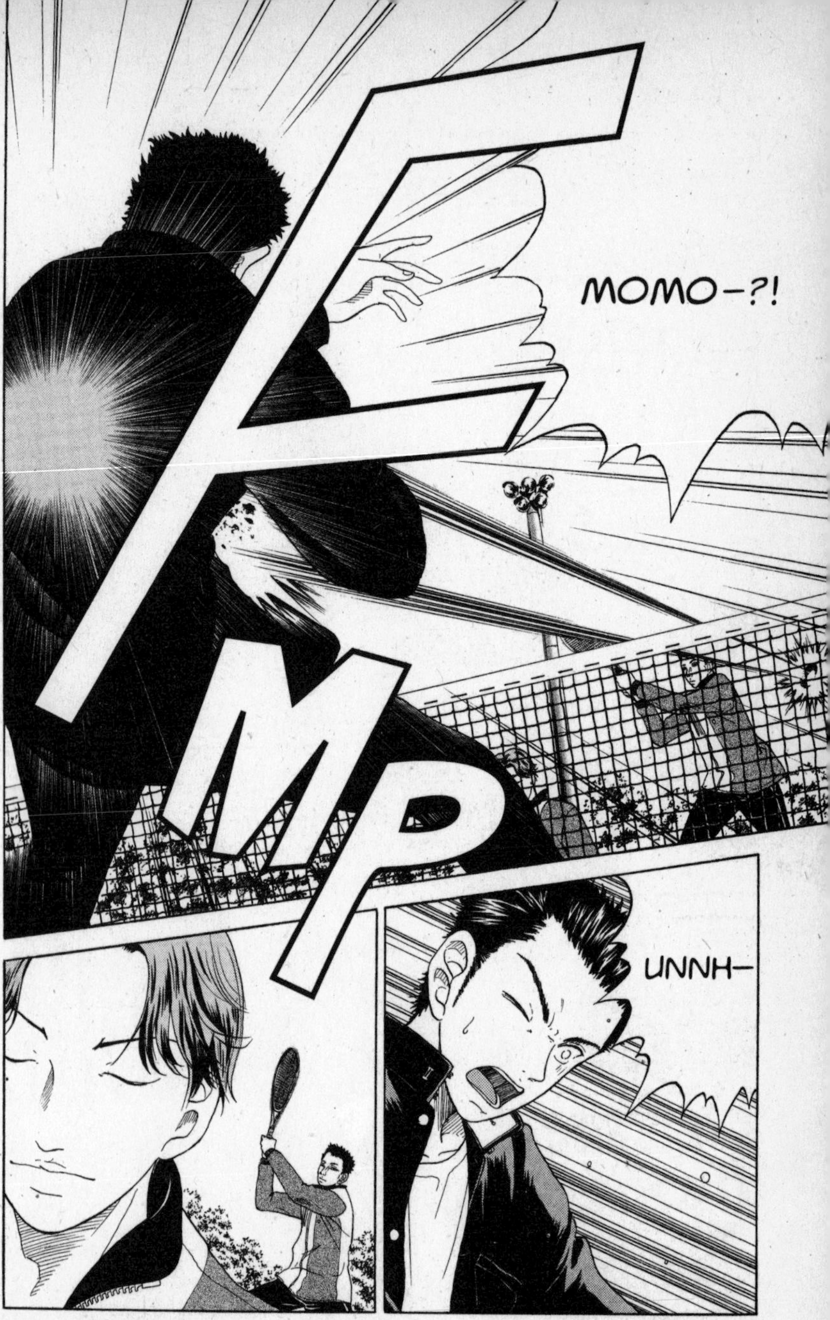
MOMO-?!
FMMP
UNNH-

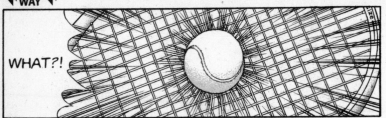

WHAT?!

HE RETURNED IT BY PURE REFLEX!!

HOW...

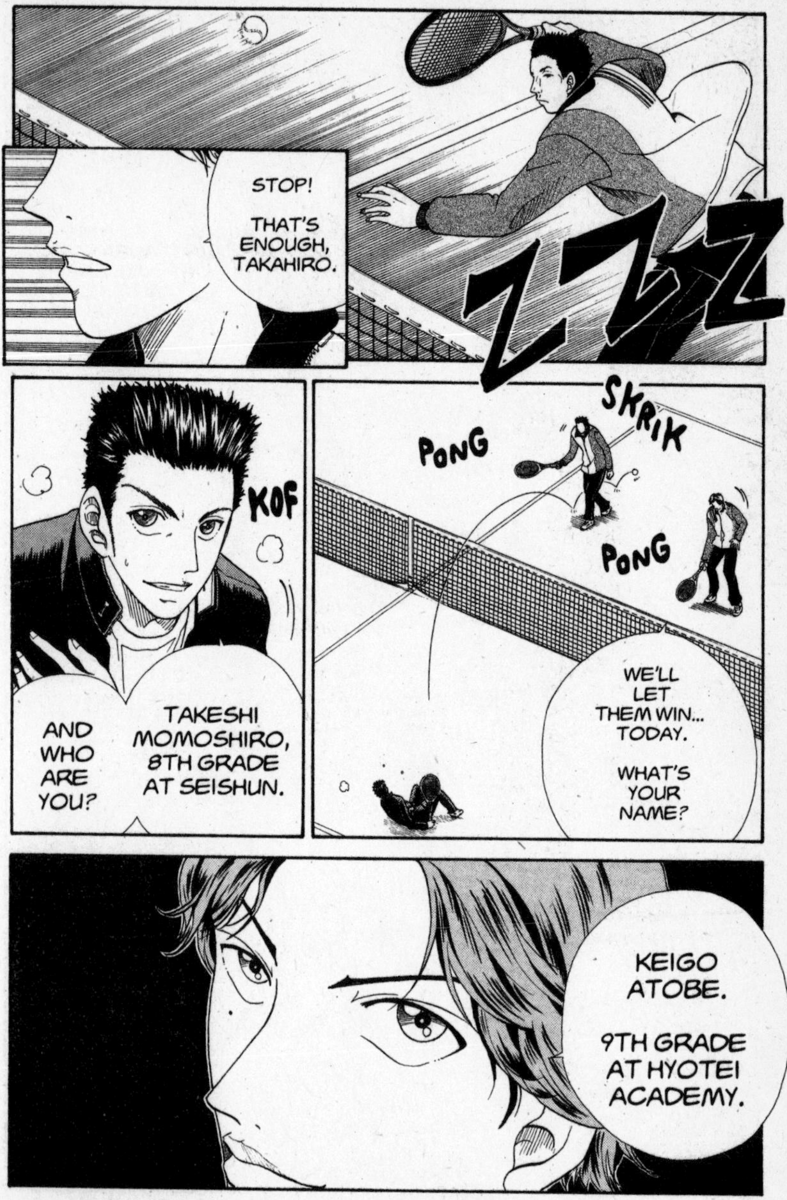
ZZZZ
STOP! THAT'S ENOUGH, TAKAHIRO.
SKRIK
PONG
PONG
WE'LL LET THEM WIN... TODAY. WHAT'S YOUR NAME?
KOF
TAKESHI MOMOSHIRO, 8TH GRADE AT SEISHUN.
AND WHO ARE YOU?
KEIGO ATOBE. 9TH GRADE AT HYOTEI ACADEMY.

READ THIS WAY

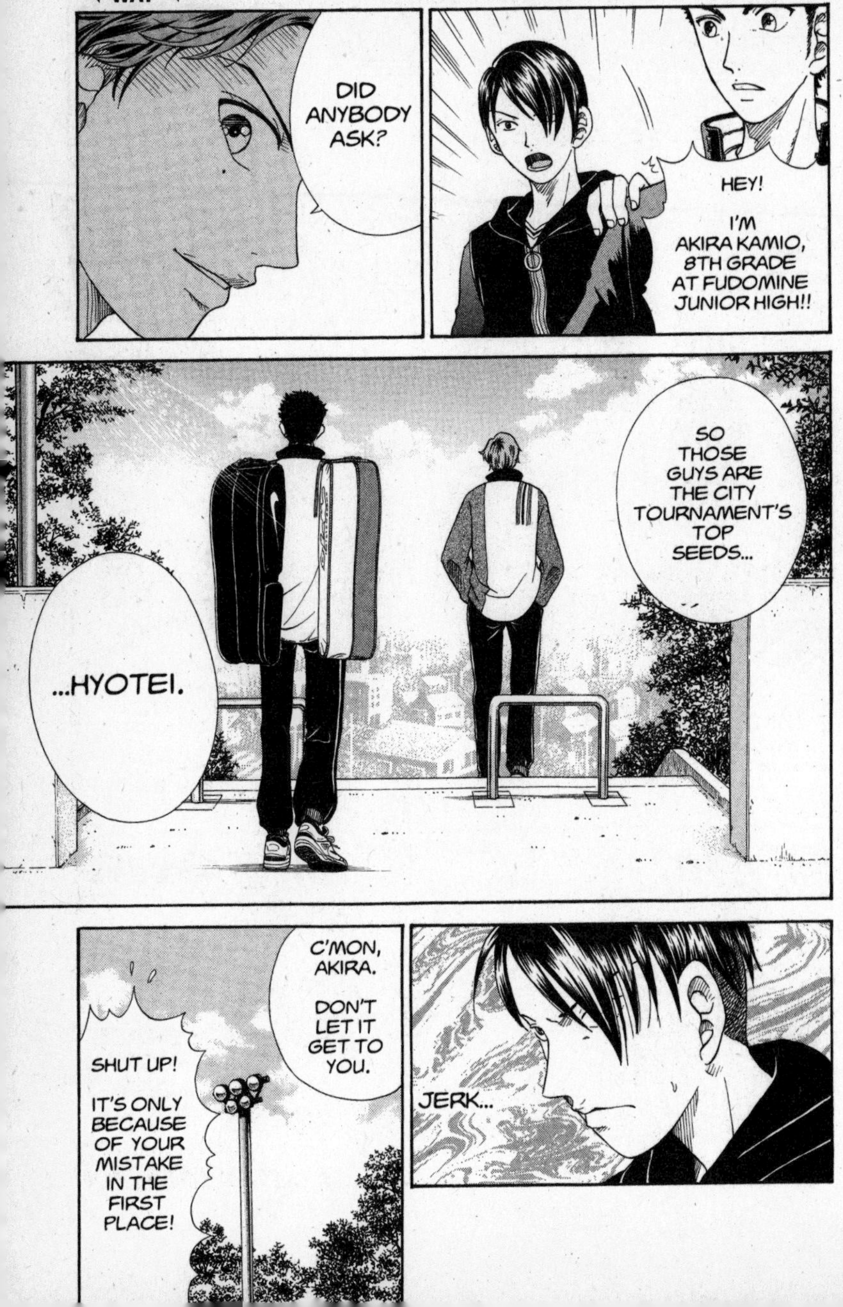
HEY!
I'M AKIRA KAMIO, 8TH GRADE AT FUDOMINE JUNIOR HIGH!!
DID ANYBODY ASK?
SO THOSE GUYS ARE THE CITY TOURNAMENT'S TOP SEEDS...
...HYOTEI.
JERK...
C'MON, AKIRA.
DON'T LET IT GET TO YOU.
SHUT UP!
IT'S ONLY BECAUSE OF YOUR MISTAKE IN THE FIRST PLACE!

THANK YOU FOR READING PRINCE OF TENNIS!
THIS MAY SOUND WEIRD, BUT I BOUGHT A WHITE BOARD A LITTLE WHILE AGO. IT'S BECAUSE OF THE PHOTO-BOOTH PICTURES I GET FROM EVERYBODY. FANS SEND LETTERS AND SAY, "YOU PROBABLY DON'T WANT A PICTURE, BUT I'LL ENCLOSE ONE ANYWAY." (BUT I DO WANT THEM!) SO...

VISIT THE STUDIO THROUGH YOUR PICTURES! IT'S EASY! JUST SEND ANY EXTRA PHOTOS LYING AROUND IN YOUR HOUSE, AND I'LL STICK THEM ON THE WHITE BOARD! (ONLY 2.5 CM X 1.5 CM, PLEASE.) IF YOU CAN'T GET TO A PHOTO BOOTH, JUST CUT A PHOTO OF YOURSELF INTO THE SIZE ABOVE. PLEASE WRITE "PHOTO ENCLOSED" ON THE OUTSIDE OF THE ENVELOPE. THE DEADLINE IS THE END OF JANUARY 2001.

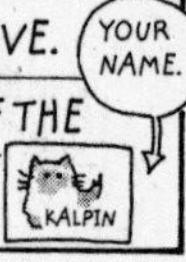
YOUR NAME.
KALPIN

* THIS PROMO WAS HELD ONLY IN JAPAN.

THE PAST "CLASSMATE" CONTEST WAS POPULAR, AND SO WAS "CHOOSE THE COVER" (ALTHOUGH TOO MANY OF YOU WROTE, ""INCLUDE EVERYBODY!"). THE RESULTS OF THIS EVENT WON'T BE PUBLISHED IN THE COMICS, BUT I WILL POST EVERY PICTURE I GET!

ANYWAY, KEEP SUPPORTING THE PRINCE OF TENNIS AND RYOMA!
SEE YOU NEXT VOLUME!

--TAKESHI KONOMI

テニスの王子様☆
T. KONOMI
2000.10.29

GENIUS 46:

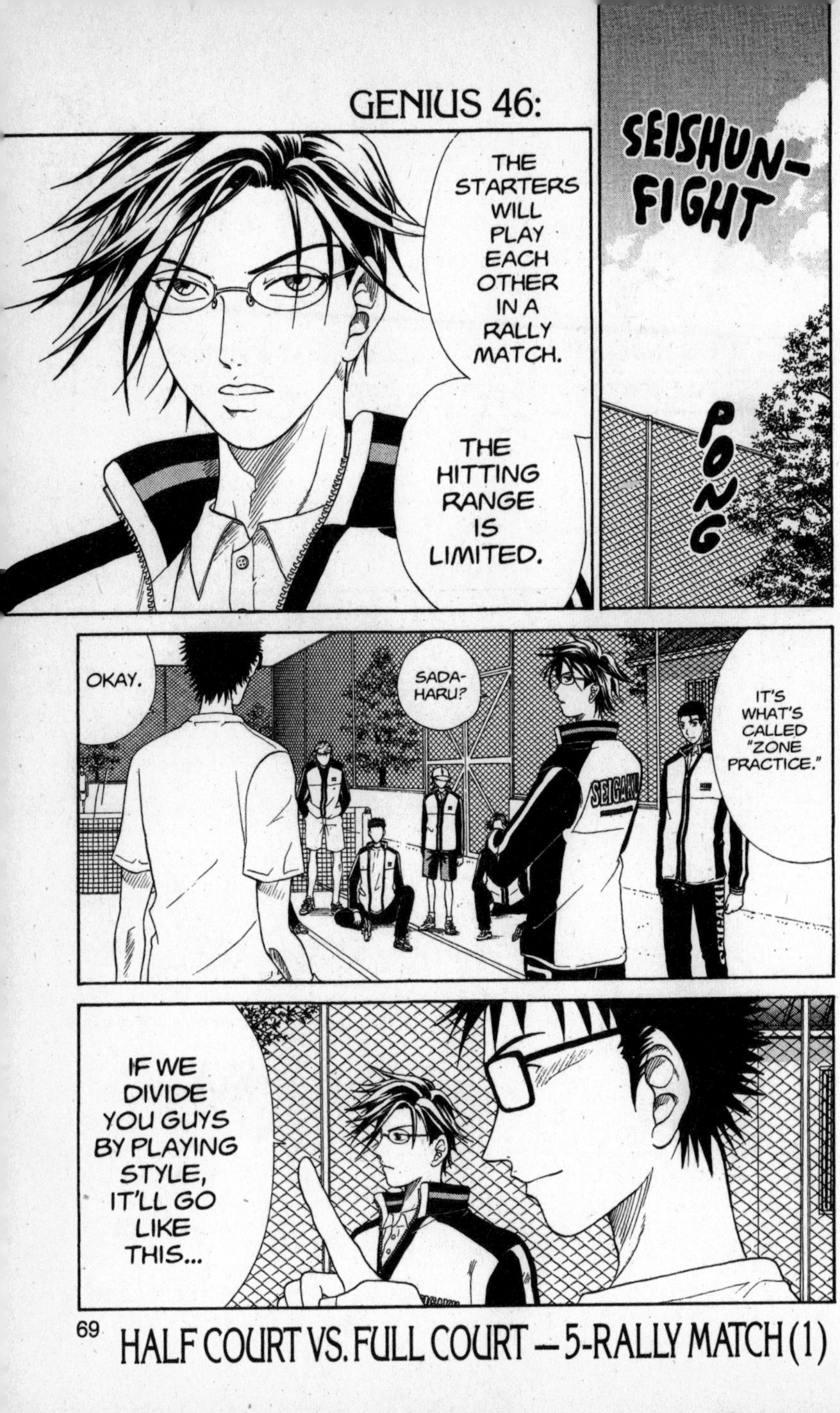
SEISHUN-FIGHT
PONG
THE STARTERS WILL PLAY EACH OTHER IN A RALLY MATCH.
THE HITTING RANGE IS LIMITED.
IT'S WHAT'S CALLED "ZONE PRACTICE."
SADA-HARU?
OKAY.
SEIGAKU
IF WE DIVIDE YOU GUYS BY PLAYING STYLE, IT'LL GO LIKE THIS...

HALF COURT VS. FULL COURT — 5-RALLY MATCH (1)

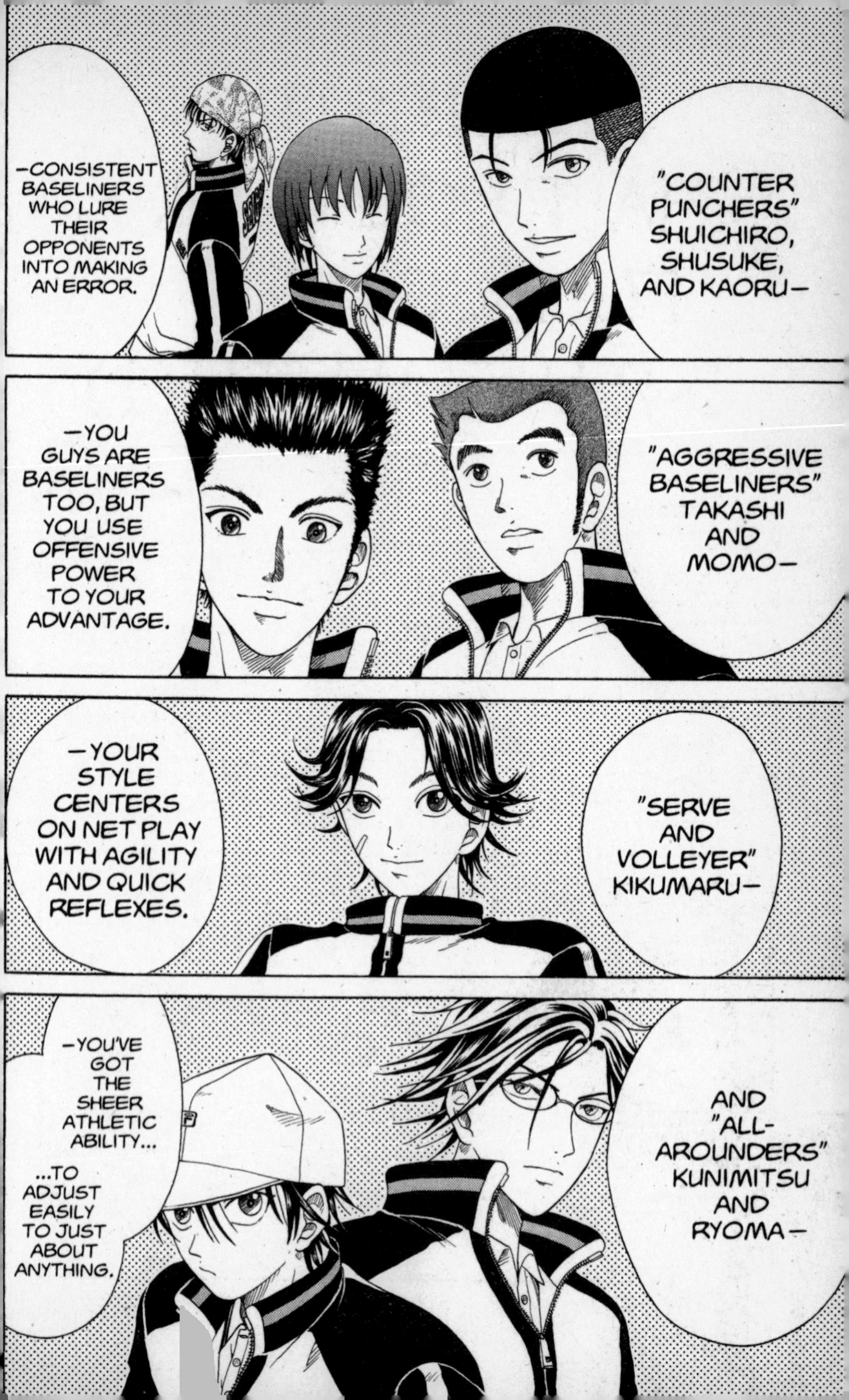
"COUNTER PUNCHERS" SHUICHIRO, SHUSUKE, AND KAORU—
—CONSISTENT BASELINERS WHO LURE THEIR OPPONENTS INTO MAKING AN ERROR.
"AGGRESSIVE BASELINERS" TAKASHI AND MOMO—
—YOU GUYS ARE BASELINERS TOO, BUT YOU USE OFFENSIVE POWER TO YOUR ADVANTAGE.
"SERVE AND VOLLEYER" KIKUMARU—
—YOUR STYLE CENTERS ON NET PLAY WITH AGILITY AND QUICK REFLEXES.
AND "ALL-AROUNDERS" KUNIMITSU AND RYOMA—
—YOU'VE GOT THE SHEER ATHLETIC ABILITY...
...TO ADJUST EASILY TO JUST ABOUT ANYTHING.

GENIUS 46: HALF COURT VS. FULL COURT — 5-RALLY MATCH (1)

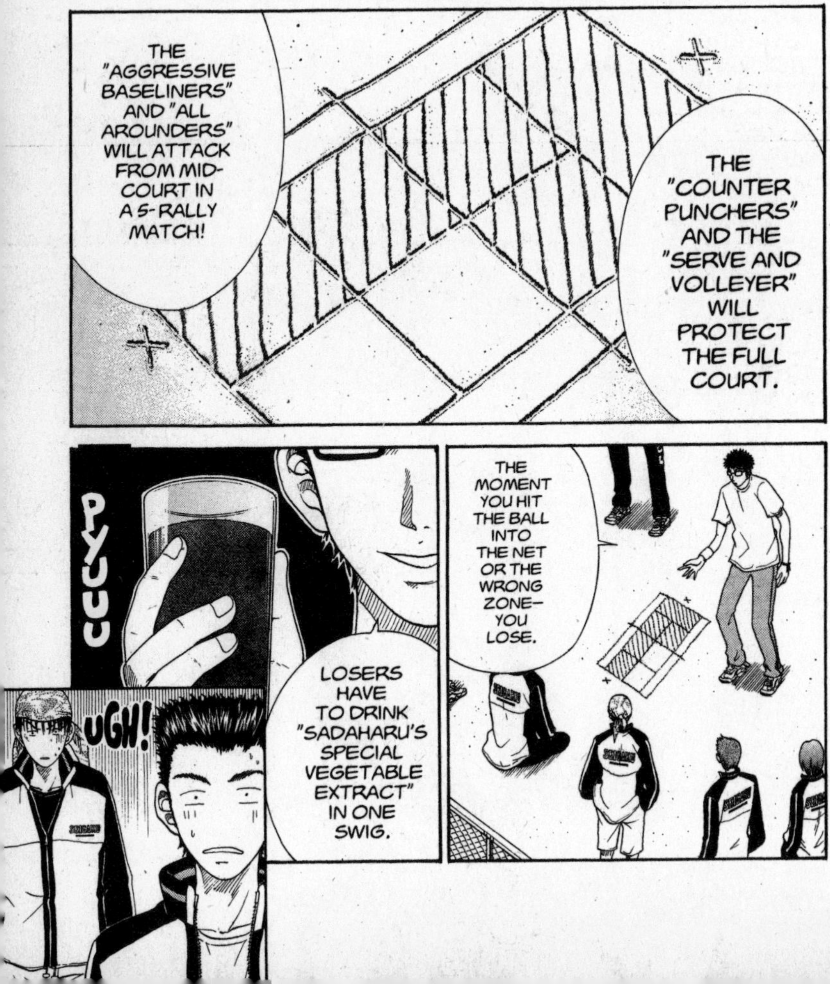
THE "AGGRESSIVE BASELINERS" AND "ALL AROUNDERS" WILL ATTACK FROM MID-COURT IN A 5-RALLY MATCH!
THE "COUNTER PUNCHERS" AND THE "SERVE AND VOLLEYER" WILL PROTECT THE FULL COURT.
THE MOMENT YOU HIT THE BALL INTO THE NET OR THE WRONG ZONE– YOU LOSE.
LOSERS HAVE TO DRINK "SADAHARU'S SPECIAL VEGETABLE EXTRACT" IN ONE SWIG.
PYUUU
UGH!

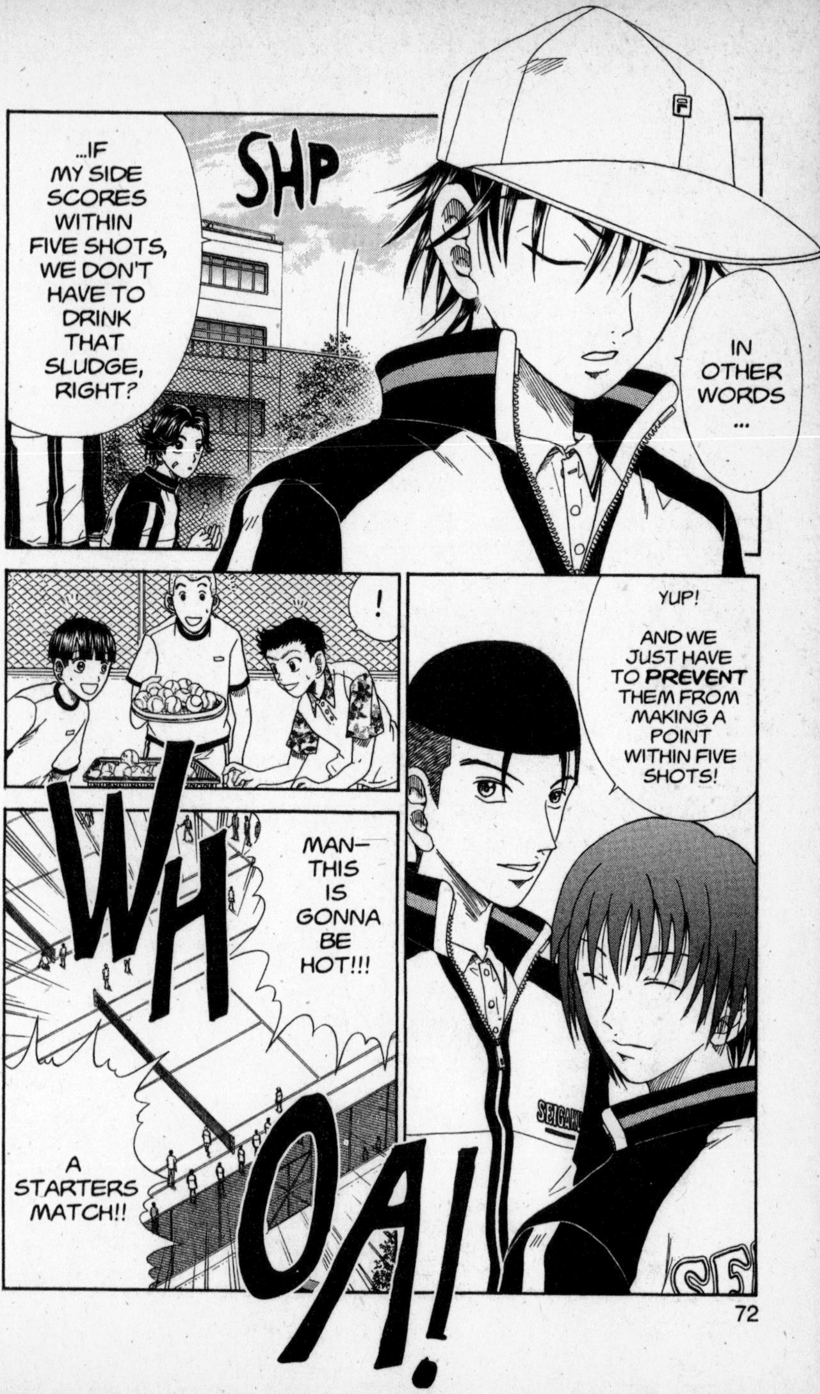

IN OTHER WORDS ...
...IF MY SIDE SCORES WITHIN FIVE SHOTS, WE DON'T HAVE TO DRINK THAT SLUDGE, RIGHT?
SHP
YUP! AND WE JUST HAVE TO PREVENT THEM FROM MAKING A POINT WITHIN FIVE SHOTS!
!
MAN— THIS IS GONNA BE HOT!!!
A STARTERS MATCH!!
WHOA!

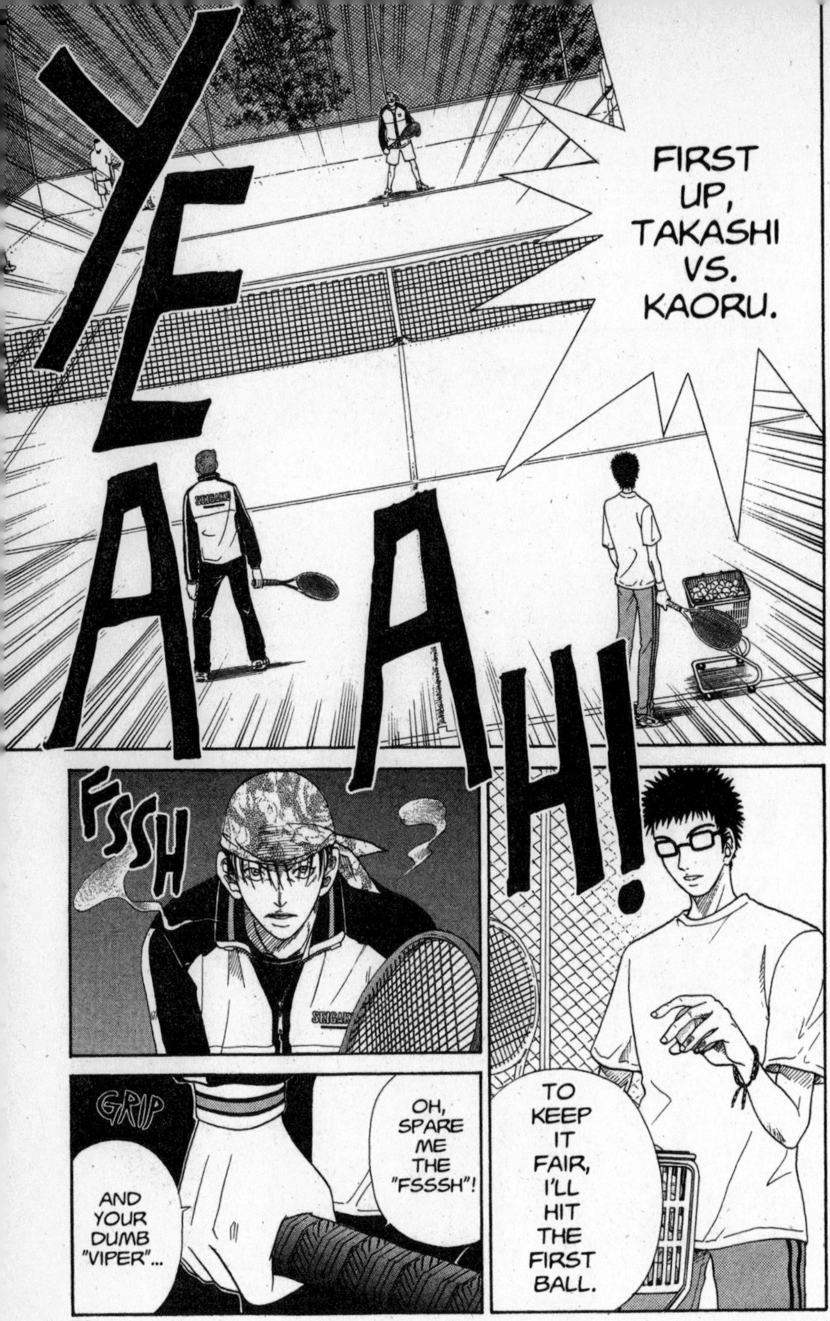
FIRST UP, TAKASHI VS. KAORU.
YEAAAH!
TO KEEP IT FAIR, I'LL HIT THE FIRST BALL.
FSSH
OH, SPARE ME THE "FSSSH"!
AND YOUR DUMB "VIPER"...
GRIP

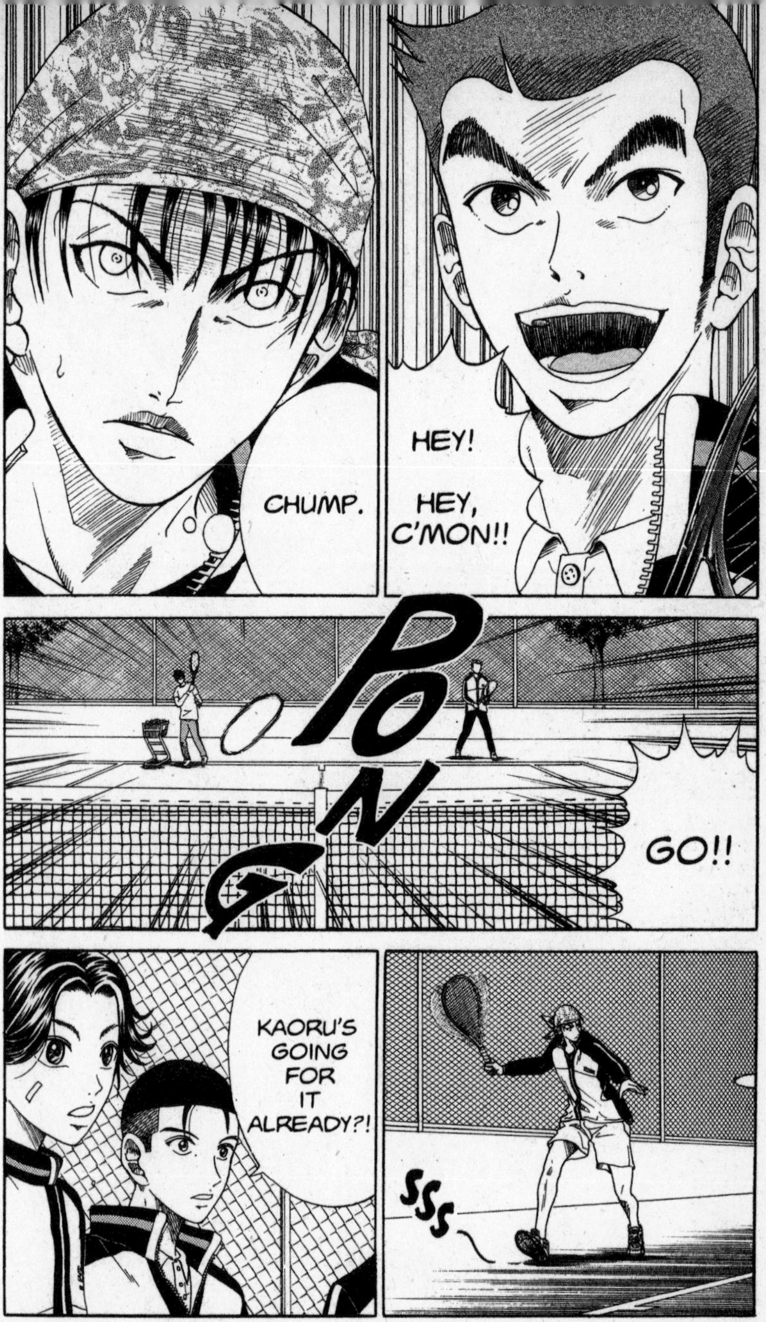
HEY!
HEY, C'MON!!
CHUMP.
PONG
GO!!
SSS
KAORU'S GOING FOR IT ALREADY?!

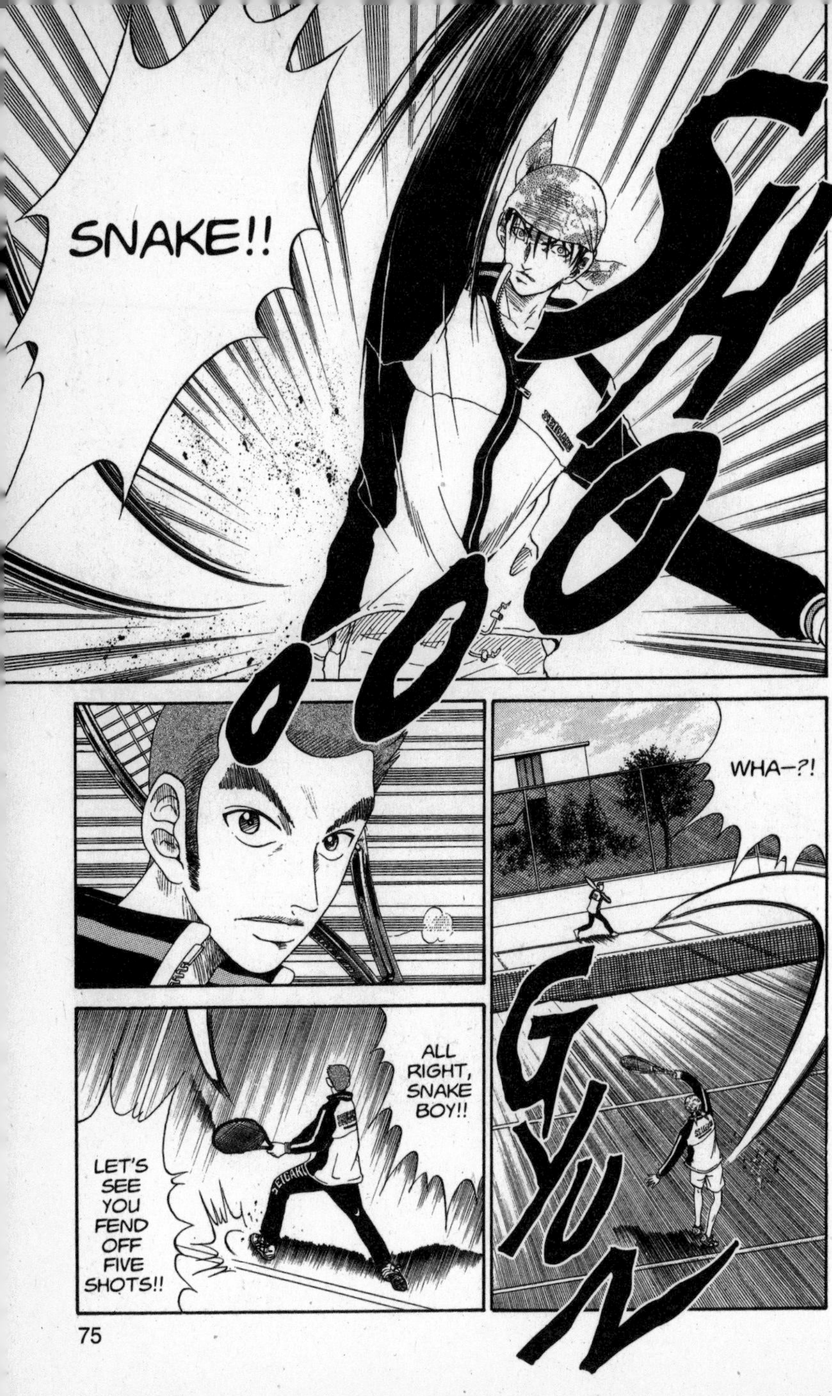
SNAKE!!
SHOOOO
WHA–?!
GYUN
ALL RIGHT, SNAKE BOY!!
LET'S SEE YOU FEND OFF FIVE SHOTS!!

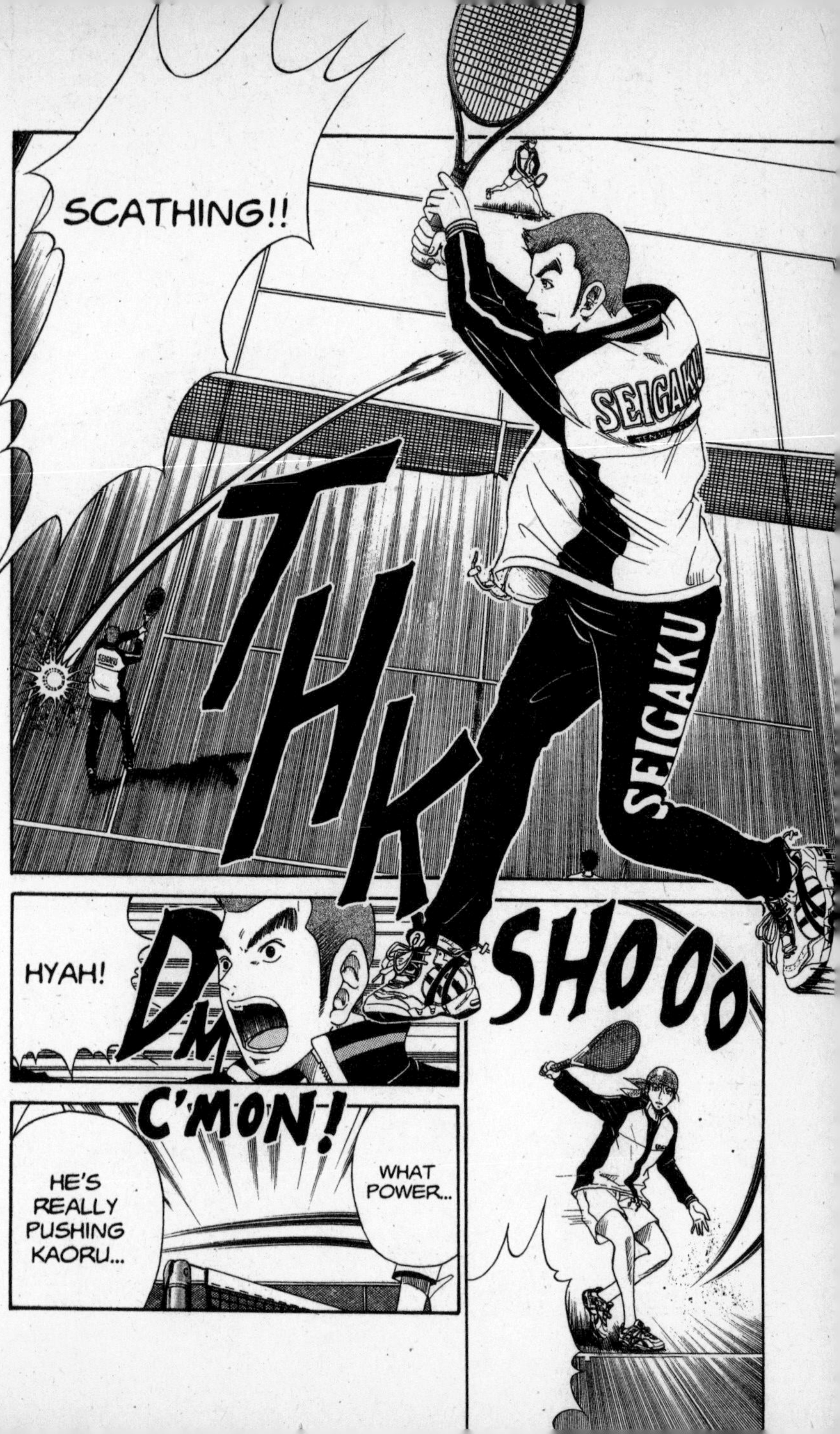
SCATHING!!
THK
SHOOOO
HYAH!
DM
C'MON!
WHAT POWER...
HE'S REALLY PUSHING KAORU...

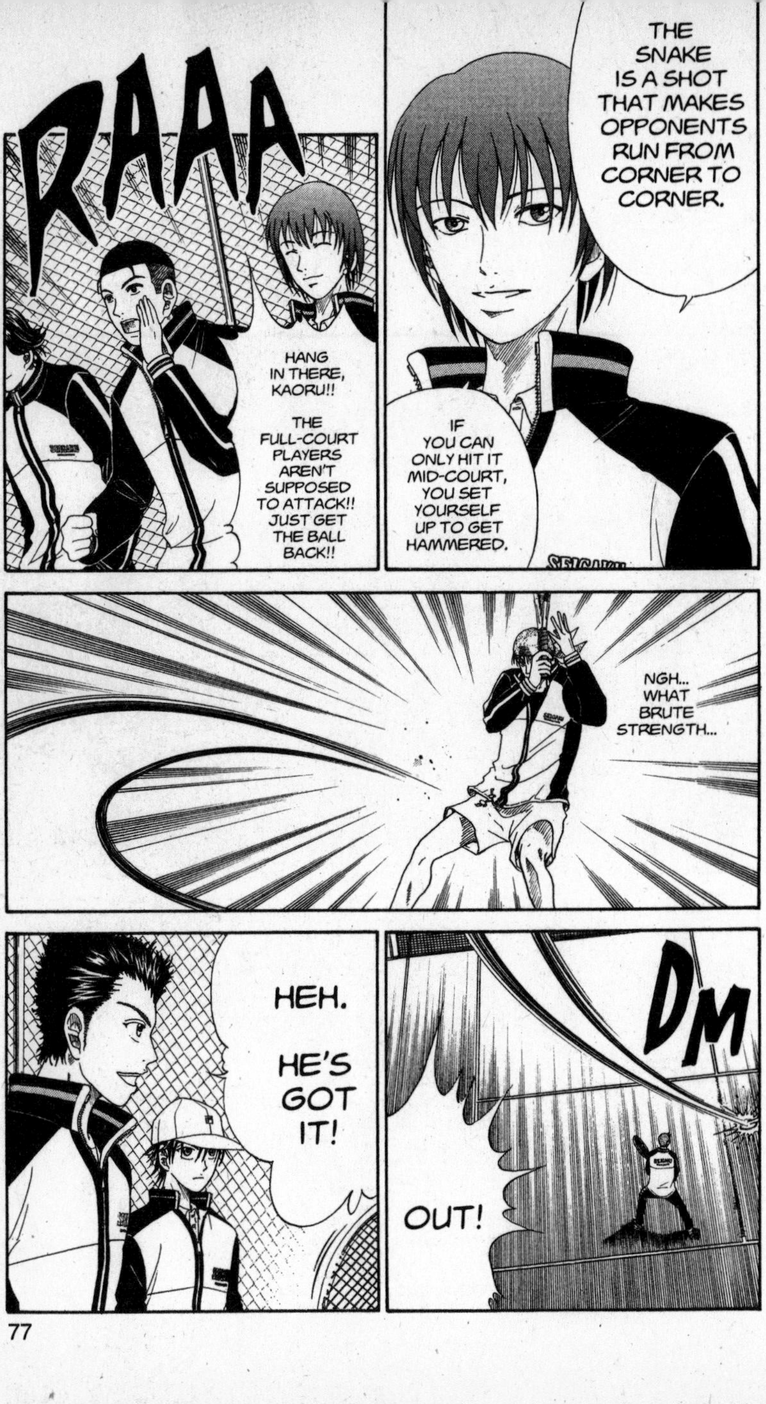
THE SNAKE IS A SHOT THAT MAKES OPPONENTS RUN FROM CORNER TO CORNER.
IF YOU CAN ONLY HIT IT MID-COURT, YOU SET YOURSELF UP TO GET HAMMERED.
RAAA
HANG IN THERE, KAORU!!
THE FULL-COURT PLAYERS AREN'T SUPPOSED TO ATTACK!! JUST GET THE BALL BACK!!
NGH... WHAT BRUTE STRENGTH...
DM
OUT!
HEH.
HE'S GOT IT!

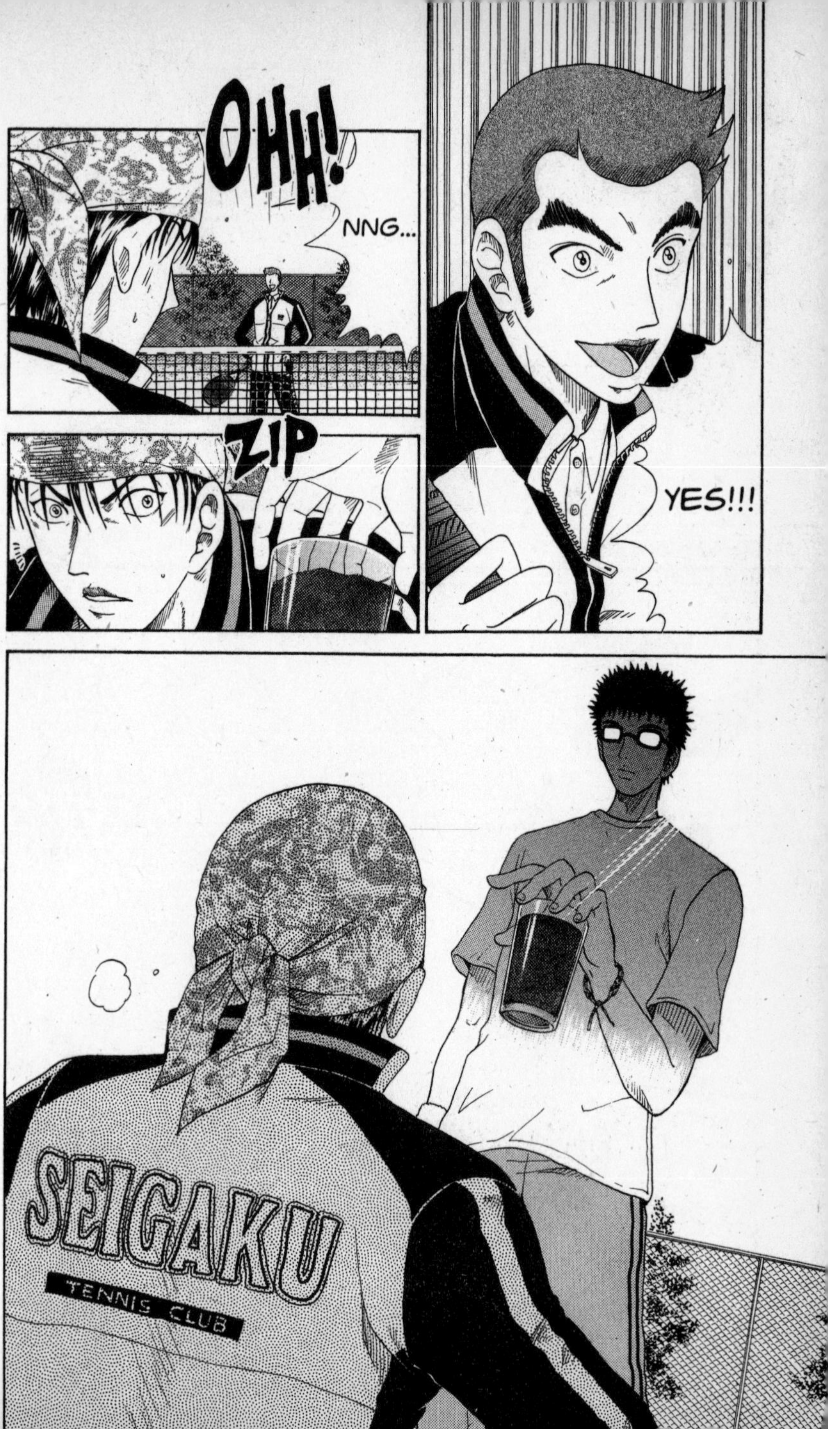
YES!!!
OHH!
NNG...
ZIP
SEIGAKU
TENNIS CLUB

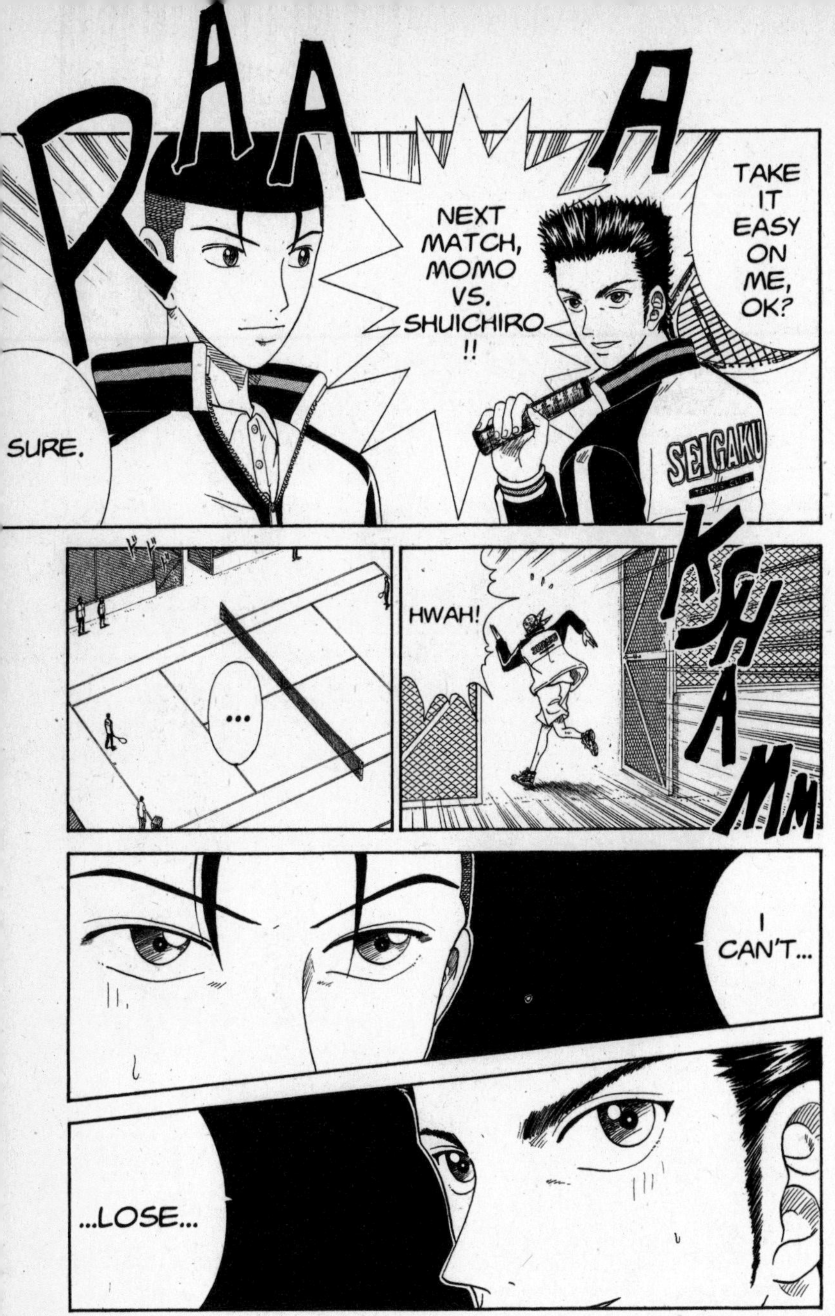
RAAAA
TAKE IT EASY ON ME, OK?
NEXT MATCH, MOMO VS. SHUICHIRO!!
SURE.
KSHAMM
HWAH!
...
I CAN'T...
...LOSE...

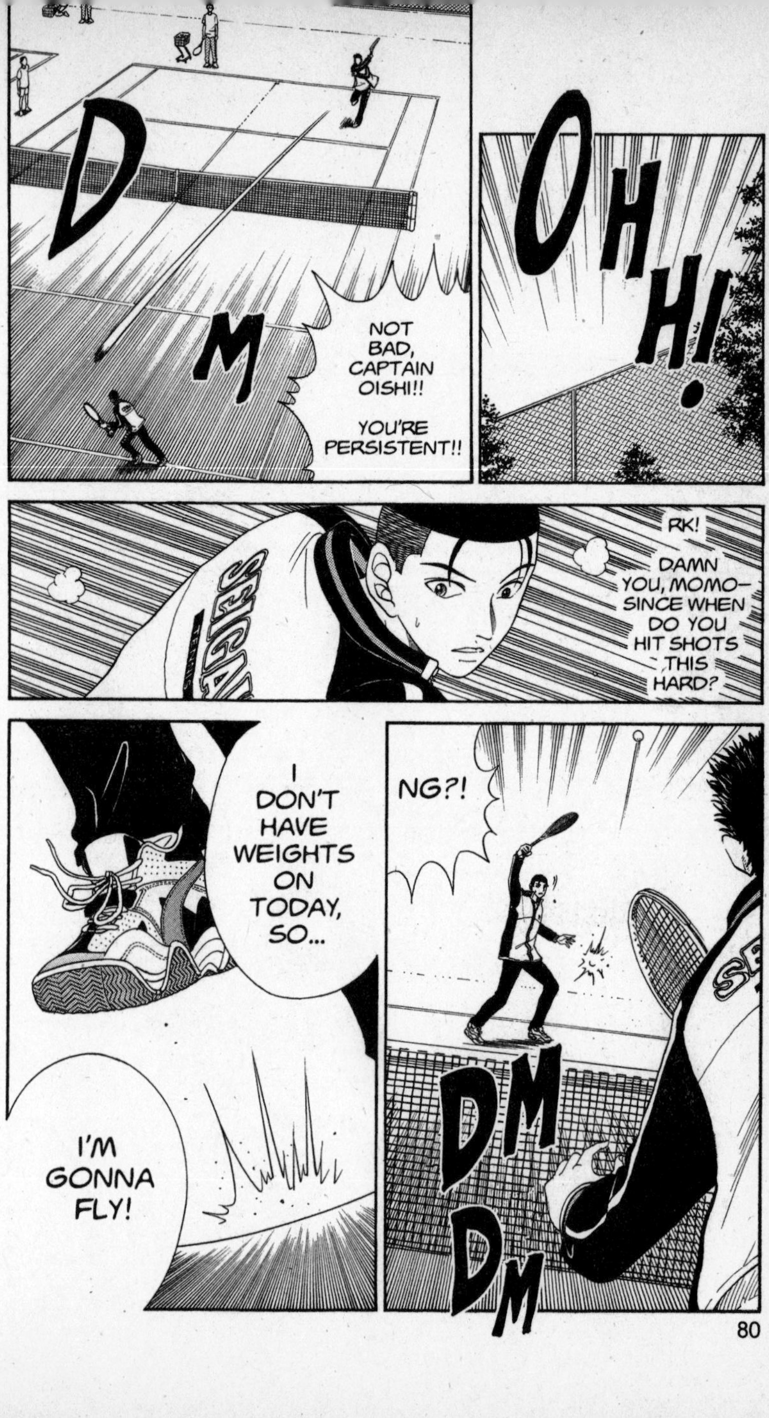
OHH!
DM
NOT BAD, CAPTAIN OISHI!!
YOU'RE PERSISTENT!!
RK!
DAMN YOU, MOMO- SINCE WHEN DO YOU HIT SHOTS THIS HARD?
NG?!
DM
DM
DM
I DON'T HAVE WEIGHTS ON TODAY, SO...
I'M GONNA FLY!

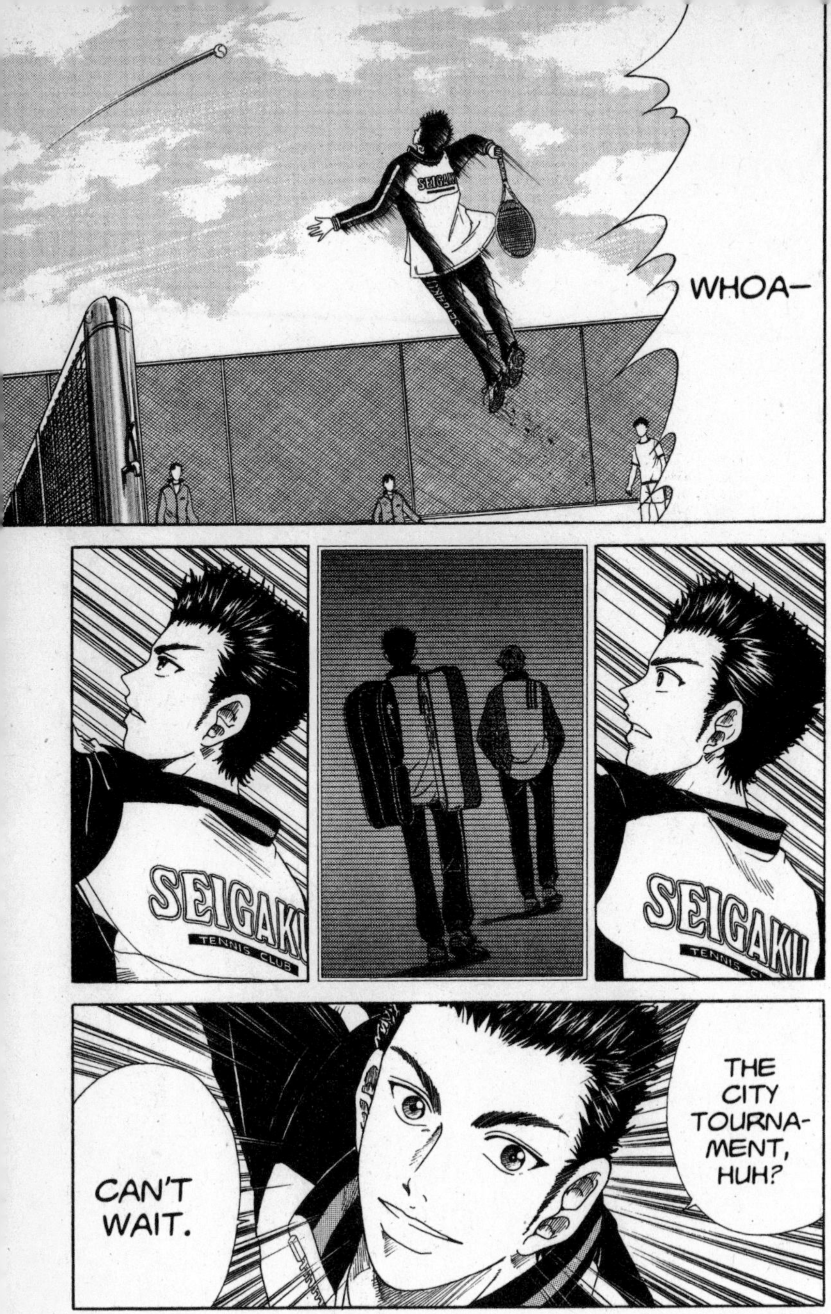
WHOA-
THE CITY TOURNAMENT, HUH?
CAN'T WAIT.

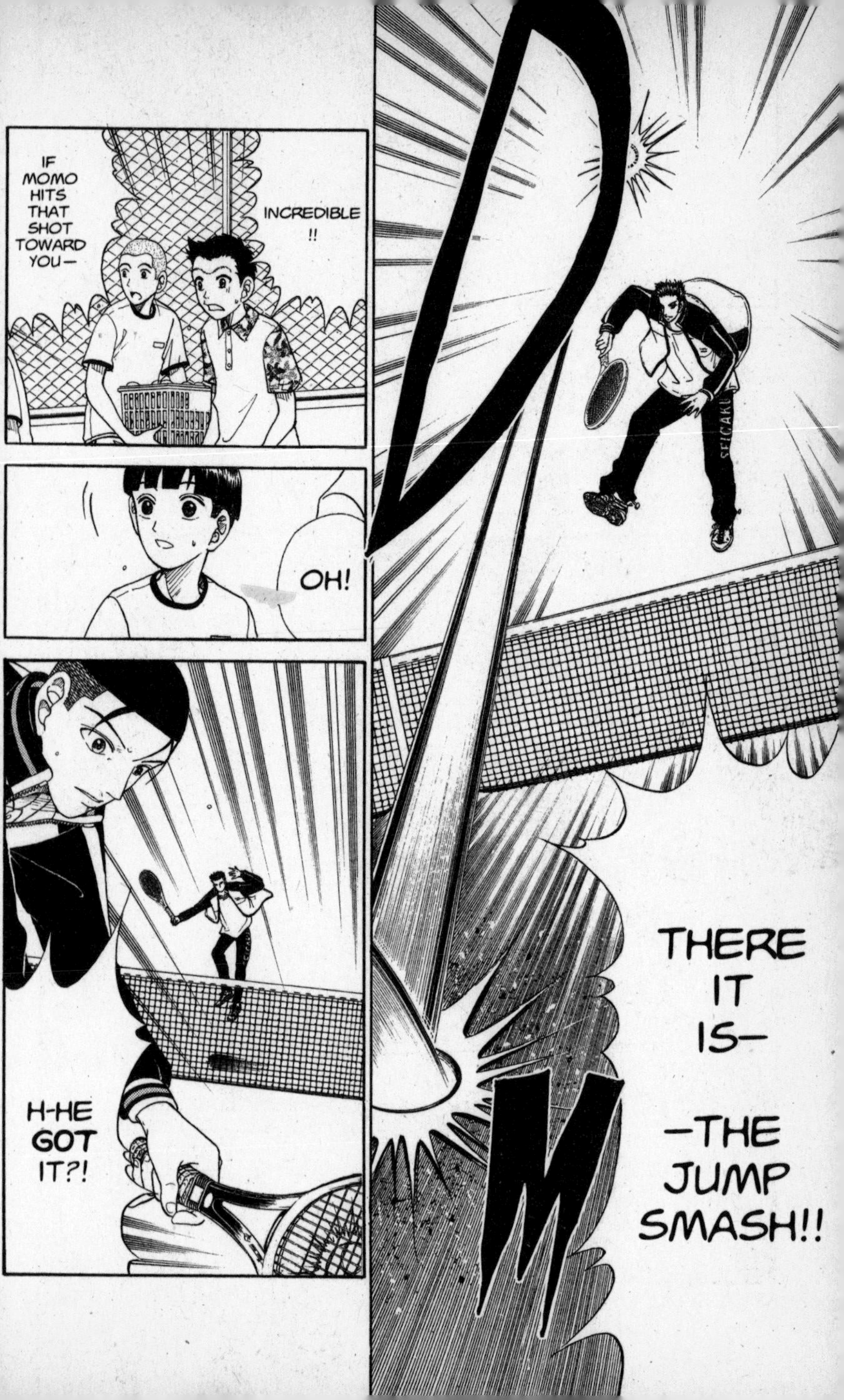
THERE IT IS—
—THE JUMP SMASH!!
INCREDIBLE!!
IF MOMO HITS THAT SHOT TOWARD YOU—
OH!
H-HE GOT IT?!

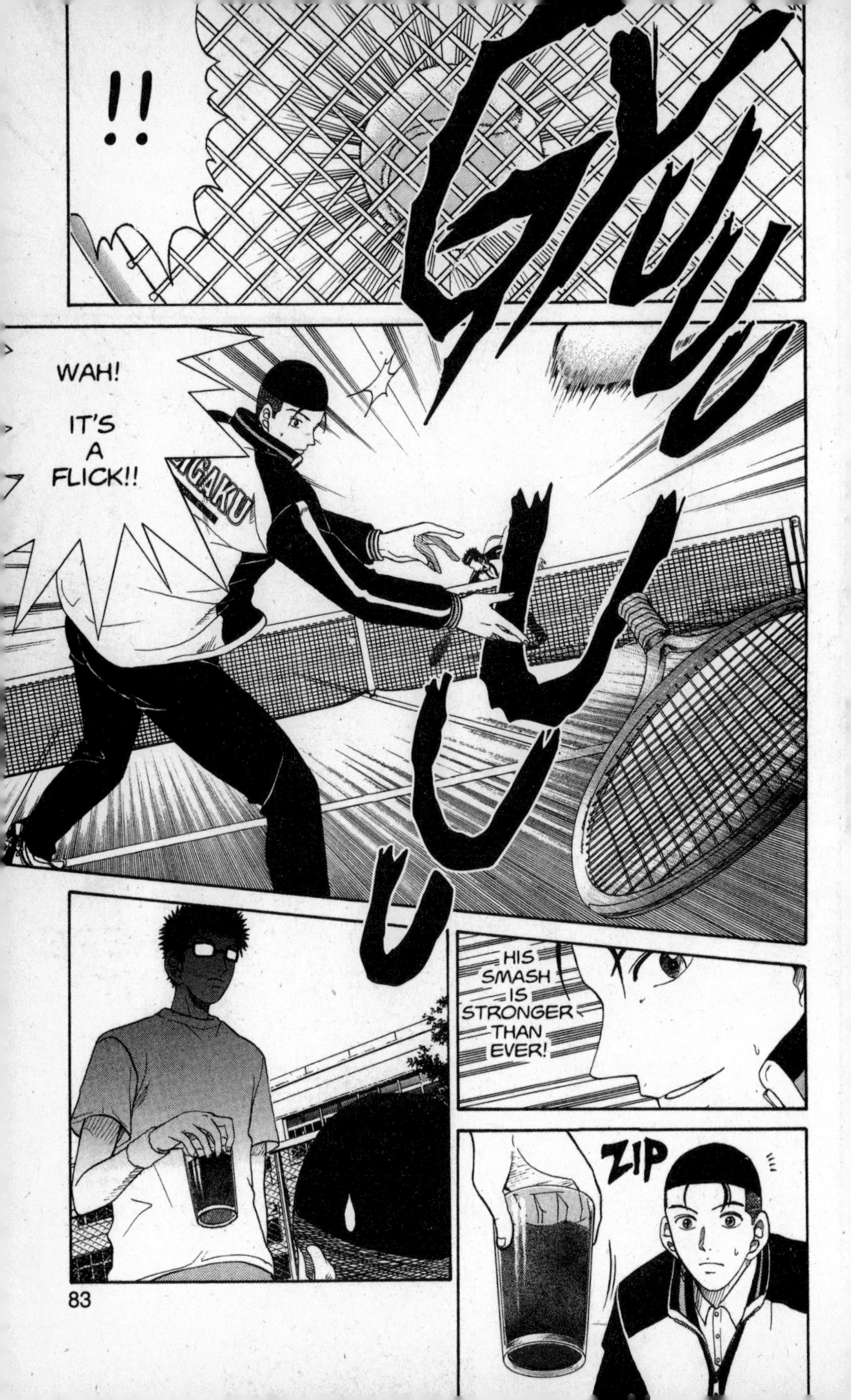
!!
WAH!
IT'S A FLICK!!
HIS SMASH IS STRONGER THAN EVER!
ZIP

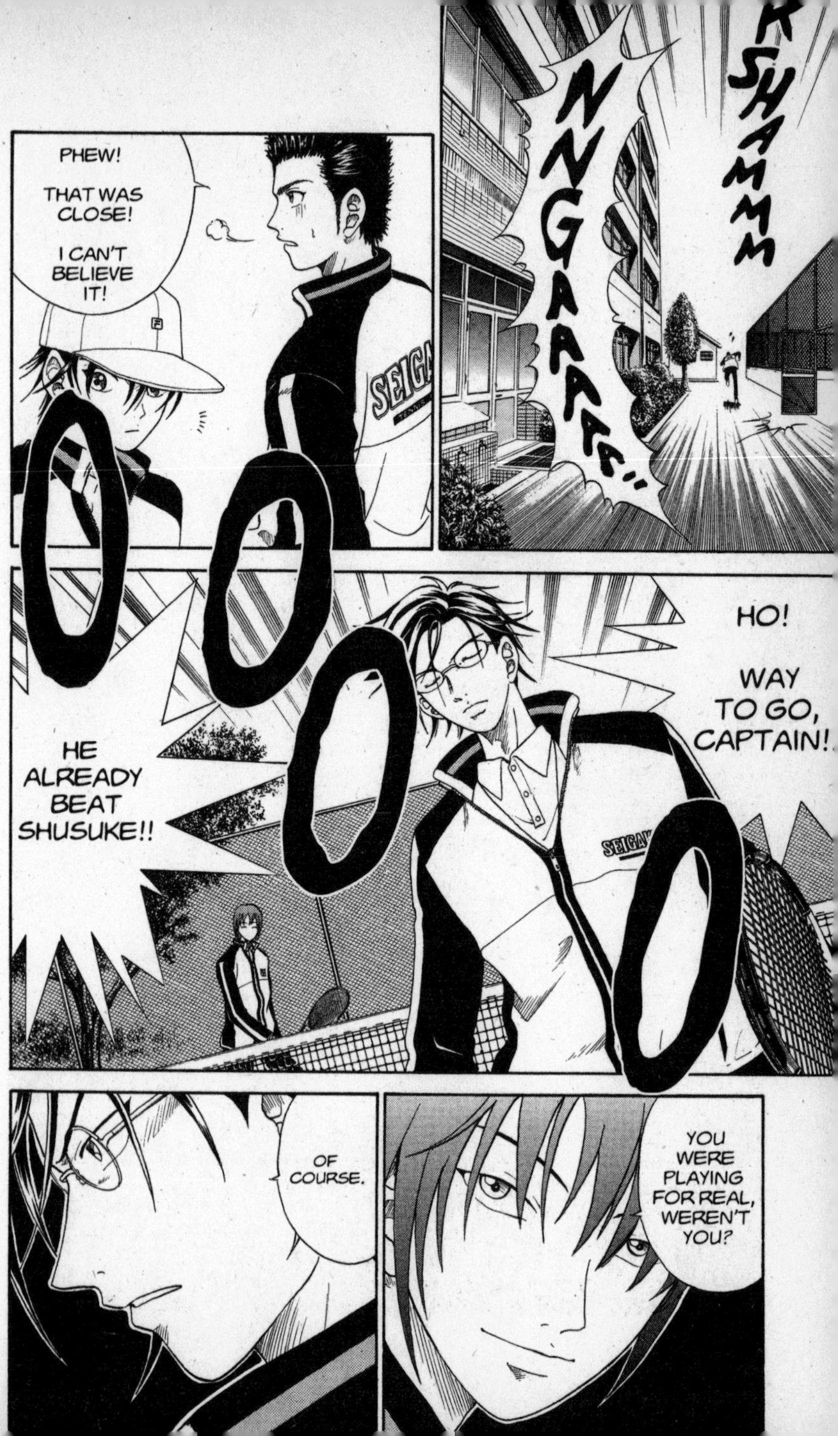
KSHAMMM
NNGAARRR!!
PHEW!
THAT WAS CLOSE!
I CAN'T BELIEVE IT!
OOOOOO
HO!
WAY TO GO, CAPTAIN!
HE ALREADY BEAT SHUSUKE!!
YOU WERE PLAYING FOR REAL, WEREN'T YOU?
OF COURSE.

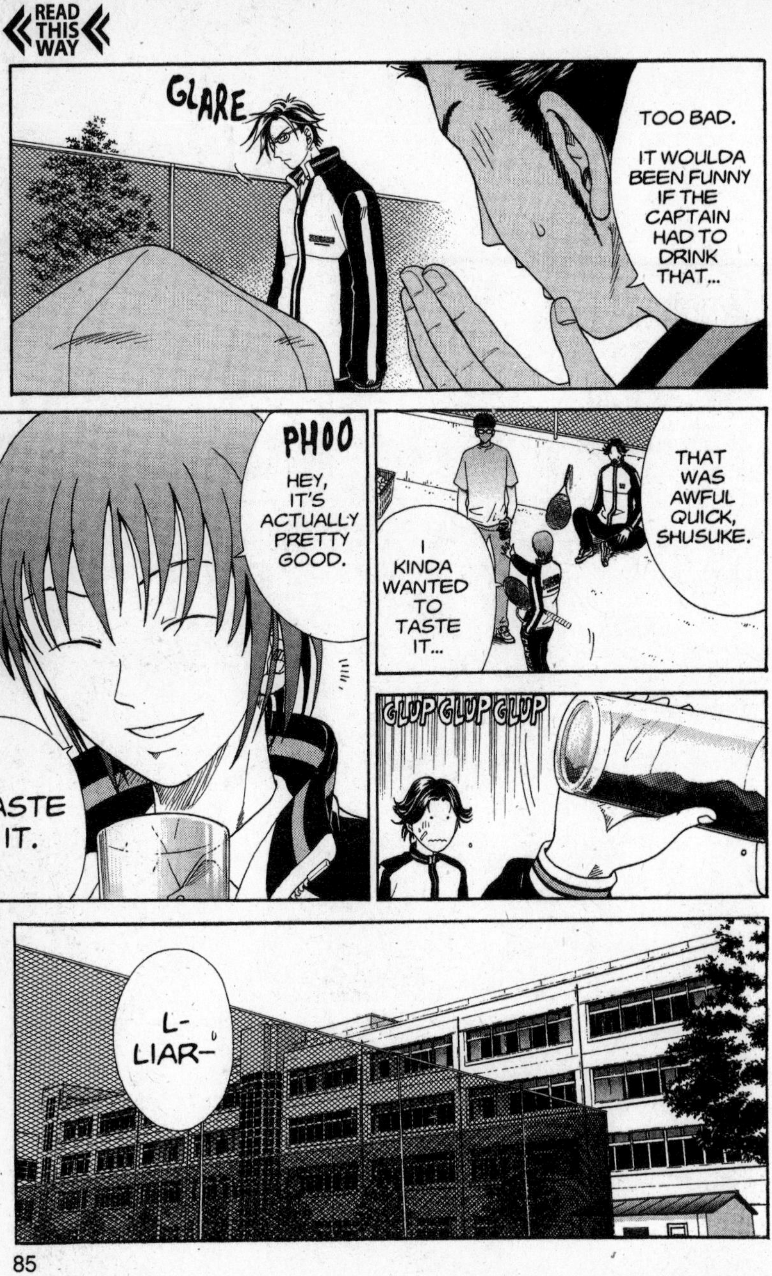
READ THIS WAY
TOO BAD.
IT WOULDA BEEN FUNNY IF THE CAPTAIN HAD TO DRINK THAT...
GLARE
THAT WAS AWFUL QUICK, SHUSUKE.
I KINDA WANTED TO TASTE IT...
GLUP GLUP GLUP
PHOO
HEY, IT'S ACTUALLY PRETTY GOOD.
TASTE IT.
L- LIAR–

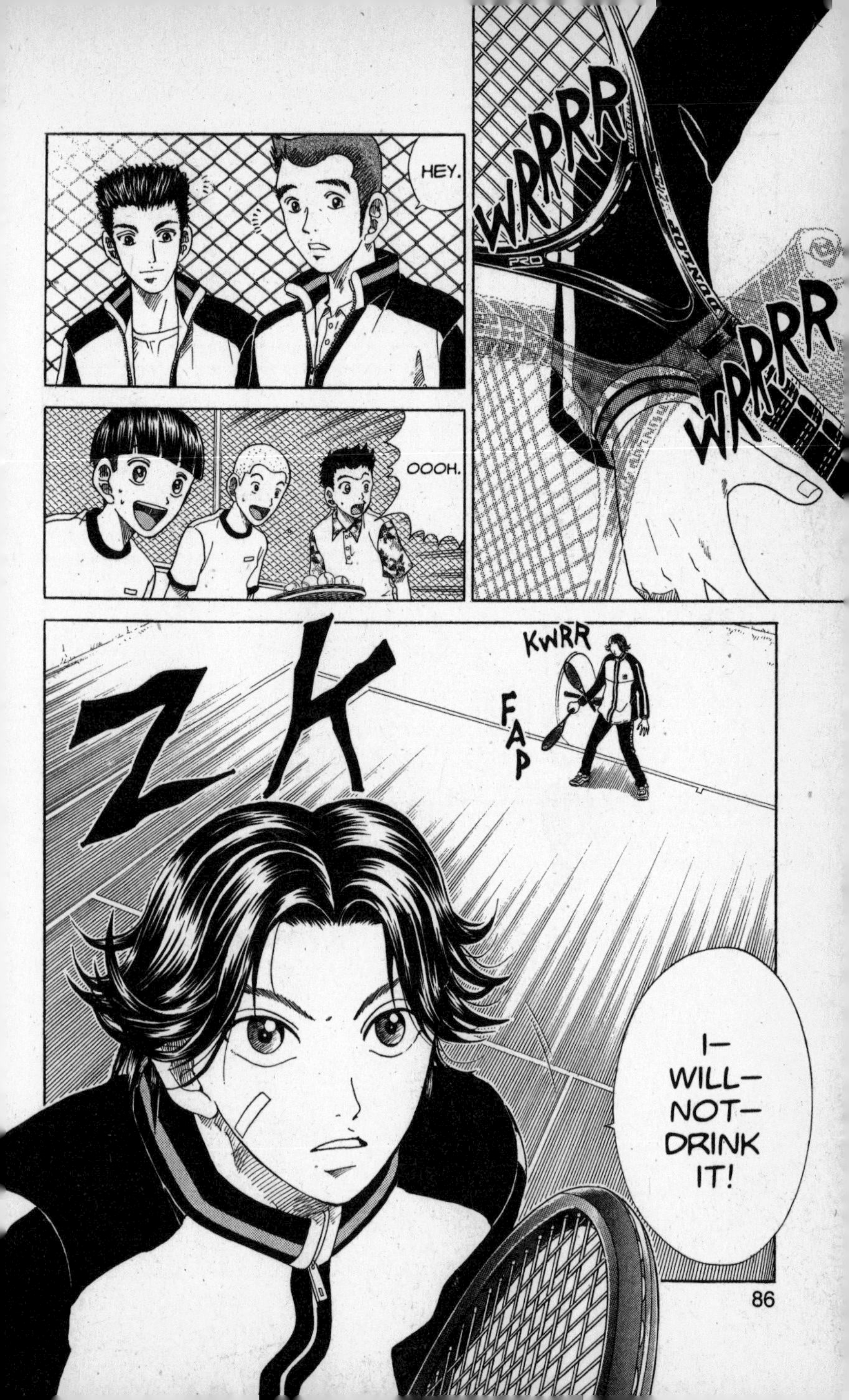
WRRRR
WRRRR
HEY.
OOOH.
KWRR
ZK
FAP
I— WILL— NOT— DRINK IT!

READ THIS WAY

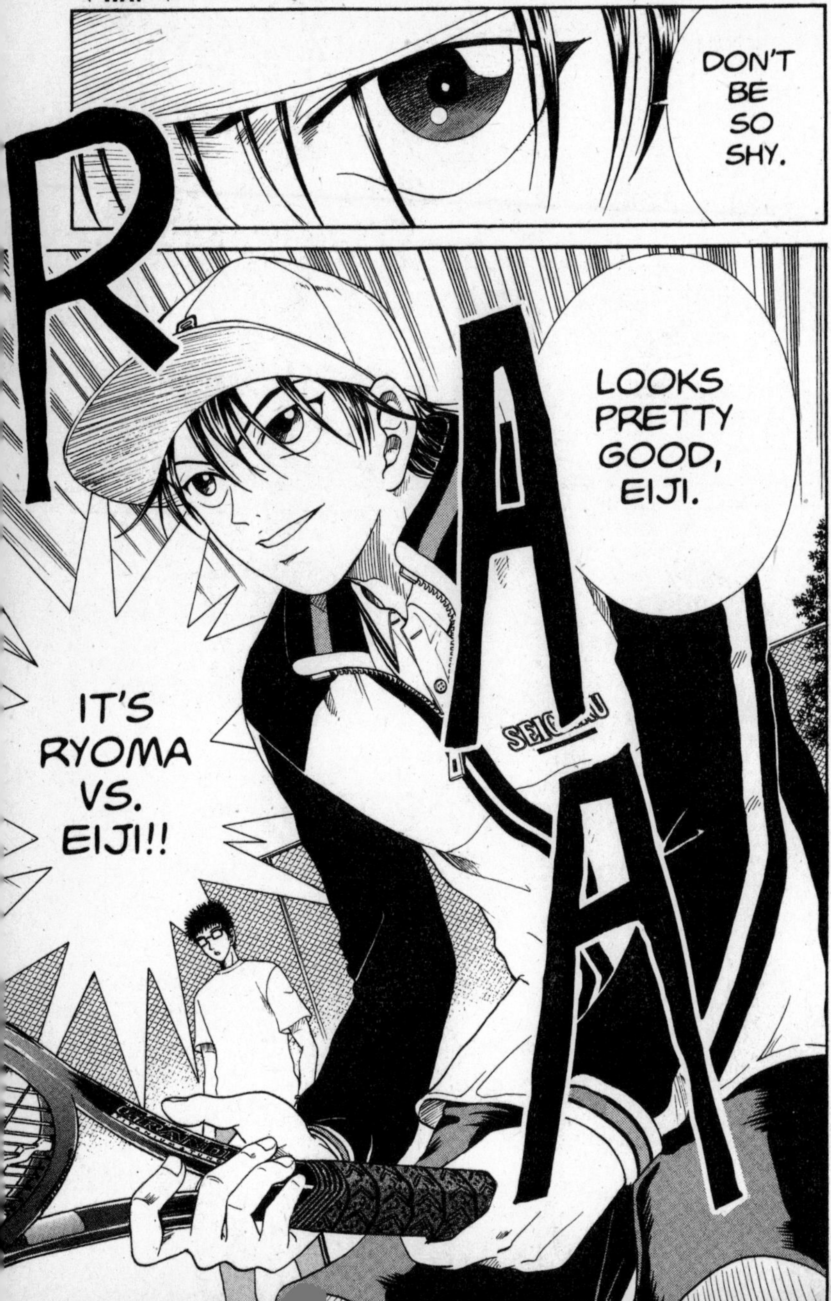
DON'T BE SO SHY.
RAAA
LOOKS PRETTY GOOD, EIJI.
IT'S RYOMA VS. EIJI!!

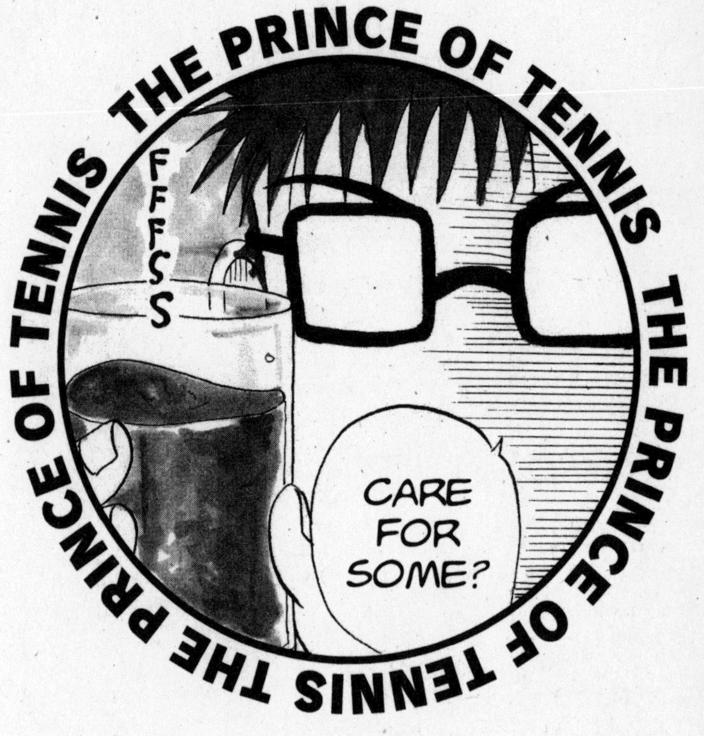
THE PRINCE OF TENNIS THE PRINCE OF TENNIS THE PRINCE OF TENNIS
FFFSS
CARE FOR SOME?

Genius 47:

HALF COURT VS. FULL COURT — 5-RALLY MATCH (2)

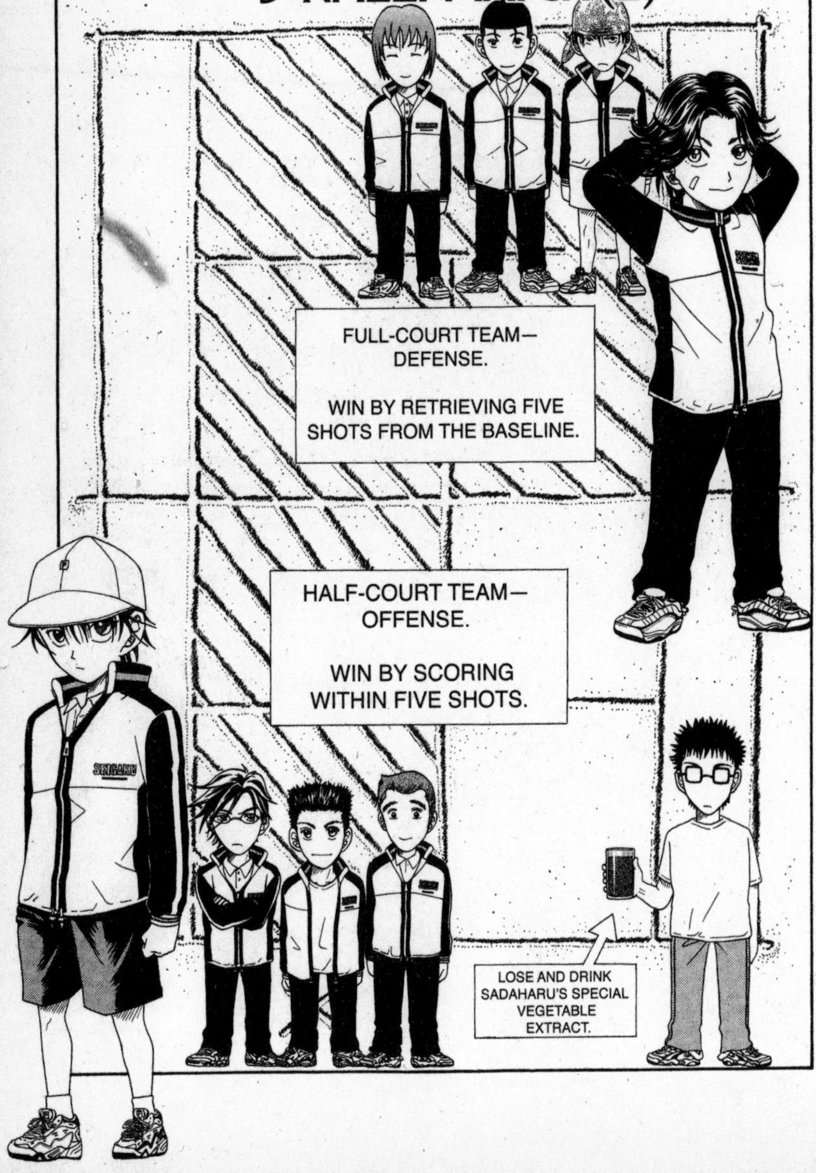
FULL-COURT TEAM—
DEFENSE.
WIN BY RETRIEVING FIVE SHOTS FROM THE BASELINE.
HALF-COURT TEAM—
OFFENSE.
WIN BY SCORING WITHIN FIVE SHOTS.
LOSE AND DRINK SADAHARU'S SPECIAL VEGETABLE EXTRACT.

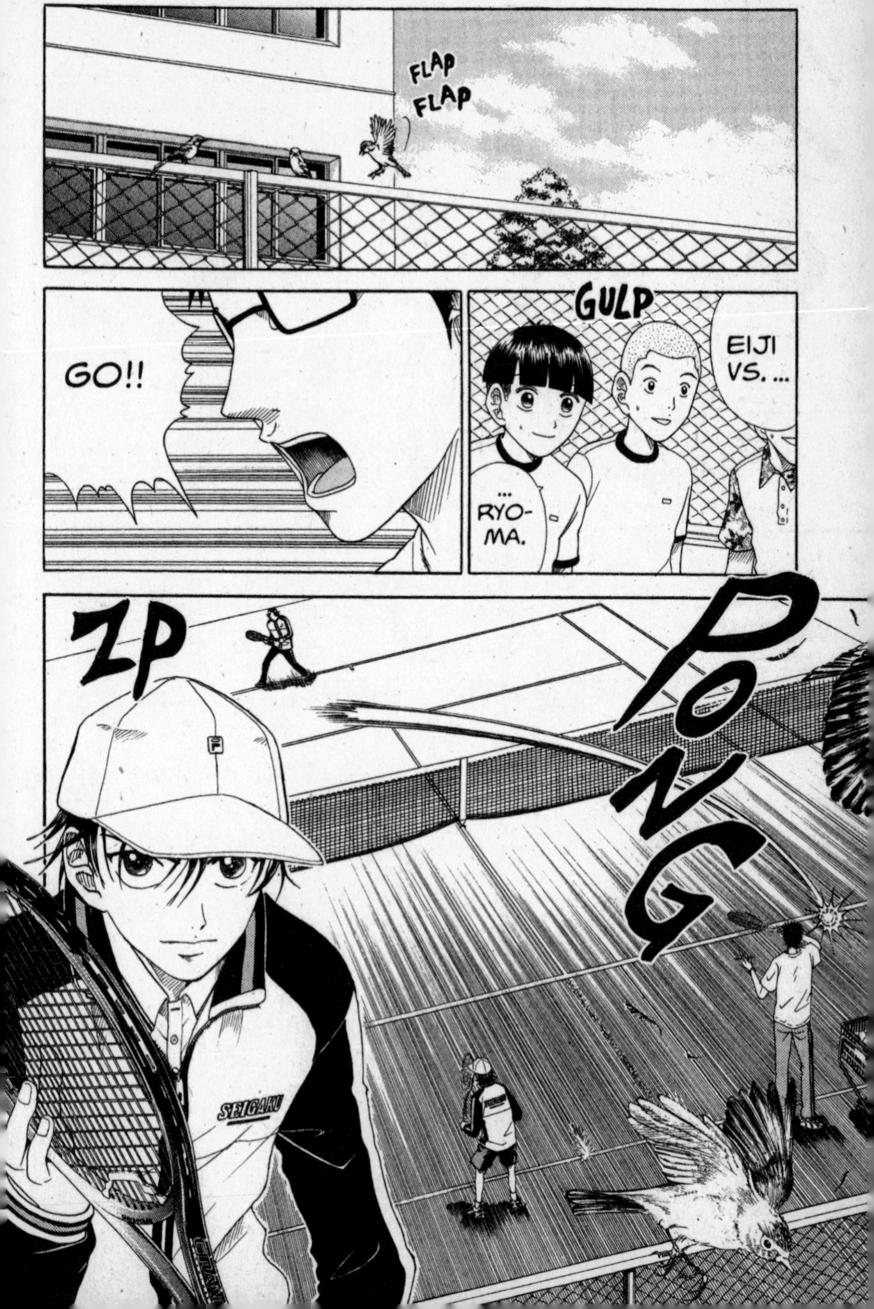
FLAP FLAP
GULP
EIJI VS. ...
... RYO-MA.
GO!!
PONG
ZP

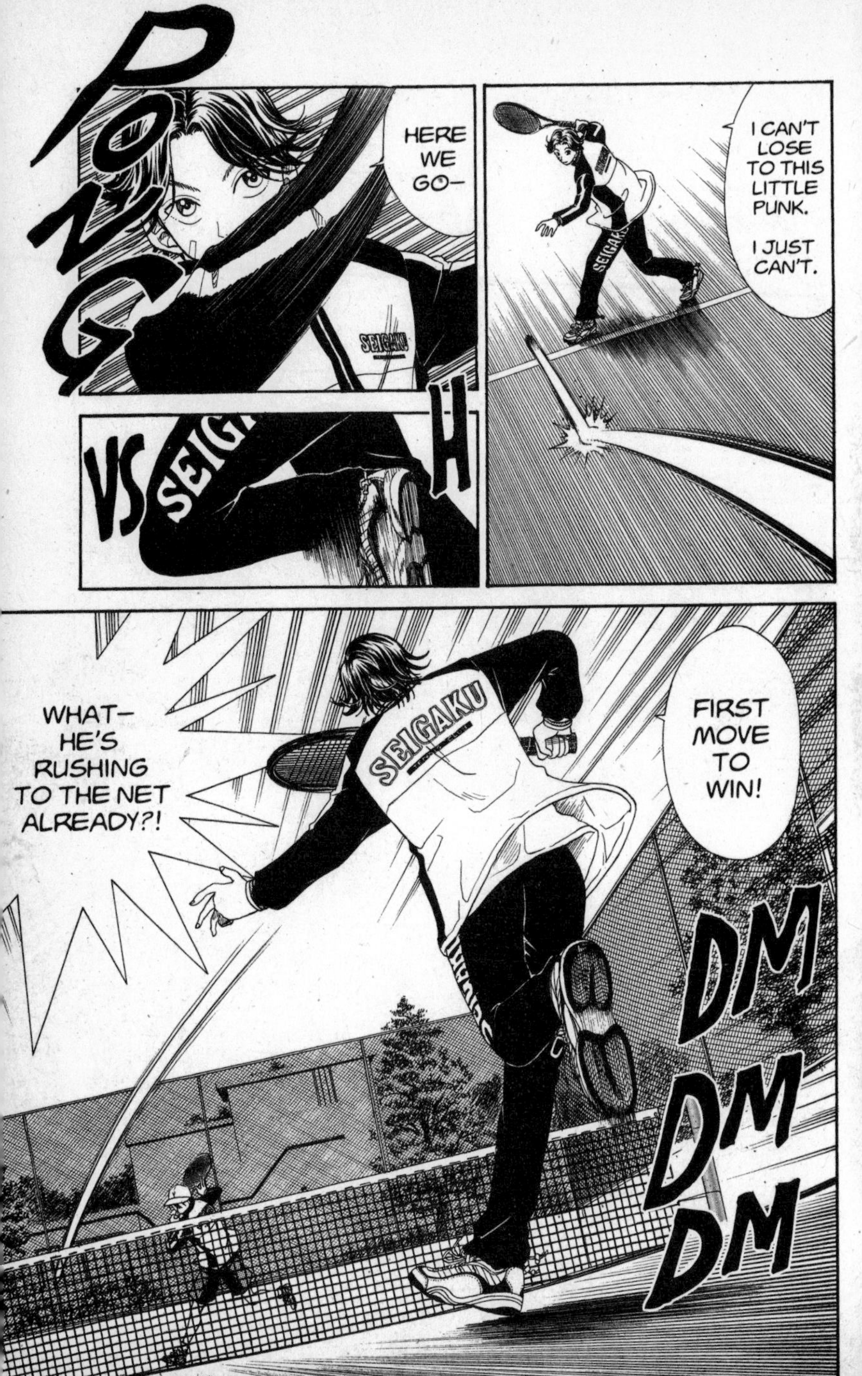
I CAN'T LOSE TO THIS LITTLE PUNK.
I JUST CAN'T.
HERE WE GO—
PONG
VS
H
FIRST MOVE TO WIN!
DM DM DM
WHAT— HE'S RUSHING TO THE NET ALREADY?!

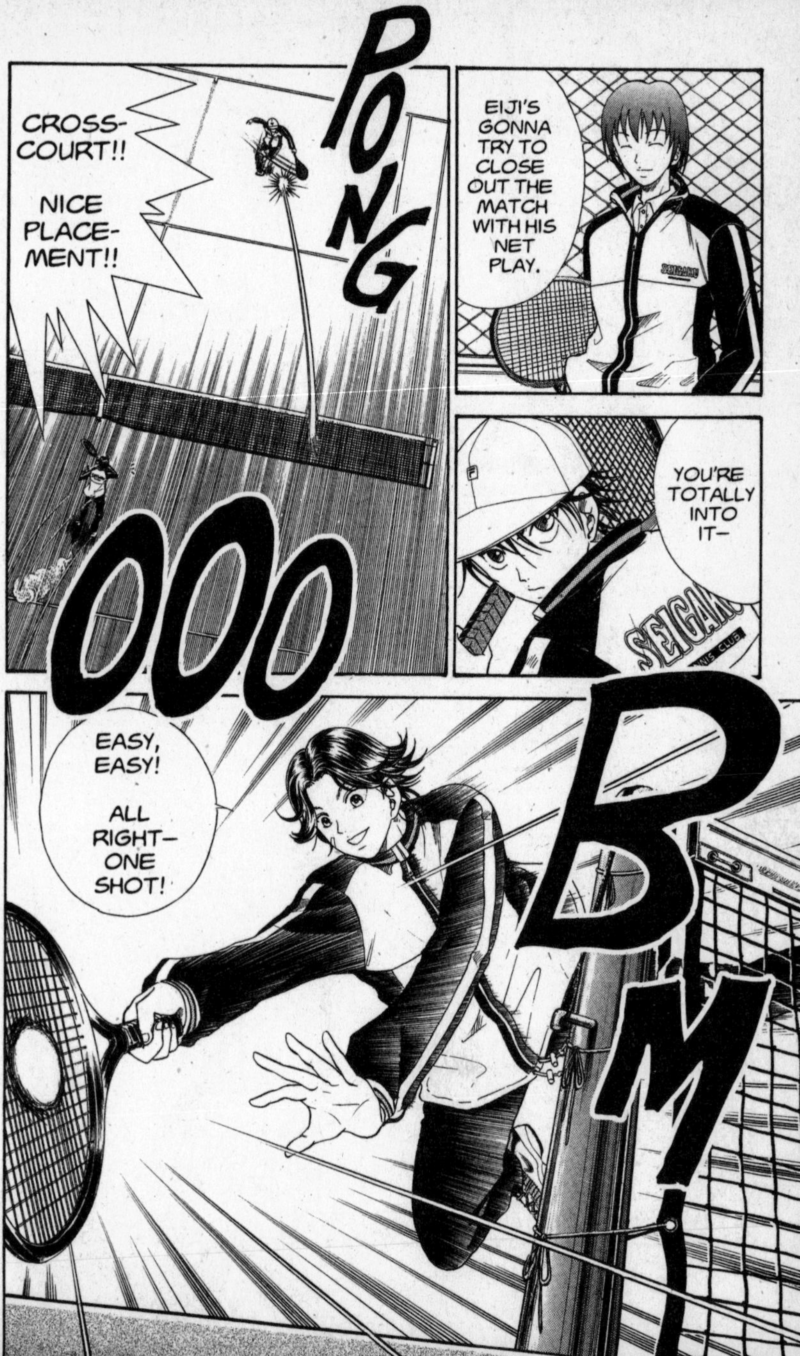
EIJI'S GONNA TRY TO CLOSE OUT THE MATCH WITH HIS NET PLAY.
YOU'RE TOTALLY INTO IT—
PONG
CROSS-COURT!!
NICE PLACE-MENT!!
OOO
B
M
EASY, EASY!
ALL RIGHT—ONE SHOT!

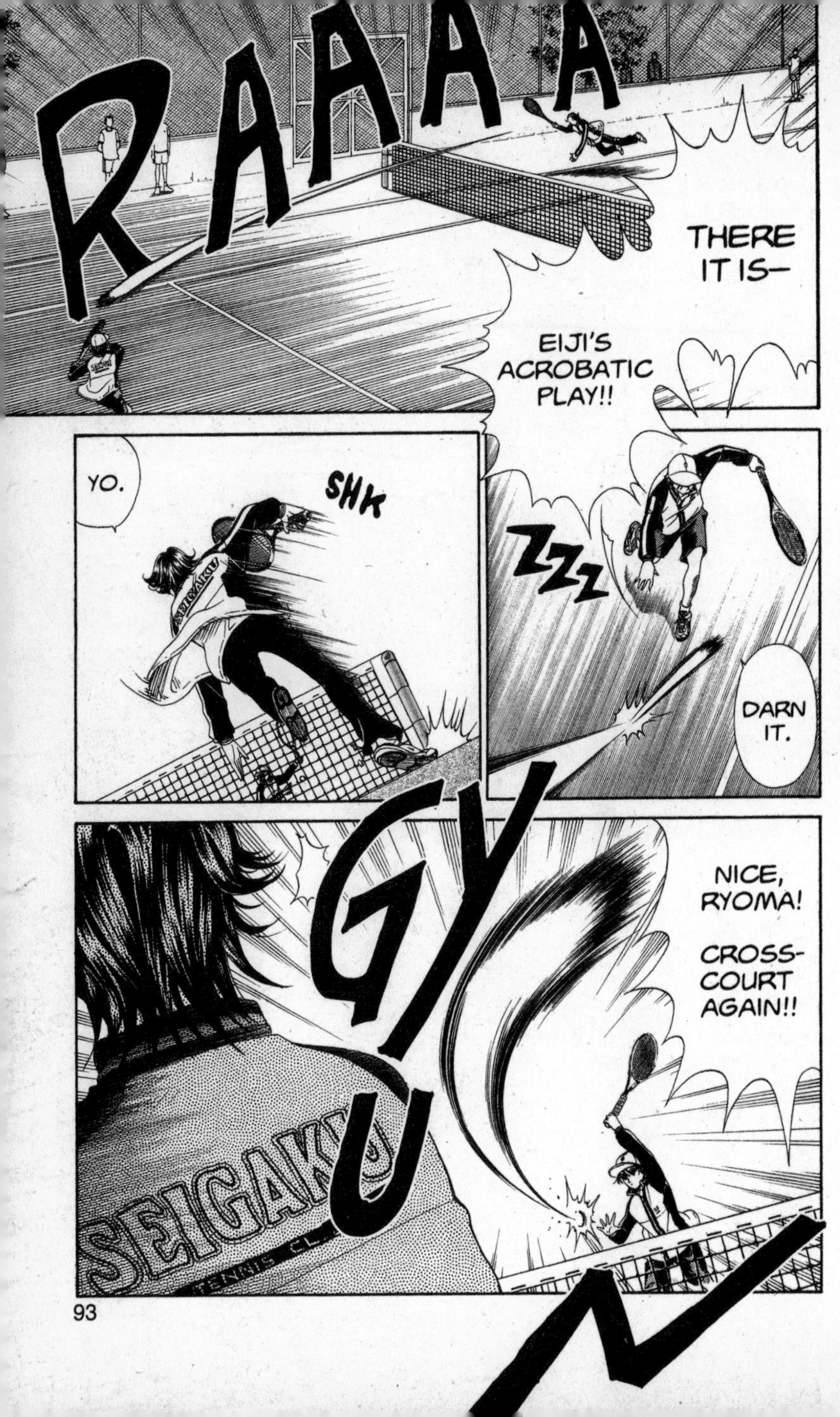
RAAAA
THERE IT IS—
EIJI'S ACROBATIC PLAY!!
ZZZ
DARN IT.
YO.
SHK
GYUN
NICE, RYOMA!
CROSS-COURT AGAIN!!

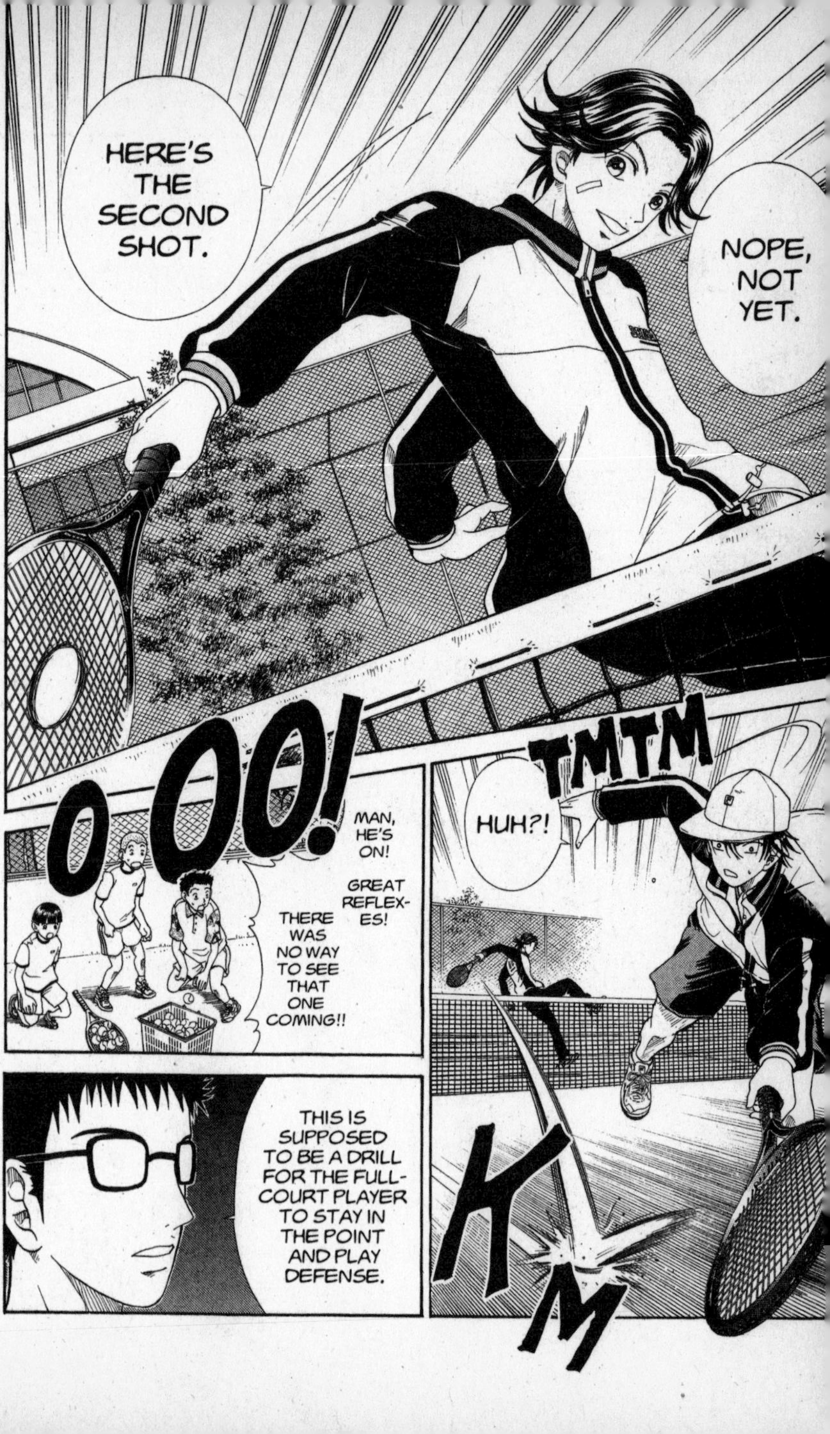
HERE'S THE SECOND SHOT.
NOPE, NOT YET.
TMTM
HUH?!
KM
OOOO!
MAN, HE'S ON!
GREAT REFLEX-ES!
THERE WAS NO WAY TO SEE THAT ONE COMING!!
THIS IS SUPPOSED TO BE A DRILL FOR THE FULL-COURT PLAYER TO STAY IN THE POINT AND PLAY DEFENSE.

READ THIS WAY

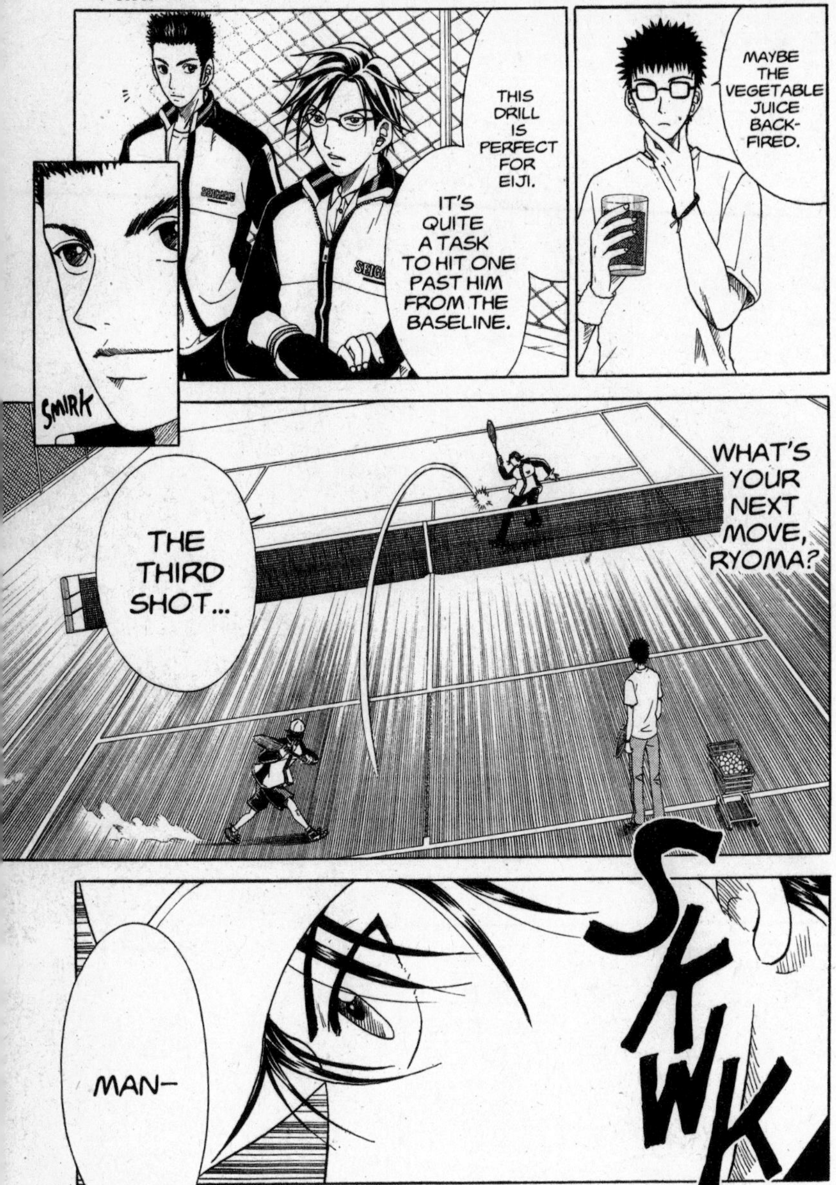
MAYBE THE VEGETABLE JUICE BACKFIRED.
THIS DRILL IS PERFECT FOR EIJI.
IT'S QUITE A TASK TO HIT ONE PAST HIM FROM THE BASELINE.
SMIRK
WHAT'S YOUR NEXT MOVE, RYOMA?
THE THIRD SHOT...
SKWK
MAN-

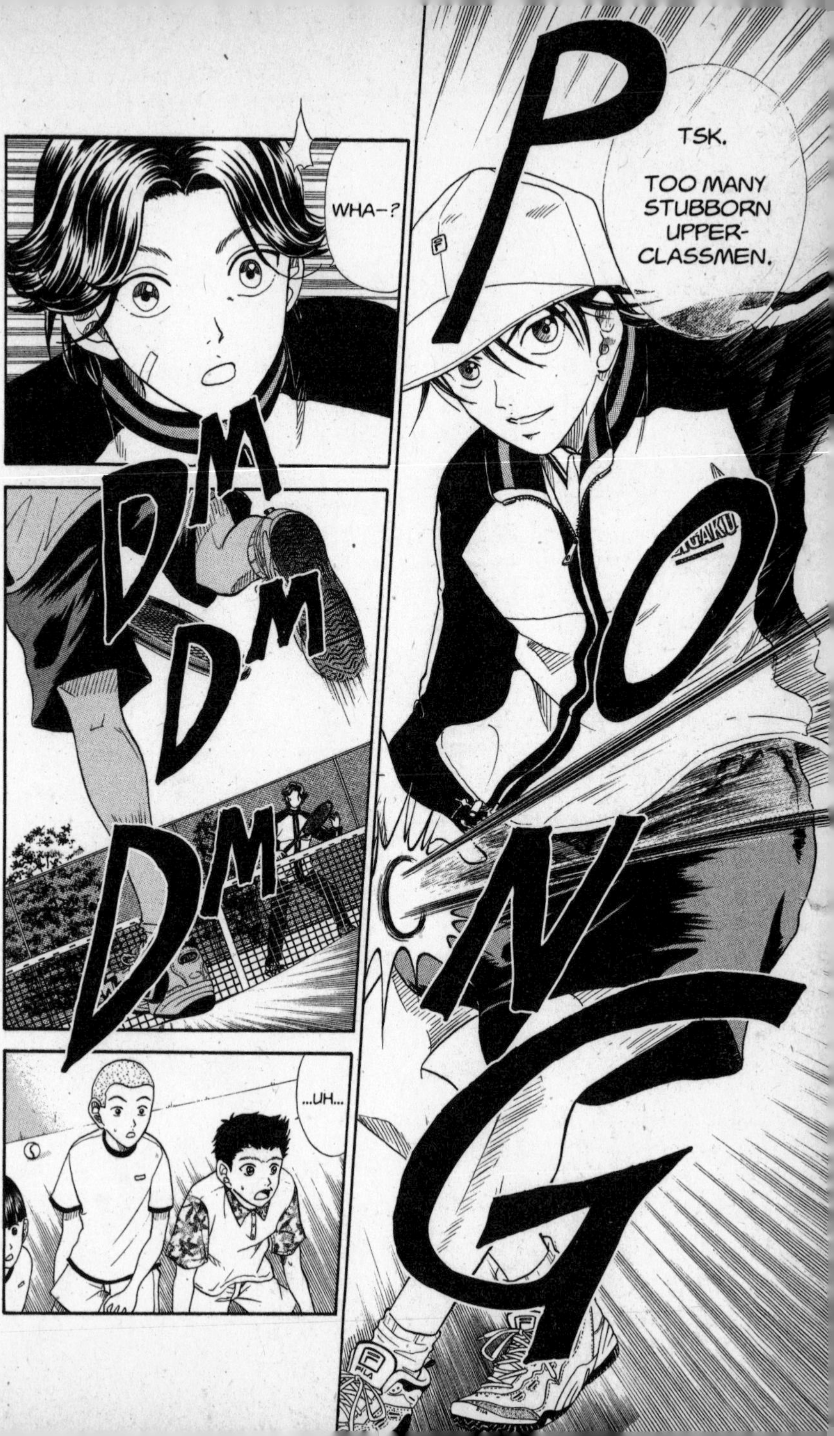
TSK.
TOO MANY STUBBORN UPPER-CLASSMEN.
PONG
WHA-?
DM DM DM
...UH...

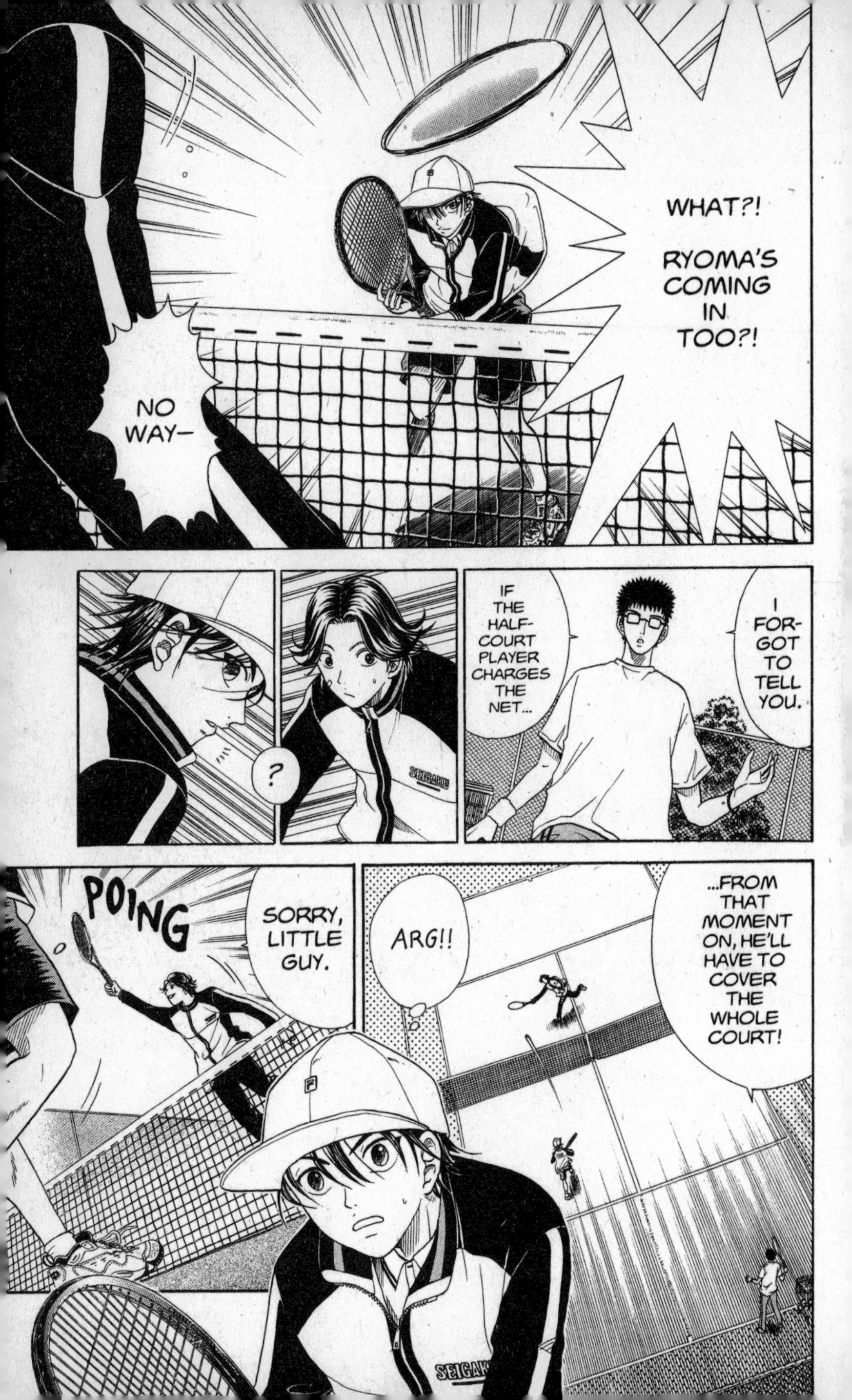
WHAT?!
RYOMA'S COMING IN TOO?!
NO WAY—
I FORGOT TO TELL YOU.
IF THE HALF-COURT PLAYER CHARGES THE NET...
?
...FROM THAT MOMENT ON, HE'LL HAVE TO COVER THE WHOLE COURT!
ARG!!
SORRY, LITTLE GUY.
POING

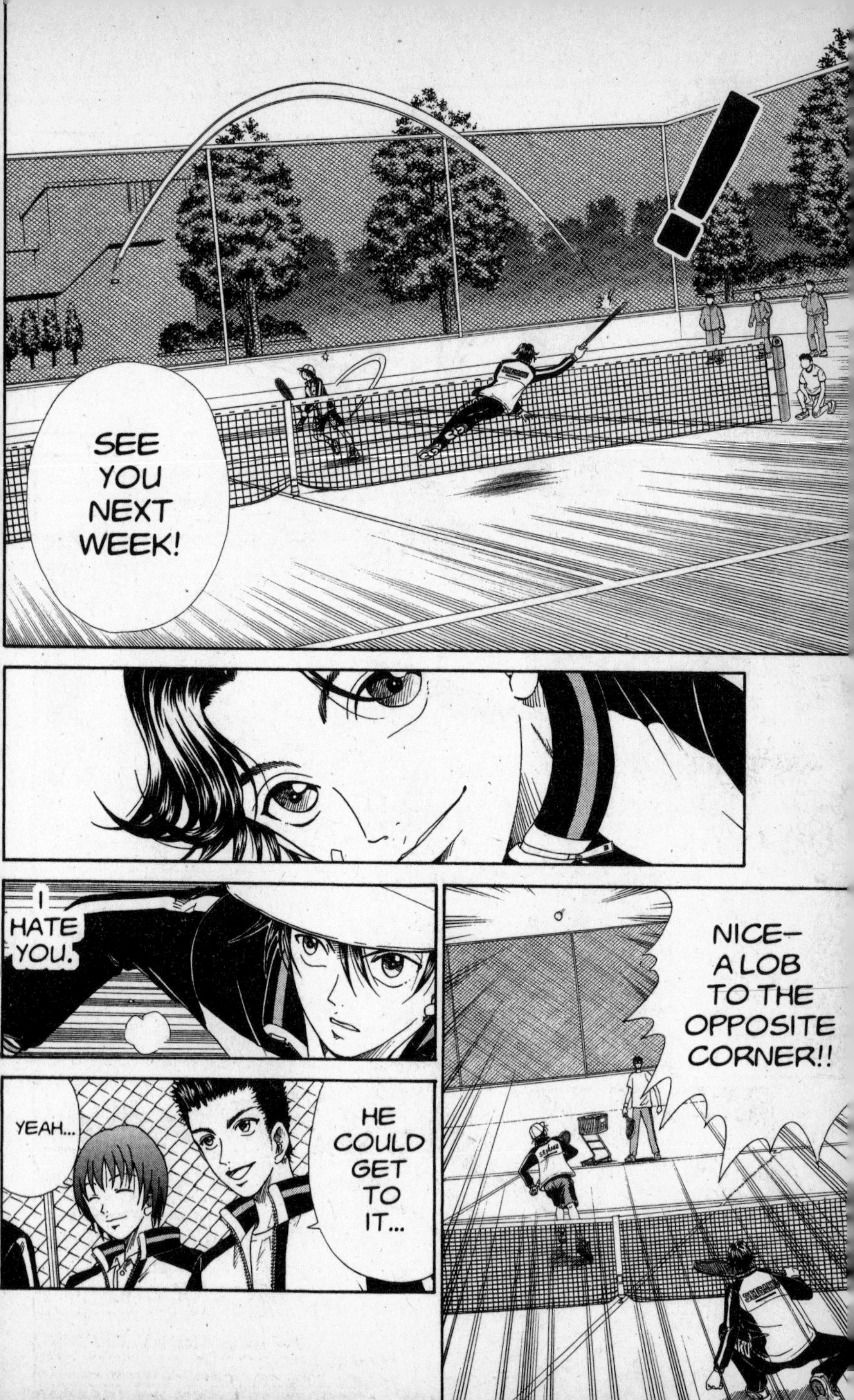
SEE YOU NEXT WEEK!
NICE— A LOB TO THE OPPOSITE CORNER!!
I HATE YOU.
HE COULD GET TO IT...
YEAH...

READ THIS WAY

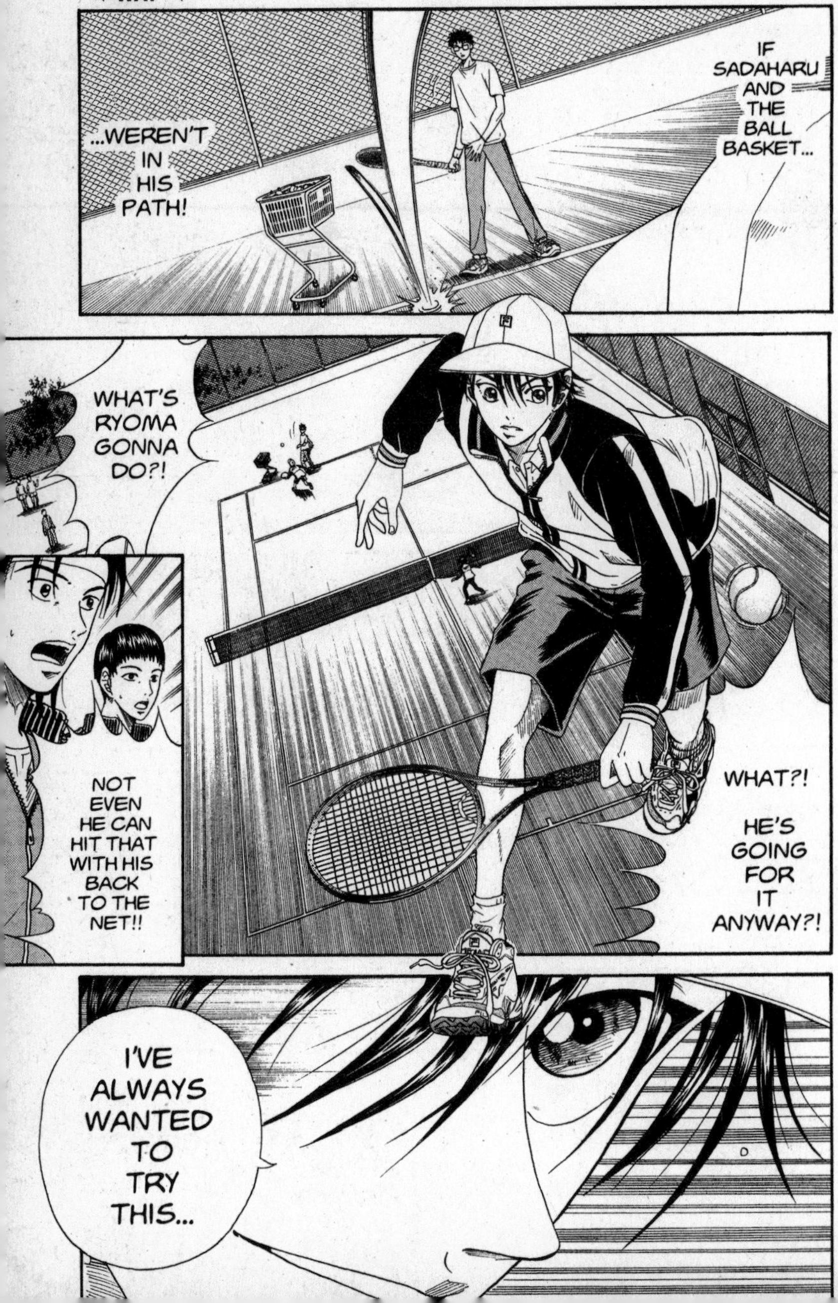
IF SADAHARU AND THE BALL BASKET...
...WEREN'T IN HIS PATH!
WHAT'S RYOMA GONNA DO?!
NOT EVEN HE CAN HIT THAT WITH HIS BACK TO THE NET!!
WHAT?! HE'S GOING FOR IT ANYWAY?!
I'VE ALWAYS WANTED TO TRY THIS...

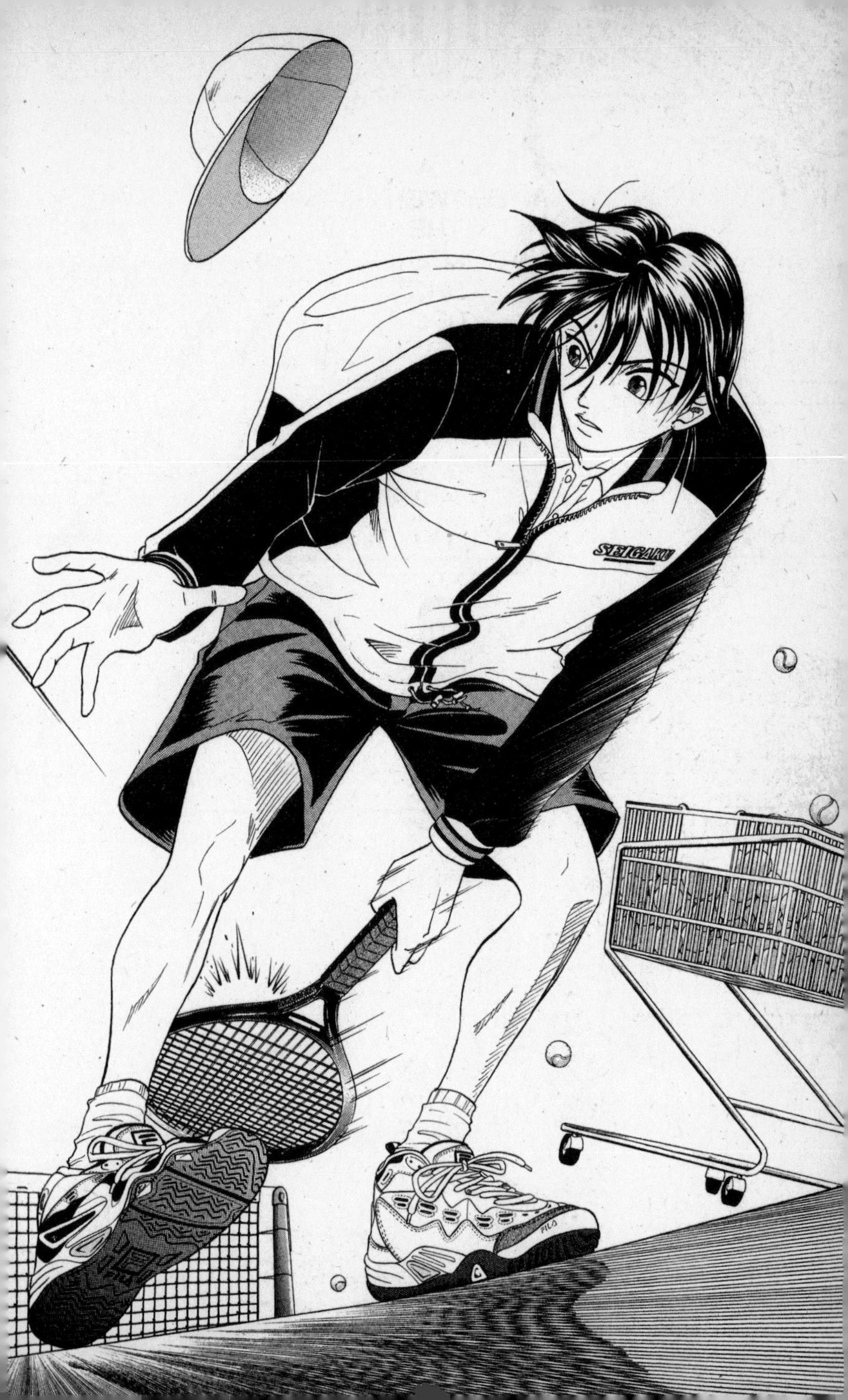
SEIGAKU
FILA

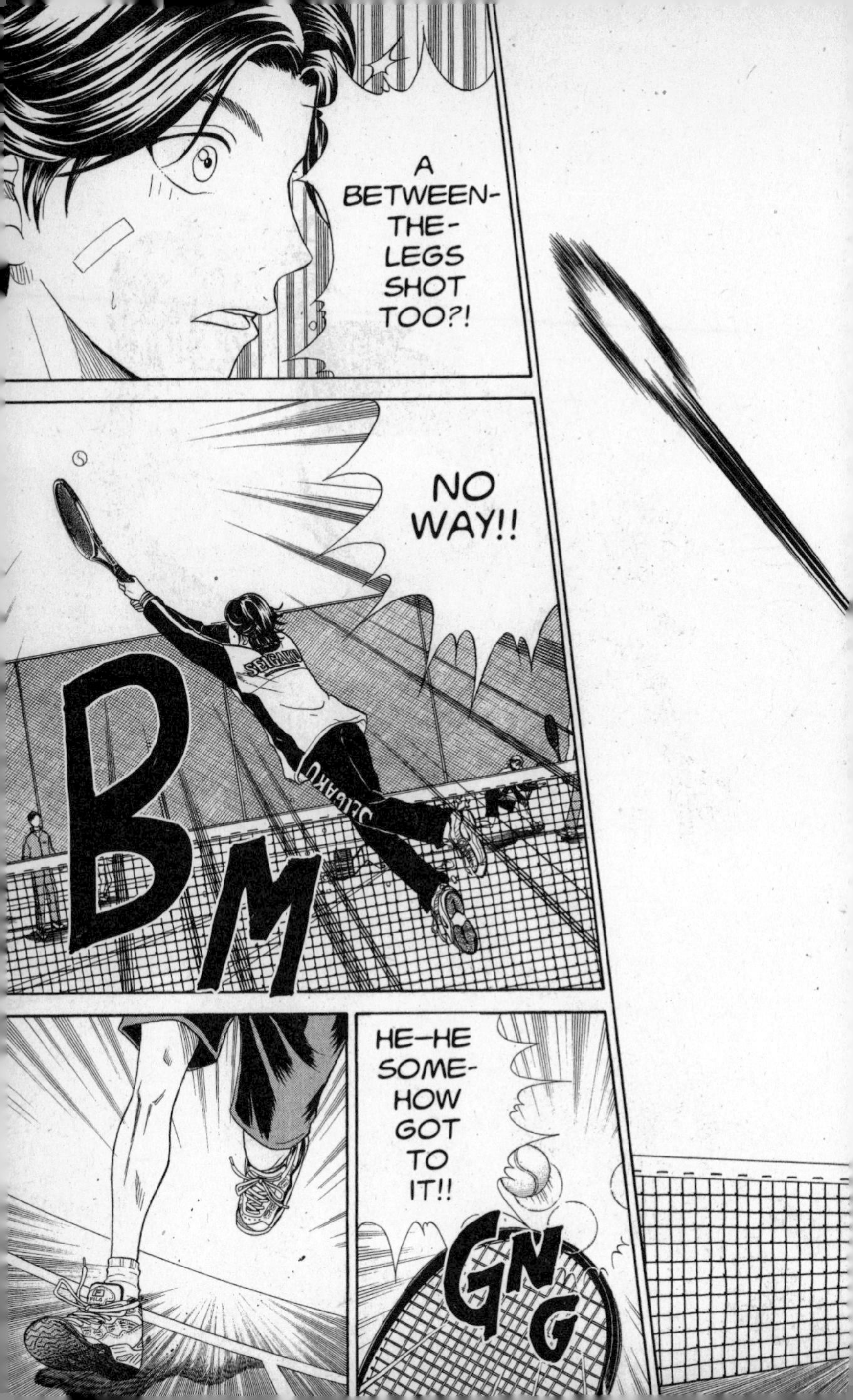
A BETWEEN-THE-LEGS SHOT TOO?!
NO WAY!!
BM
HE-HE SOME-HOW GOT TO IT!!
GNG

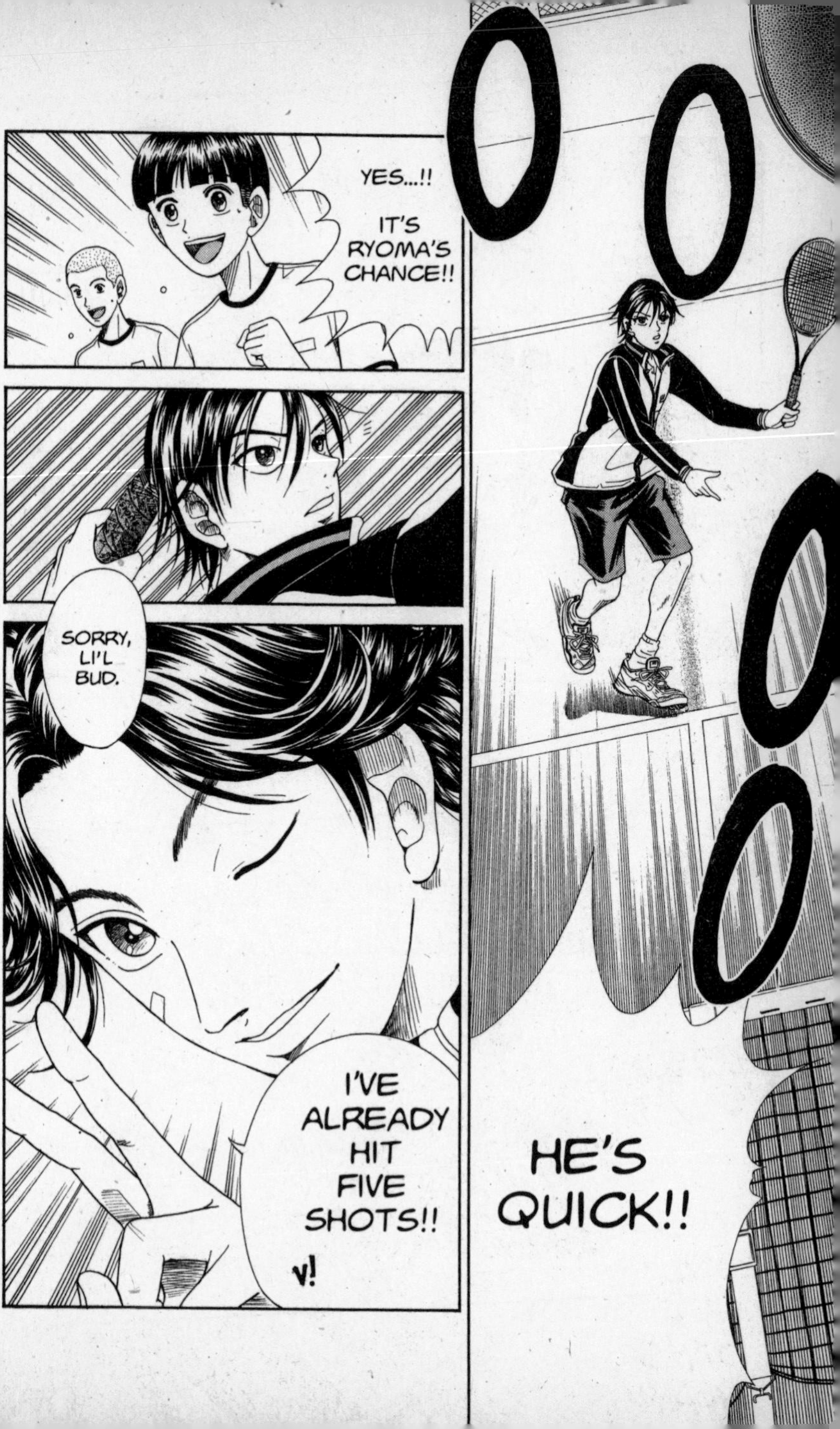
HE'S QUICK!!
YES...!!
IT'S RYOMA'S CHANCE!!
SORRY, LI'L BUD.
I'VE ALREADY HIT FIVE SHOTS!!
V!

READ THIS WAY

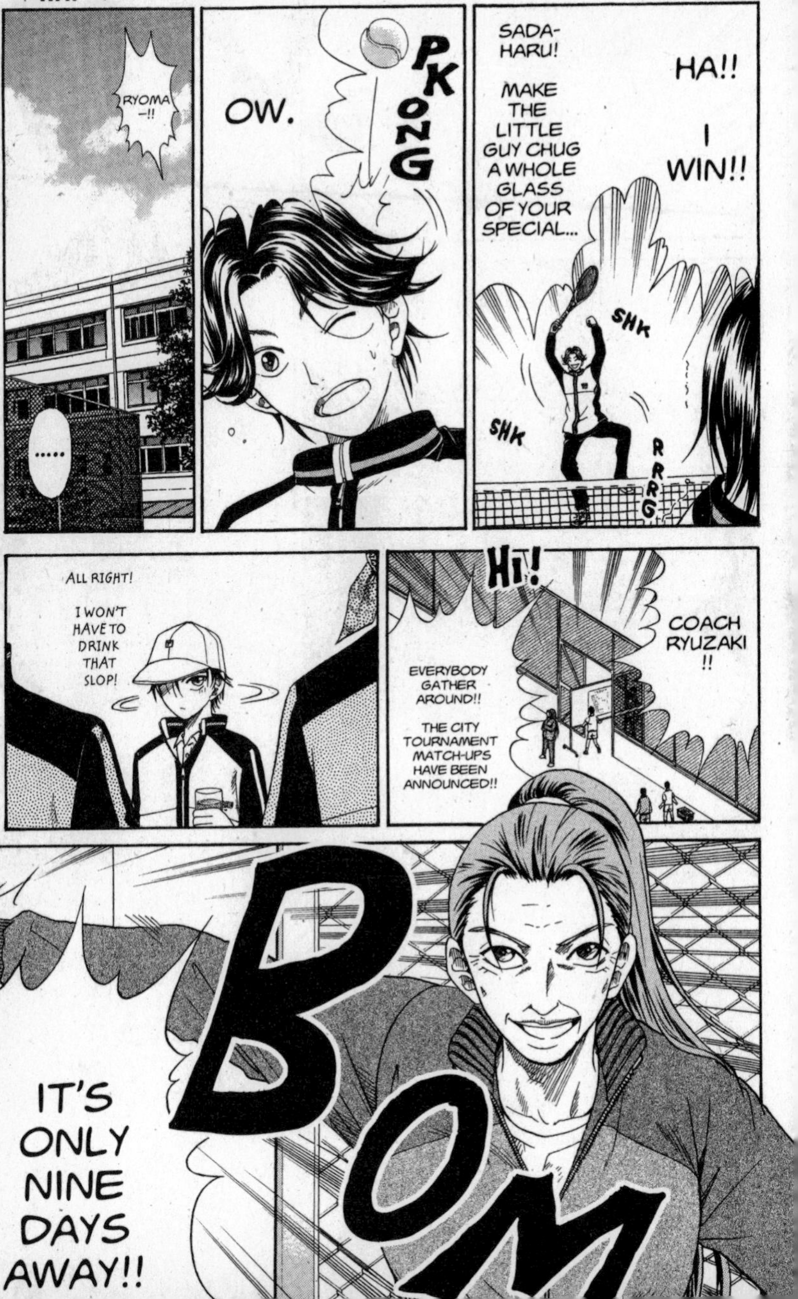
HA!!
I WIN!!
SADA-HARU!
MAKE THE LITTLE GUY CHUG A WHOLE GLASS OF YOUR SPECIAL...
SHK
SHK
RRRG
PKONG
OW.
RYOMA—!!
......
HI!
COACH RYUZAKI!!
EVERYBODY GATHER AROUND!!
THE CITY TOURNAMENT MATCH-UPS HAVE BEEN ANNOUNCED!!
ALL RIGHT!
I WON'T HAVE TO DRINK THAT SLOP!
BOM
IT'S ONLY NINE DAYS AWAY!!

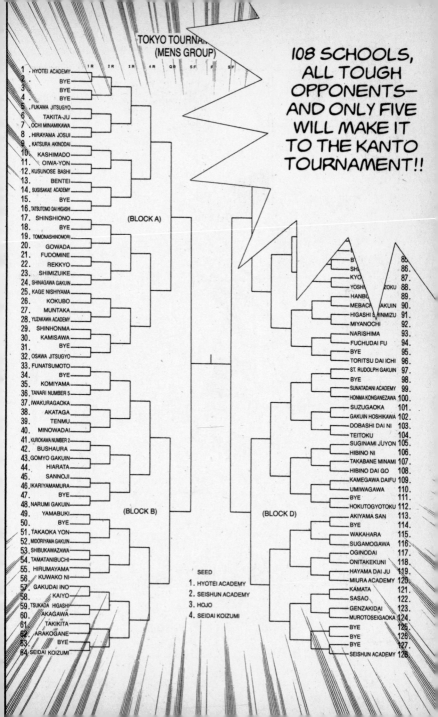

TOKYO TOURNAMENT
(MENS GROUP)

108 SCHOOLS,
ALL TOUGH
OPPONENTS—
AND ONLY FIVE
WILL MAKE IT
TO THE KANTO
TOURNAMENT!!

1R   2R   3R   4R   QR   SF   F   SF

1. HYOTEI ACADEMY
2. BYE
3. BYE
4. BYE
5. FUKAWA JITSUGYO
6. TAKITA-JU
7. OCHI MINAMIKAWA
8. HIRAYAMA JOSUI
9. KATSURA AKINODAI
10. KASHIMADO
11. OIWA-YON
12. KUSUNOSE BASHI
13. BENTEI
14. SUGISAKAE ACADEMY
15. BYE
16. TATSUTOMO DAI HIGASHI
17. SHINSHIONO
18. BYE
19. TOMONASHINOMORI
20. GOWADA
21. FUDOMINE
22. REKKYO
23. SHIMIZUIKE
24. SHINAGAWA GAKUIN
25. KAGE NISHIYAMA
26. KOKUBO
27. MUNTAKA
28. YUZAKAWA ACADEMY
29. SHINHONMA
30. KAMISAWA
31. BYE
32. OSAWA JITSUGYO
33. FUNATSUMOTO
34. BYE
35. KOMIYAMA
36. TANARI NUMBER 5
37. IWAKURAGAOKA
38. AKATAGA
39. TENMU
40. MINOWADAI
41. KUROKAWA NUMBER 2
42. BUSHAURA
43. GOMYO GAKUIN
44. HIARATA
45. SANNOJI
46. IKARIYAMAMURA
47. BYE
48. NARUMI GAKUIN
49. YAMABUKI
50. BYE
51. TAKAOKA YON
52. MIDORIYAMA GAKUIN
53. SHIBUKAWAZAWA
54. TAMATANIBUCHI
55. HIRUMAYAMA
56. KUWAKO NI
57. GAKUDAI INO
58. KAIYO
59. TSUKADA HIGASHI
60. AKAGAWA
61. TAKIKITA
62. ARAKOGANE
63. BYE
64. SEIDAI KOIZUMI

(BLOCK A)

(BLOCK B)

B   85.
SH   86.
KYO   87.
YOSHI ZOKU 88.
HANBU   89.
MEBACA GAKUIN 90.
HIGASHI SHINMIZU 91.
MIYANOCHI 92.
NARISHIMA 93.
FUCHUDAI FU 94.
BYE   95.
TORITSU DAI ICHI 96.
ST. RUDOLPH GAKUIN 97.
BYE   98.
SUNATADANI ACADEMY 99.
HONMA KONGANEZAWA 100.
SUZUGAOKA 101.
GAKUIN HOSHIKAWA 102.
DOBASHI DAI NI 103.
TEITOKU 104.
SUGINAMI JUYON 105.
HIBINO NI 106.
TAKABANE MINAMI 107.
HIBINO DAI GO 108.
KAMEGAWA DAIFU 109.
UMIWAGAWA 110.
BYE   111.
HOKUTOGYOTOKU 112.
AKIYAMA SAN 113.
BYE   114.
WAKAHARA 115.
SUGAMOGAWA 116.
OGINODAI 117.
ONITAKEKUNI 118.
HAYAMA DAI JU 119.
MIURA ACADEMY 120.
KAMATA 121.
SASAO 122.
GENZAKIDAI 123.
MUROTOSEIGAOKA 124.
BYE   125.
BYE   126.
BYE   127.
SEISHUN ACADEMY 128.

(BLOCK D)

SEED

1. HYOTEI ACADEMY
2. SEISHUN ACADEMY
3. HOJO
4. SEIDAI KOIZUMI

READ THIS WAY

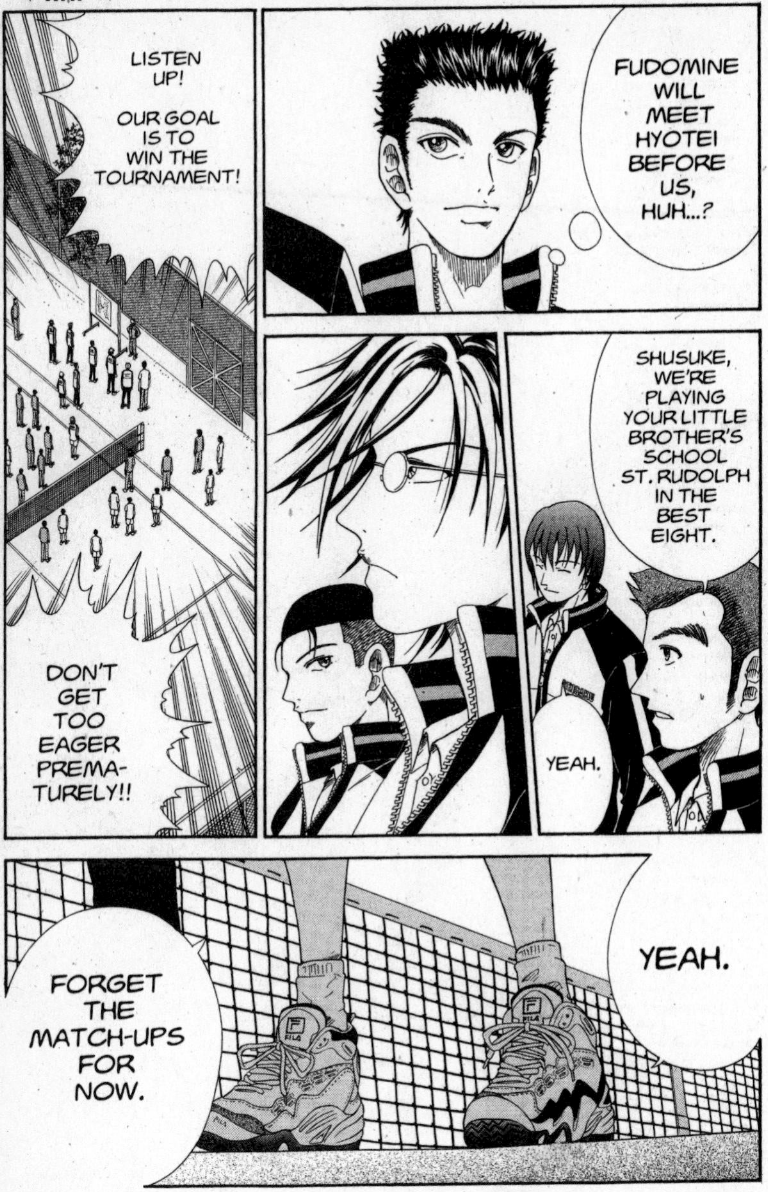
FUDOMINE WILL MEET HYOTEI BEFORE US, HUH...?
SHUSUKE, WE'RE PLAYING YOUR LITTLE BROTHER'S SCHOOL ST. RUDOLPH IN THE BEST EIGHT.
YEAH.
LISTEN UP!
OUR GOAL IS TO WIN THE TOURNAMENT!
DON'T GET TOO EAGER PREMA-TURELY!!
FORGET THE MATCH-UPS FOR NOW.
YEAH.

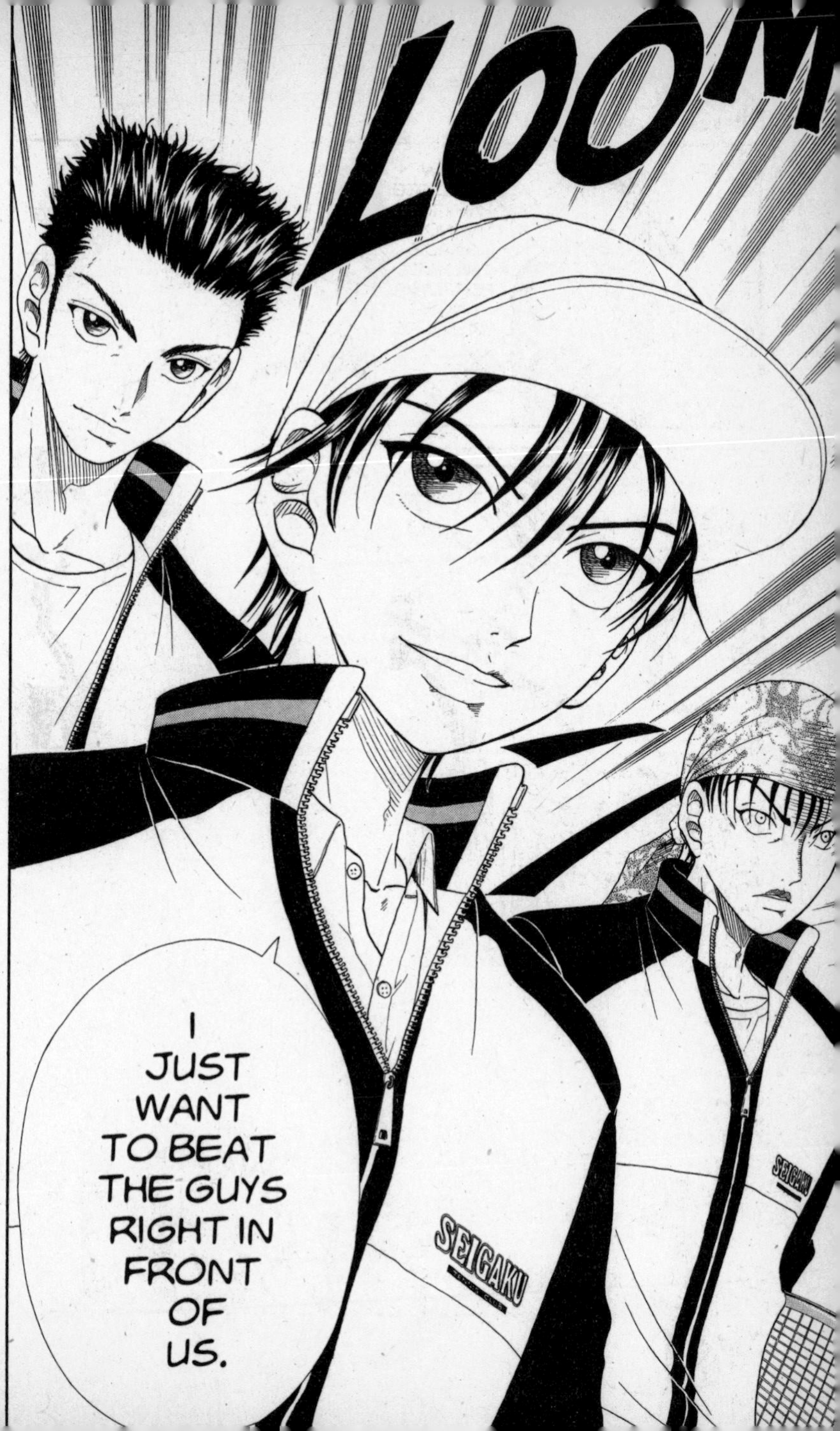
LOOM
I JUST WANT TO BEAT THE GUYS RIGHT IN FRONT OF US.
SEIGAKU
SEIGAKU

READ THIS WAY

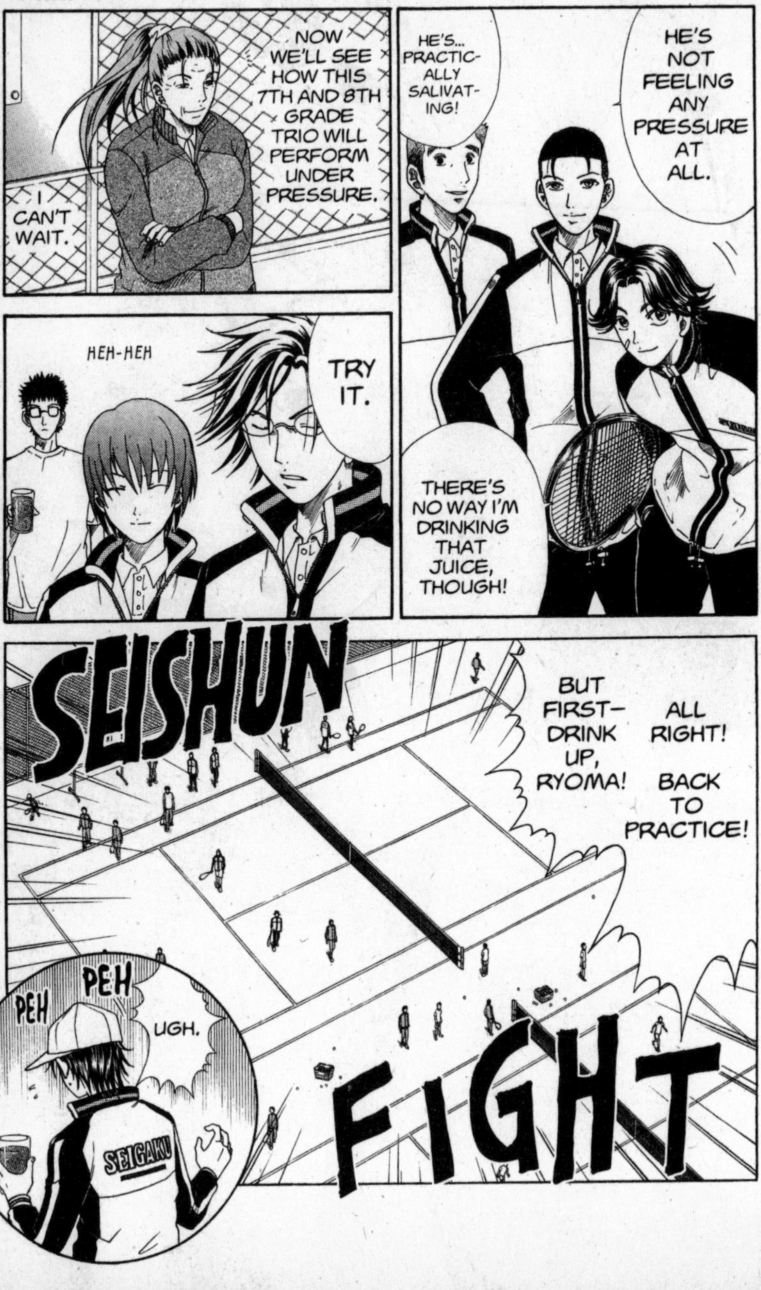
HE'S NOT FEELING ANY PRESSURE AT ALL.
HE'S... PRACTICALLY SALIVATING!
THERE'S NO WAY I'M DRINKING THAT JUICE, THOUGH!
NOW WE'LL SEE HOW THIS 7TH AND 8TH GRADE TRIO WILL PERFORM UNDER PRESSURE.
I CAN'T WAIT.
TRY IT.
HEH-HEH
ALL RIGHT! BACK TO PRACTICE!
BUT FIRST- DRINK UP, RYOMA!
SEISHUN
FIGHT
PEH PEH
UGH.

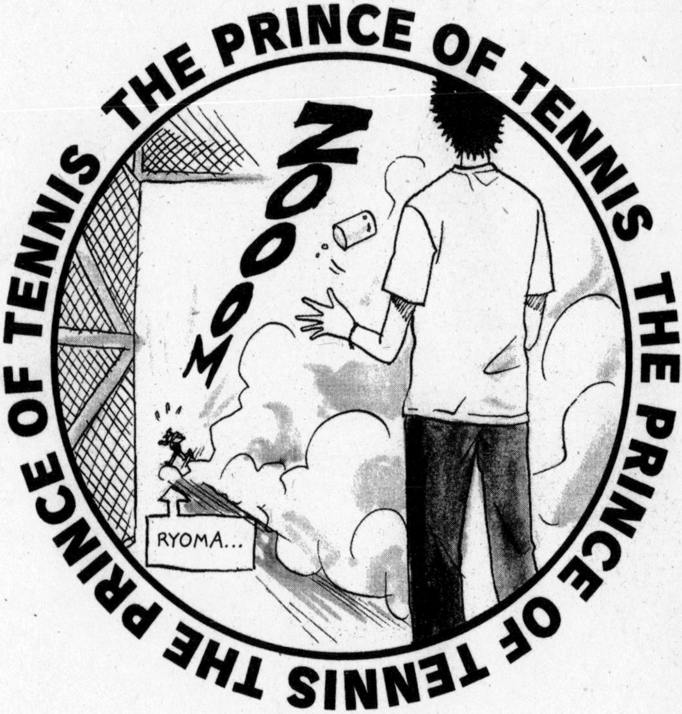
THE PRINCE OF TENNIS THE PRINCE OF TENNIS THE PRINCE OF TENNIS
ZOOOOM
RYOMA...

GENIUS 48: KALPIN'S BIG ADVENTURE (THE DAY BEFORE THE TOURNAMENT)

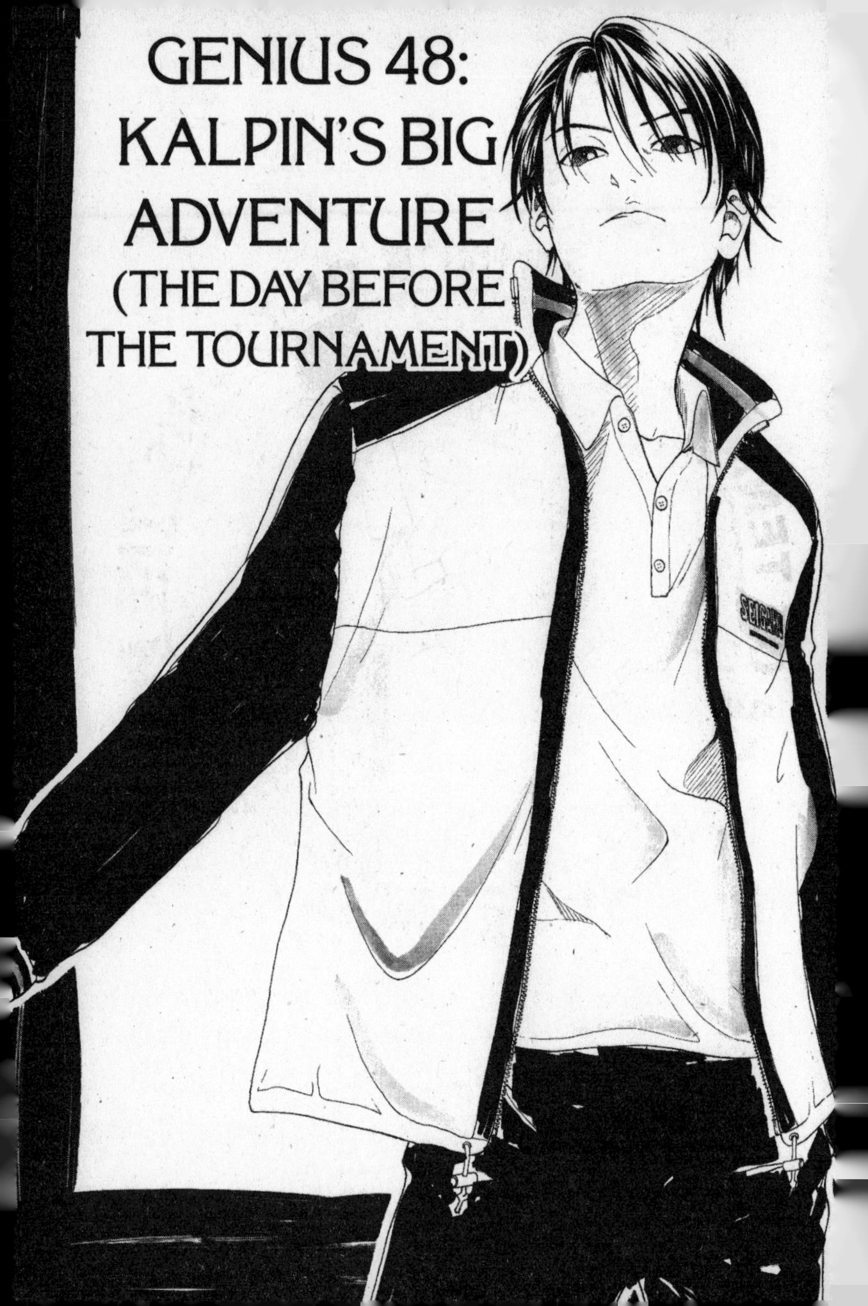

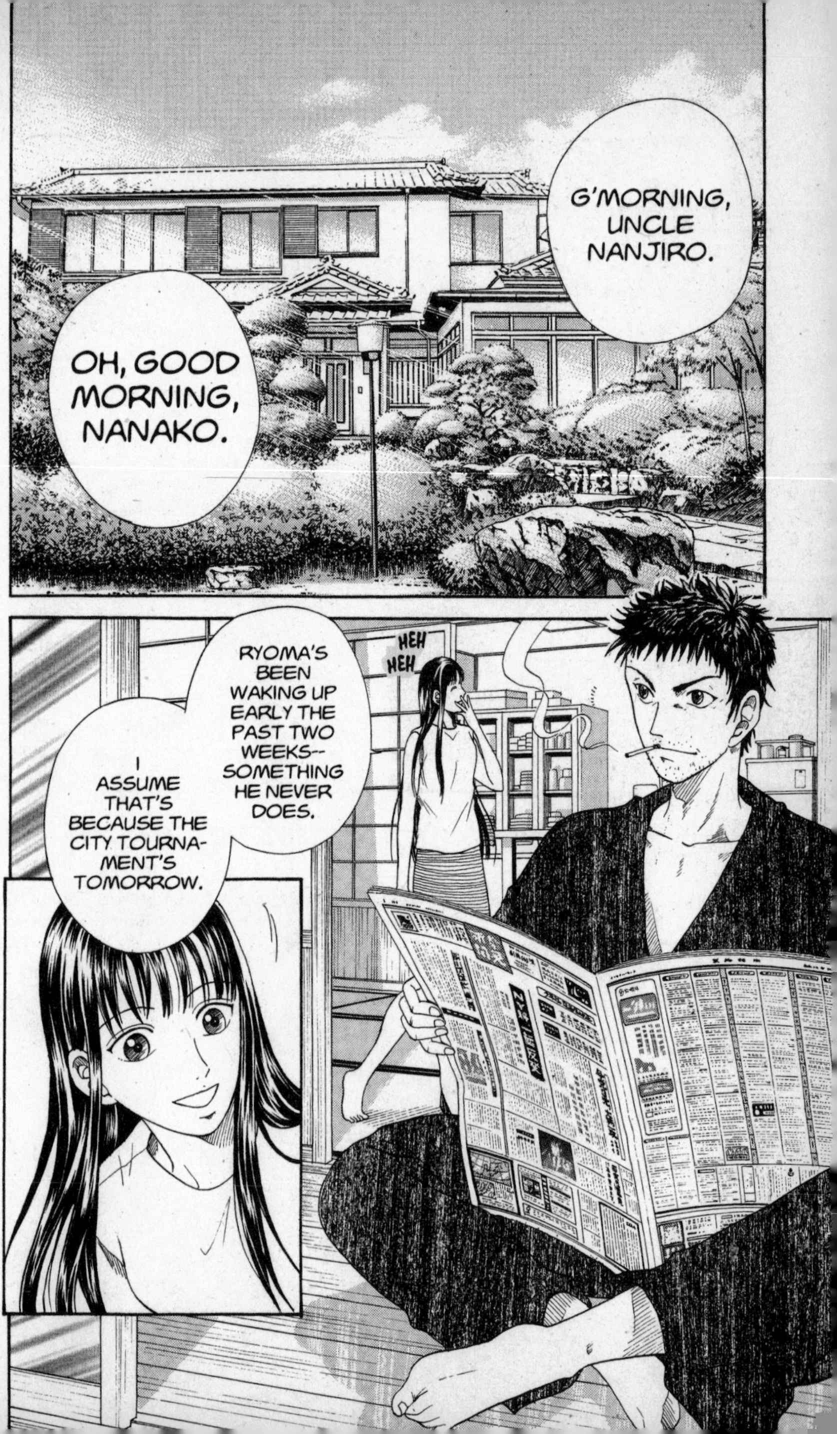
G'MORNING, UNCLE NANJIRO.
OH, GOOD MORNING, NANAKO.
HEH HEH
RYOMA'S BEEN WAKING UP EARLY THE PAST TWO WEEKS-- SOMETHING HE NEVER DOES.
I ASSUME THAT'S BECAUSE THE CITY TOURNA-MENT'S TOMORROW.

READ THIS WAY

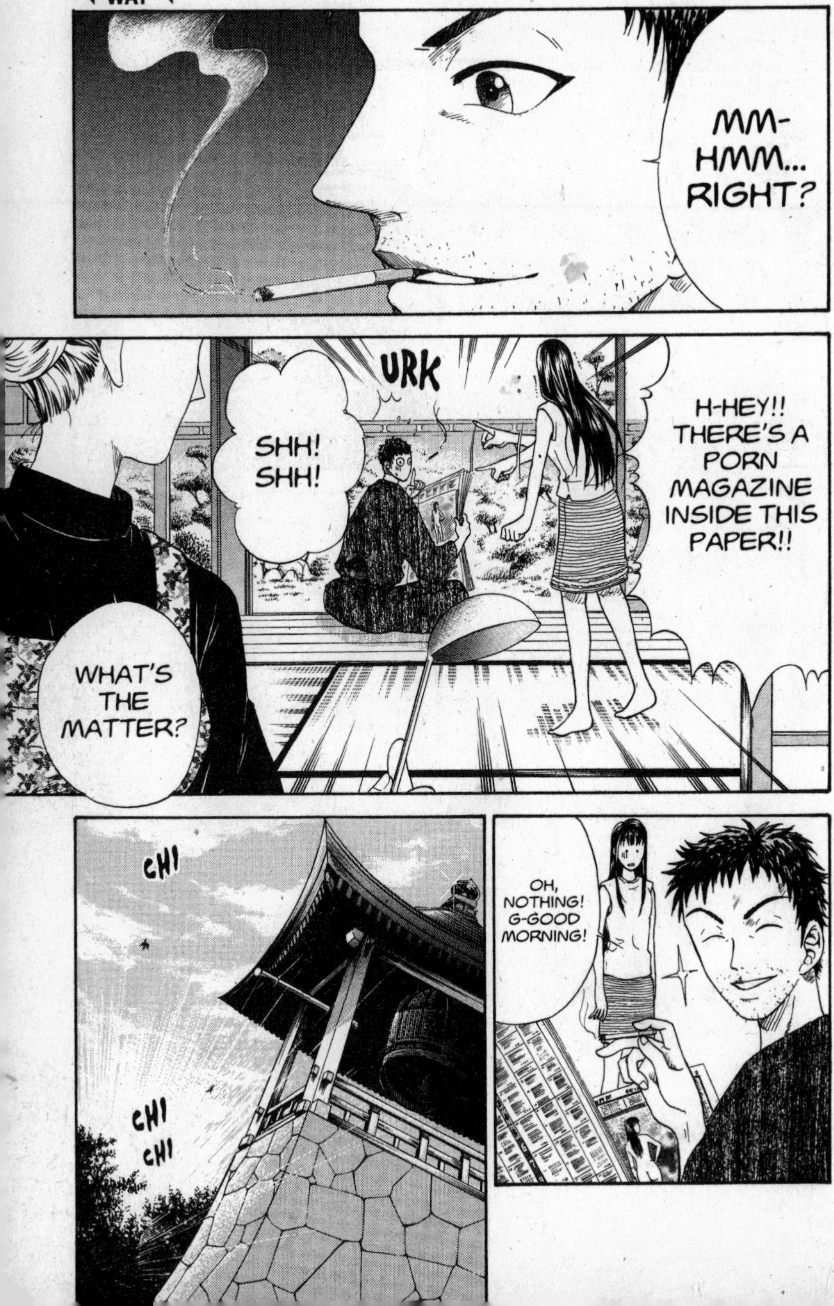
MM-HMM... RIGHT?
H-HEY!! THERE'S A PORN MAGAZINE INSIDE THIS PAPER!!
URK
SHH! SHH!
WHAT'S THE MATTER?
OH, NOTHING! G-GOOD MORNING!
CHI
CHI CHI

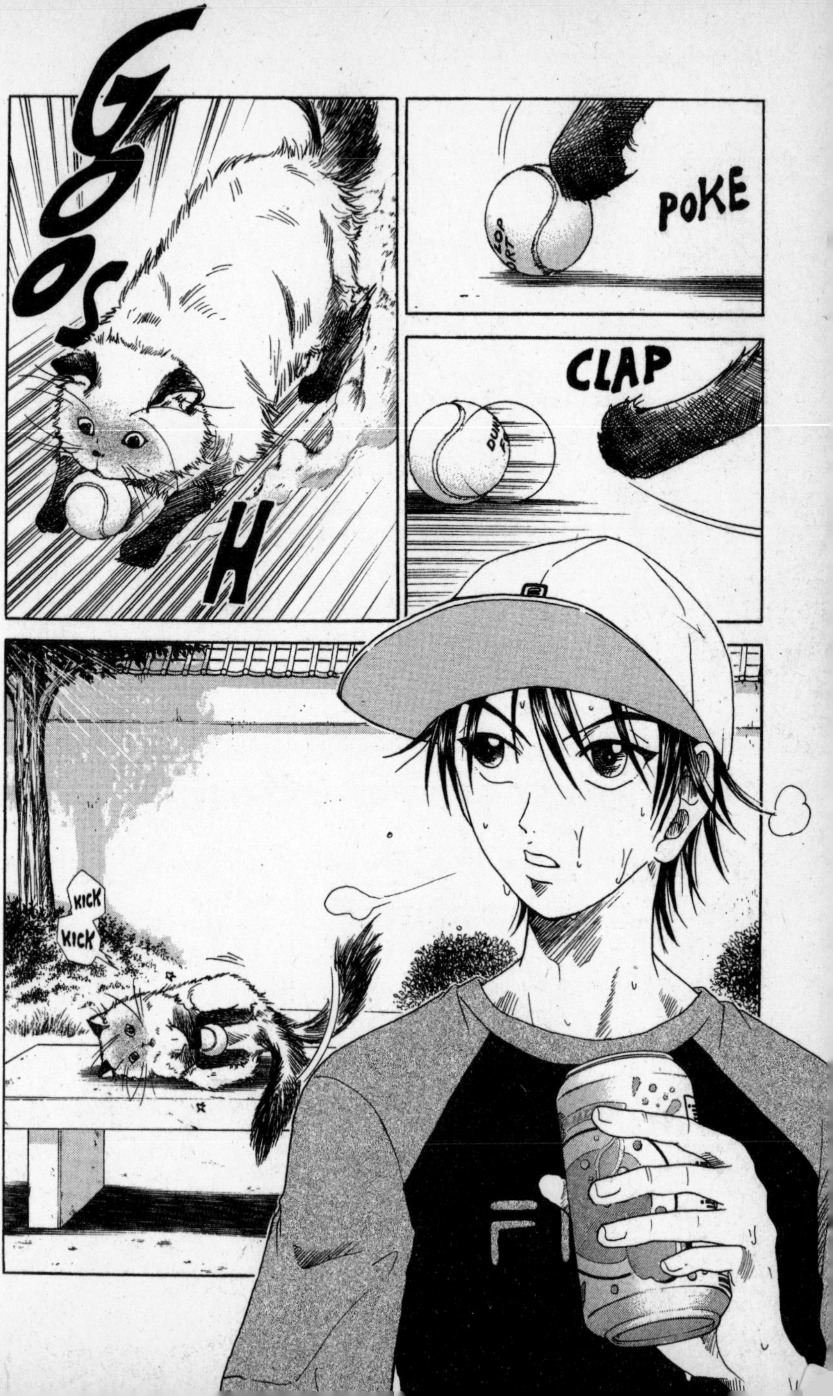
POKE
CLAP
GOOSH
KICK
KICK

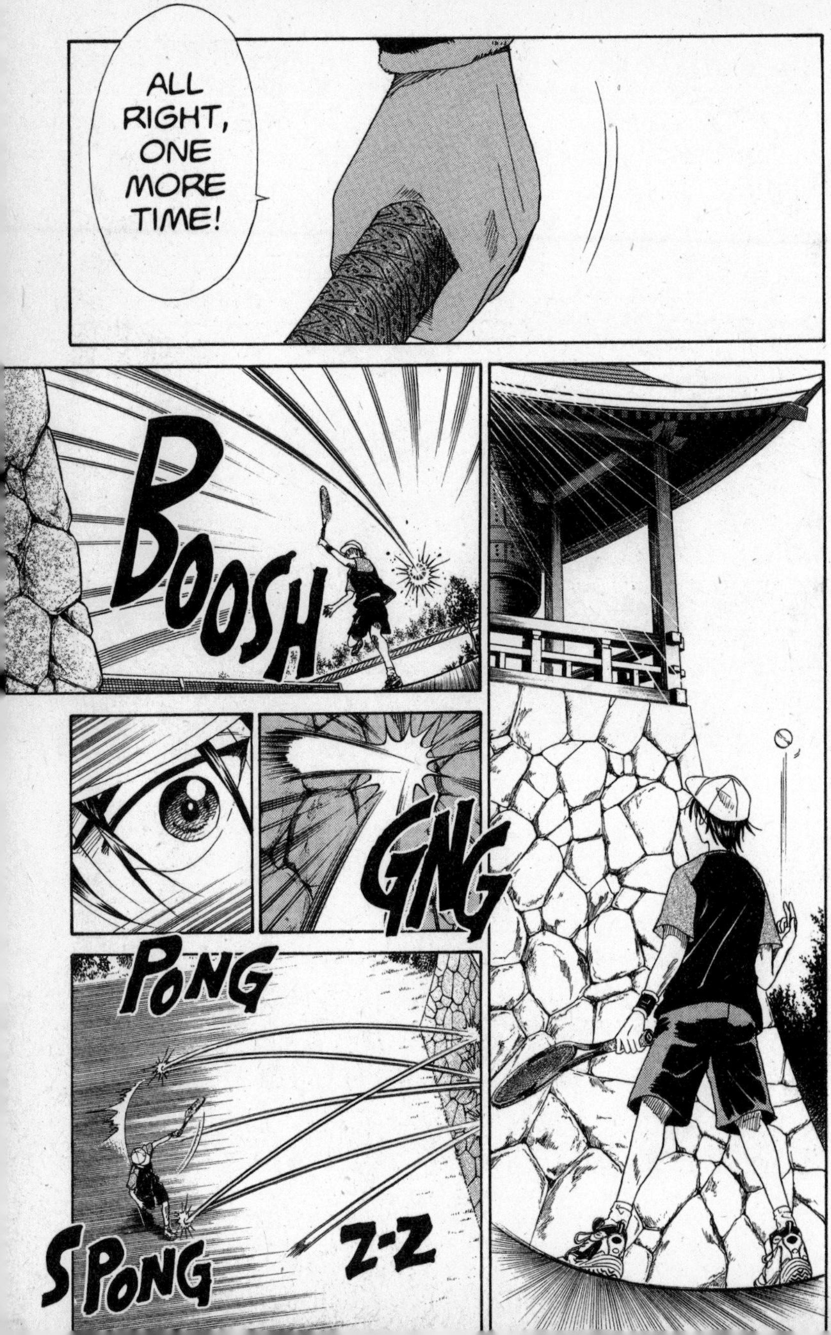
ALL RIGHT, ONE MORE TIME!
BOOSH
GNG
PONG
Z-Z
SPONG

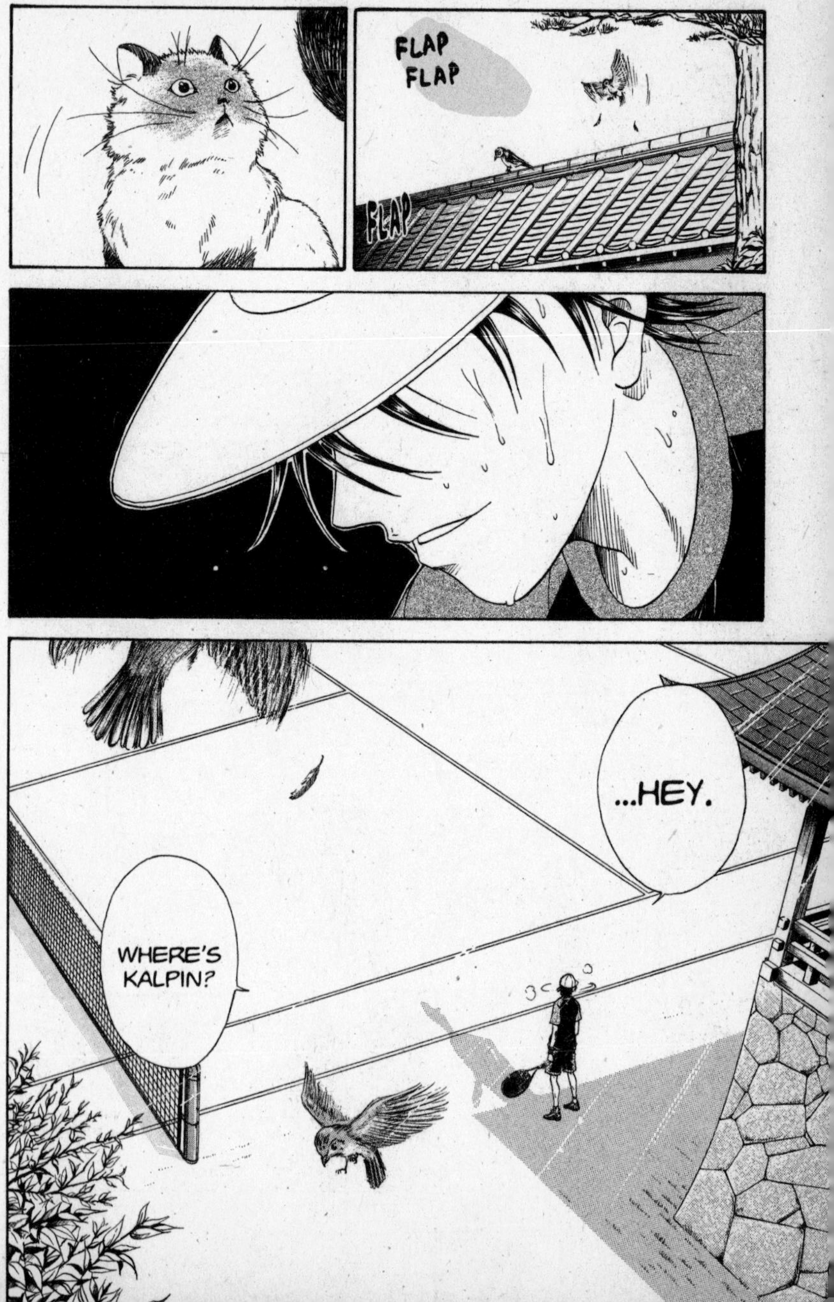
FLAP
FLAP
FLAP
...HEY.
WHERE'S KALPIN?

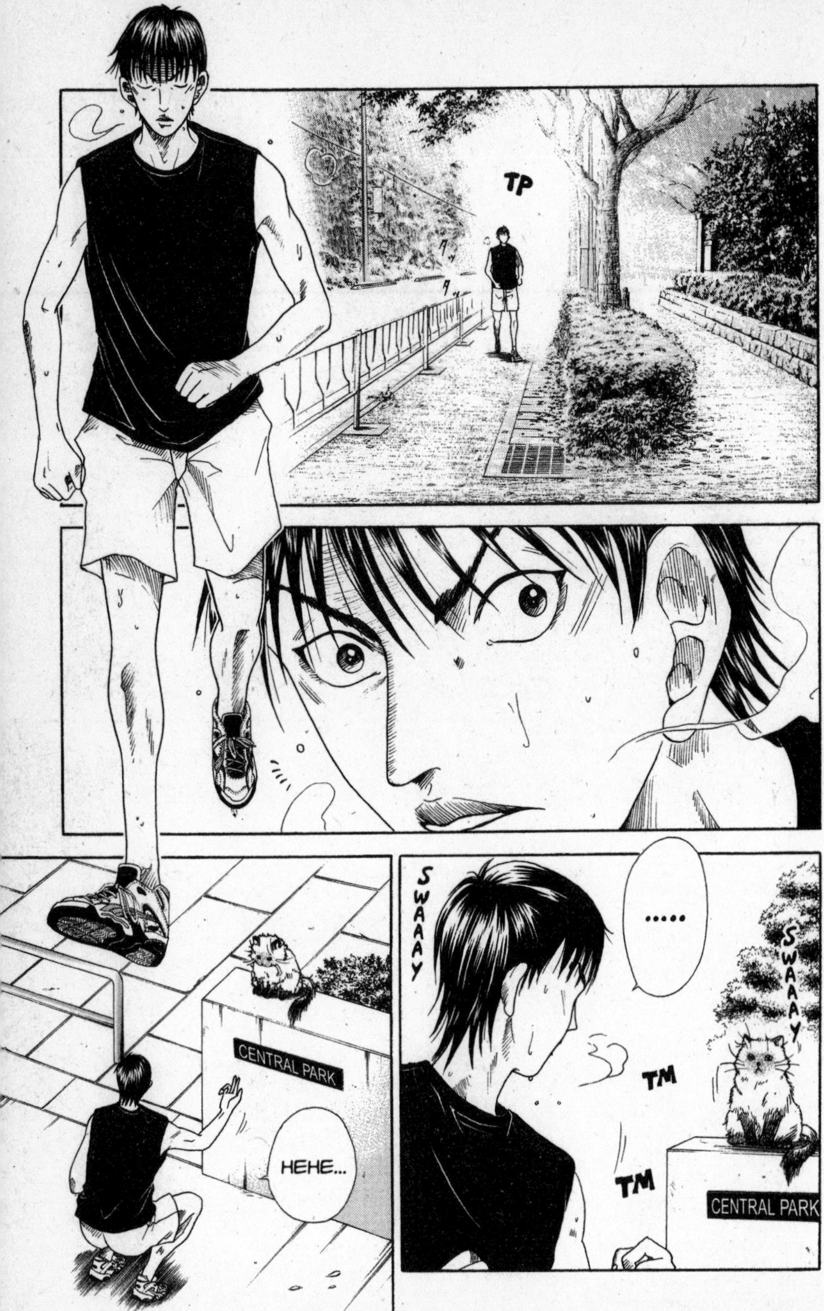
TP
SWAAAY
......
SWAAAY
TM
TM
CENTRAL PARK
CENTRAL PARK
HEHE...

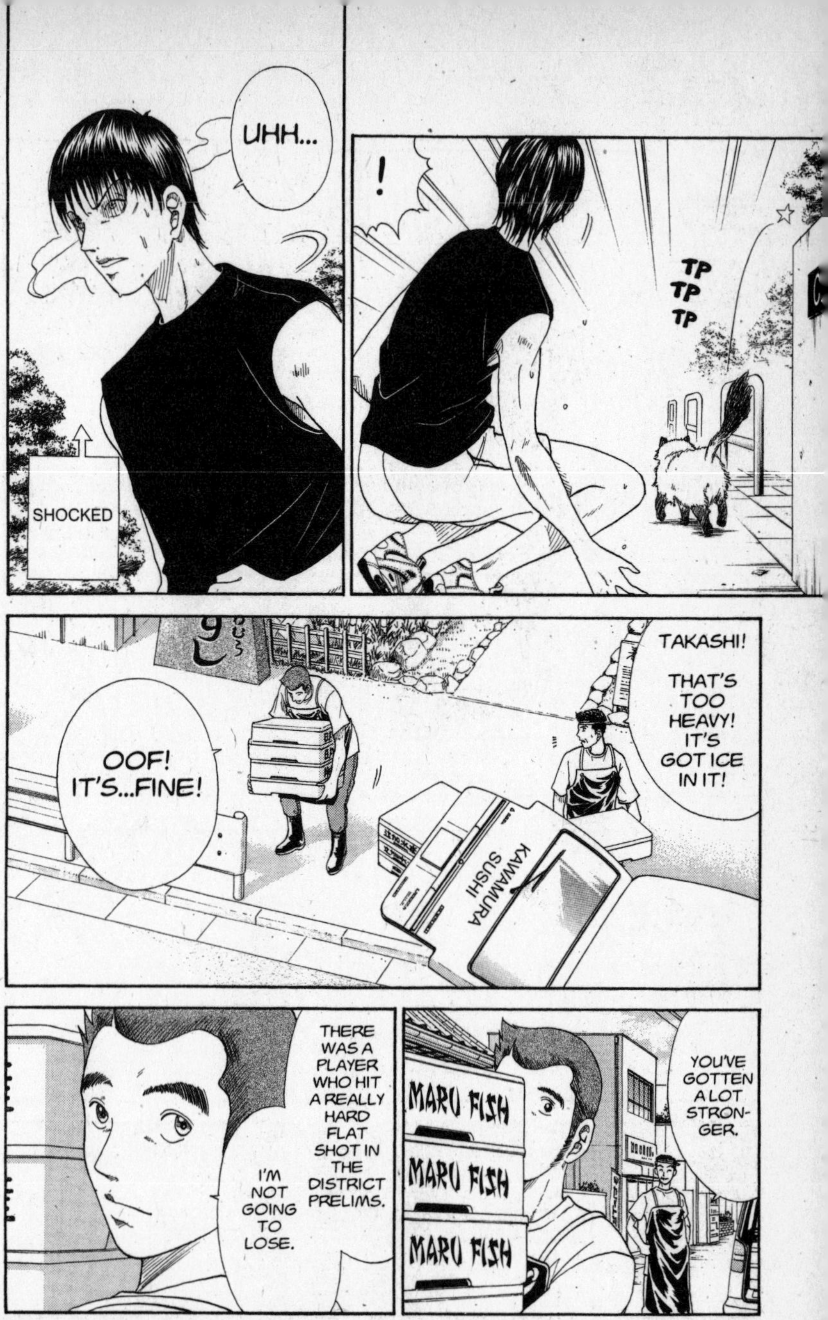
!
TP TP TP
UHH...
SHOCKED
TAKASHI! THAT'S TOO HEAVY! IT'S GOT ICE IN IT!
KAWAMURA SUSHI
OOF! IT'S...FINE!
YOU'VE GOTTEN A LOT STRONGER.
MARU FISH
MARU FISH
MARU FISH
THERE WAS A PLAYER WHO HIT A REALLY HARD FLAT SHOT IN THE DISTRICT PRELIMS.
I'M NOT GOING TO LOSE.

READ THIS WAY

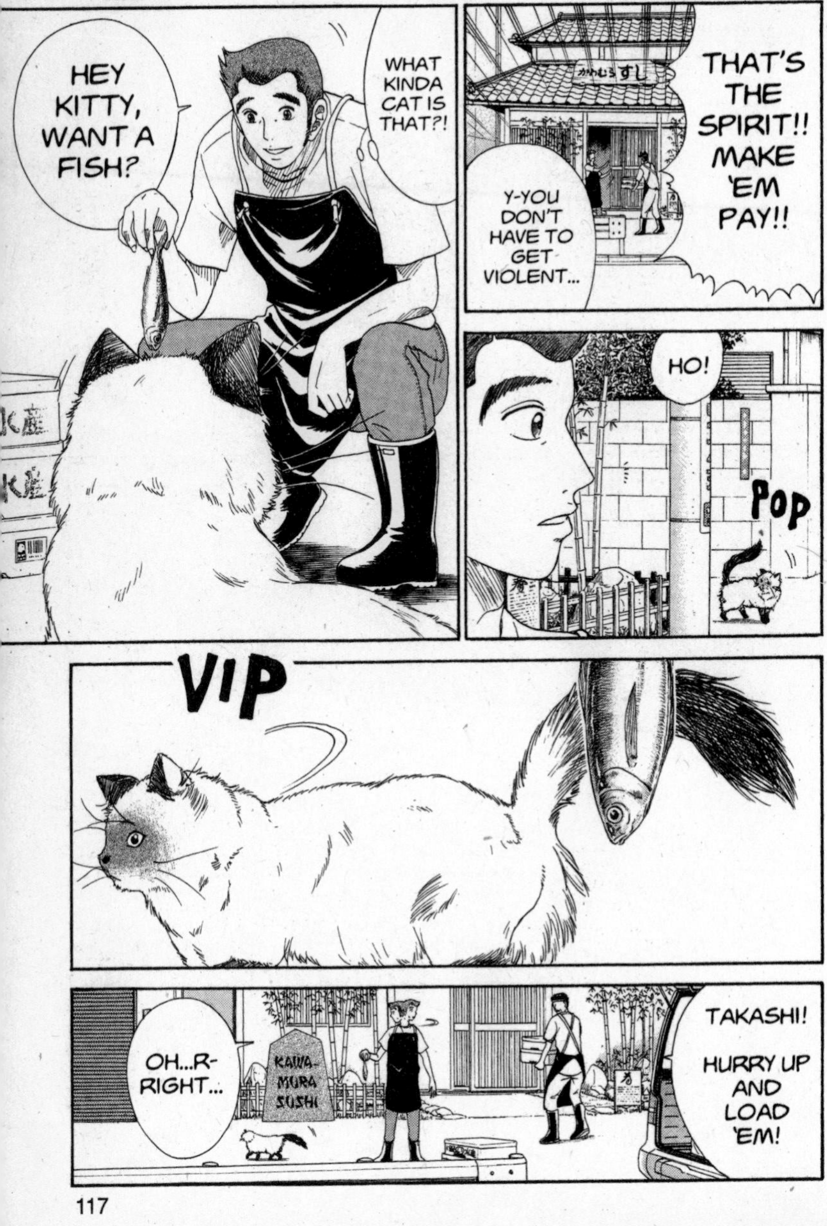

かわむらすし
THAT'S THE SPIRIT!! MAKE 'EM PAY!!
Y-YOU DON'T HAVE TO GET VIOLENT...
HO!
POP
WHAT KINDA CAT IS THAT?!
HEY KITTY, WANT A FISH?
VIP
TAKASHI!
HURRY UP AND LOAD 'EM!
OH...R-RIGHT...
KAWA-MURA SUSHI

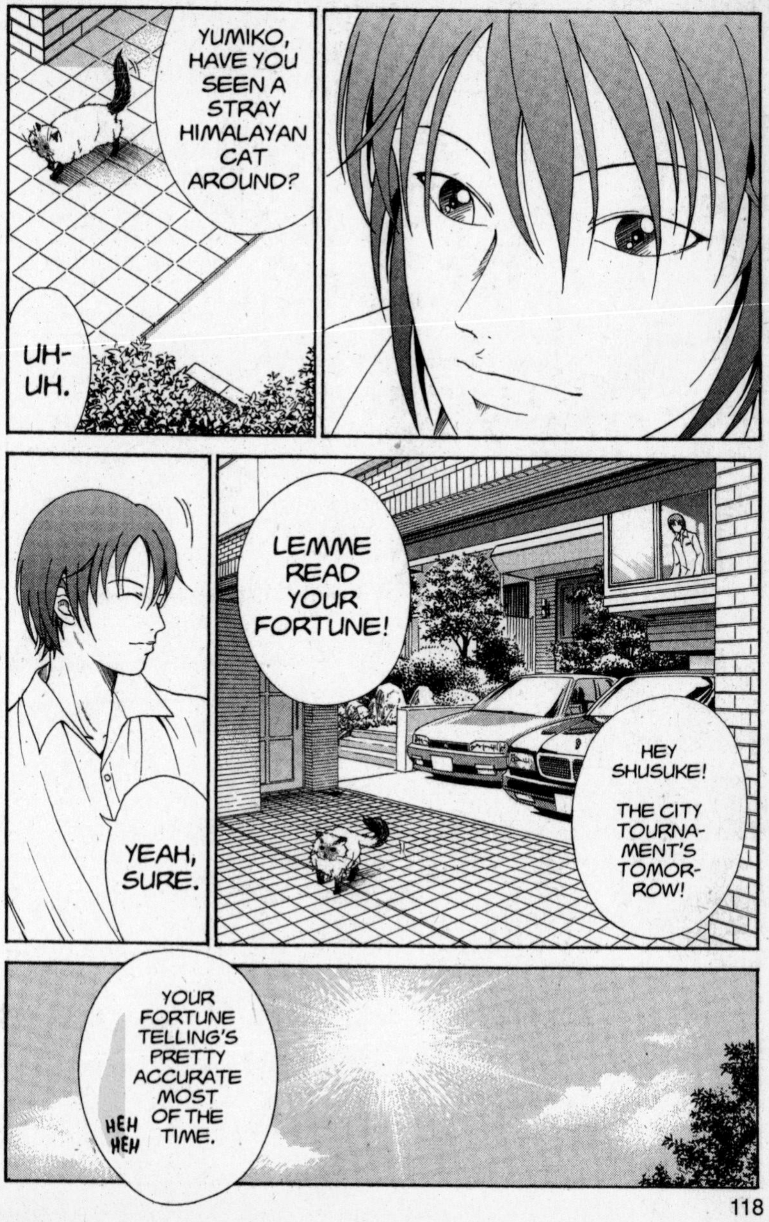
YUMIKO, HAVE YOU SEEN A STRAY HIMALAYAN CAT AROUND?
UH-UH.
HEY SHUSUKE! THE CITY TOURNAMENT'S TOMORROW!
LEMME READ YOUR FORTUNE!
YEAH, SURE.
YOUR FORTUNE TELLING'S PRETTY ACCURATE MOST OF THE TIME.
HEH HEH

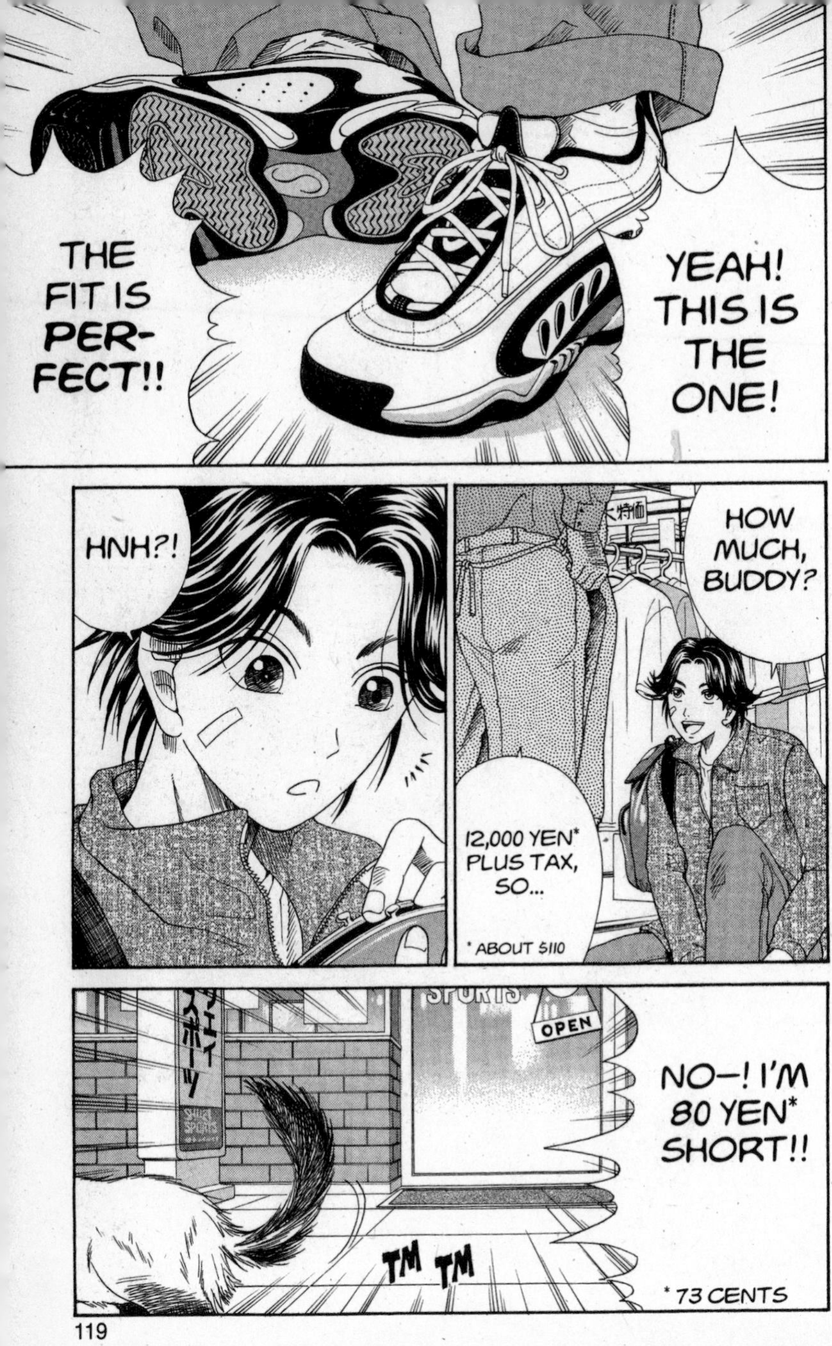
YEAH! THIS IS THE ONE!
THE FIT IS PER-FECT!!
HOW MUCH, BUDDY?
12,000 YEN* PLUS TAX, SO...
* ABOUT $110
HNH?!
OPEN
NO—! I'M 80 YEN* SHORT!!
TM TM
* 73 CENTS

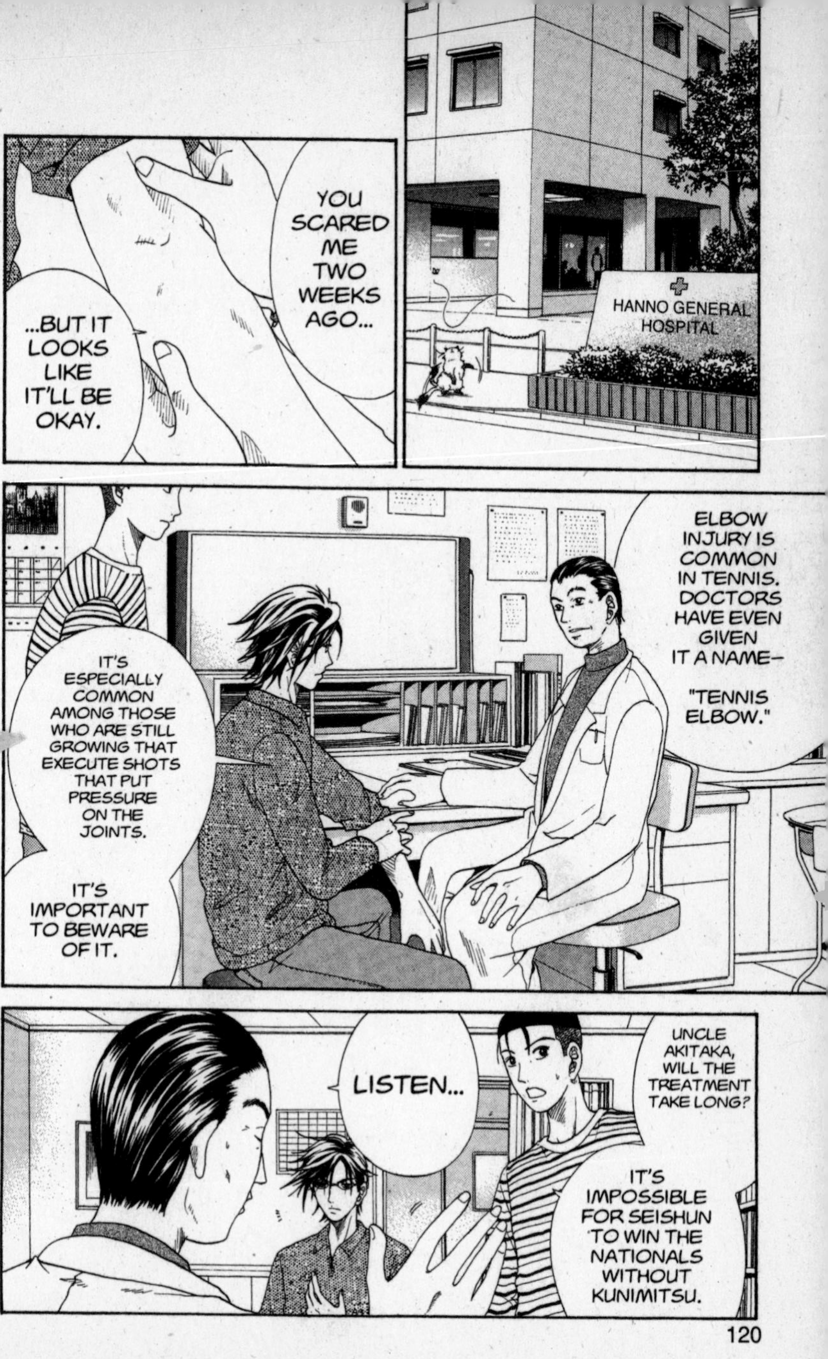
HANNO GENERAL HOSPITAL
YOU SCARED ME TWO WEEKS AGO...
...BUT IT LOOKS LIKE IT'LL BE OKAY.
ELBOW INJURY IS COMMON IN TENNIS. DOCTORS HAVE EVEN GIVEN IT A NAME–
"TENNIS ELBOW."
IT'S ESPECIALLY COMMON AMONG THOSE WHO ARE STILL GROWING THAT EXECUTE SHOTS THAT PUT PRESSURE ON THE JOINTS.
IT'S IMPORTANT TO BEWARE OF IT.
UNCLE AKITAKA, WILL THE TREATMENT TAKE LONG?
IT'S IMPOSSIBLE FOR SEISHUN TO WIN THE NATIONALS WITHOUT KUNIMITSU.
LISTEN...

READ THIS WAY

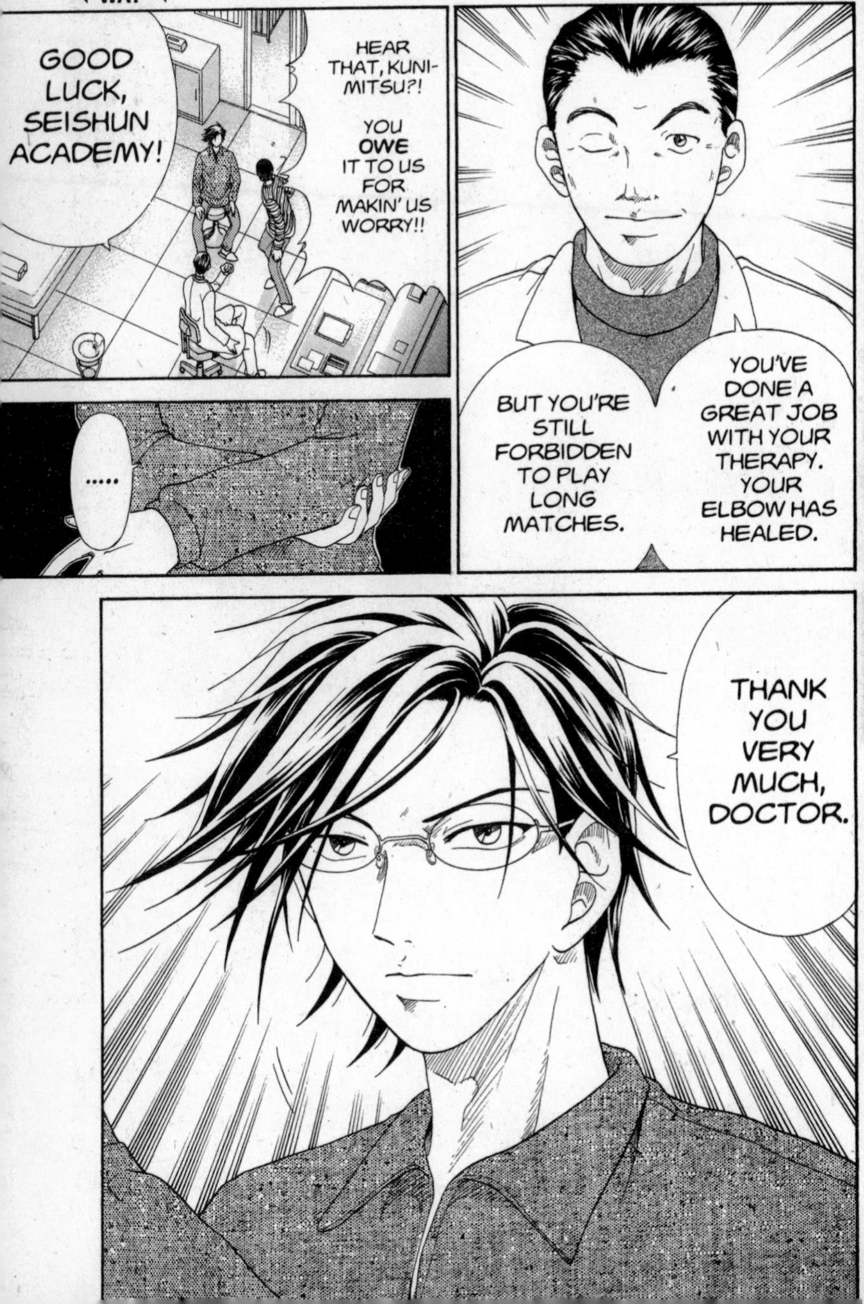
YOU'VE DONE A GREAT JOB WITH YOUR THERAPY. YOUR ELBOW HAS HEALED.
BUT YOU'RE STILL FORBIDDEN TO PLAY LONG MATCHES.
HEAR THAT, KUNI-MITSU?! YOU OWE IT TO US FOR MAKIN' US WORRY!!
GOOD LUCK, SEISHUN ACADEMY!
......
THANK YOU VERY MUCH, DOCTOR.

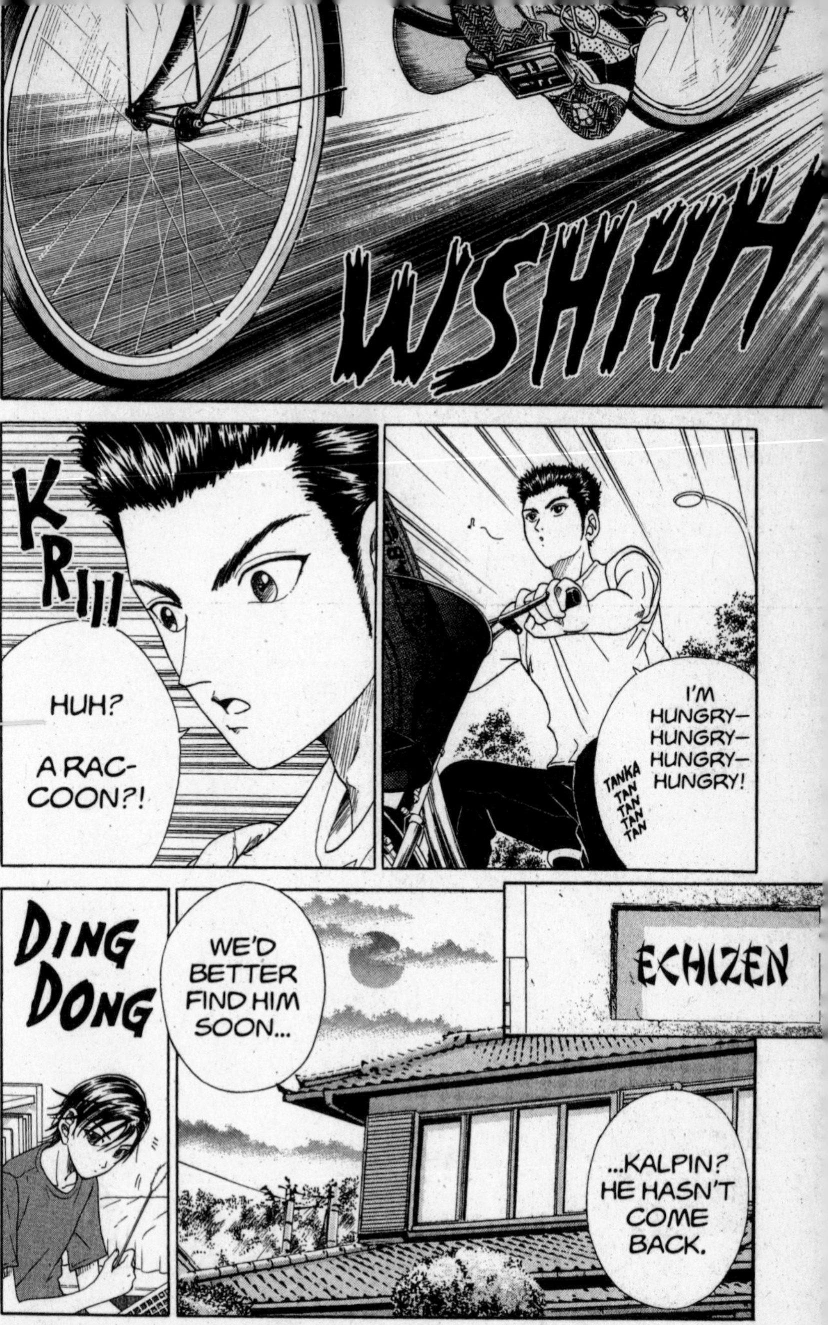
WSHHH
I'M HUNGRY—HUNGRY—HUNGRY—HUNGRY!
TANKA TAN TAN TAN TAN
KRIII
HUH?
A RAC-COON?!
ECHIZEN
...KALPIN? HE HASN'T COME BACK.
WE'D BETTER FIND HIM SOON...
DING DONG

DOESN'T THIS CAT LIVE HERE?

HEY... RYOMA!!

WRRR?

THANKS, MOMO!

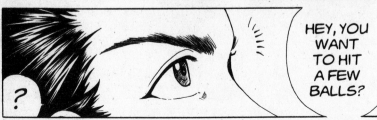

?

HEY, YOU WANT TO HIT A FEW BALLS?

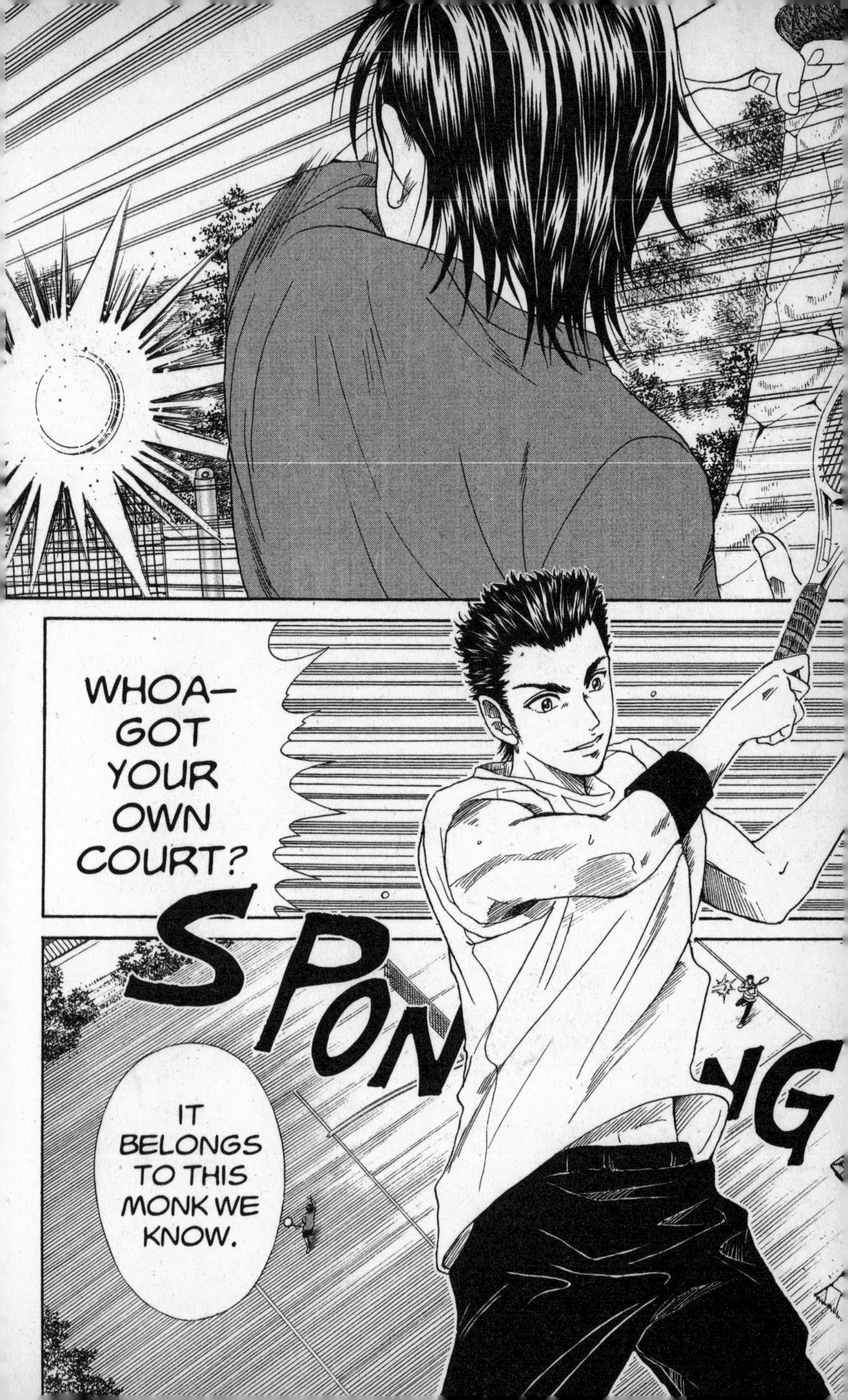
WHOA- GOT YOUR OWN COURT?
SPONNG
IT BELONGS TO THIS MONK WE KNOW.

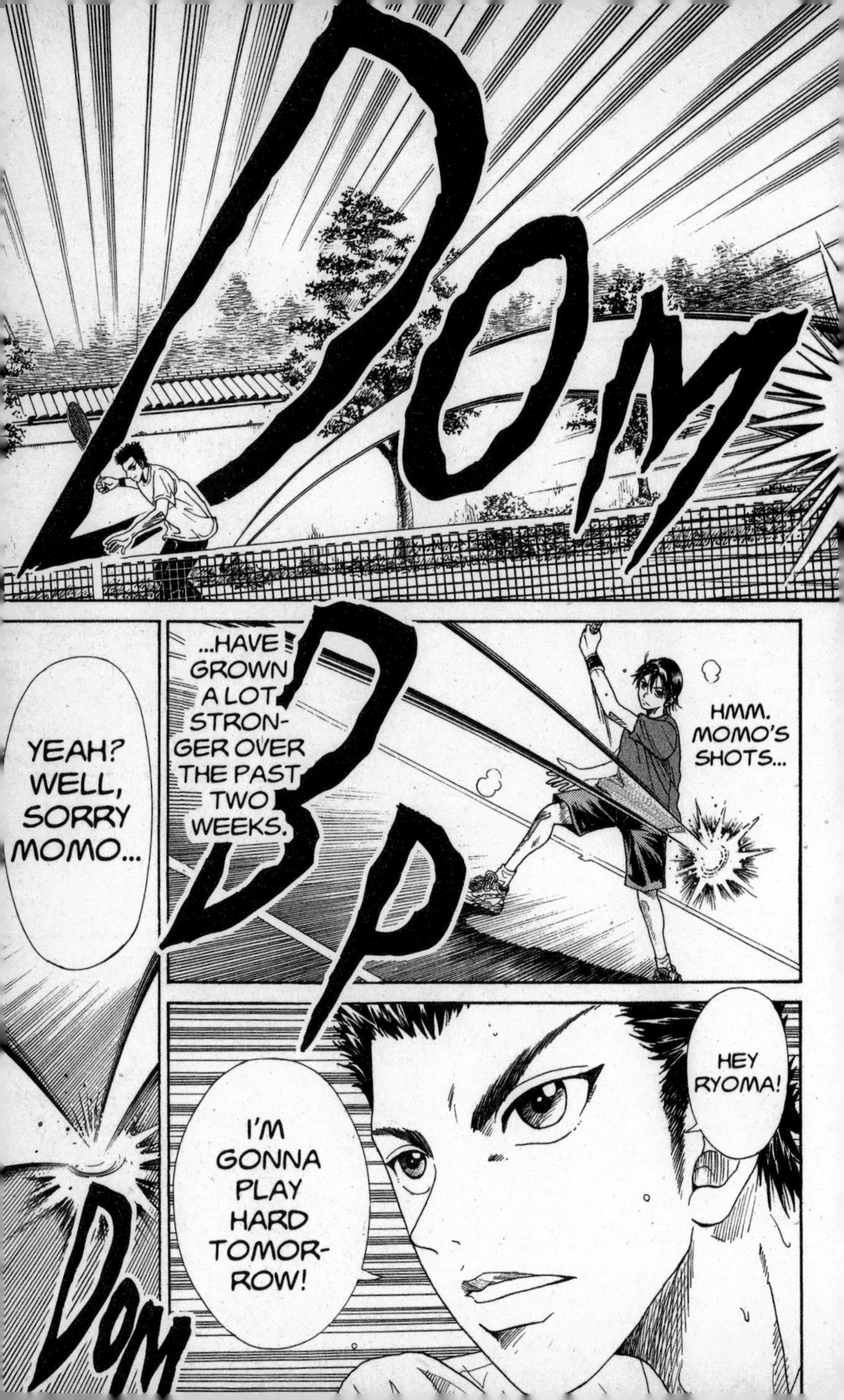
DOM
HMM. MOMO'S SHOTS...
...HAVE GROWN A LOT STRONGER OVER THE PAST TWO WEEKS.
DOP
YEAH? WELL, SORRY MOMO...
HEY RYOMA!
I'M GONNA PLAY HARD TOMORROW!
DOM

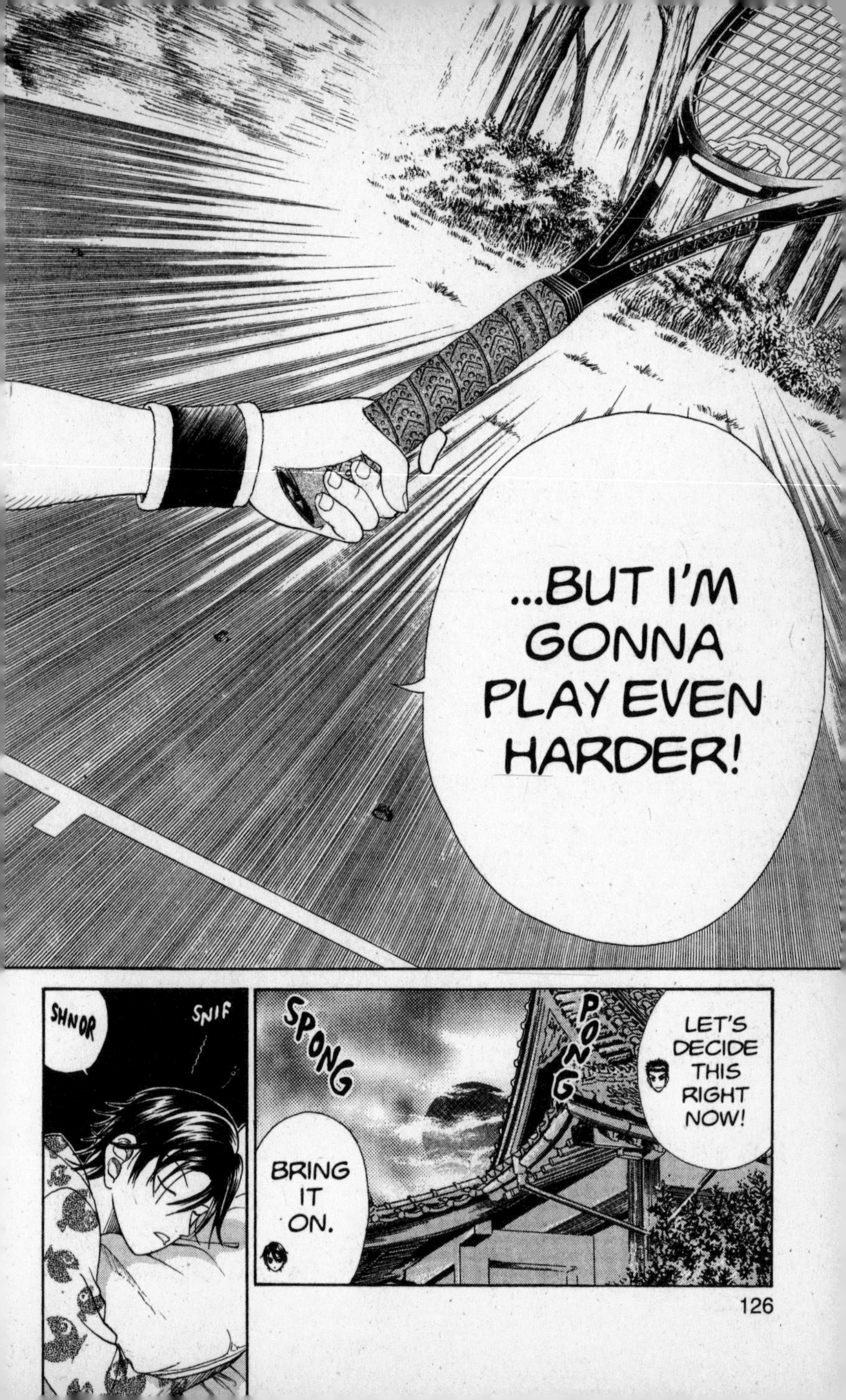
...BUT I'M GONNA PLAY EVEN HARDER!
LET'S DECIDE THIS RIGHT NOW!
PONG
SPONG
BRING IT ON.
SNIF
SHNOR

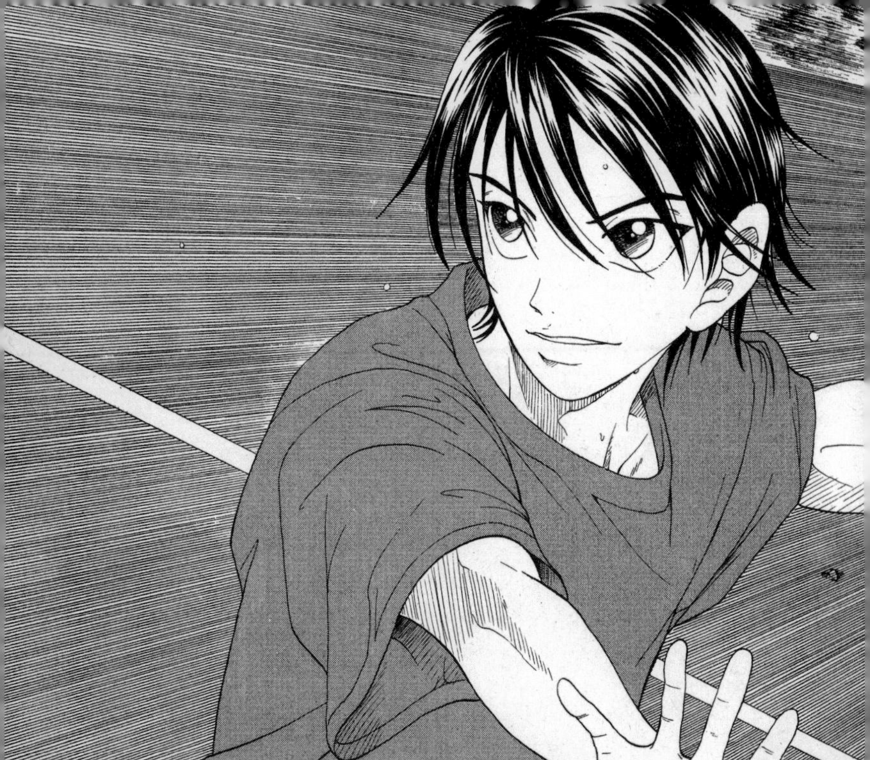

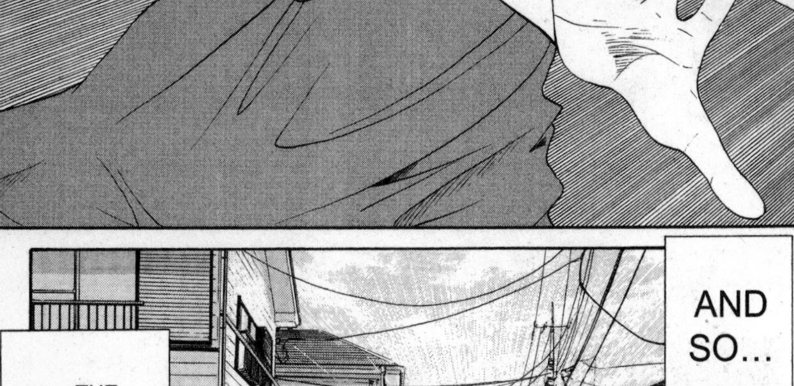
AND SO...
...THE MORNING OF THE CITY TOURNAMENT ARRIVES.

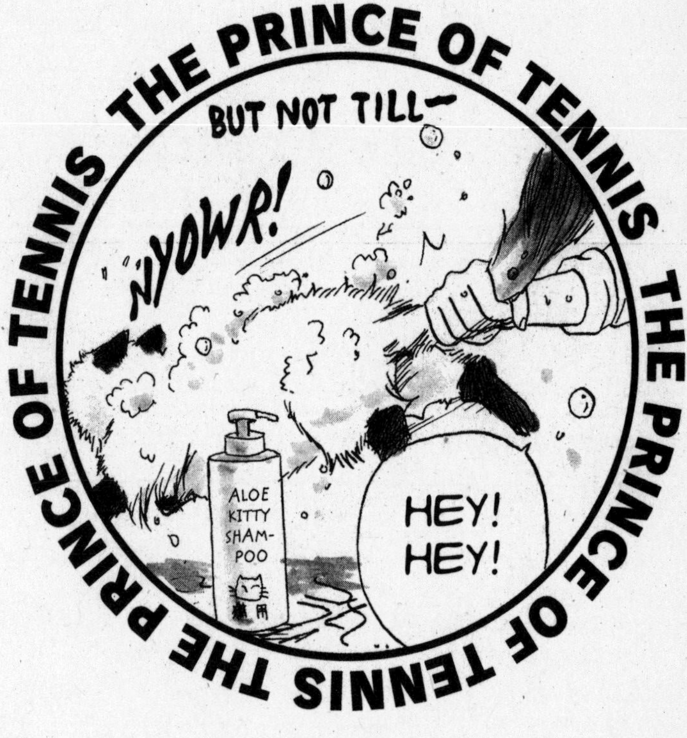
THE PRINCE OF TENNIS THE PRINCE OF TENNIS THE PRINCE OF TENNIS
BUT NOT TILL—
N'YOWR!
HEY! HEY!
ALOE KITTY SHAM-POO
猫用

GENIUS 49:

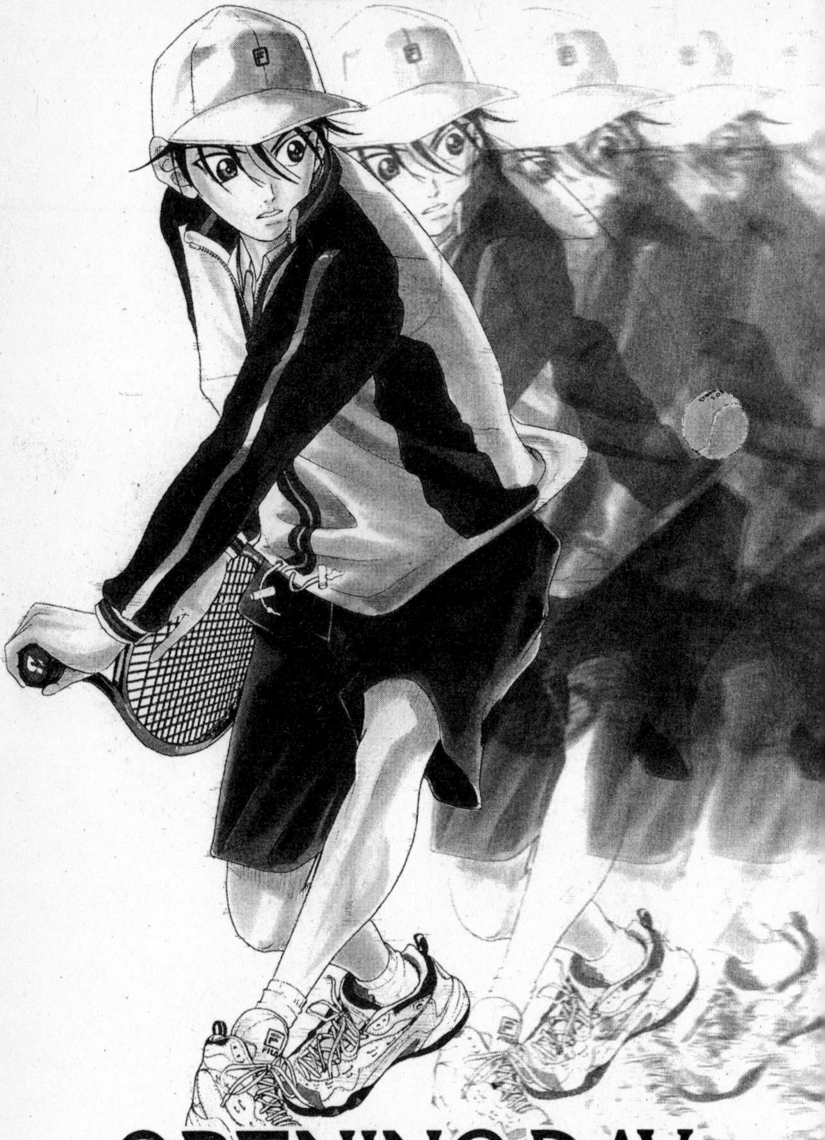

OPENING DAY

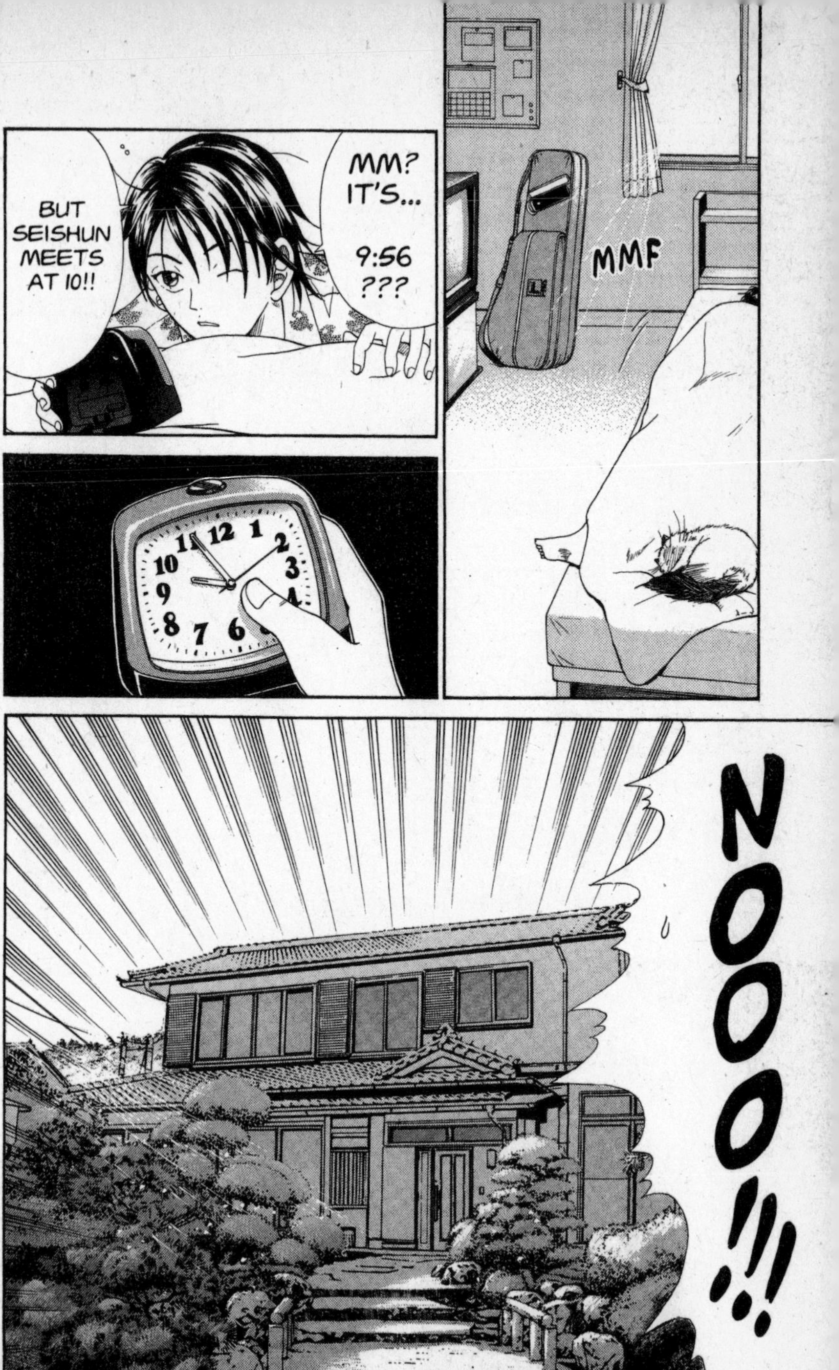
MMF
MM? IT'S... 9:56 ???
BUT SEISHUN MEETS AT 10!!
NOOO!!!

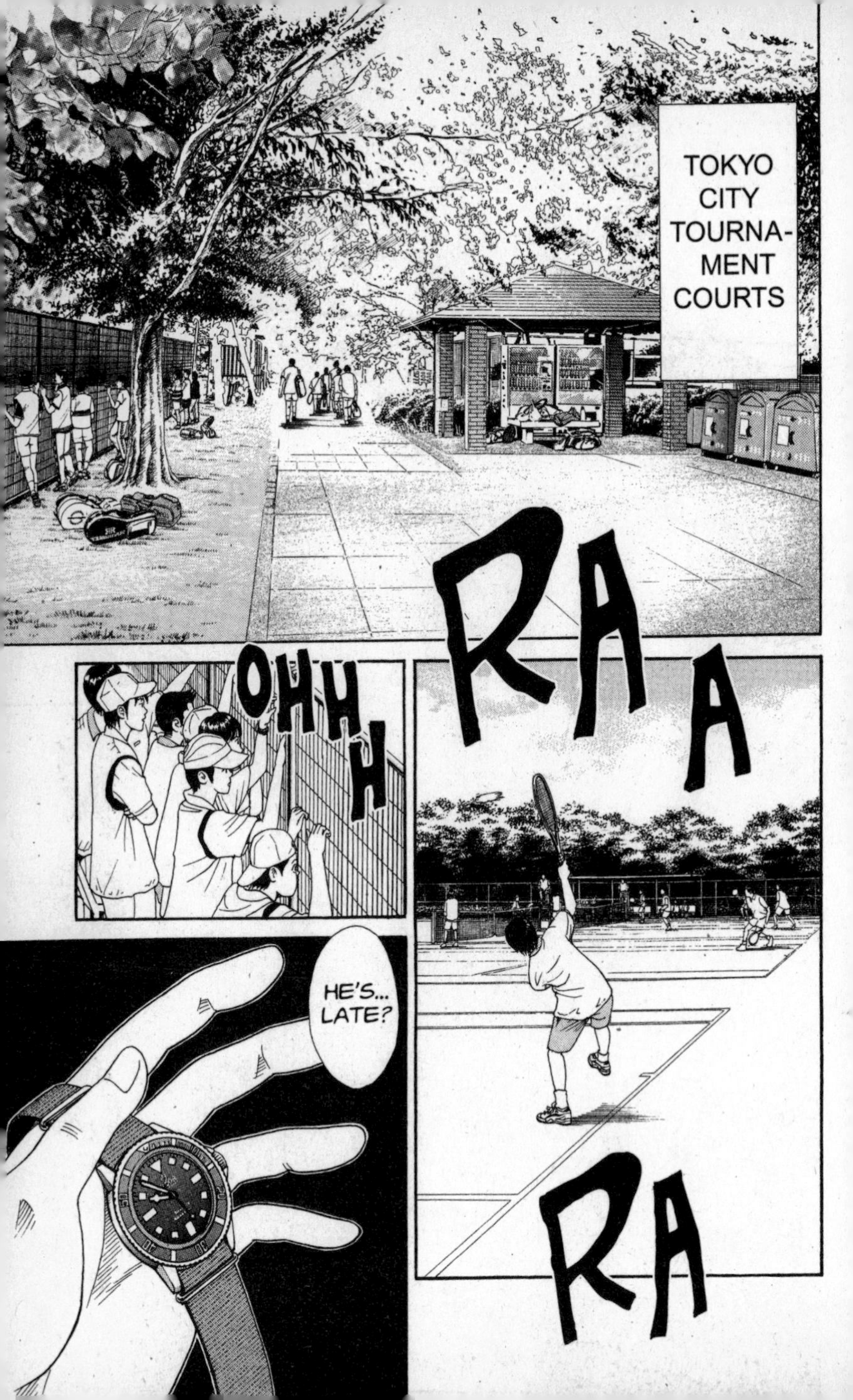
TOKYO CITY TOURNAMENT COURTS
RAAA
RA
OHHH
HE'S... LATE?

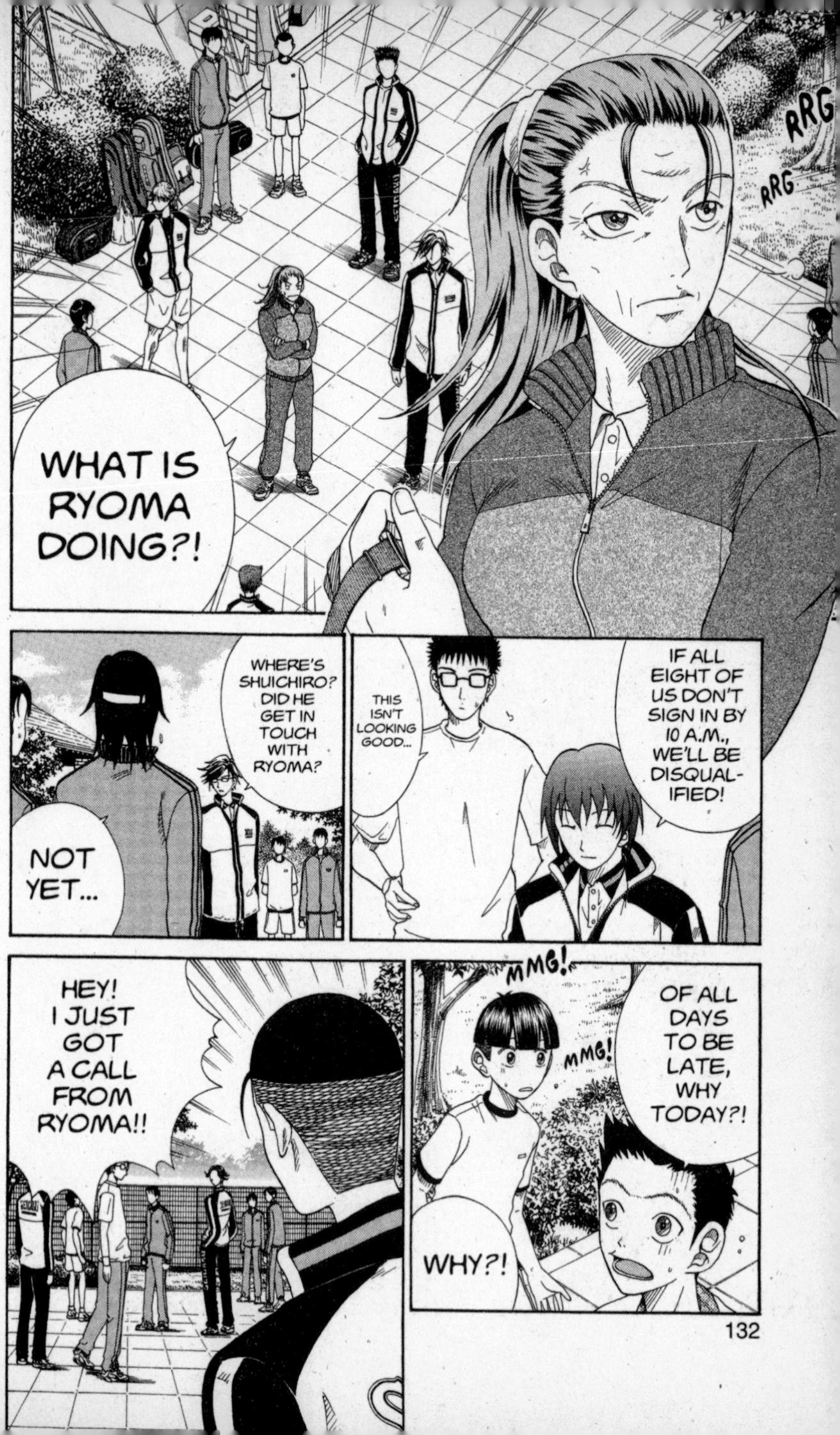
RRG
RRG
WHAT IS RYOMA DOING?!
IF ALL EIGHT OF US DON'T SIGN IN BY 10 A.M., WE'LL BE DISQUALIFIED!
THIS ISN'T LOOKING GOOD...
WHERE'S SHUICHIRO? DID HE GET IN TOUCH WITH RYOMA?
NOT YET...
MMG!
MMG!
OF ALL DAYS TO BE LATE, WHY TODAY?!
WHY?!
HEY! I JUST GOT A CALL FROM RYOMA!!

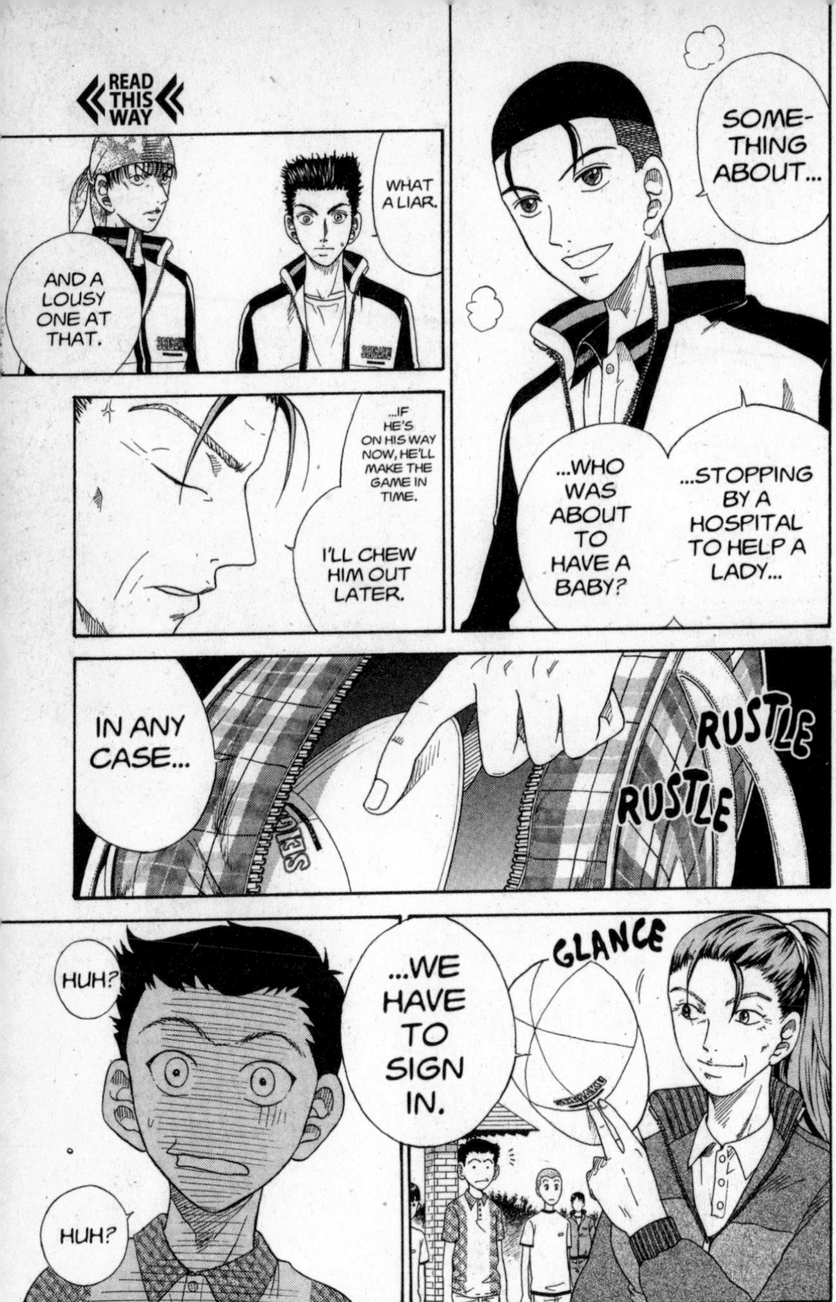
READ THIS WAY
SOME-THING ABOUT...
...STOPPING BY A HOSPITAL TO HELP A LADY...
...WHO WAS ABOUT TO HAVE A BABY?
WHAT A LIAR.
AND A LOUSY ONE AT THAT.
...IF HE'S ON HIS WAY NOW, HE'LL MAKE THE GAME IN TIME.
I'LL CHEW HIM OUT LATER.
IN ANY CASE...
RUSTLE
RUSTLE
GLANCE
...WE HAVE TO SIGN IN.
HUH?
HUH?

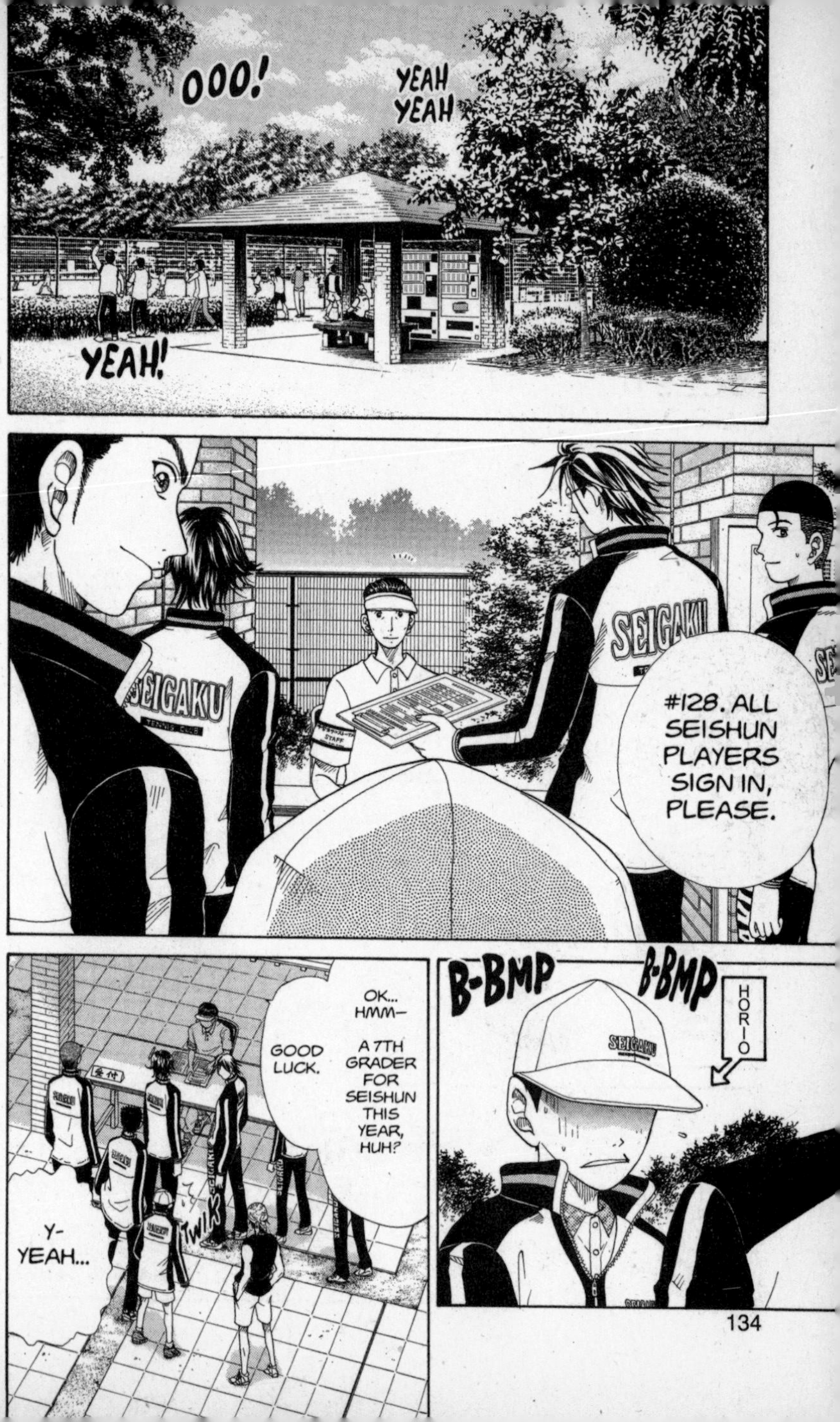
YEAH YEAH
OOO!
YEAH!
#128. ALL SEISHUN PLAYERS SIGN IN, PLEASE.
B-BMP
B-BMP
HORIO
OK... HMM— A 7TH GRADER FOR SEISHUN THIS YEAR, HUH?
GOOD LUCK.
TWIK
Y-YEAH...

READ THIS WAY

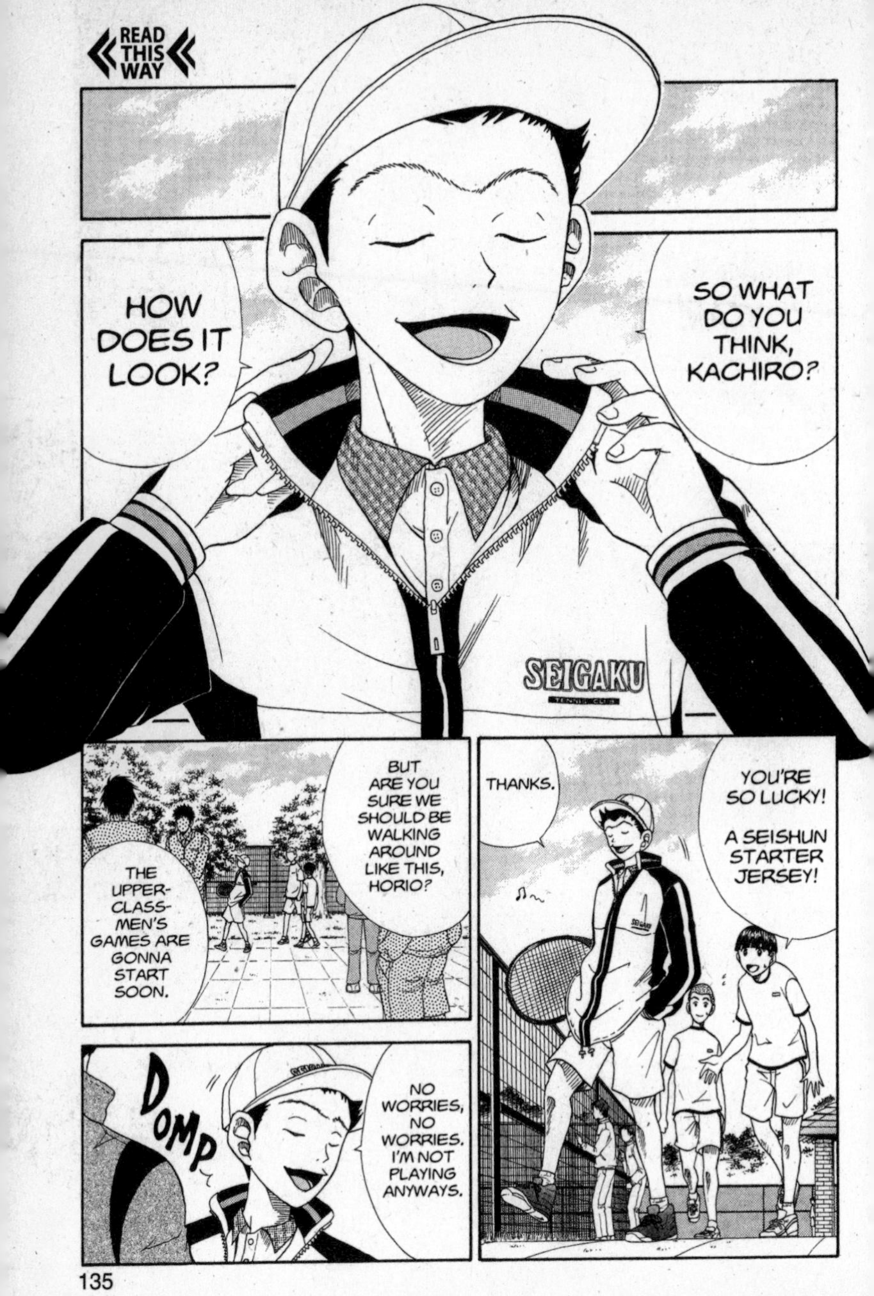

SO WHAT DO YOU THINK, KACHIRO?
HOW DOES IT LOOK?
SEIGAKU
YOU'RE SO LUCKY!
A SEISHUN STARTER JERSEY!
THANKS.
BUT ARE YOU SURE WE SHOULD BE WALKING AROUND LIKE THIS, HORIO?
THE UPPER-CLASSMEN'S GAMES ARE GONNA START SOON.
NO WORRIES, NO WORRIES. I'M NOT PLAYING ANYWAYS.
DOMP

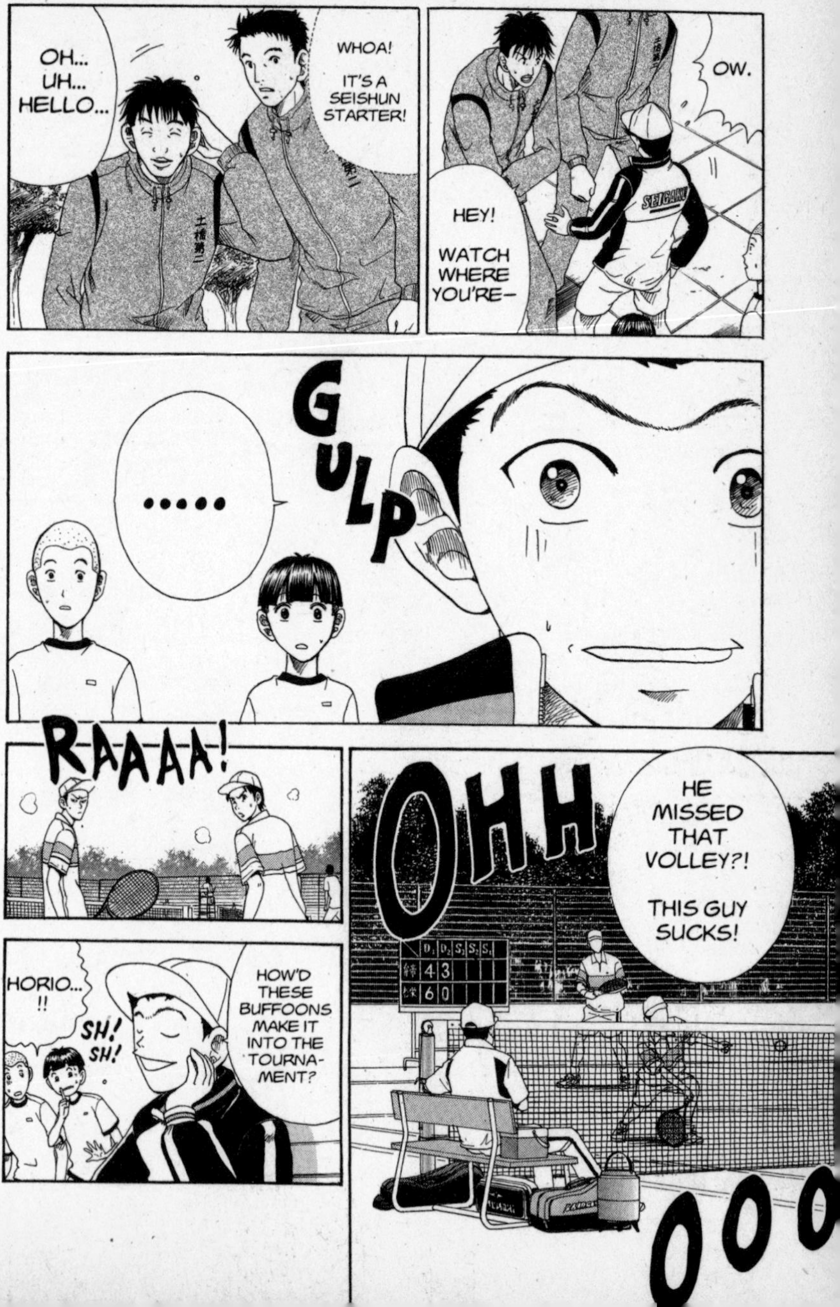
OW.
HEY! WATCH WHERE YOU'RE–
WHOA! IT'S A SEISHUN STARTER!
OH... UH... HELLO...
GULP
.....
OHH
HE MISSED THAT VOLLEY?! THIS GUY SUCKS!
OOO
RAAAA!
HOW'D THESE BUFFOONS MAKE IT INTO THE TOURNAMENT?
HORIO... !!
SH! SH!

READ THIS WAY

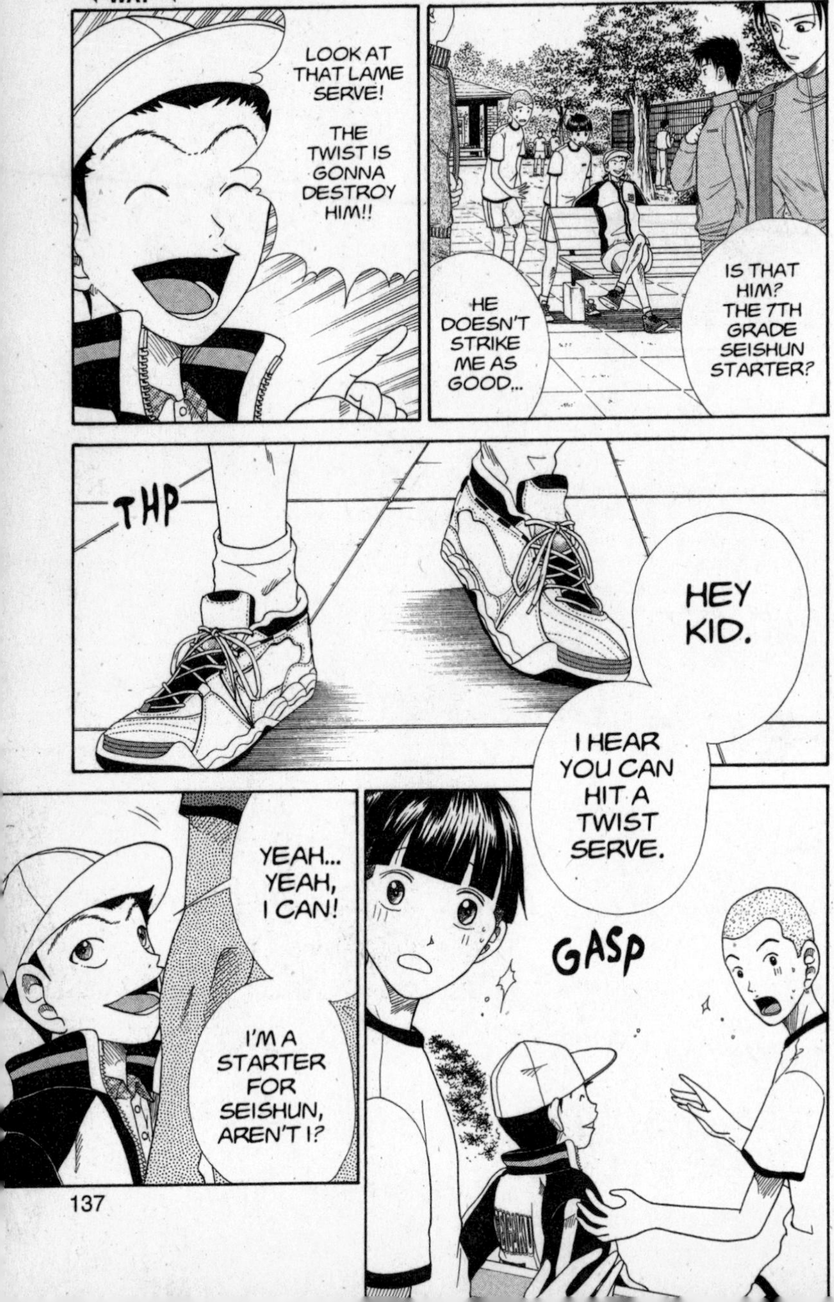
IS THAT HIM? THE 7TH GRADE SEISHUN STARTER?
HE DOESN'T STRIKE ME AS GOOD...
LOOK AT THAT LAME SERVE!
THE TWIST IS GONNA DESTROY HIM!!
THP
HEY KID.
I HEAR YOU CAN HIT A TWIST SERVE.
GASP
YEAH... YEAH, I CAN!
I'M A STARTER FOR SEISHUN, AREN'T I?

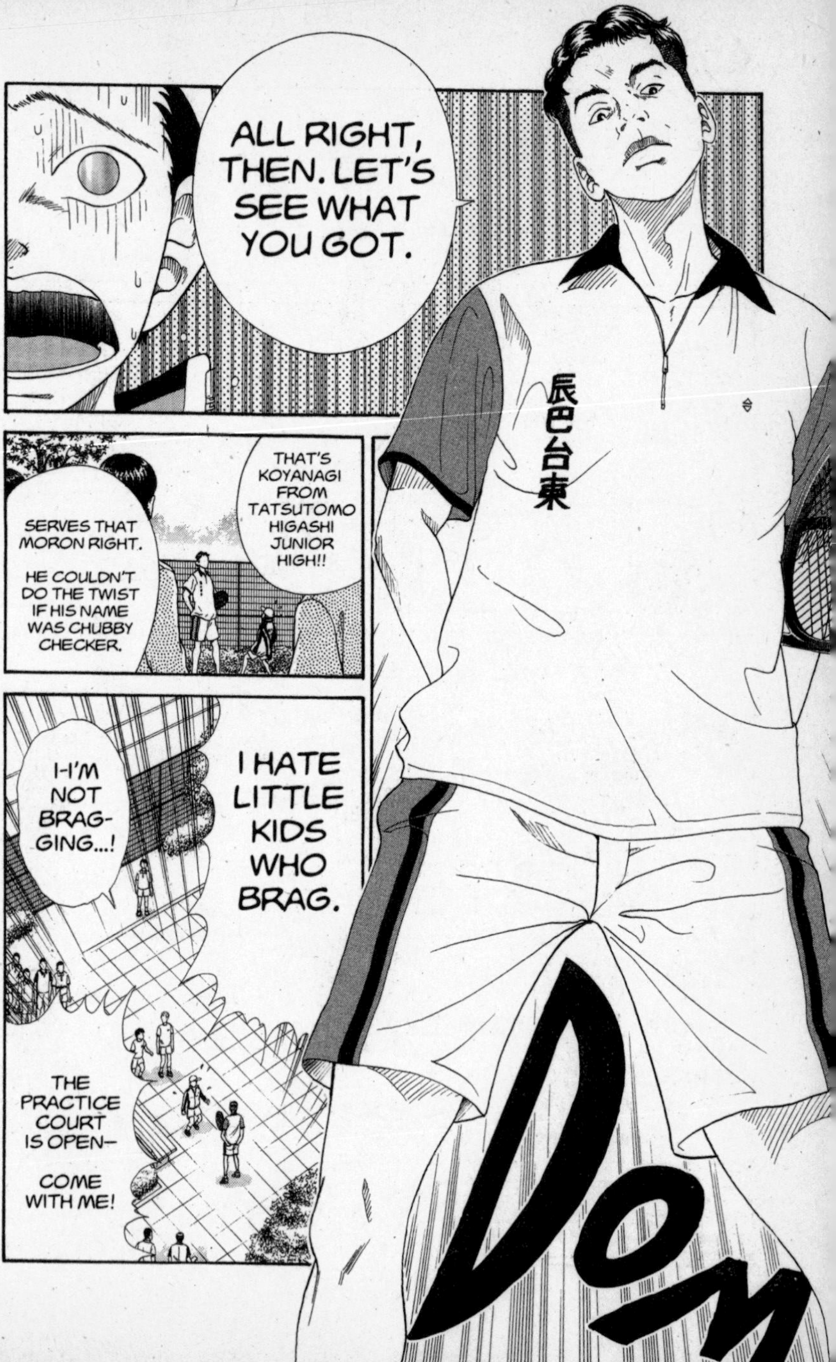
ALL RIGHT, THEN. LET'S SEE WHAT YOU GOT.
THAT'S KOYANAGI FROM TATSUTOMO HIGASHI JUNIOR HIGH!!
SERVES THAT MORON RIGHT.
HE COULDN'T DO THE TWIST IF HIS NAME WAS CHUBBY CHECKER.
I HATE LITTLE KIDS WHO BRAG.
I-I'M NOT BRAG-GING...!
THE PRACTICE COURT IS OPEN—
COME WITH ME!
辰巳台東
DOM

READ THIS WAY

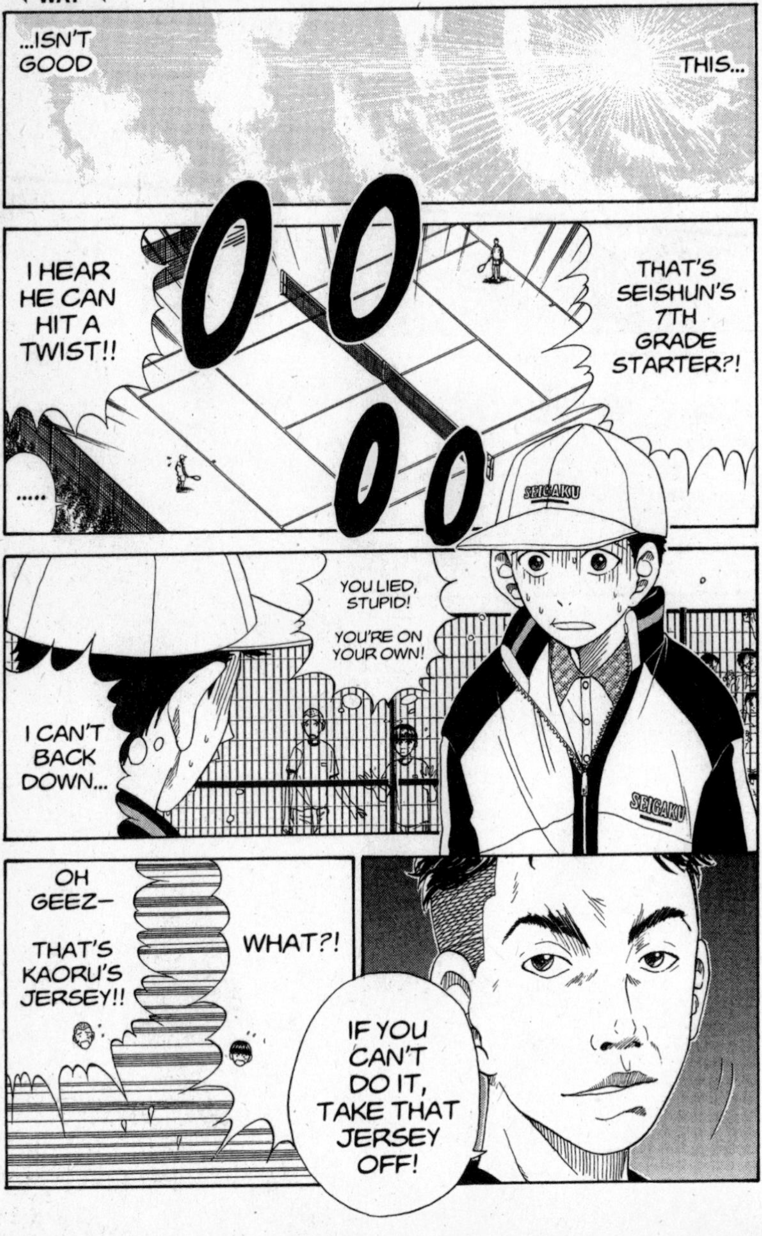
THIS...
...ISN'T GOOD
THAT'S SEISHUN'S 7TH GRADE STARTER?!
I HEAR HE CAN HIT A TWIST!!
.....
YOU LIED, STUPID!
YOU'RE ON YOUR OWN!
I CAN'T BACK DOWN...
SEIGAKU
IF YOU CAN'T DO IT, TAKE THAT JERSEY OFF!
WHAT?!
OH GEEZ—
THAT'S KAORU'S JERSEY!!

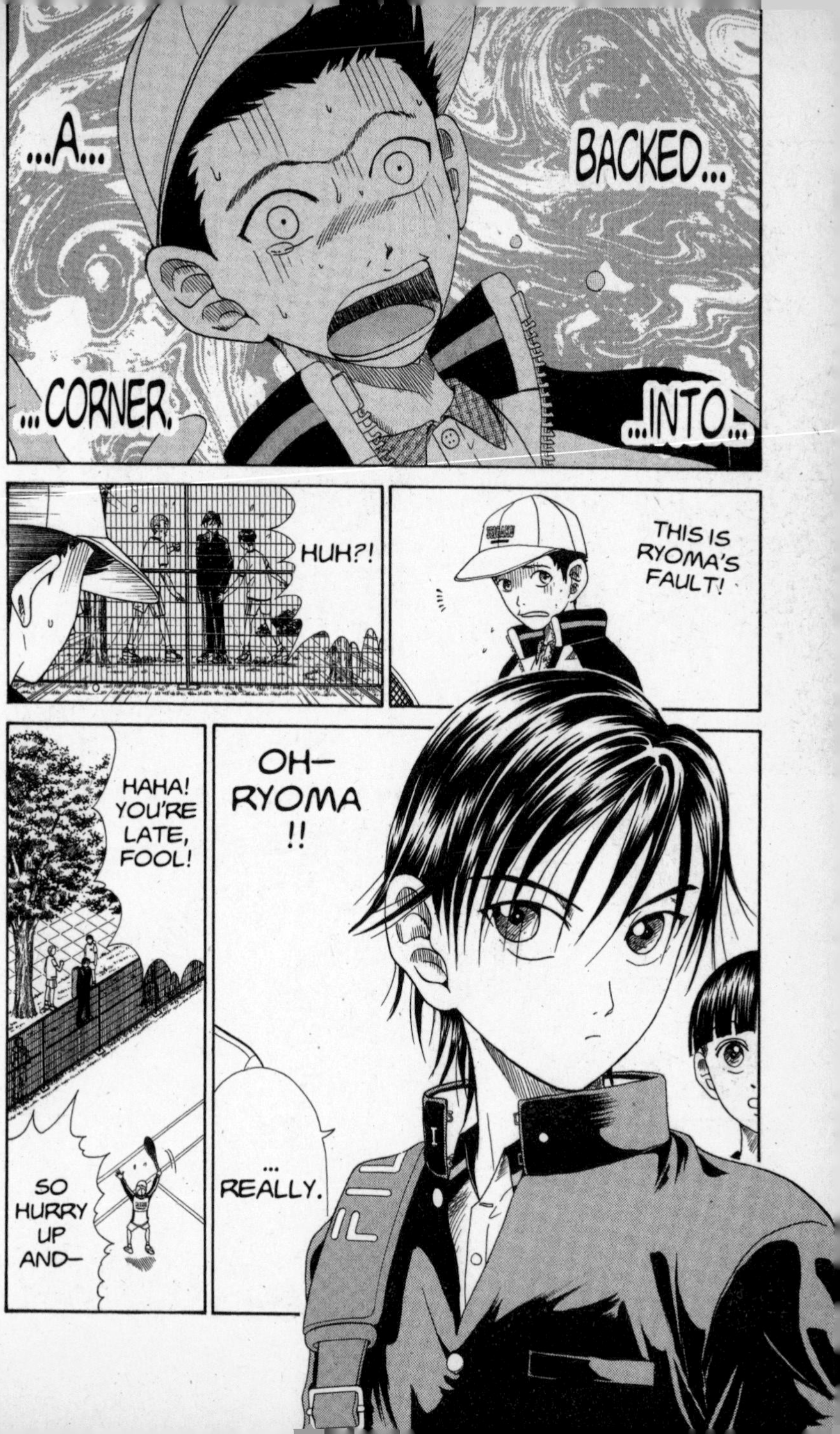
BACKED...
...INTO...
...A...
...CORNER.
THIS IS RYOMA'S FAULT!
HUH?!
OH— RYOMA!!
...REALLY.
HAHA! YOU'RE LATE, FOOL!
SO HURRY UP AND—

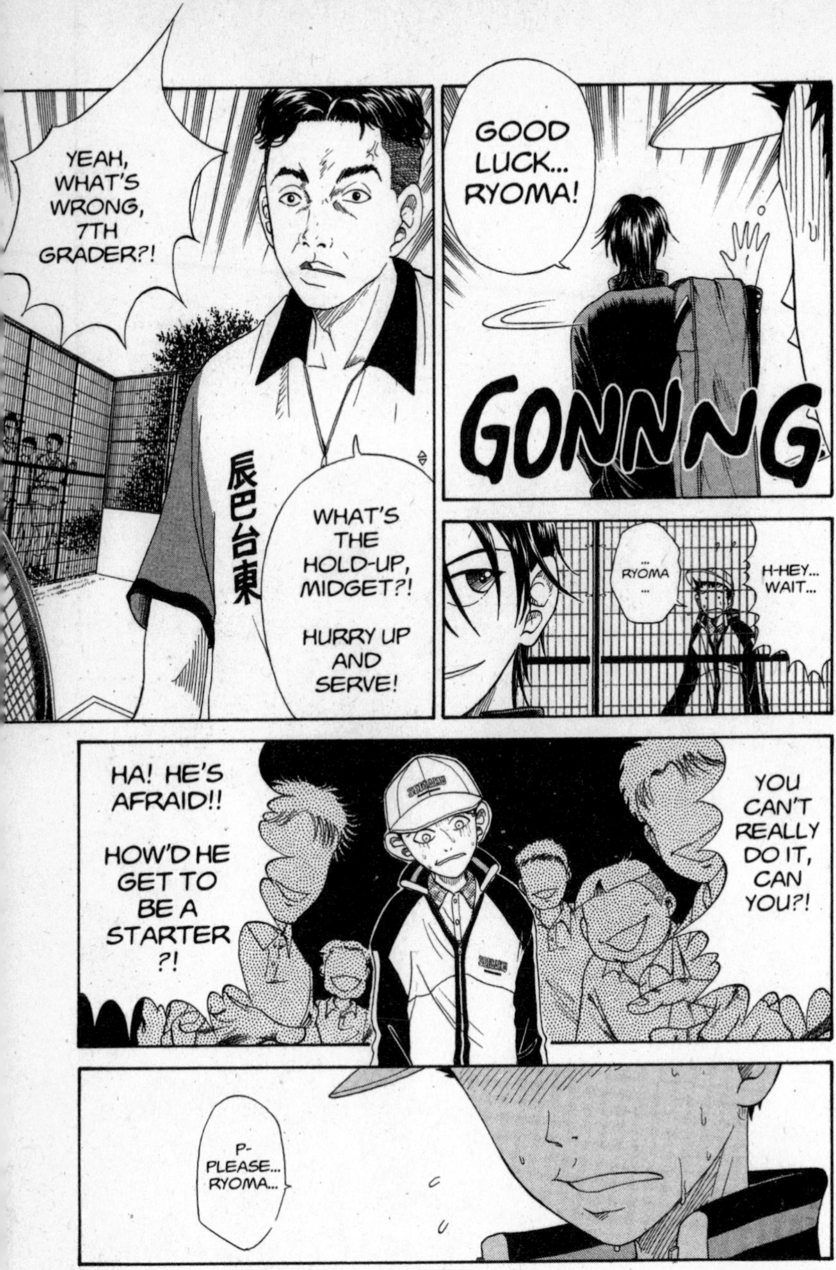
GOOD LUCK... RYOMA!
GONNNG
H-HEY... WAIT...
... RYOMA ...
YEAH, WHAT'S WRONG, 7TH GRADER?!
辰巳台東
WHAT'S THE HOLD-UP, MIDGET?!
HURRY UP AND SERVE!
YOU CAN'T REALLY DO IT, CAN YOU?!
HA! HE'S AFRAID!!
HOW'D HE GET TO BE A STARTER ?!
P- PLEASE... RYOMA...

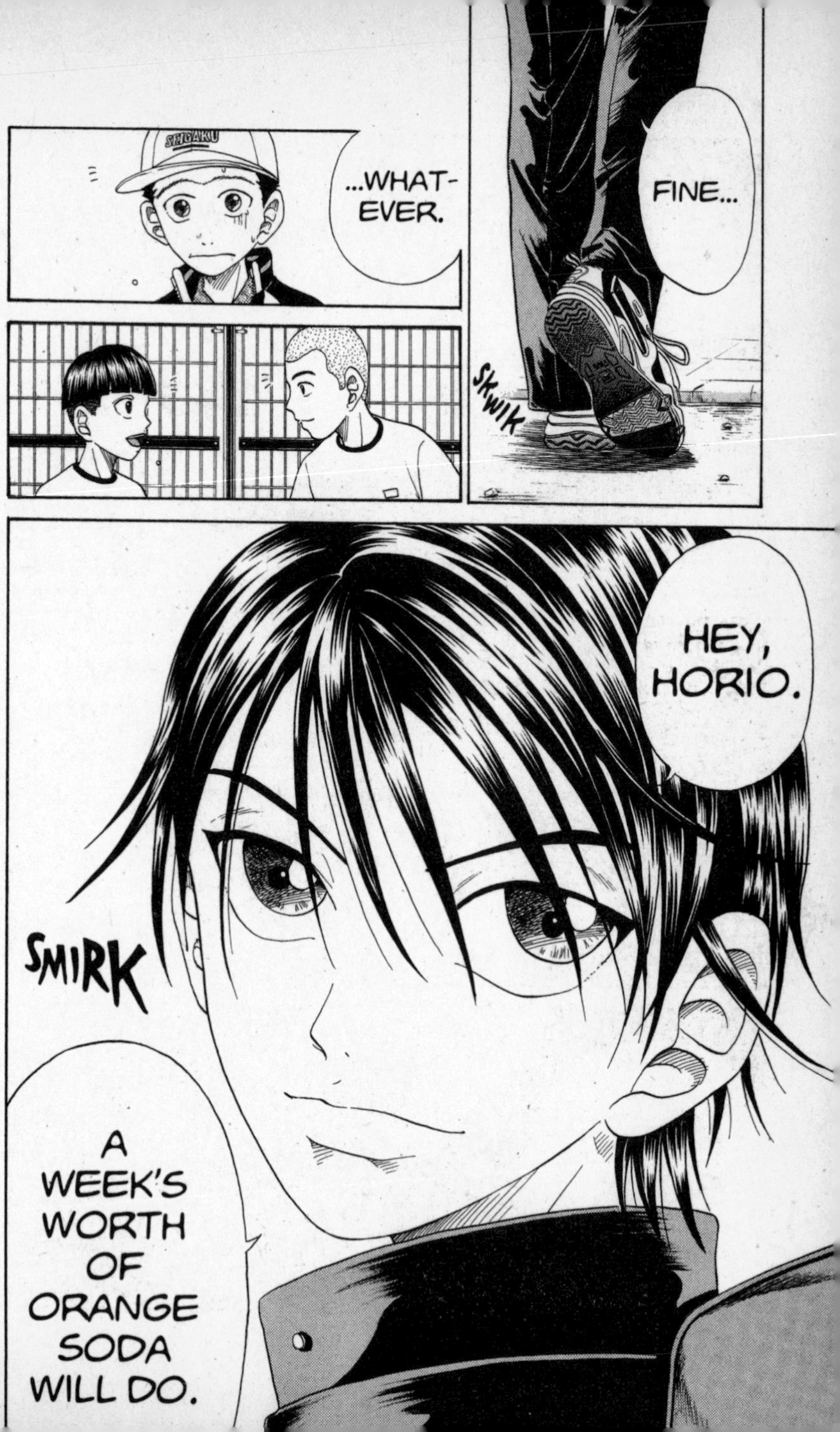
FINE...
SKWIK
...WHAT-
EVER.
HEY,
HORIO.
SMIRK
A
WEEK'S
WORTH
OF
ORANGE
SODA
WILL DO.

READ THIS WAY

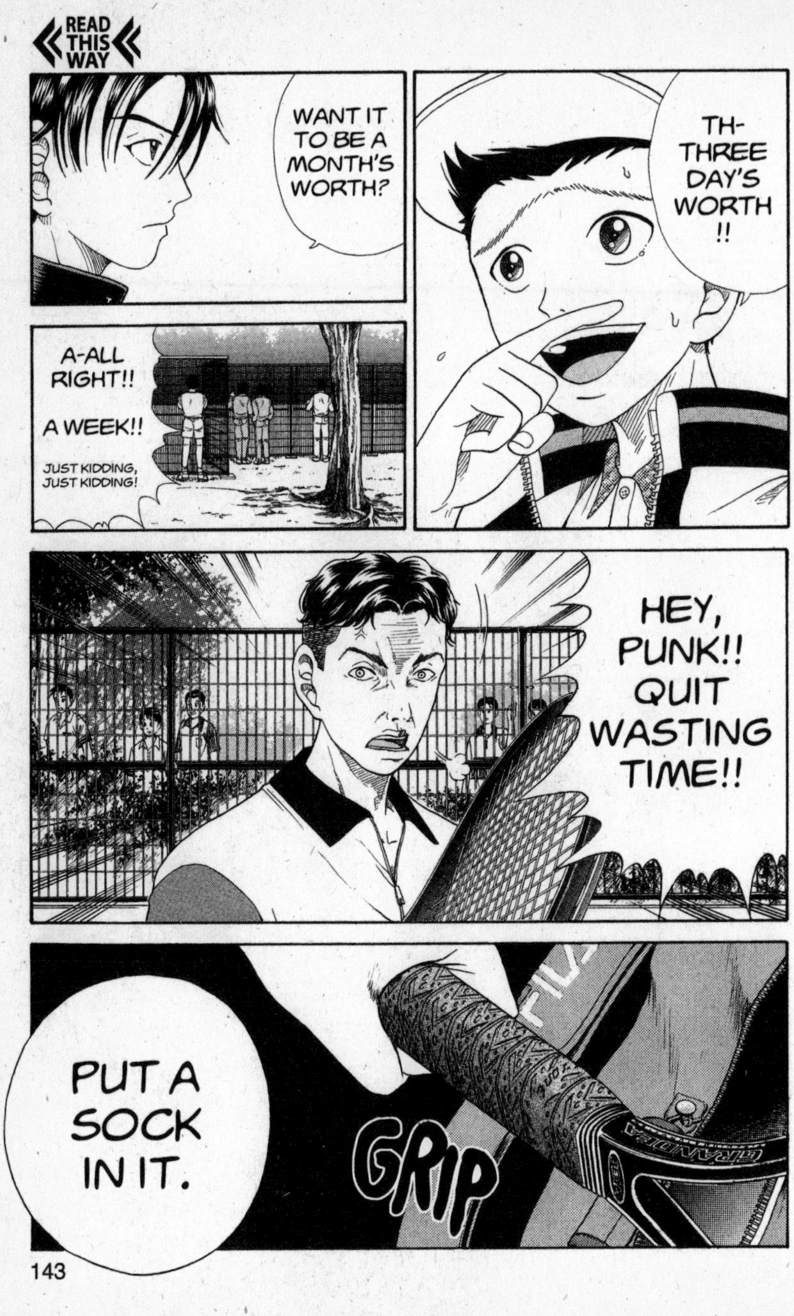
TH- THREE DAY'S WORTH !!
WANT IT TO BE A MONTH'S WORTH?
A-ALL RIGHT!!
A WEEK!!
JUST KIDDING, JUST KIDDING!
HEY, PUNK!! QUIT WASTING TIME!!
PUT A SOCK IN IT.
GRIP

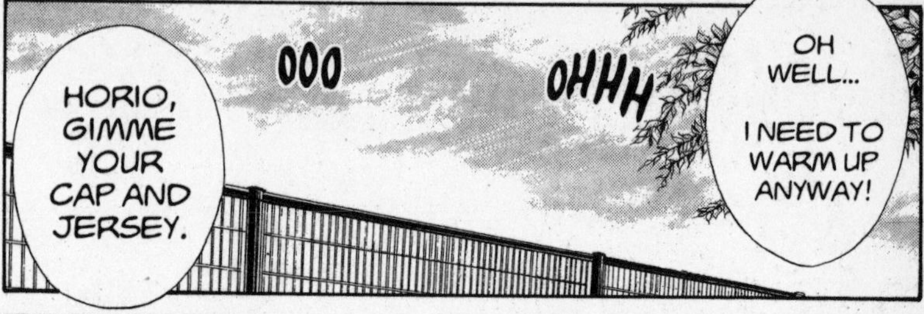
OH WELL... I NEED TO WARM UP ANYWAY!
OHHH
OOO
HORIO, GIMME YOUR CAP AND JERSEY.

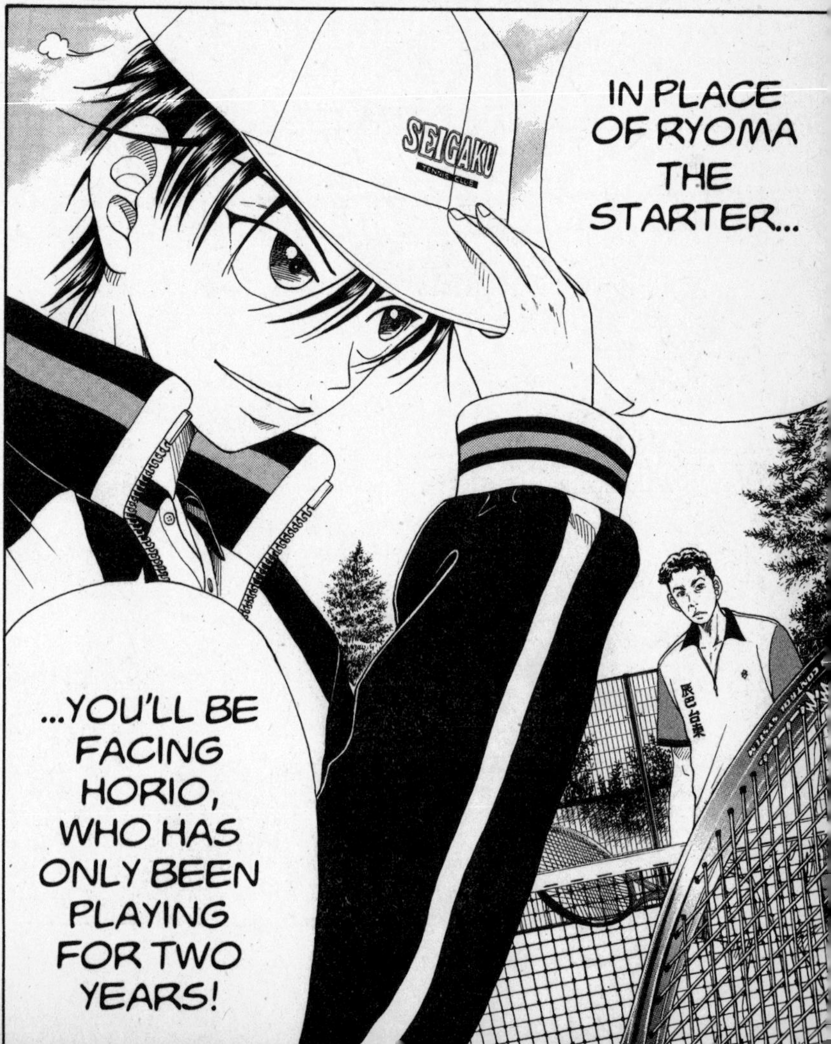
SEIGAKU TENNIS CLUB
IN PLACE OF RYOMA THE STARTER...
...YOU'LL BE FACING HORIO, WHO HAS ONLY BEEN PLAYING FOR TWO YEARS!

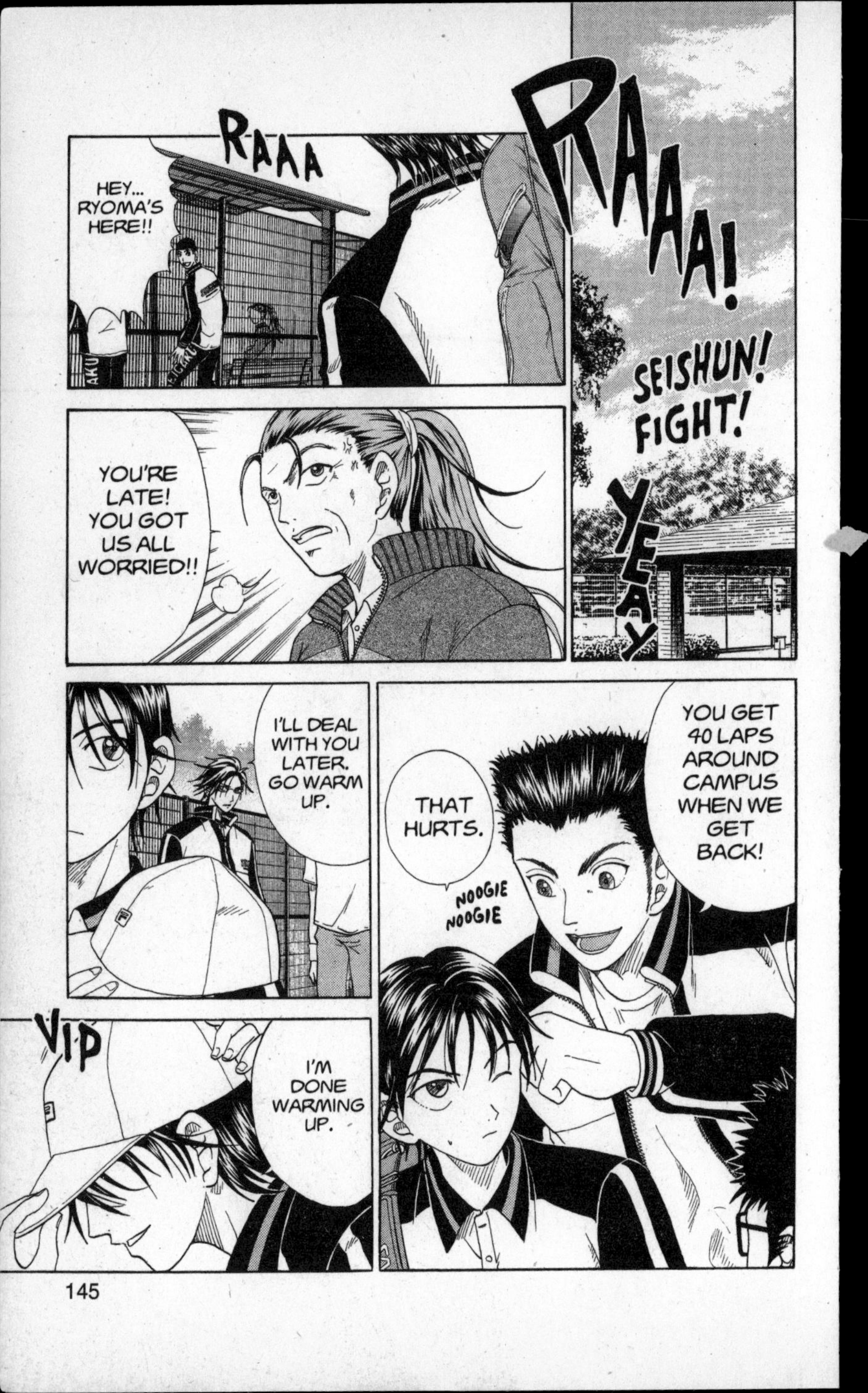
RAAAAI!
SEISHUN! FIGHT!
YEAY
RAAA
HEY... RYOMA'S HERE!!
YOU'RE LATE! YOU GOT US ALL WORRIED!!
YOU GET 40 LAPS AROUND CAMPUS WHEN WE GET BACK!
THAT HURTS.
NOOGIE NOOGIE
I'LL DEAL WITH YOU LATER. GO WARM UP.
VIP
I'M DONE WARMING UP.

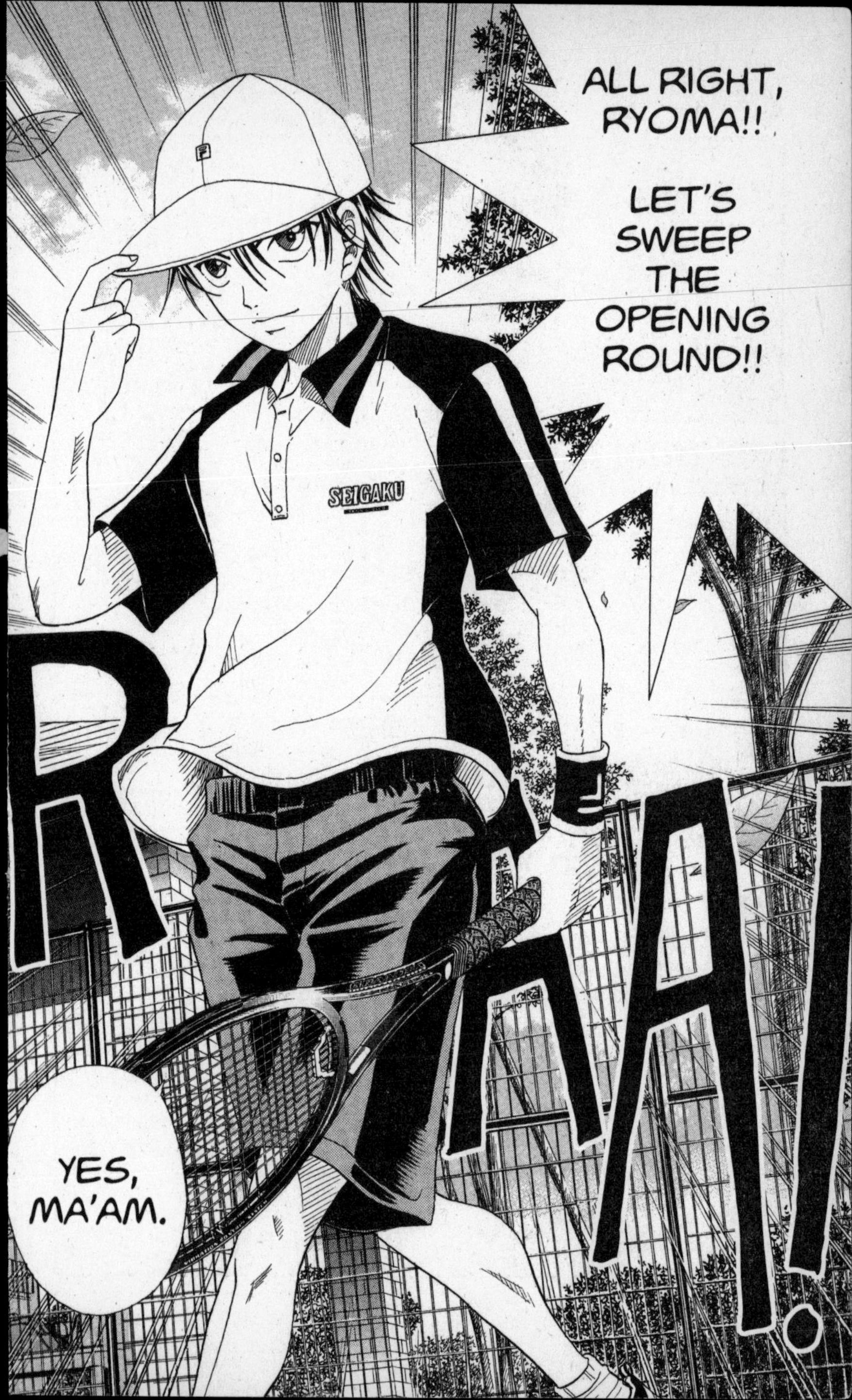
ALL RIGHT, RYOMA!!
LET'S SWEEP THE OPENING ROUND!!
RAA!
SEIGAKU
YES, MA'AM.

READ THIS WAY

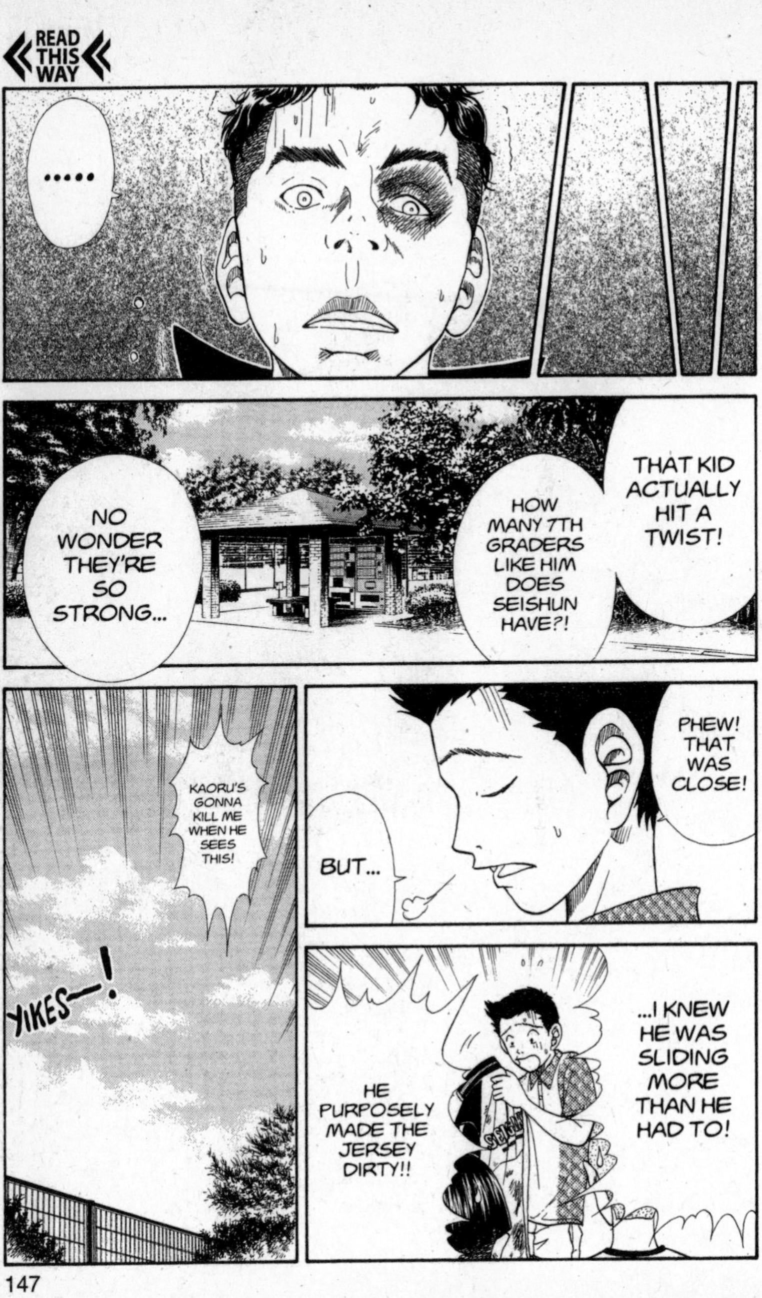
.....
THAT KID ACTUALLY HIT A TWIST!
HOW MANY 7TH GRADERS LIKE HIM DOES SEISHUN HAVE?!
NO WONDER THEY'RE SO STRONG...
PHEW! THAT WAS CLOSE!
BUT...
...I KNEW HE WAS SLIDING MORE THAN HE HAD TO!
HE PURPOSELY MADE THE JERSEY DIRTY!!
KAORU'S GONNA KILL ME WHEN HE SEES THIS!
YIKES—!

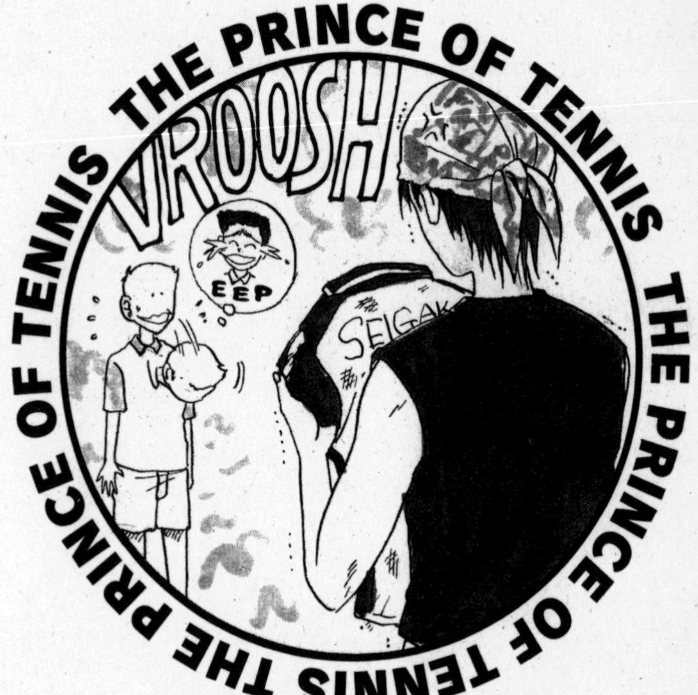
THE PRINCE OF TENNIS THE PRINCE OF TENNIS THE PRINCE OF TENNIS
VROOSH
EEP
SEIGAK

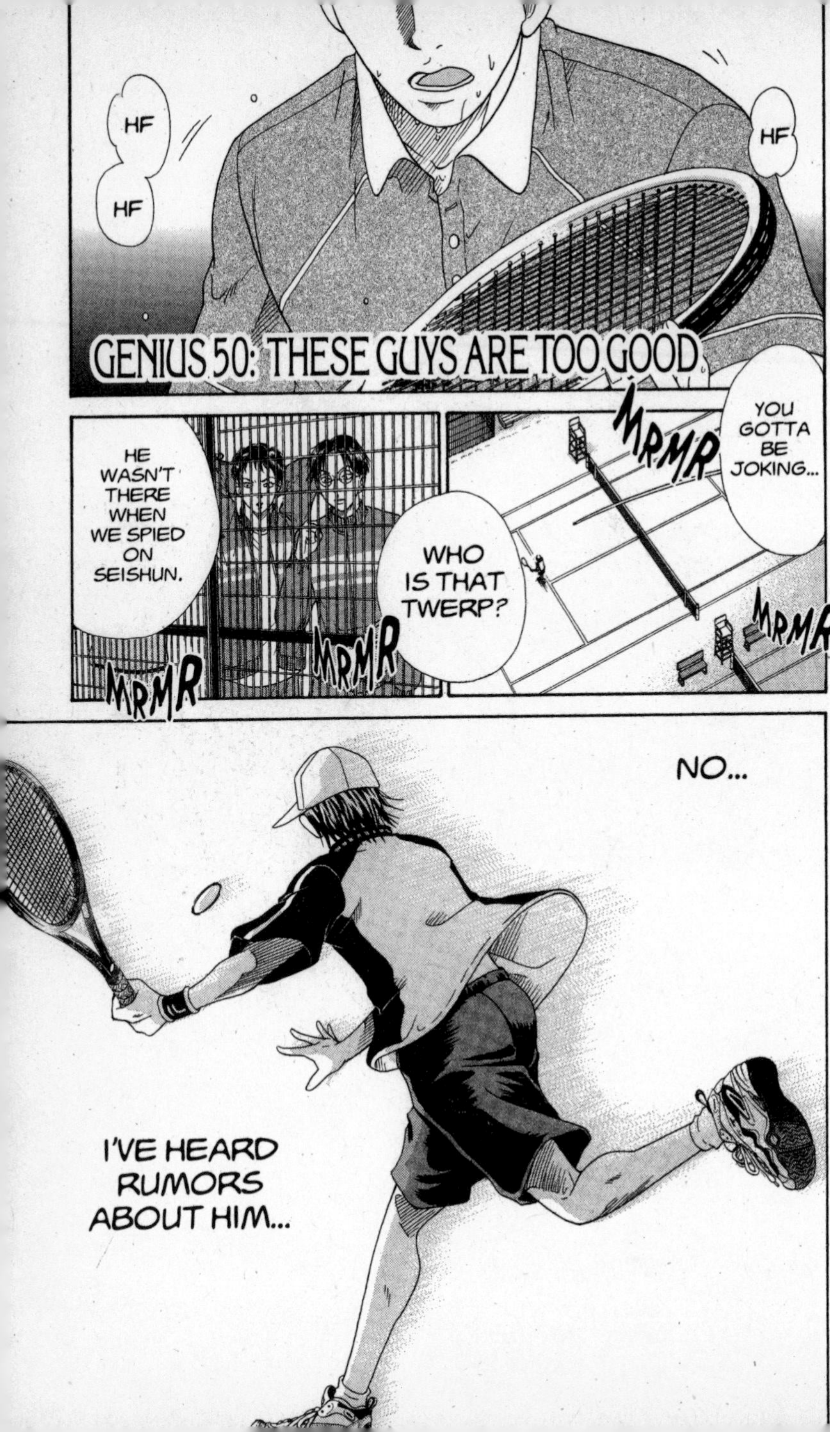
HF
HF
HF
GENIUS 50: THESE GUYS ARE TOO GOOD
MRMR
YOU GOTTA BE JOKING...
WHO IS THAT TWERP?
MRMR
HE WASN'T THERE WHEN WE SPIED ON SEISHUN.
MRMR
MRMR
NO...
I'VE HEARD RUMORS ABOUT HIM...

GENIUS 50: THESE GUYS ARE TOO GOOD

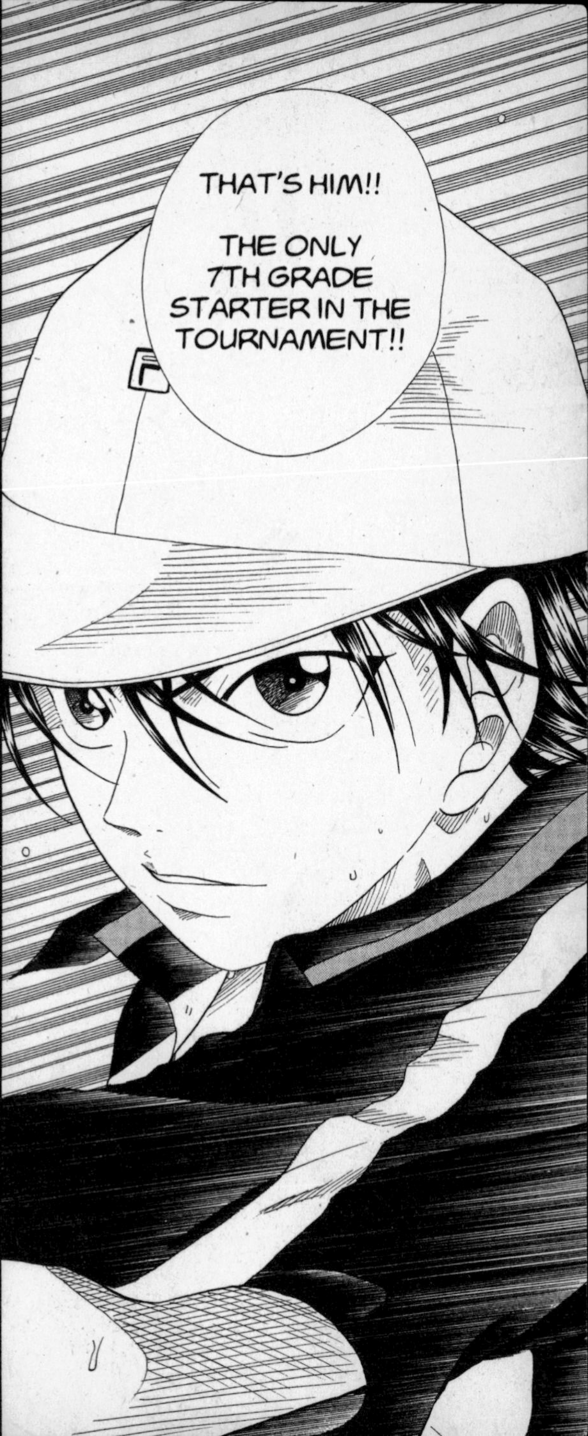
THAT'S HIM!!
THE ONLY 7TH GRADE STARTER IN THE TOURNAMENT!!

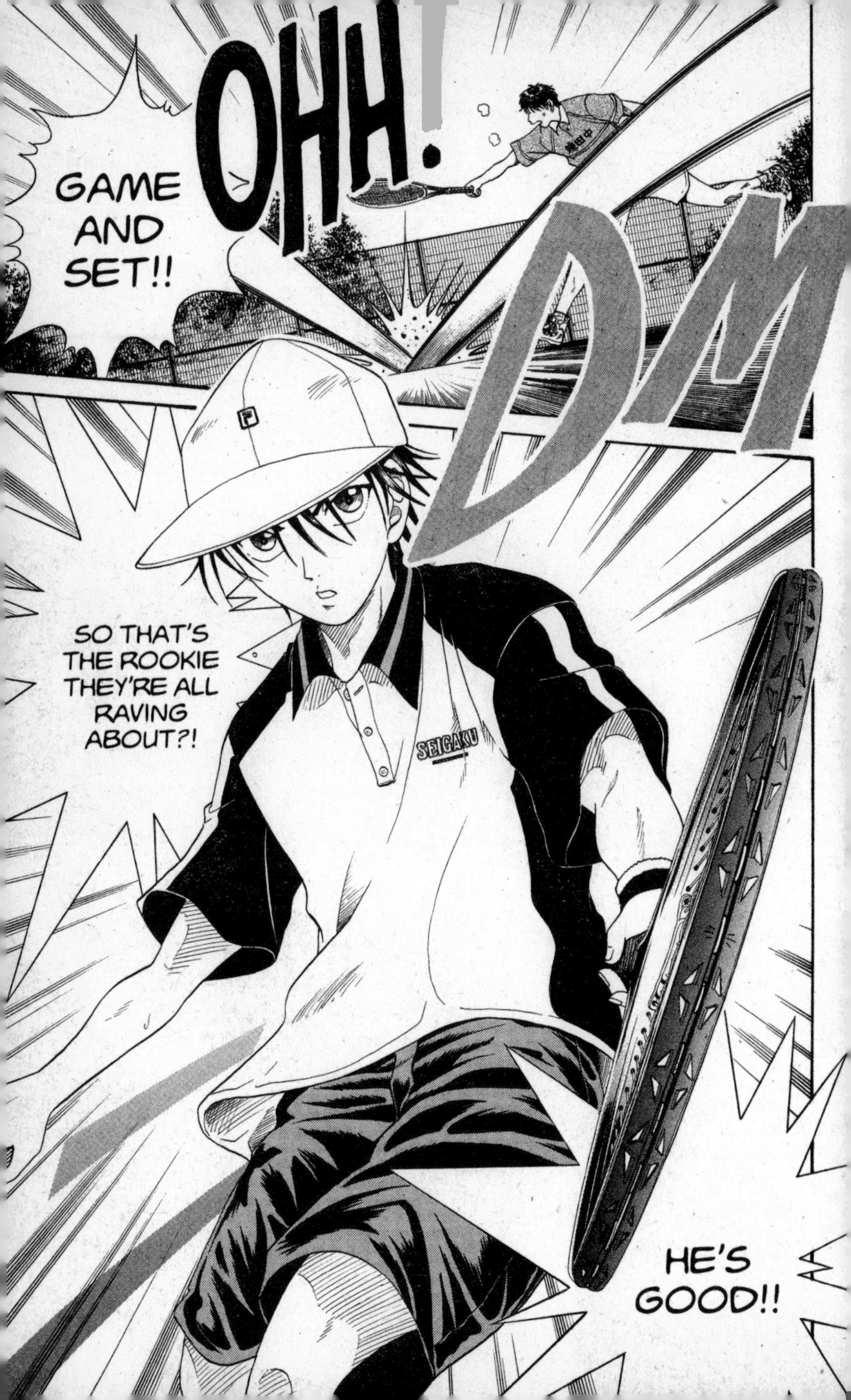
OHH!
GAME AND SET!!
DM
SO THAT'S THE ROOKIE THEY'RE ALL RAVING ABOUT?!
SEIGAKU
HE'S GOOD!!

YEAAH!

YES!!

RYOMA WINS A LOPSIDED MATCH !!!

THAT MAKES FOUR WINS AND ZERO LOSSES FOR SEISHUN.

SEISHUN SEISHUN

GAME NAME	D$_2$	D$_1$	S$_3$	S$_2$	S$_1$	TOTAL
KAMATA	0	0	0	0		
SEISHUN	6	6	6	6		

THE NEXT PLAYER CAN CLOSE IT OUT...

THANKS.

NICE GAME, RYOMA.

TP

READ THIS WAY

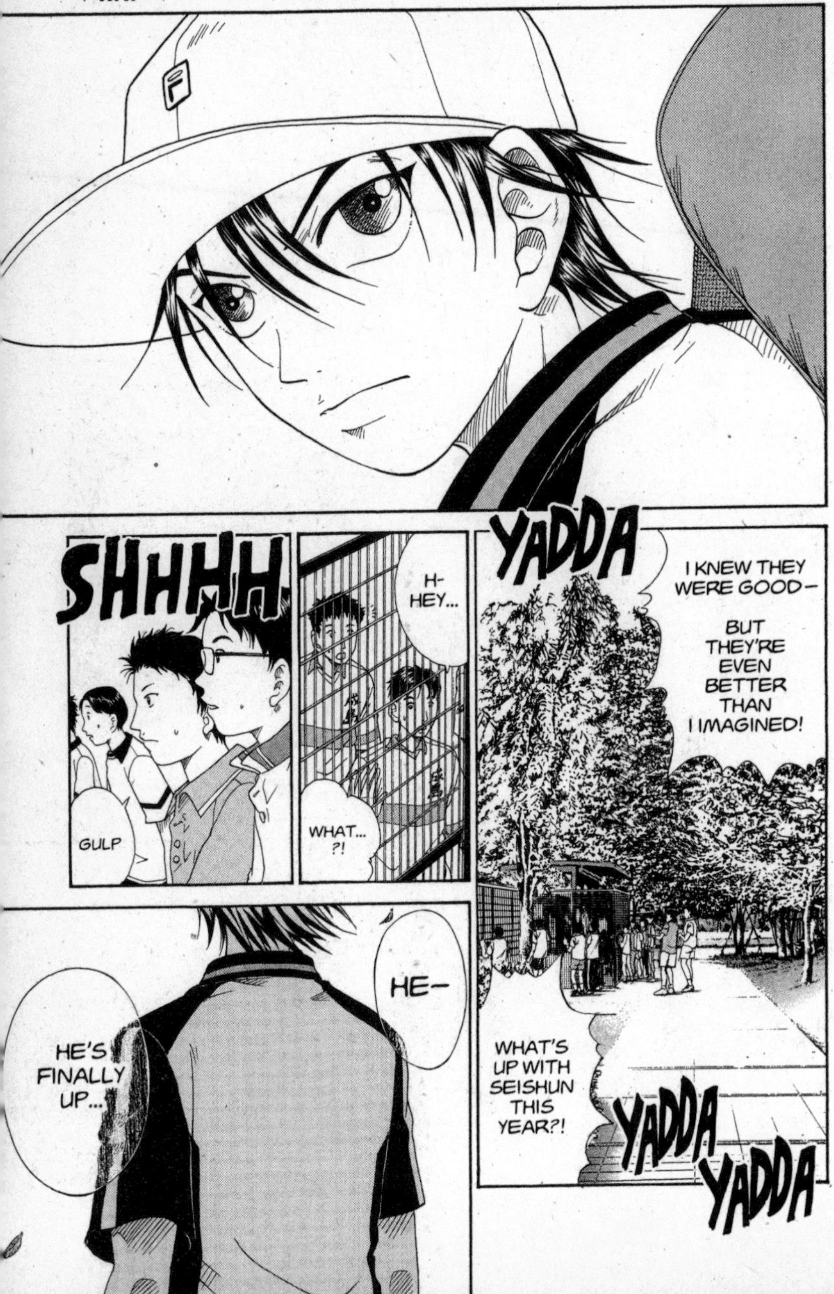
YADDA
I KNEW THEY WERE GOOD—
BUT THEY'RE EVEN BETTER THAN I IMAGINED!
WHAT'S UP WITH SEISHUN THIS YEAR?!
YADDA YADDA
H-HEY...
WHAT...?!
SHHHH
GULP
HE—
HE'S FINALLY UP...

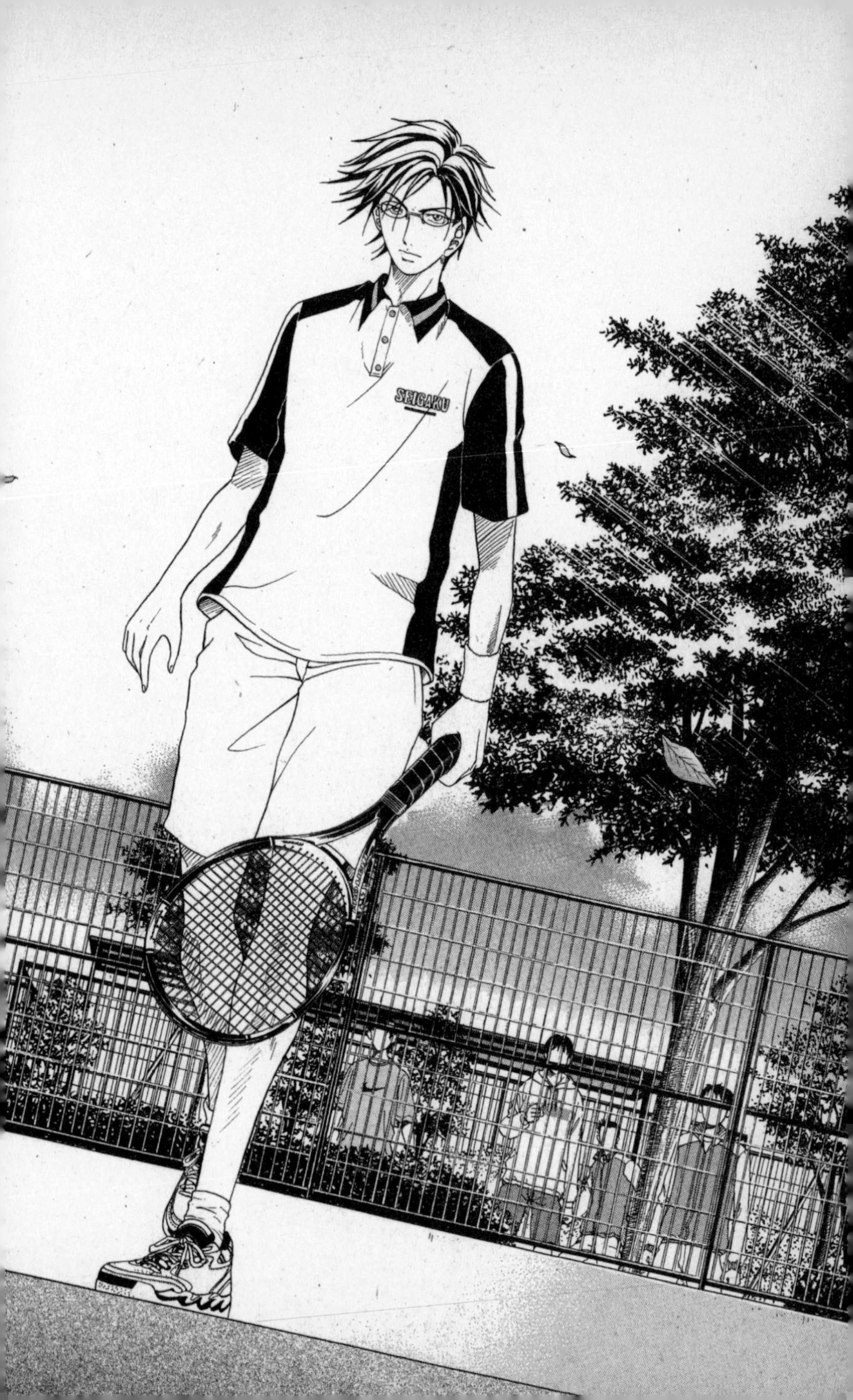
SEIGAKU

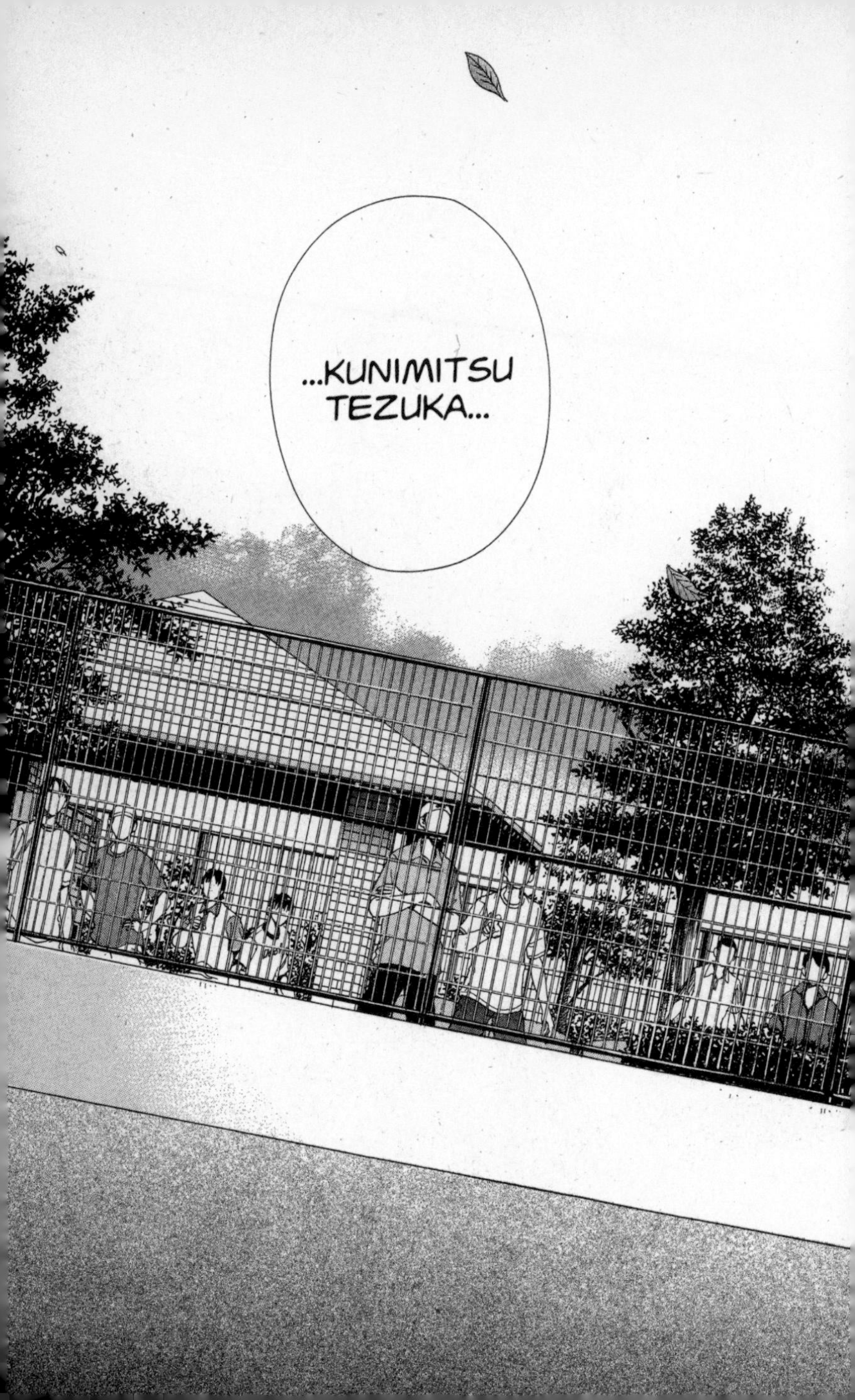
...KUNIMITSU TEZUKA...

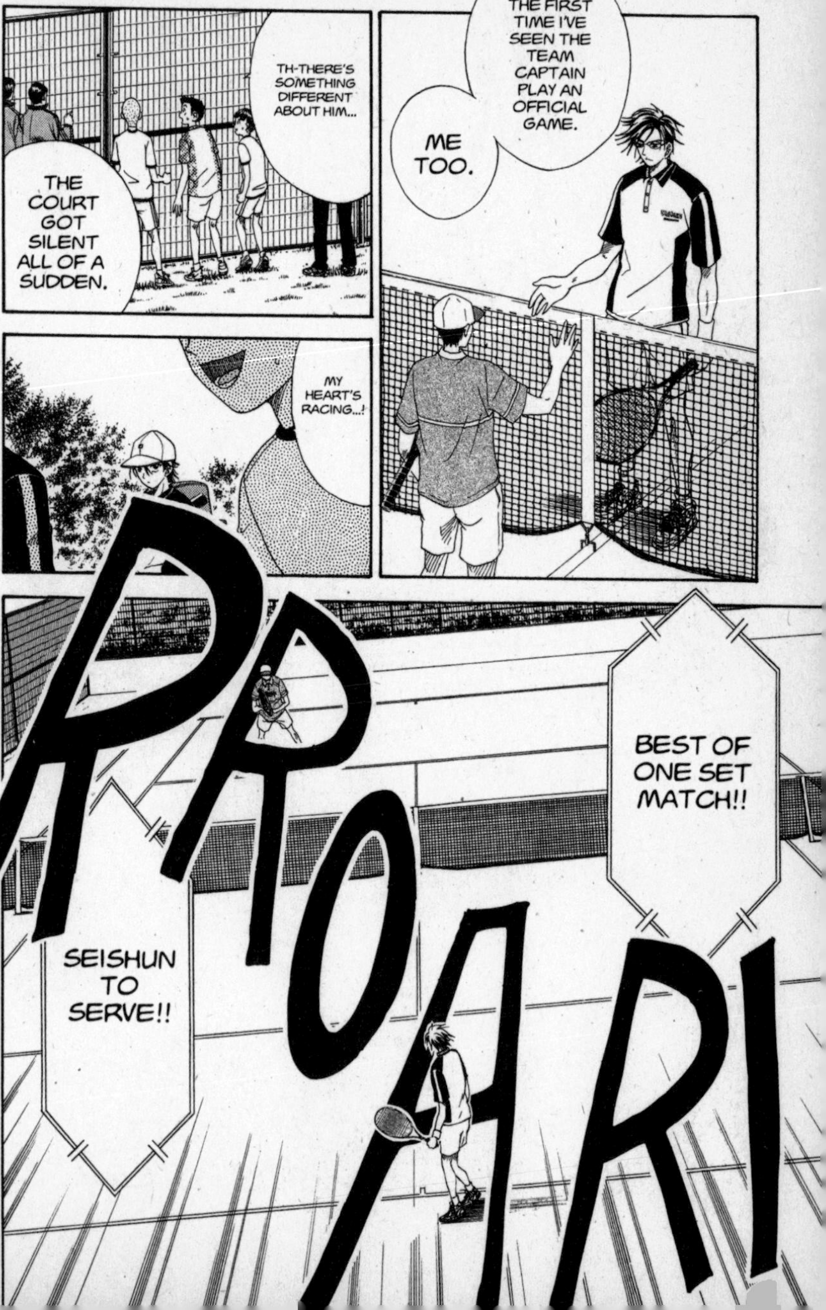
IT'S THE FIRST TIME I'VE SEEN THE TEAM CAPTAIN PLAY AN OFFICIAL GAME.
ME TOO.
TH-THERE'S SOMETHING DIFFERENT ABOUT HIM...
THE COURT GOT SILENT ALL OF A SUDDEN.
MY HEART'S RACING...!
BEST OF ONE SET MATCH!!
SEISHUN TO SERVE!!

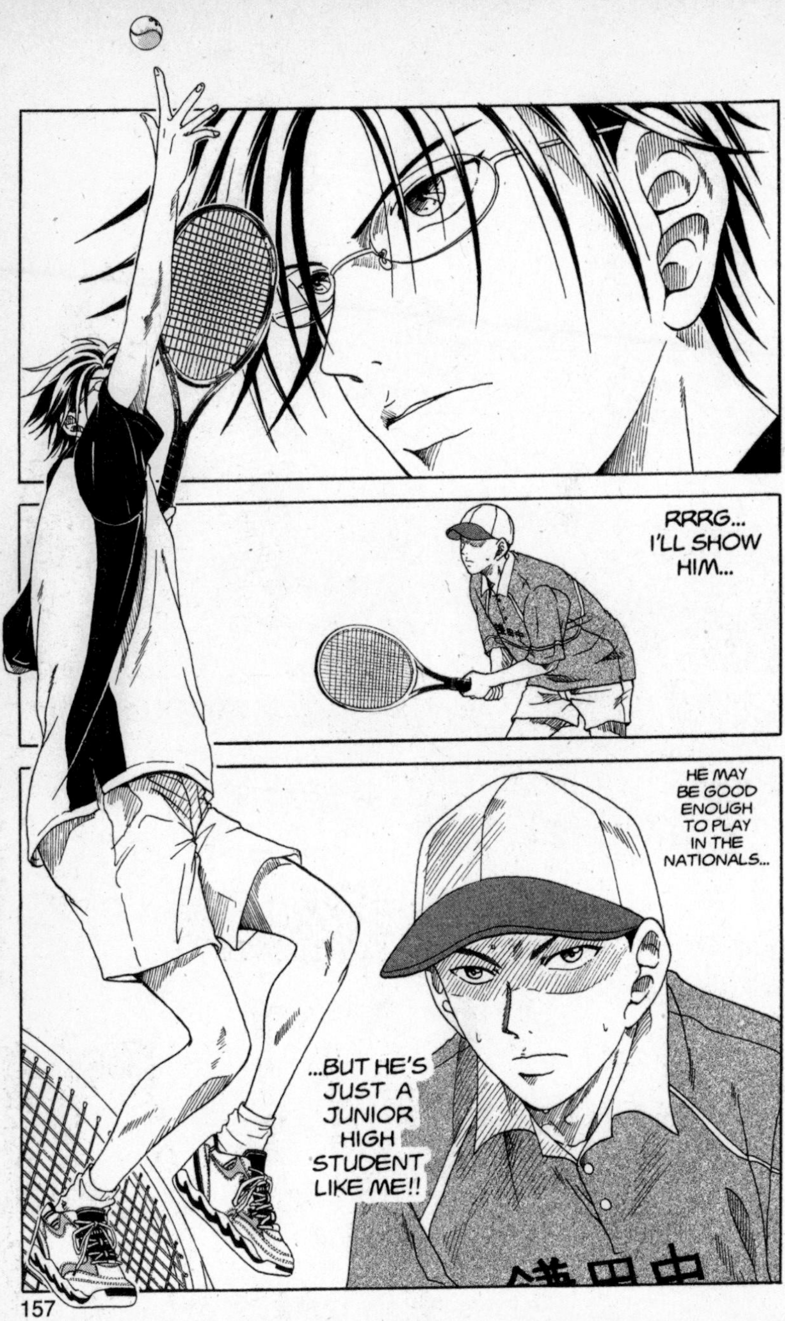
RRRG... I'LL SHOW HIM...
HE MAY BE GOOD ENOUGH TO PLAY IN THE NATIONALS...
...BUT HE'S JUST A JUNIOR HIGH STUDENT LIKE ME!!

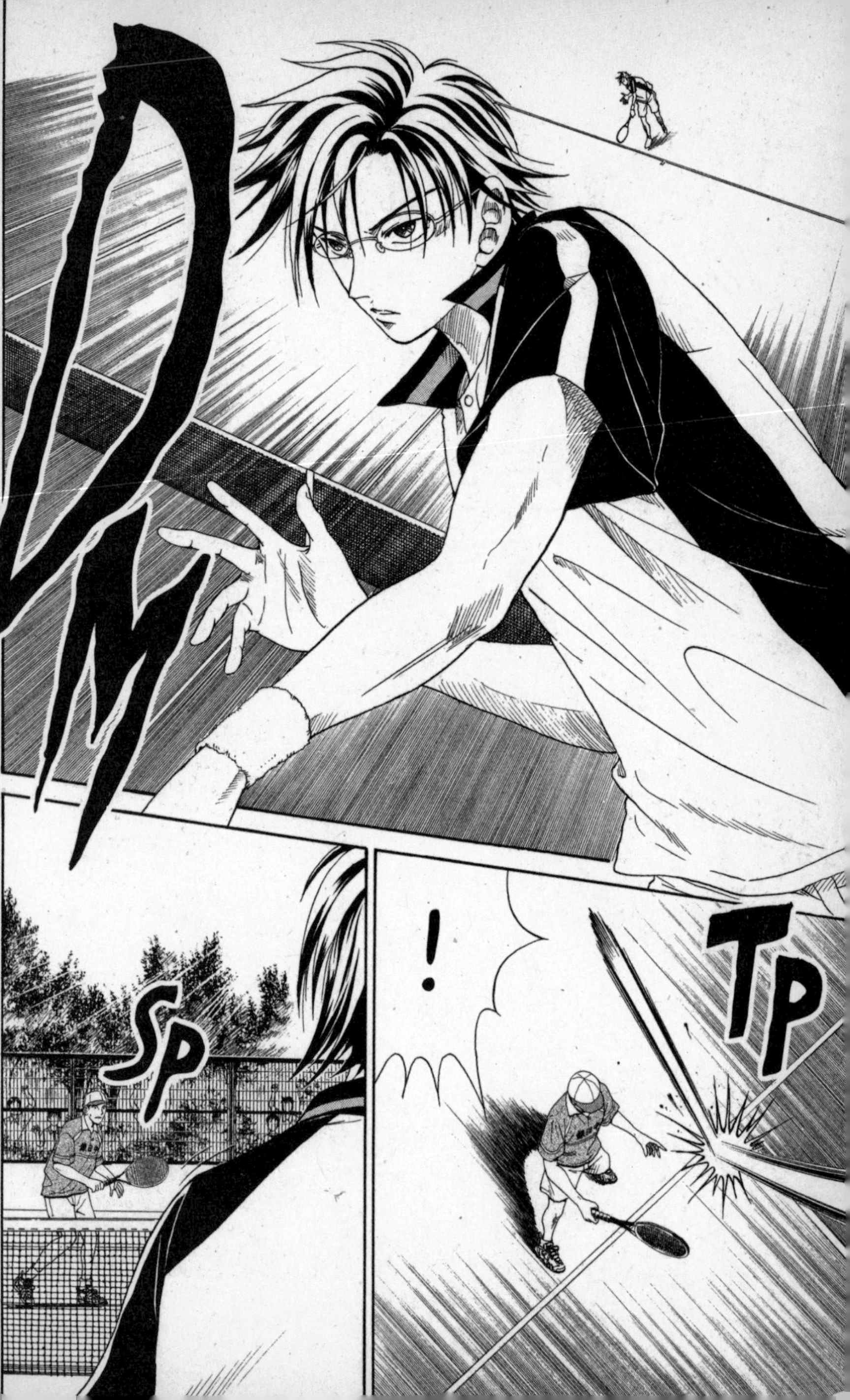
TP
!
SP

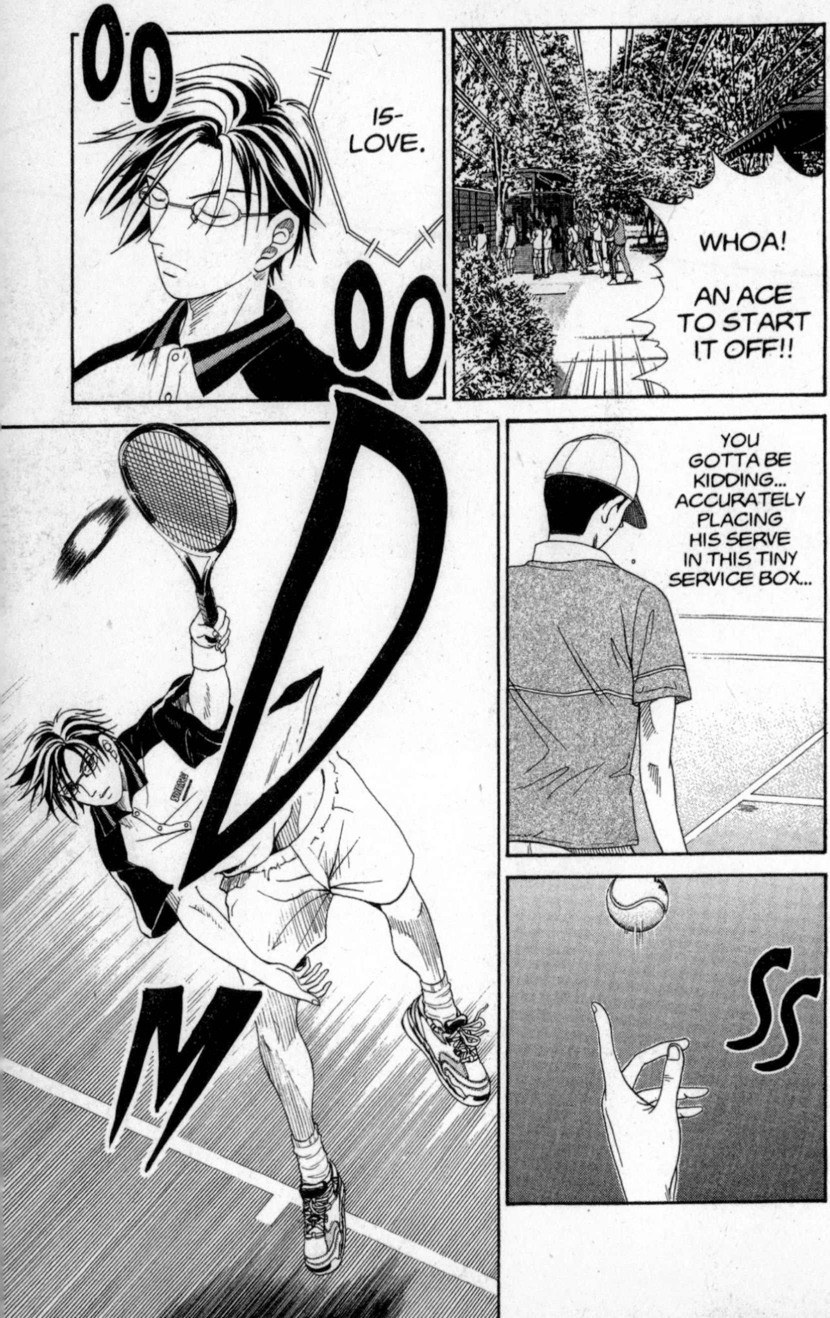
WHOA!
AN ACE TO START IT OFF!!
IS- LOVE.
OO
OO
YOU GOTTA BE KIDDING... ACCURATELY PLACING HIS SERVE IN THIS TINY SERVICE BOX...
SS
D
O
M

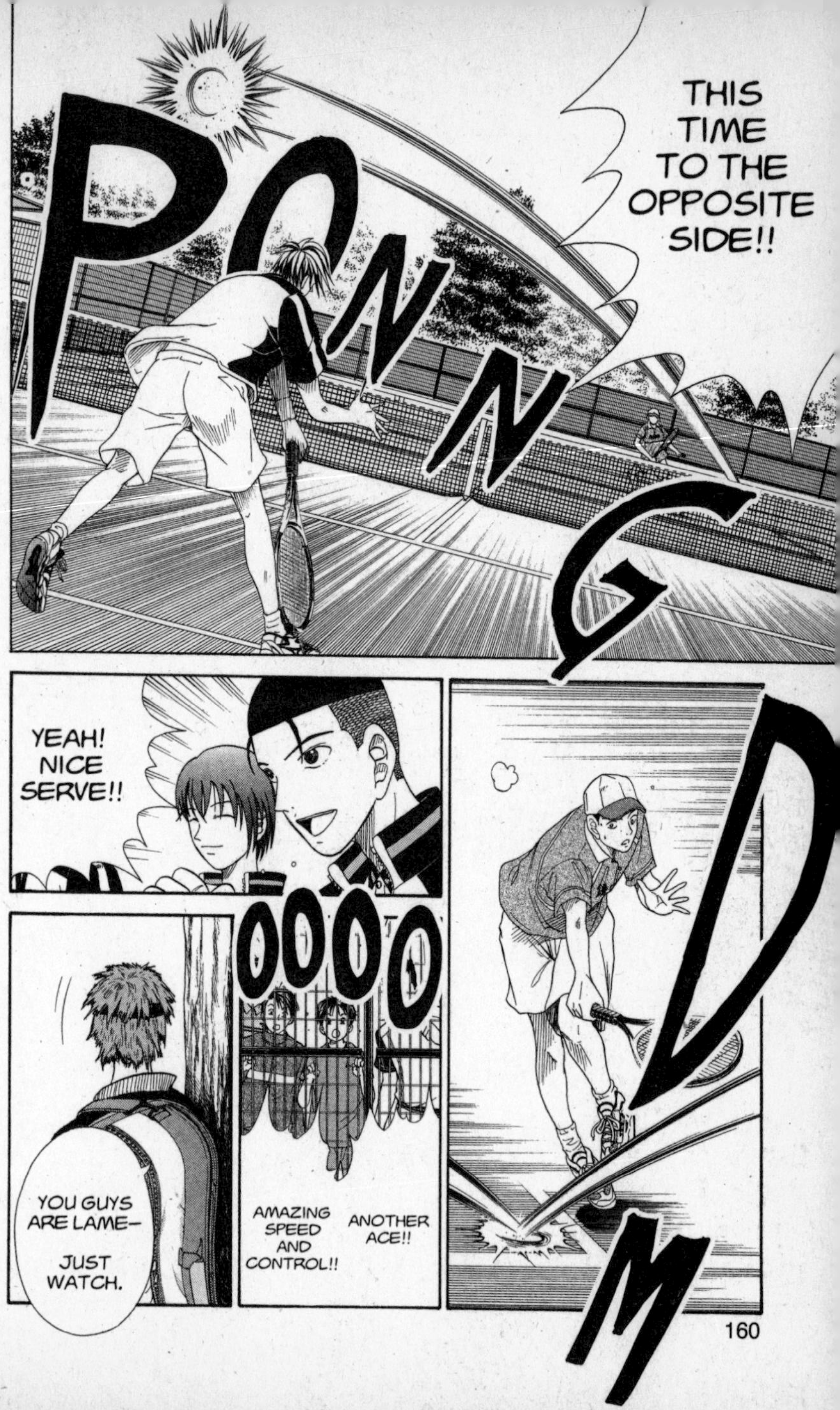
THIS TIME TO THE OPPOSITE SIDE!!
PONNG
DOOOOM
YEAH! NICE SERVE!!
ANOTHER ACE!!
AMAZING SPEED AND CONTROL!!
YOU GUYS ARE LAME—
JUST WATCH.

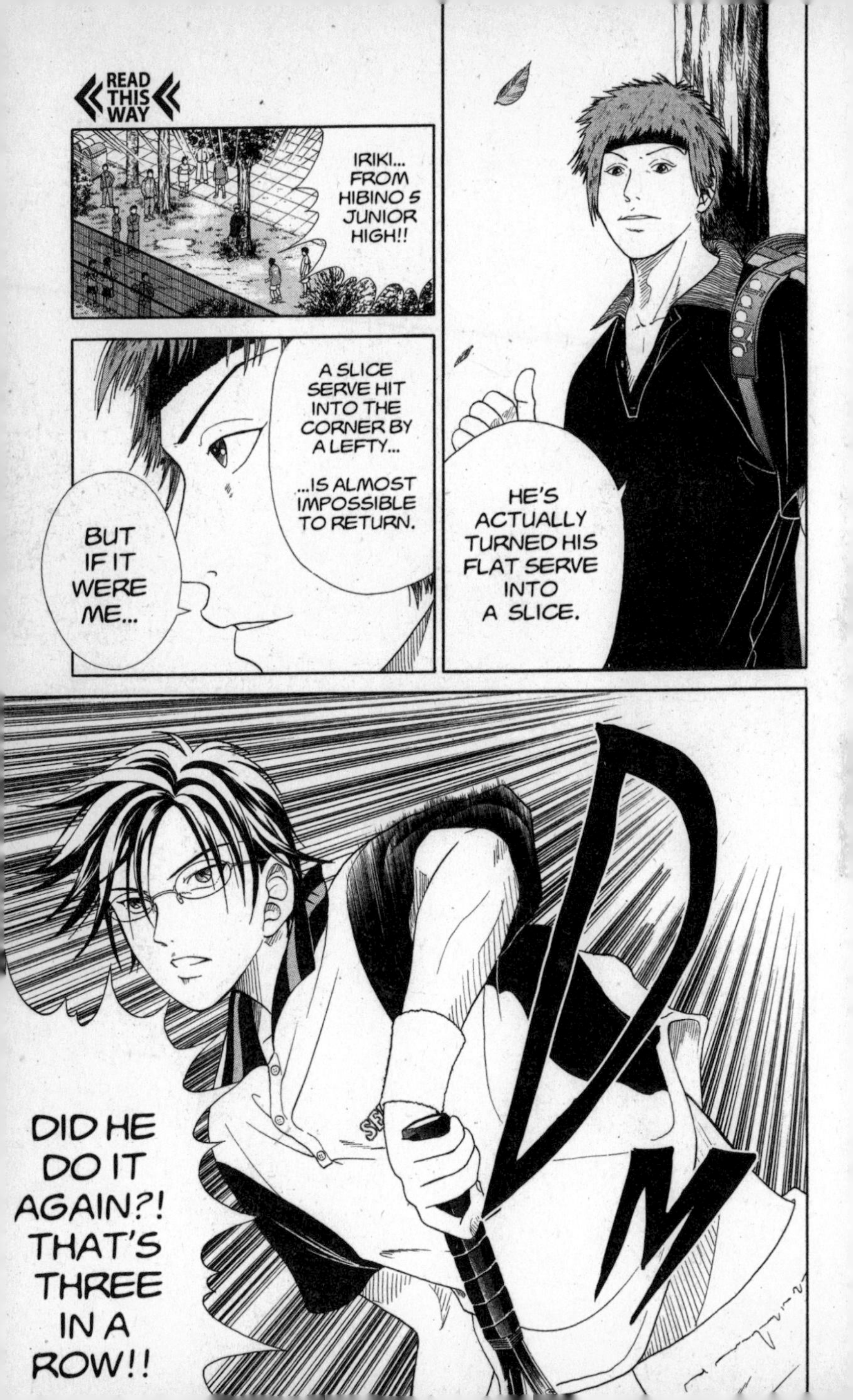
READ THIS WAY
HE'S ACTUALLY TURNED HIS FLAT SERVE INTO A SLICE.
IRIKI... FROM HIBINO 5 JUNIOR HIGH!!
A SLICE SERVE HIT INTO THE CORNER BY A LEFTY...
...IS ALMOST IMPOSSIBLE TO RETURN.
BUT IF IT WERE ME...
DID HE DO IT AGAIN?! THAT'S THREE IN A ROW!!

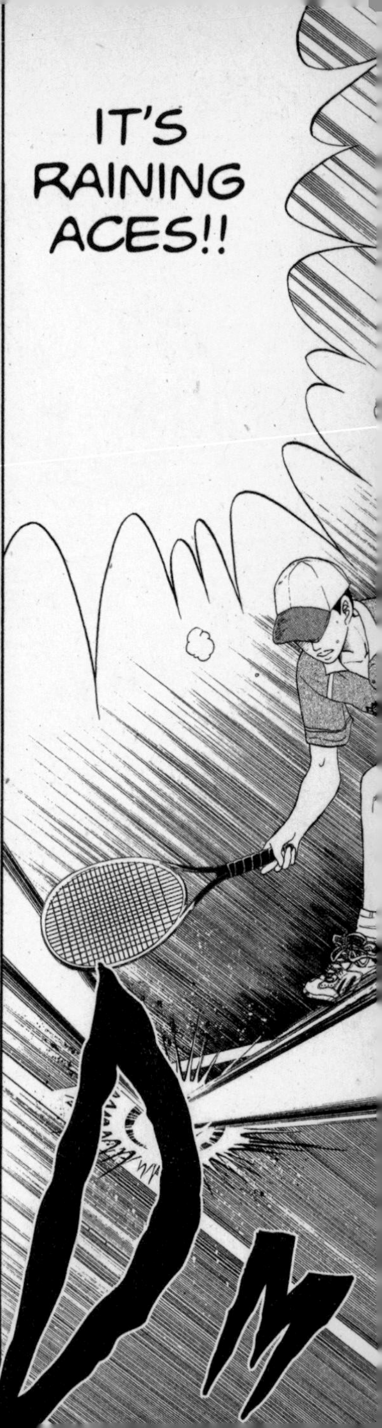
IT'S RAINING ACES!!

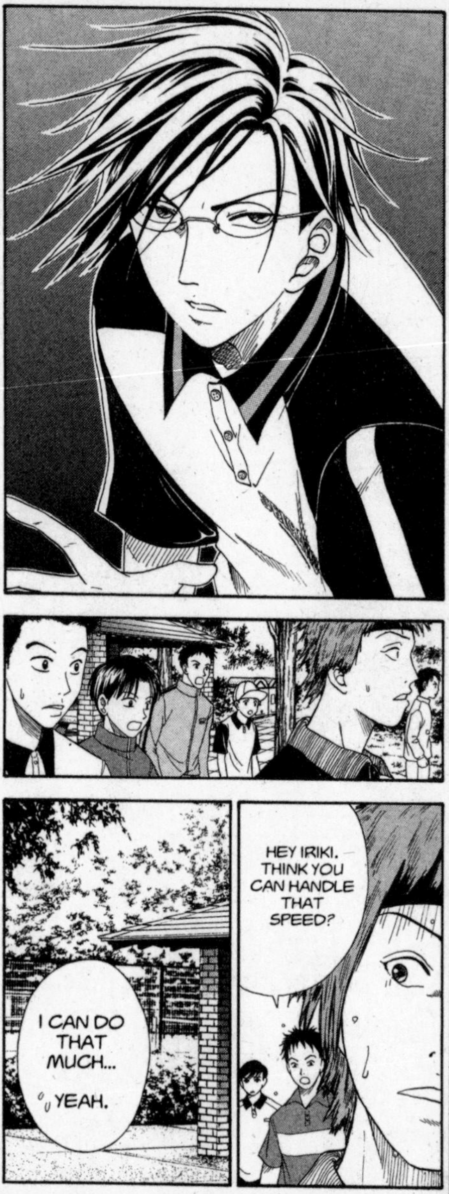
HEY IRIKI. THINK YOU CAN HANDLE THAT SPEED?
I CAN DO THAT MUCH... YEAH.

READ THIS WAY

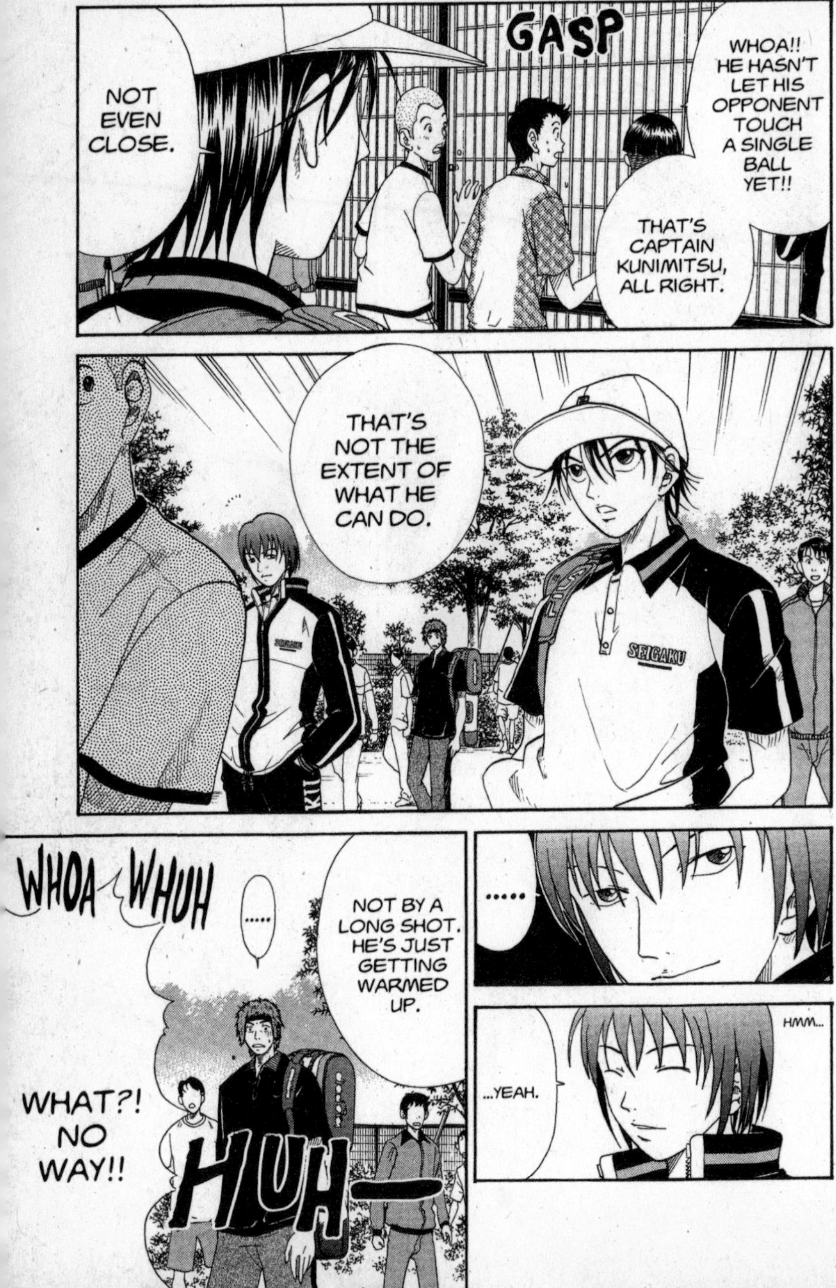
GASP
WHOA!! HE HASN'T LET HIS OPPONENT TOUCH A SINGLE BALL YET!!
THAT'S CAPTAIN KUNIMITSU, ALL RIGHT.
NOT EVEN CLOSE.
THAT'S NOT THE EXTENT OF WHAT HE CAN DO.
.....
HMM...
...YEAH.
NOT BY A LONG SHOT. HE'S JUST GETTING WARMED UP.
......
WHOA WHUH
WHAT?! NO WAY!!
HUH—

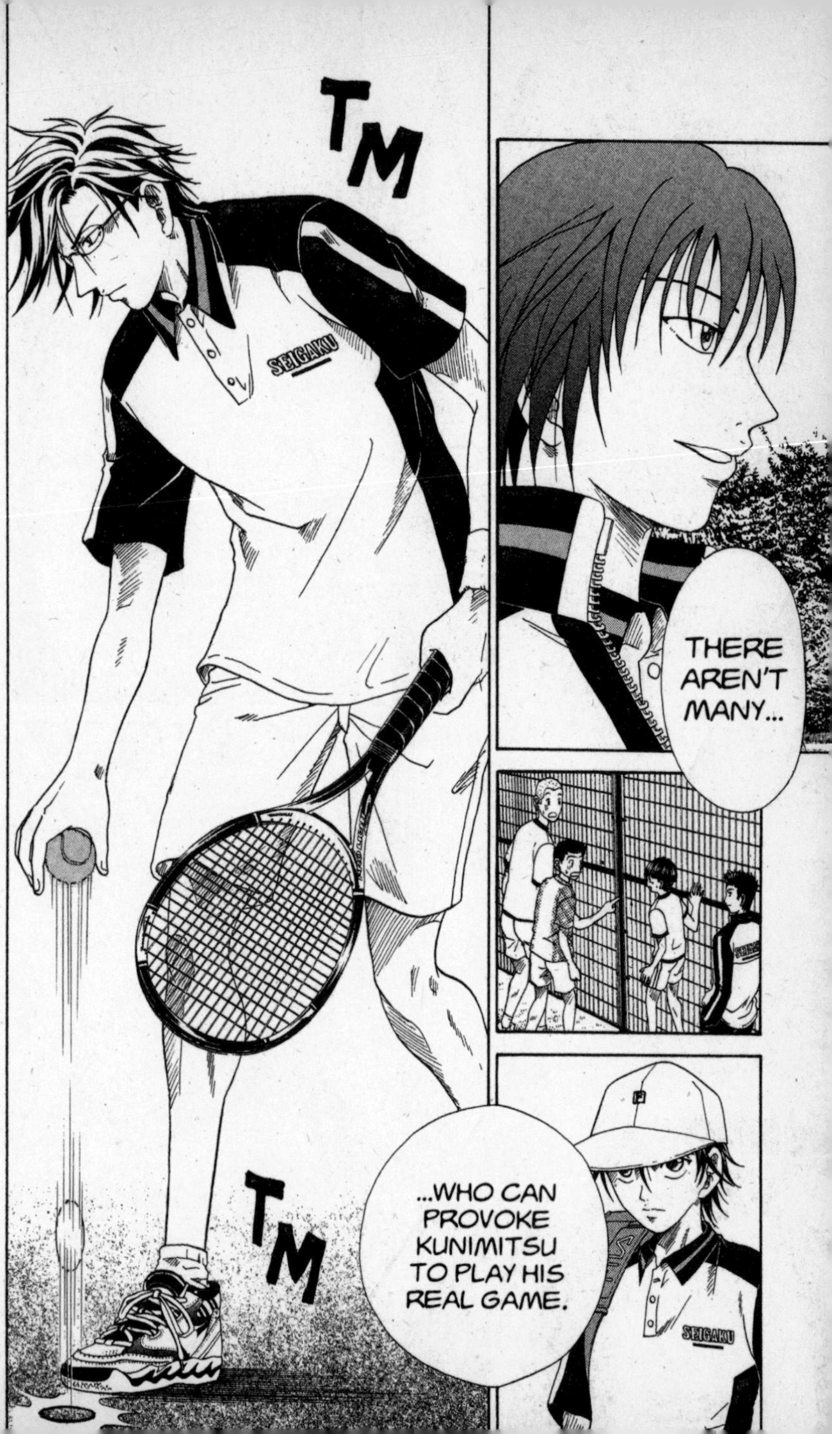
THERE AREN'T MANY...
...WHO CAN PROVOKE KUNIMITSU TO PLAY HIS REAL GAME.
TM
TM

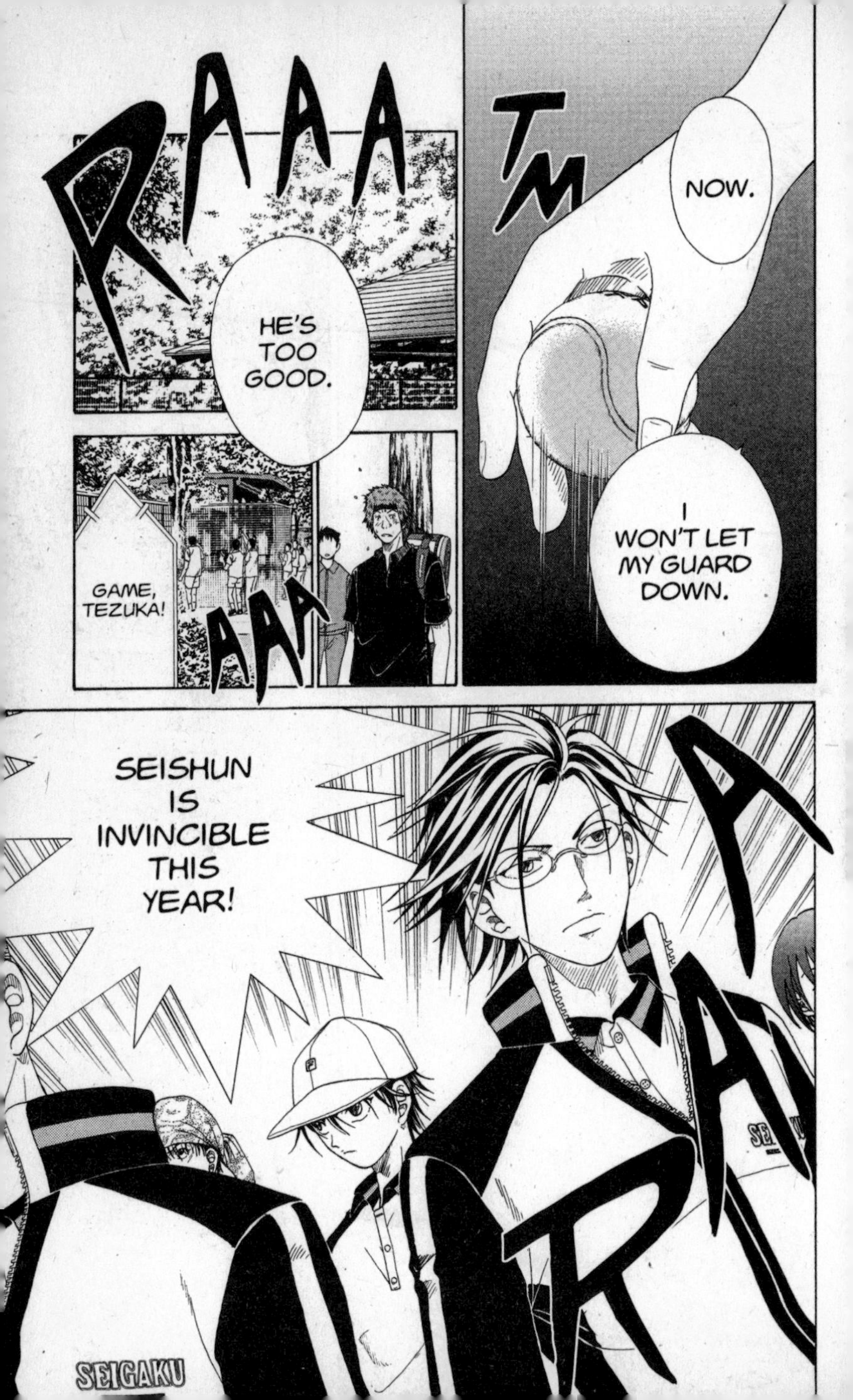
NOW.
I WON'T LET MY GUARD DOWN.
RAAA
HE'S TOO GOOD.
GAME, TEZUKA!
SEISHUN IS INVINCIBLE THIS YEAR!
SEIGAKU

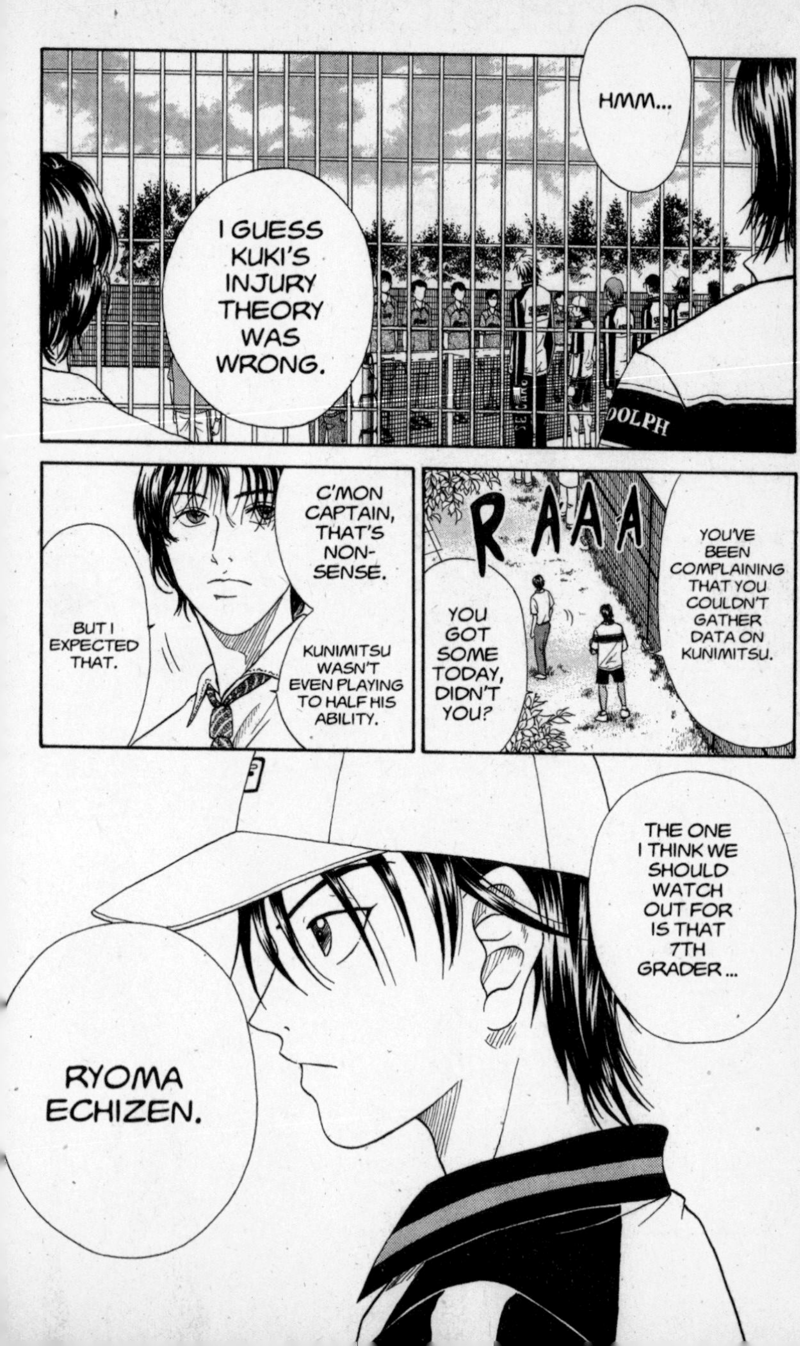
HMM...
I GUESS KUKI'S INJURY THEORY WAS WRONG.
YOU'VE BEEN COMPLAINING THAT YOU COULDN'T GATHER DATA ON KUNIMITSU.
RAAA
YOU GOT SOME TODAY, DIDN'T YOU?
C'MON CAPTAIN, THAT'S NON-SENSE.
KUNIMITSU WASN'T EVEN PLAYING TO HALF HIS ABILITY.
BUT I EXPECTED THAT.
THE ONE I THINK WE SHOULD WATCH OUT FOR IS THAT 7TH GRADER...
RYOMA ECHIZEN.

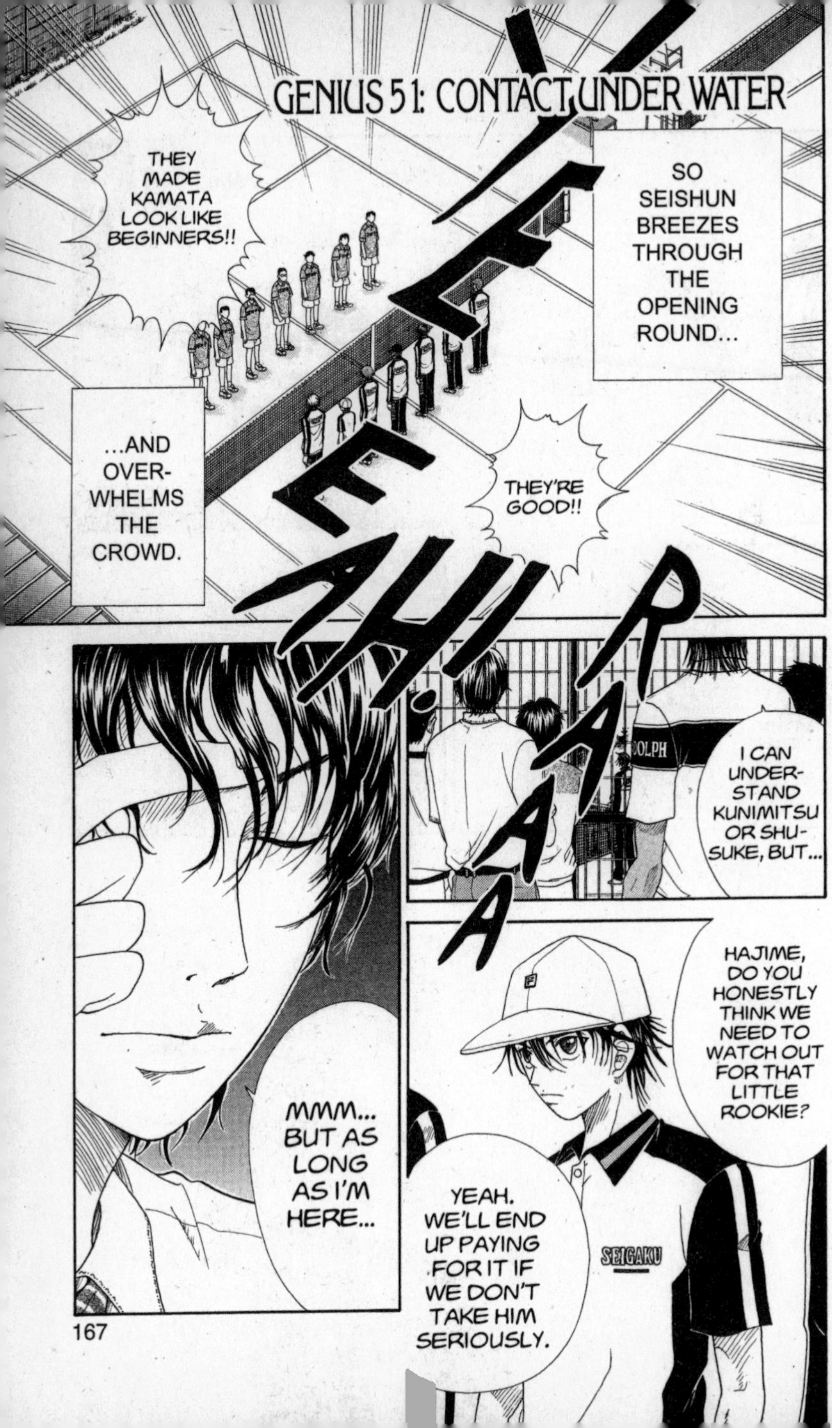

GENIUS 51: CONTACT UNDER WATER
SO SEISHUN BREEZES THROUGH THE OPENING ROUND...
THEY MADE KAMATA LOOK LIKE BEGINNERS!!
THEY'RE GOOD!!
...AND OVER-WHELMS THE CROWD.
I CAN UNDER-STAND KUNIMITSU OR SHU-SUKE, BUT...
HAJIME, DO YOU HONESTLY THINK WE NEED TO WATCH OUT FOR THAT LITTLE ROOKIE?
YEAH. WE'LL END UP PAYING FOR IT IF WE DON'T TAKE HIM SERIOUSLY.
MMM... BUT AS LONG AS I'M HERE...

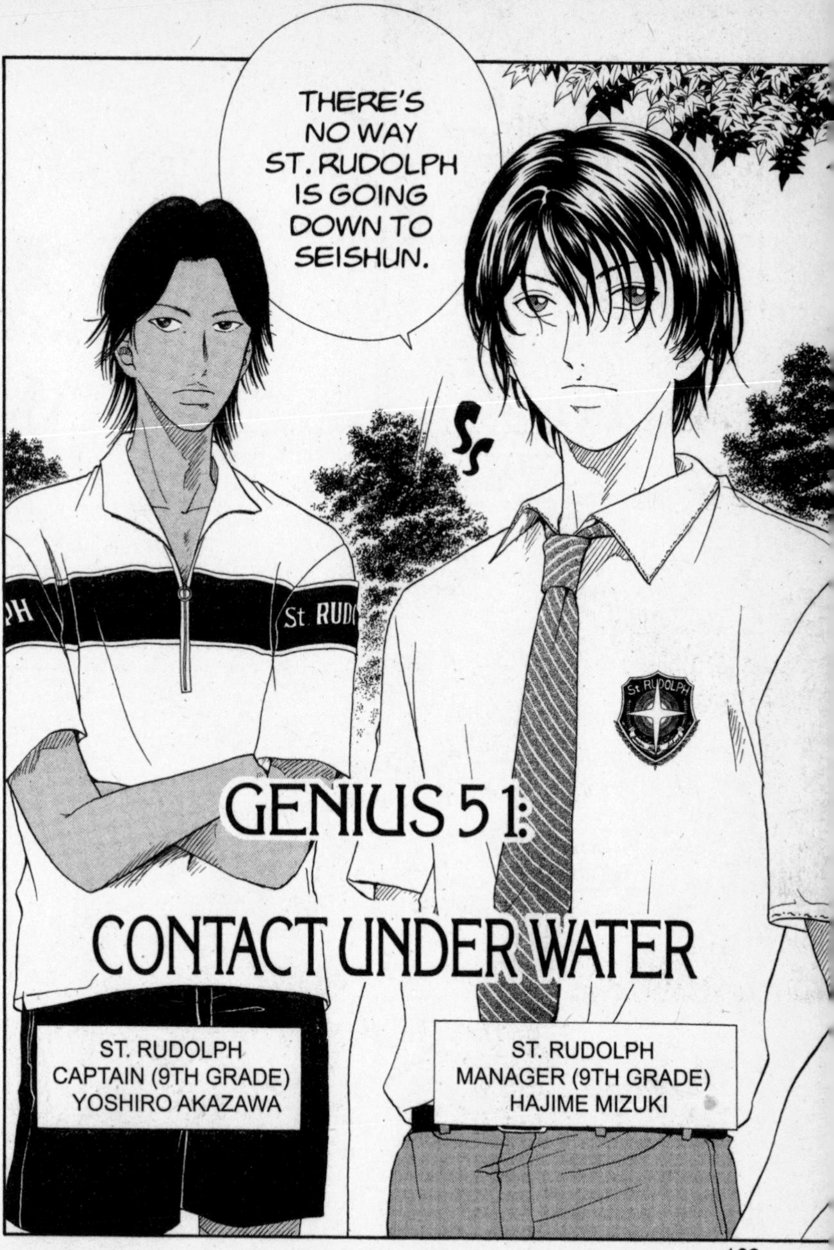
THERE'S NO WAY ST. RUDOLPH IS GOING DOWN TO SEISHUN.
GENIUS 51:
CONTACT UNDER WATER
ST. RUDOLPH MANAGER (9TH GRADE) HAJIME MIZUKI
ST. RUDOLPH CAPTAIN (9TH GRADE) YOSHIRO AKAZAWA

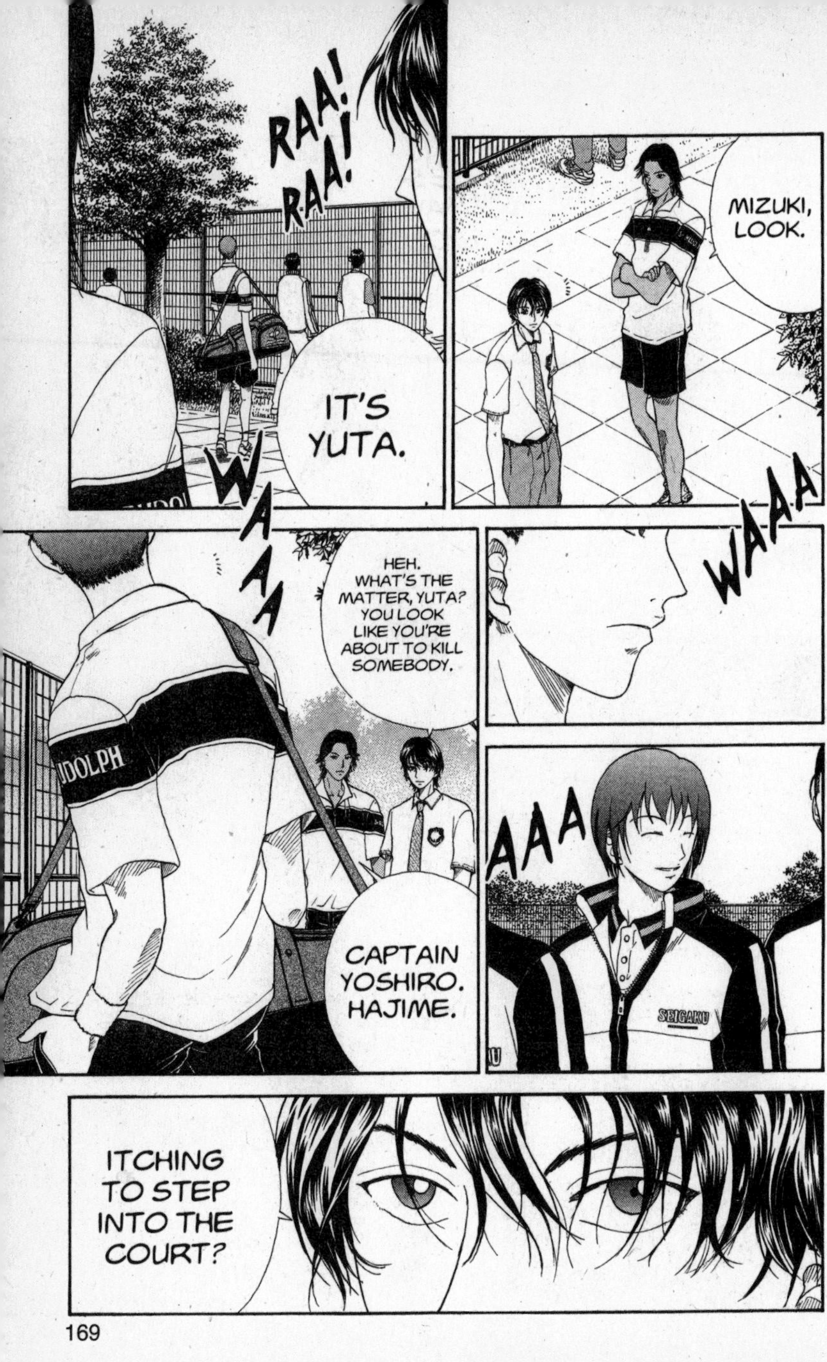
MIZUKI, LOOK.
WAAA
RAA! RAA!
IT'S YUTA.
WAAA
WAAA
AAA
HEH. WHAT'S THE MATTER, YUTA? YOU LOOK LIKE YOU'RE ABOUT TO KILL SOMEBODY.
CAPTAIN YOSHIRO. HAJIME.
ITCHING TO STEP INTO THE COURT?

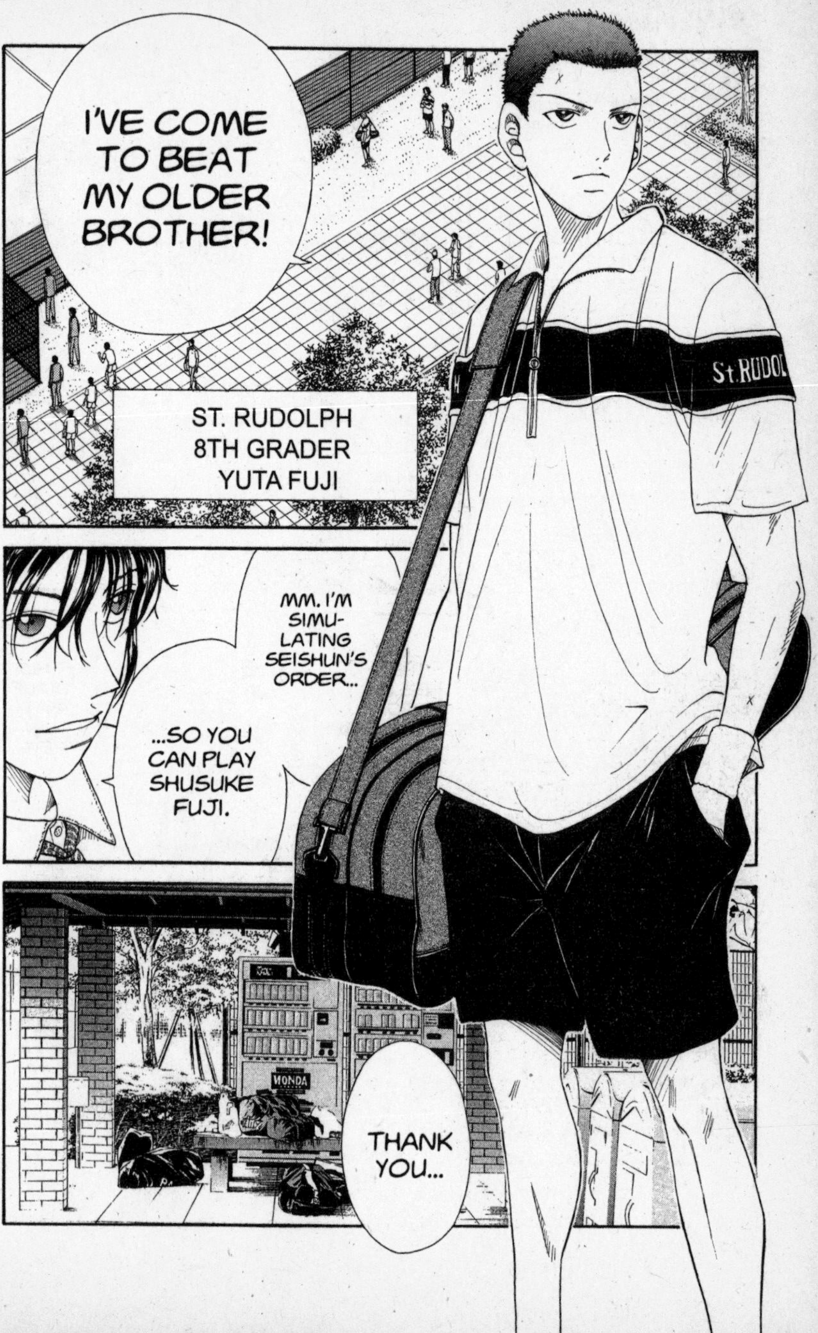
I'VE COME TO BEAT MY OLDER BROTHER!
ST. RUDOLPH 8TH GRADER YUTA FUJI
St. RUDOL
MM. I'M SIMU-LATING SEISHUN'S ORDER...
...SO YOU CAN PLAY SHUSUKE FUJI.
THANK YOU...

READ THIS WAY

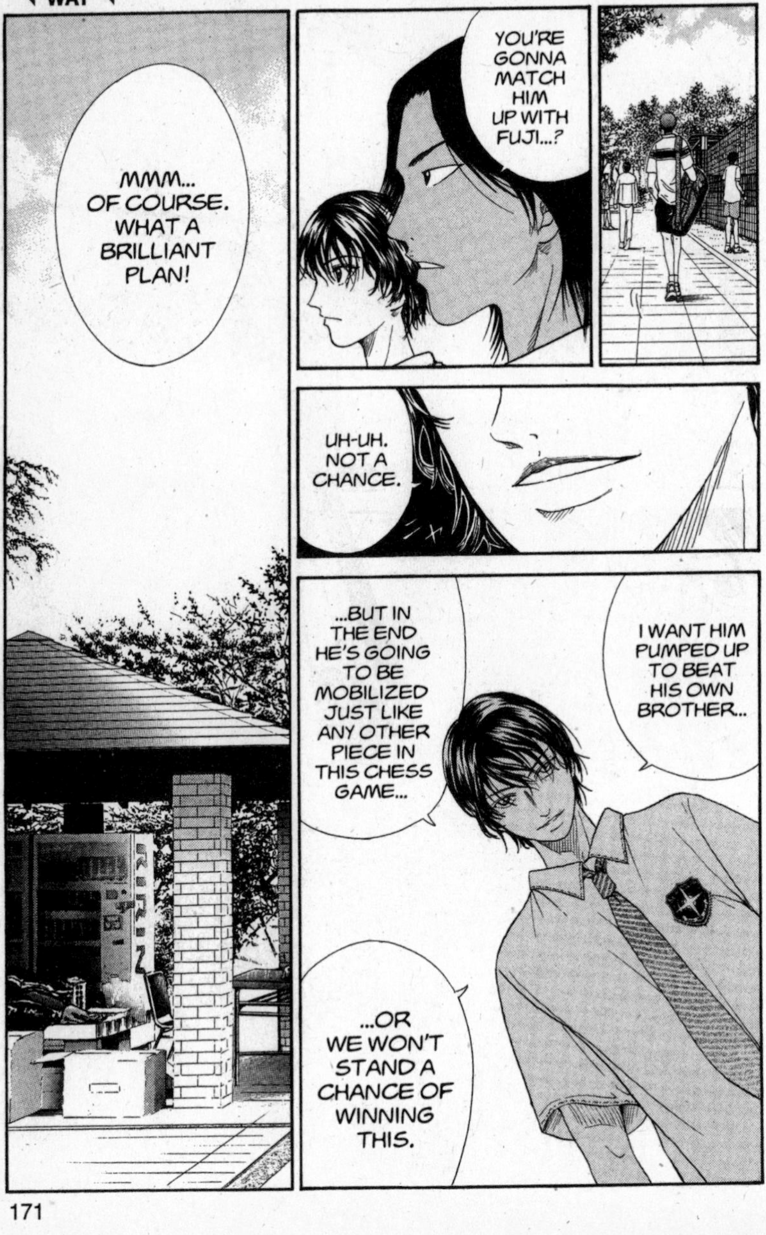
YOU'RE GONNA MATCH HIM UP WITH FUJI...?
UH-UH. NOT A CHANCE.
I WANT HIM PUMPED UP TO BEAT HIS OWN BROTHER...
...BUT IN THE END HE'S GOING TO BE MOBILIZED JUST LIKE ANY OTHER PIECE IN THIS CHESS GAME...
...OR WE WON'T STAND A CHANCE OF WINNING THIS.
MMM... OF COURSE. WHAT A BRILLIANT PLAN!

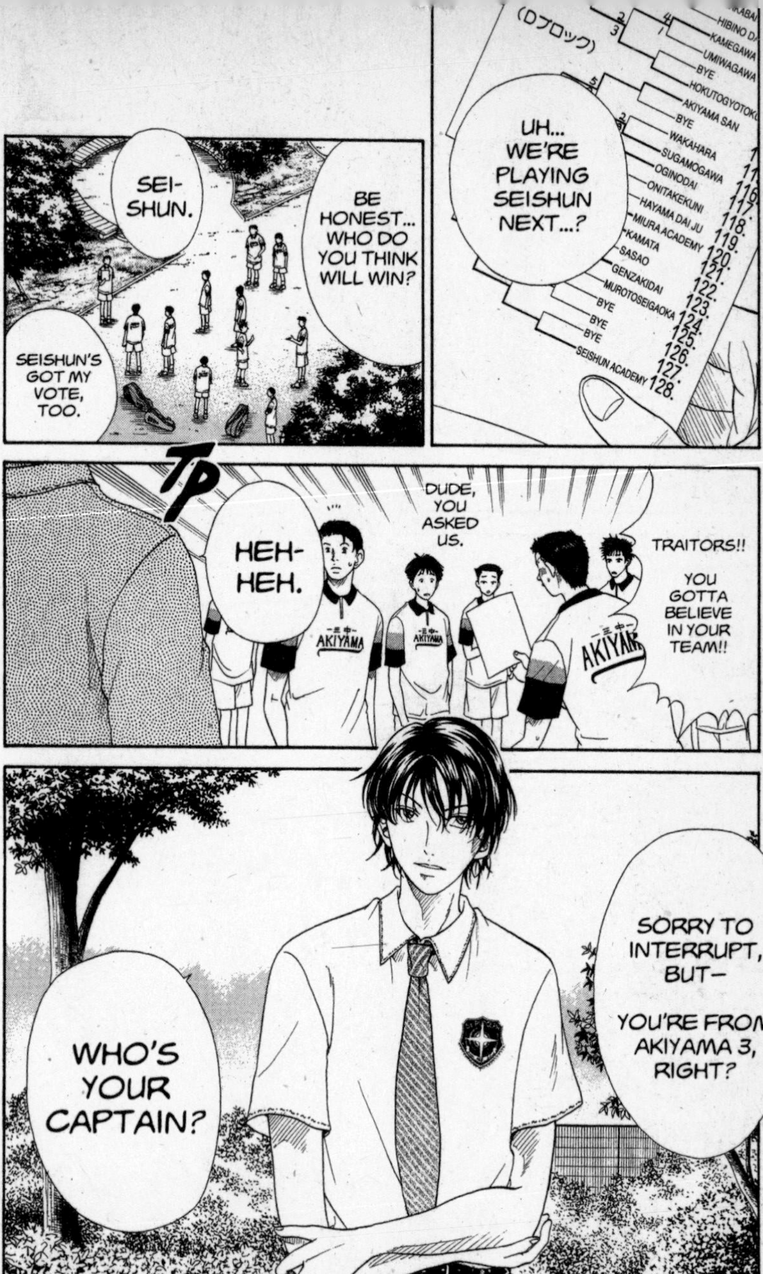
(Dブロック)
KAMEGAWA
UMIWAGAWA
BYE
HOKUTOGYOTOKU
AKIYAMA SAN
BYE
WAKAHARA
SUGAMOGAWA
OGINODAI
ONITAKEKUNI
HAYAMA DAI JU
MIURA ACADEMY
KAMATA
SASAO
GENZAKIDAI
MUROTOSEIGAOKA
BYE
BYE
BYE
SEISHUN ACADEMY
117.
118.
119.
120.
121.
122.
123.
124.
125.
126.
127.
128.
UH... WE'RE PLAYING SEISHUN NEXT...?
BE HONEST... WHO DO YOU THINK WILL WIN?
SEI-SHUN.
SEISHUN'S GOT MY VOTE, TOO.
TRAITORS!!
YOU GOTTA BELIEVE IN YOUR TEAM!!
DUDE, YOU ASKED US.
HEH-HEH.
TP
SORRY TO INTERRUPT, BUT—
YOU'RE FROM AKIYAMA 3, RIGHT?
WHO'S YOUR CAPTAIN?

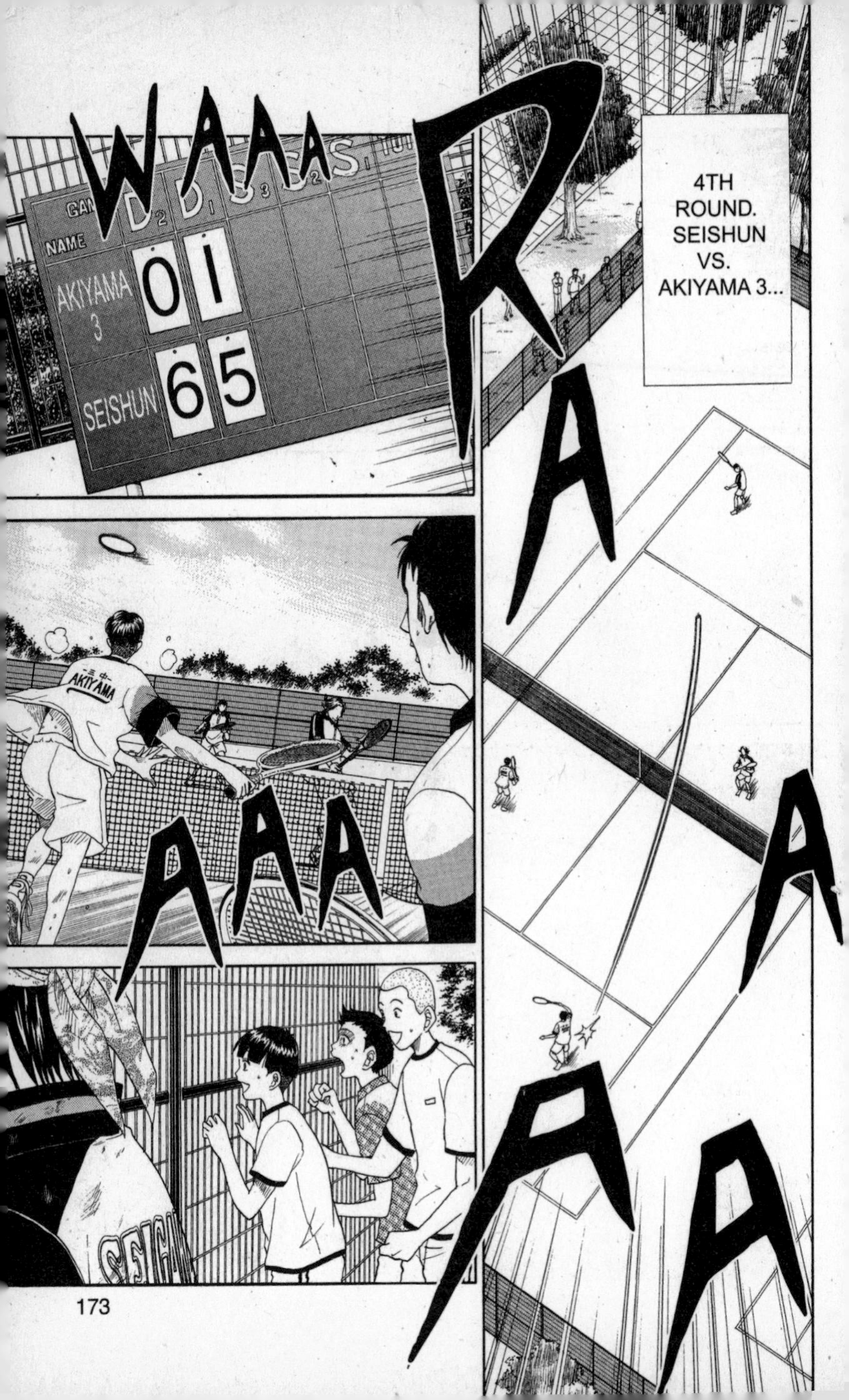
4TH ROUND. SEISHUN VS. AKIYAMA 3...
WAAARAAAAAA
NAME
AKIYAMA 3
SEISHUN
0 1
6 5
AKIYAMA

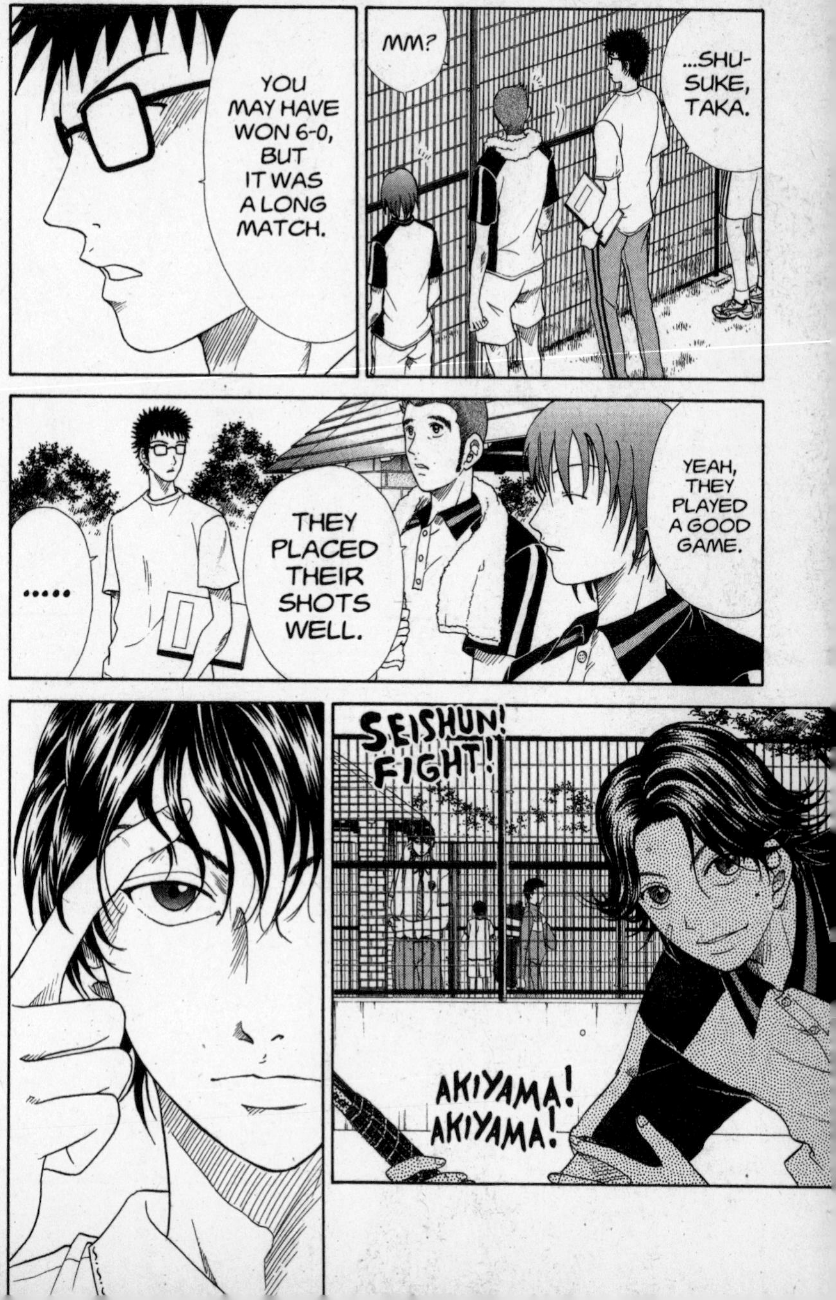
...SHU-SUKE, TAKA.
MM?
YOU MAY HAVE WON 6-0, BUT IT WAS A LONG MATCH.
YEAH, THEY PLAYED A GOOD GAME.
THEY PLACED THEIR SHOTS WELL.
.....
SEISHUN! FIGHT!
AKIYAMA! AKIYAMA!

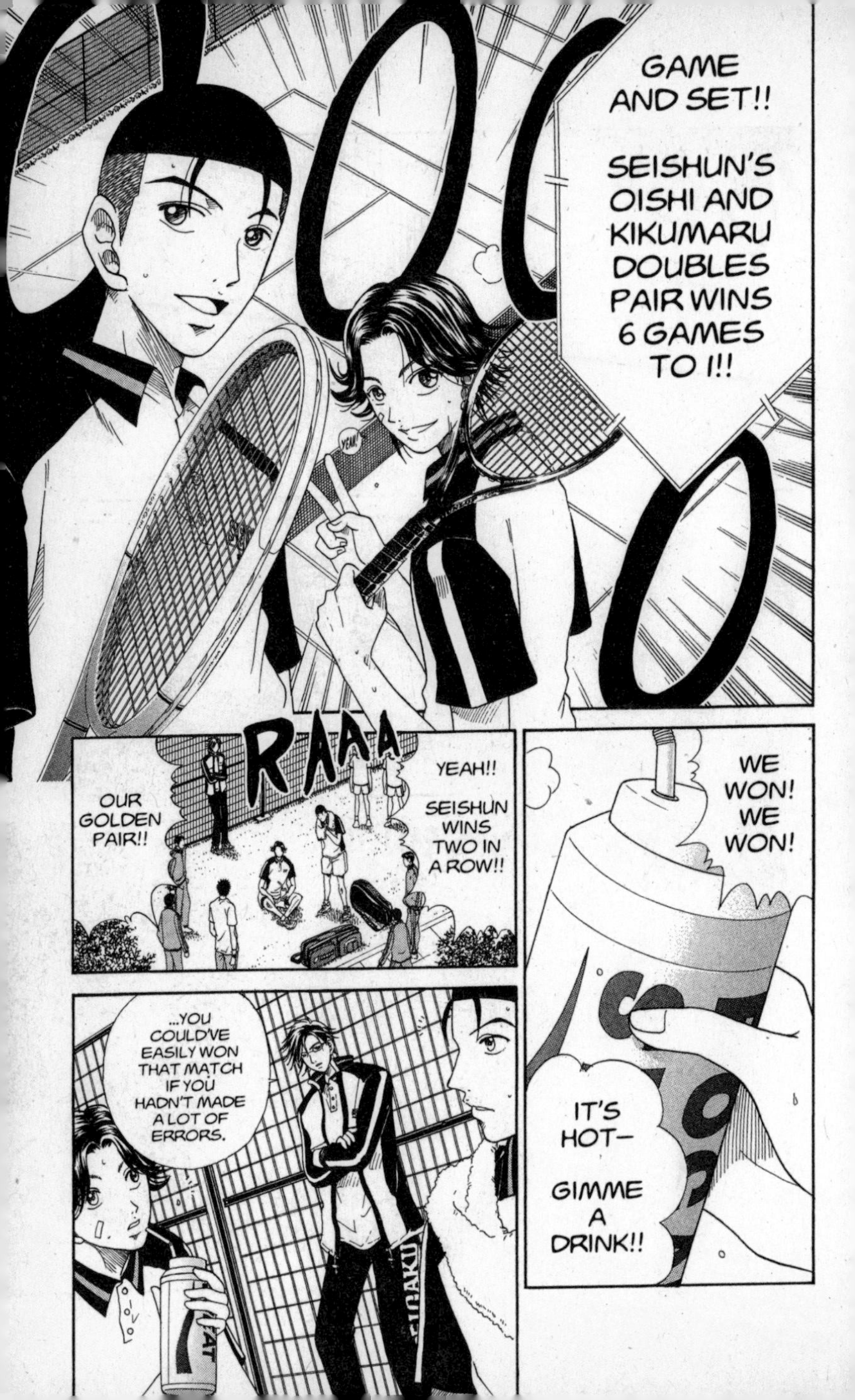
GAME AND SET!!
SEISHUN'S OISHI AND KIKUMARU DOUBLES PAIR WINS 6 GAMES TO 1!!
YEAH!
WE WON! WE WON!
IT'S HOT—
GIMME A DRINK!!
YEAH!!
SEISHUN WINS TWO IN A ROW!!
RAAA
OUR GOLDEN PAIR!!
...YOU COULD'VE EASILY WON THAT MATCH IF YOU HADN'T MADE A LOT OF ERRORS.

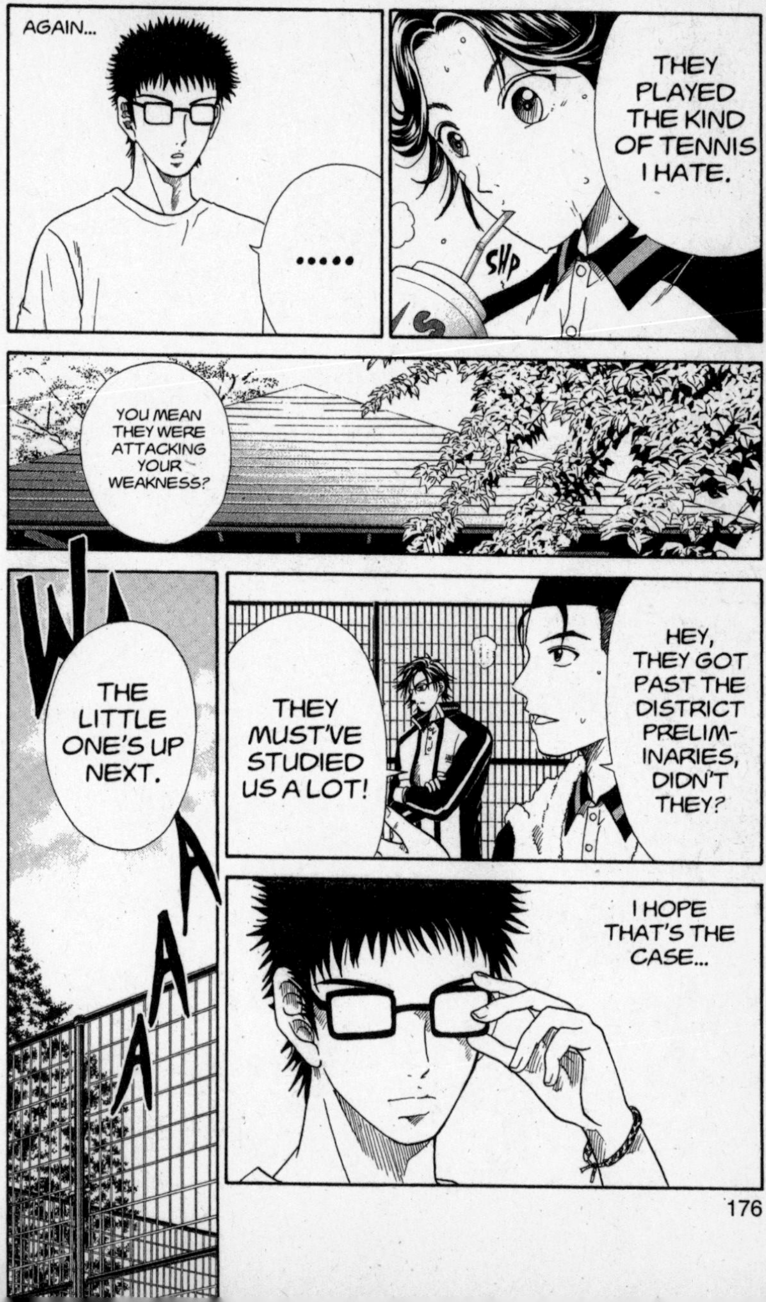
THEY PLAYED THE KIND OF TENNIS I HATE.
SHP
AGAIN...
.....
YOU MEAN THEY WERE ATTACKING YOUR WEAKNESS?
HEY, THEY GOT PAST THE DISTRICT PRELIM- INARIES, DIDN'T THEY?
THEY MUST'VE STUDIED US A LOT!
I HOPE THAT'S THE CASE...
WAAAA
THE LITTLE ONE'S UP NEXT.

READ THIS WAY

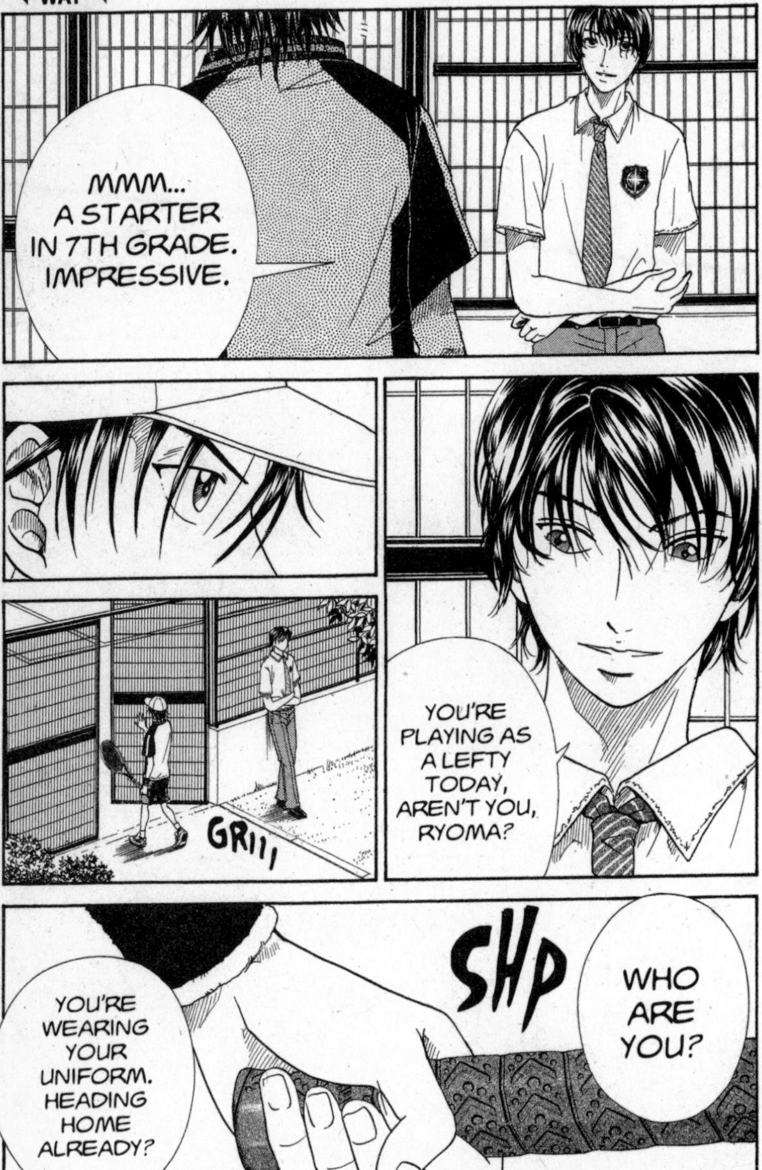
MMM... A STARTER IN 7TH GRADE. IMPRESSIVE.
YOU'RE PLAYING AS A LEFTY TODAY, AREN'T YOU, RYOMA?
GRIII
SHP
WHO ARE YOU?
YOU'RE WEARING YOUR UNIFORM. HEADING HOME ALREADY?

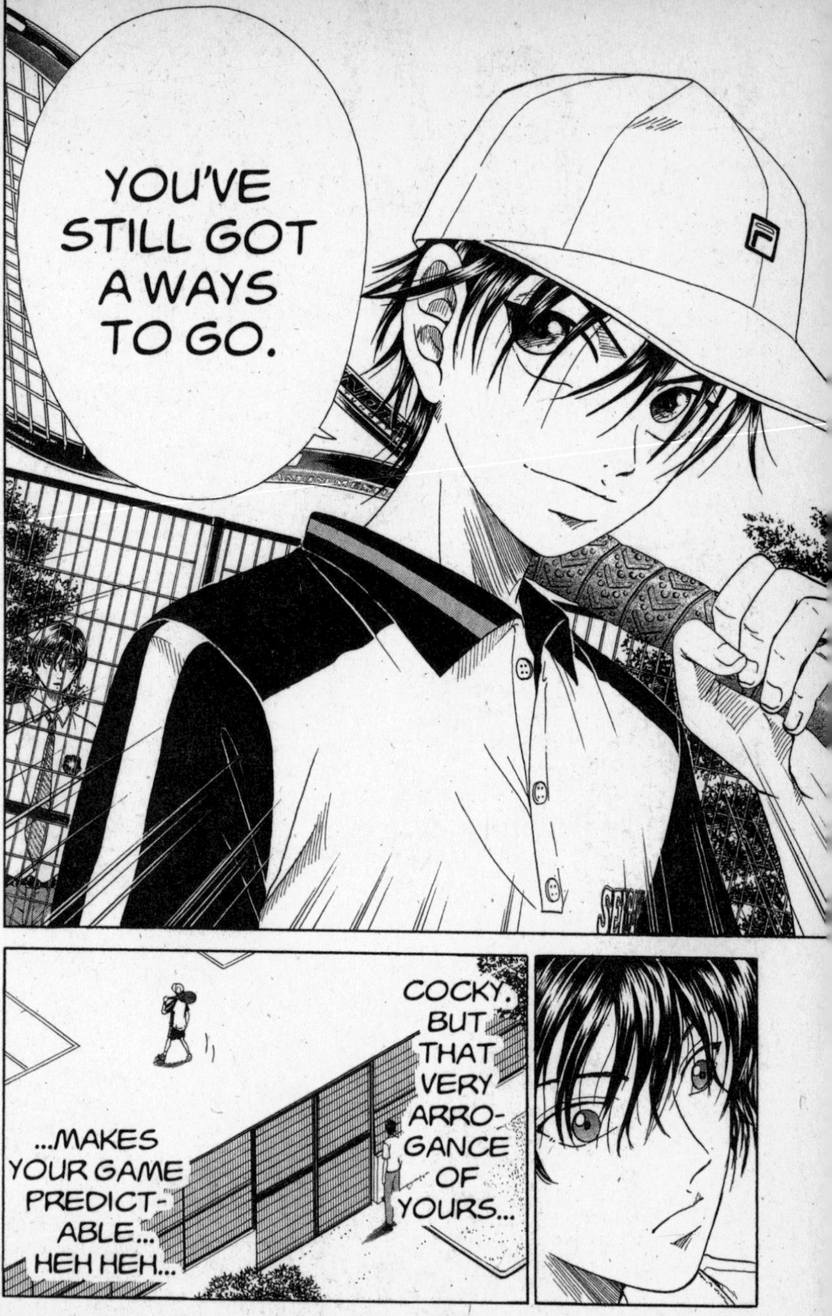
YOU'VE STILL GOT A WAYS TO GO.
COCKY. BUT THAT VERY ARRO-GANCE OF YOURS...
...MAKES YOUR GAME PREDICT-ABLE... HEH HEH...

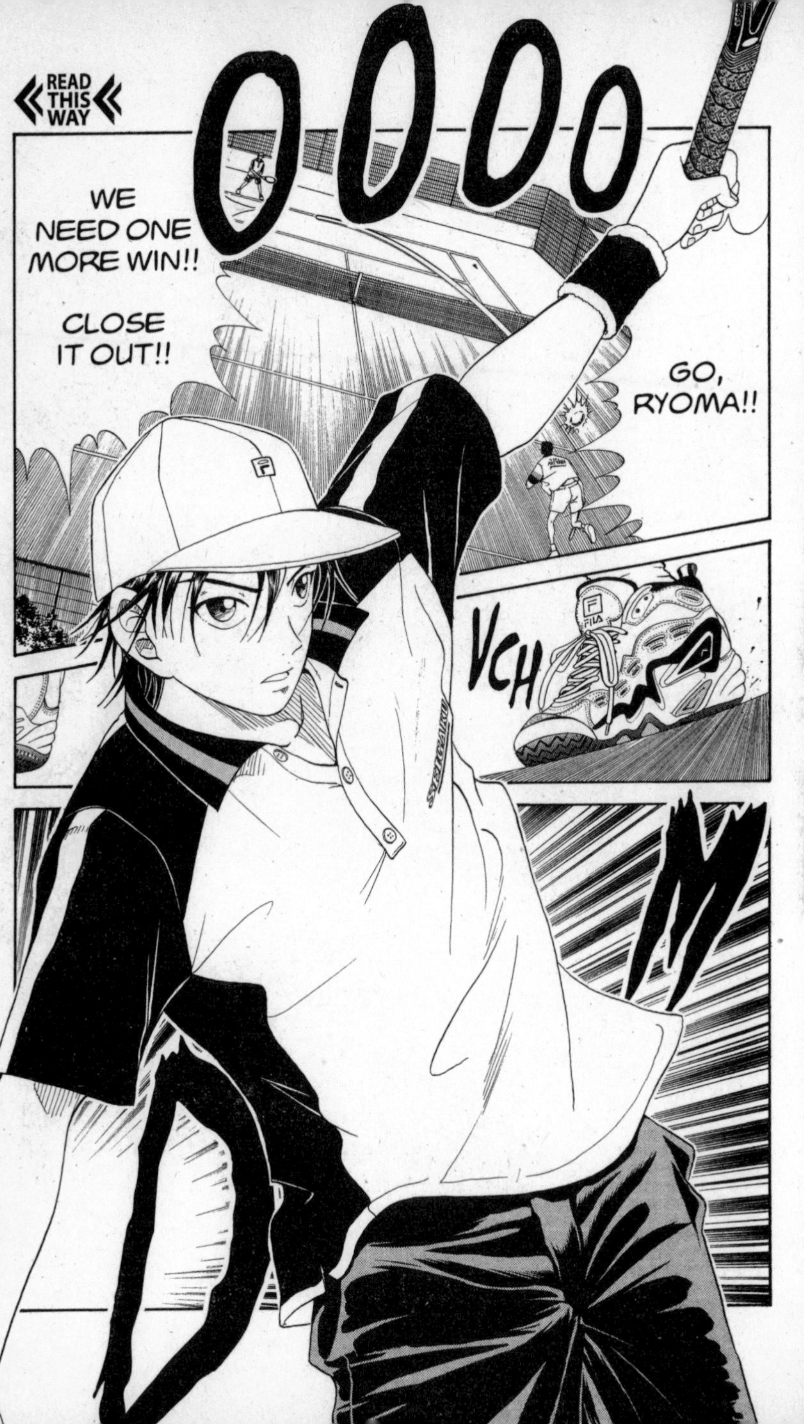
READ THIS WAY
OOOO!
GO, RYOMA!!
WE NEED ONE MORE WIN!!
CLOSE IT OUT!!
VCH

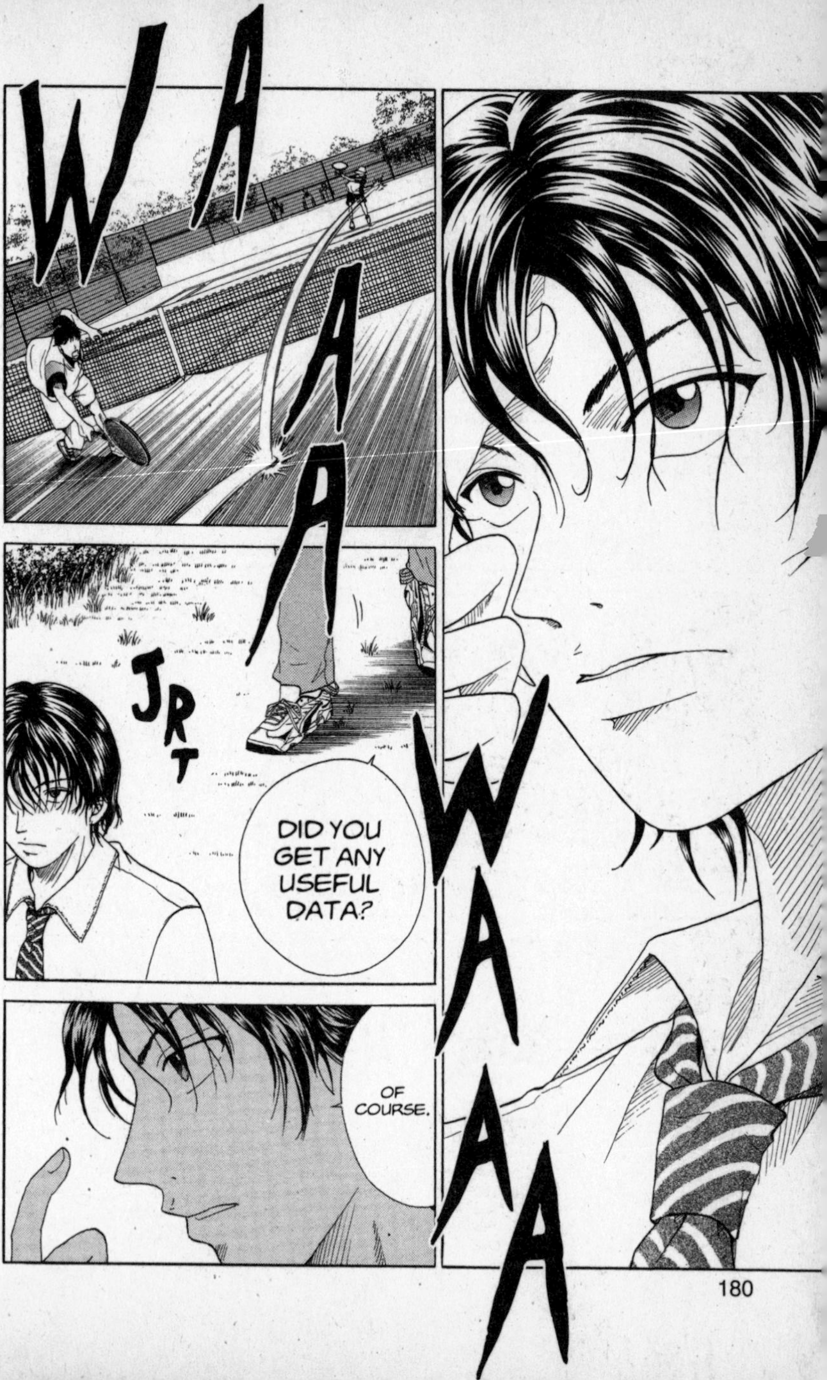
WAAAA
WAAA
JRT
DID YOU GET ANY USEFUL DATA?
OF COURSE.

READ THIS WAY

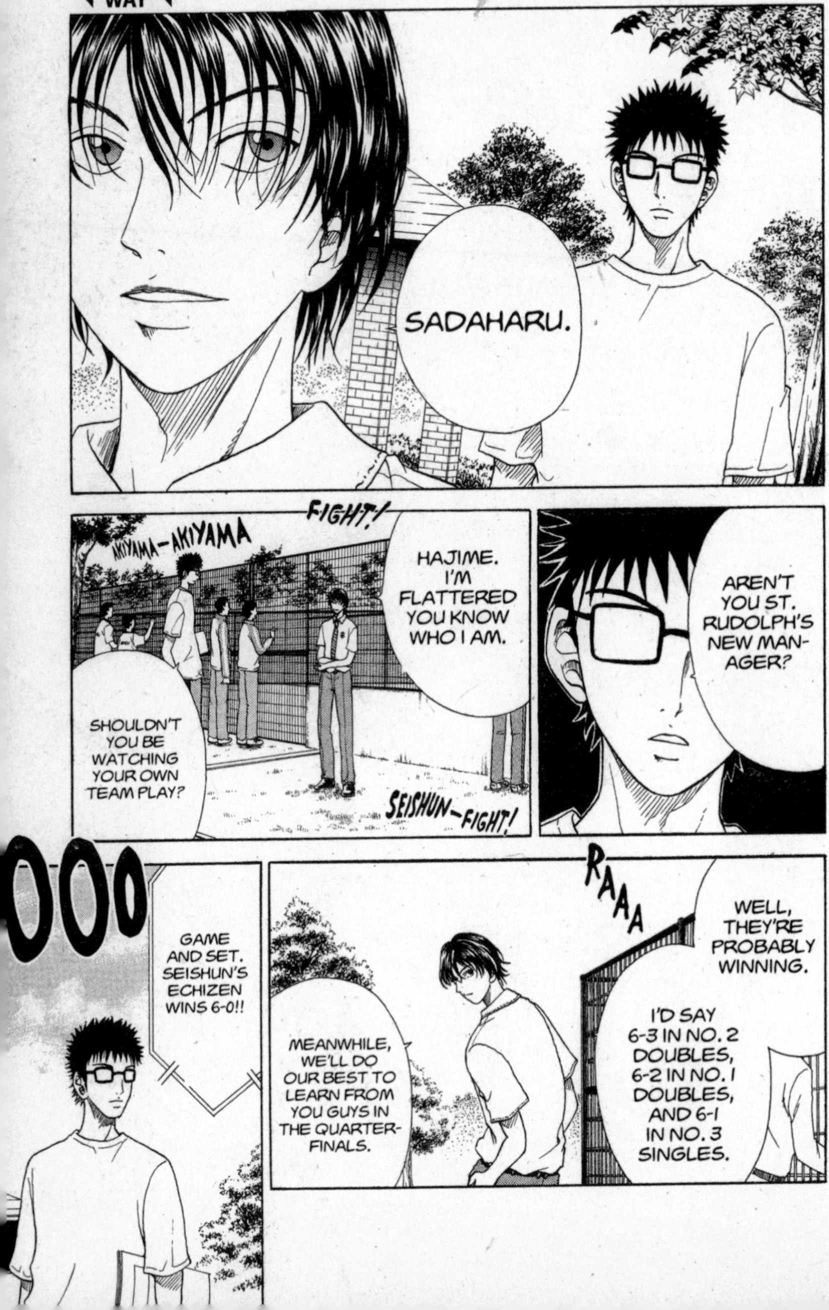
SADAHARU.
AREN'T YOU ST. RUDOLPH'S NEW MANAGER?
FIGHT!
HAJIME. I'M FLATTERED YOU KNOW WHO I AM.
AKIYAMA-AKIYAMA
SHOULDN'T YOU BE WATCHING YOUR OWN TEAM PLAY?
SEISHUN-FIGHT!
RAAA
WELL, THEY'RE PROBABLY WINNING.
I'D SAY 6-3 IN NO. 2 DOUBLES, 6-2 IN NO. 1 DOUBLES, AND 6-1 IN NO. 3 SINGLES.
MEANWHILE, WE'LL DO OUR BEST TO LEARN FROM YOU GUYS IN THE QUARTER-FINALS.
OOO
GAME AND SET. SEISHUN'S ECHIZEN WINS 6-0!!

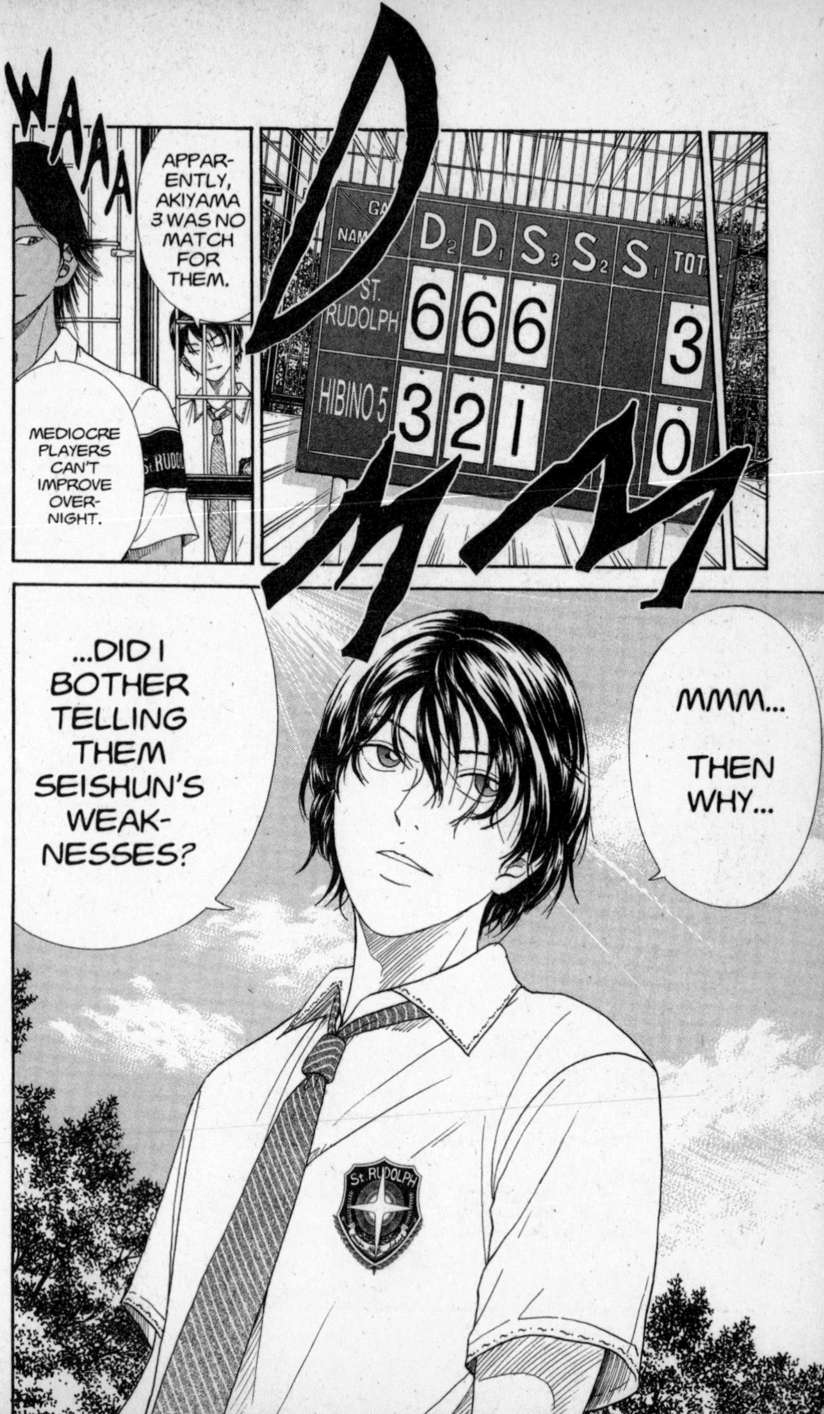
DMM
ST. RUDOLPH 6 6 6 3
HIBINO 5 3 2 1 0
WAAAA
APPARENTLY, AKIYAMA 3 WAS NO MATCH FOR THEM.
MEDIOCRE PLAYERS CAN'T IMPROVE OVERNIGHT.
MMM... THEN WHY...
...DID I BOTHER TELLING THEM SEISHUN'S WEAKNESSES?

READ THIS WAY

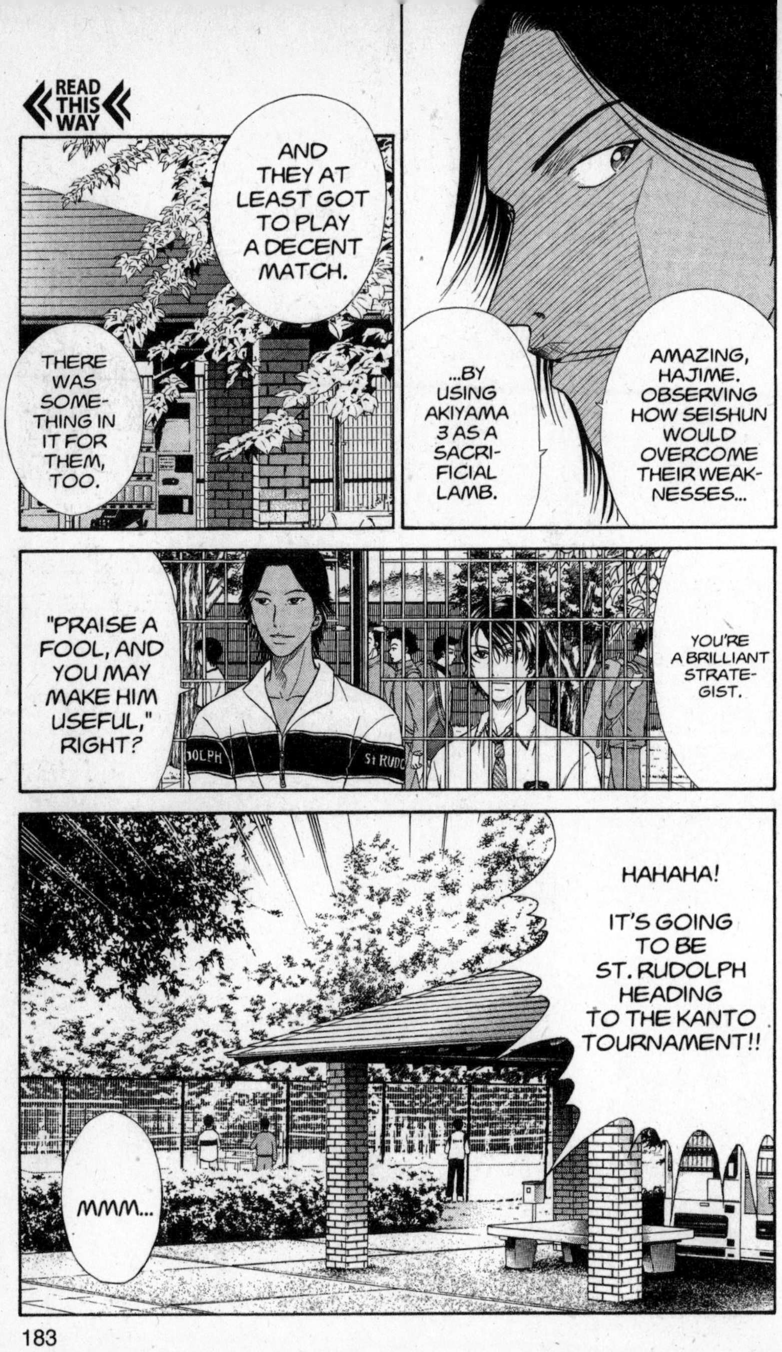
AMAZING, HAJIME. OBSERVING HOW SEISHUN WOULD OVERCOME THEIR WEAKNESSES...
...BY USING AKIYAMA 3 AS A SACRIFICIAL LAMB.
AND THEY AT LEAST GOT TO PLAY A DECENT MATCH.
THERE WAS SOMETHING IN IT FOR THEM, TOO.
YOU'RE A BRILLIANT STRATEGIST.
"PRAISE A FOOL, AND YOU MAY MAKE HIM USEFUL," RIGHT?
HAHAHA!
IT'S GOING TO BE ST. RUDOLPH HEADING TO THE KANTO TOURNAMENT!!
MMM...

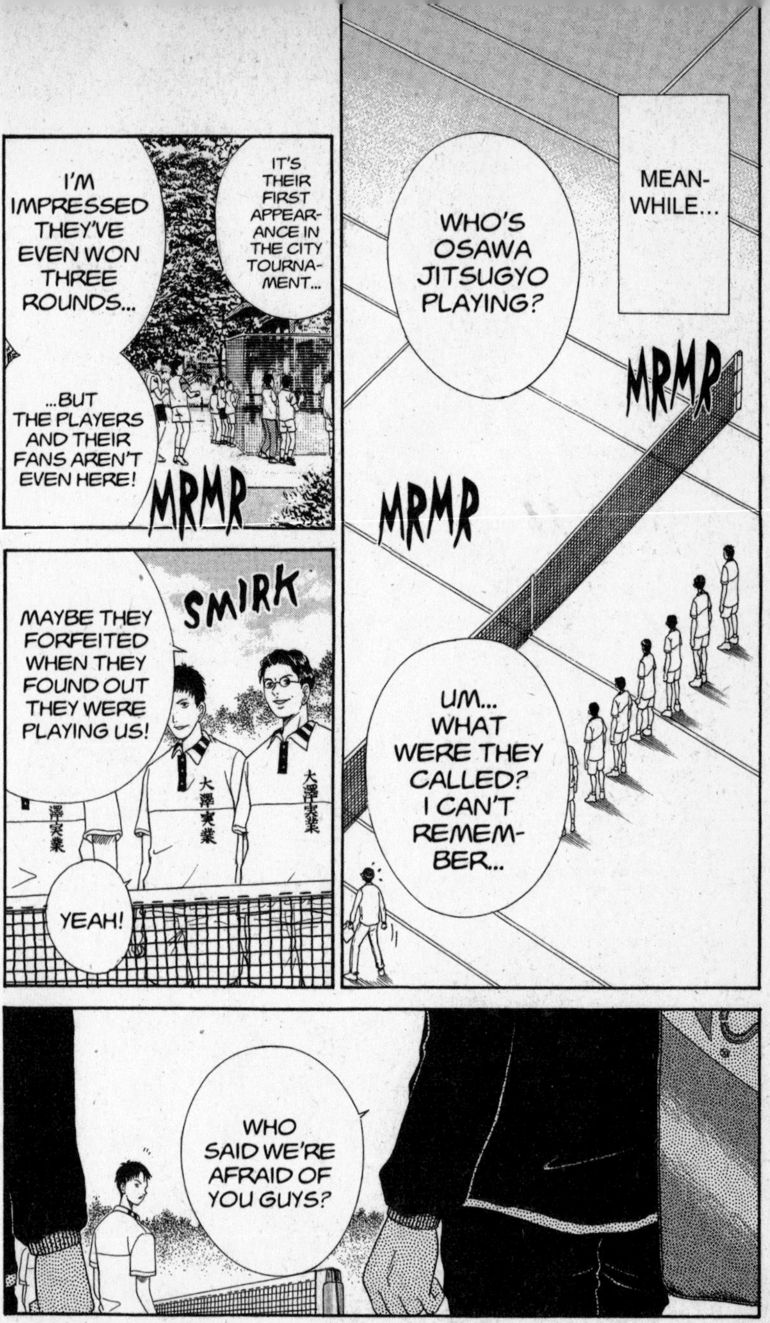
MEAN-WHILE…
WHO'S OSAWA JITSUGYO PLAYING?
MRMR
MRMR
UM... WHAT WERE THEY CALLED? I CAN'T REMEMBER...
IT'S THEIR FIRST APPEARANCE IN THE CITY TOURNAMENT...
I'M IMPRESSED THEY'VE EVEN WON THREE ROUNDS...
...BUT THE PLAYERS AND THEIR FANS AREN'T EVEN HERE!
MRMR
SMIRK
MAYBE THEY FORFEITED WHEN THEY FOUND OUT THEY WERE PLAYING US!
YEAH!
WHO SAID WE'RE AFRAID OF YOU GUYS?

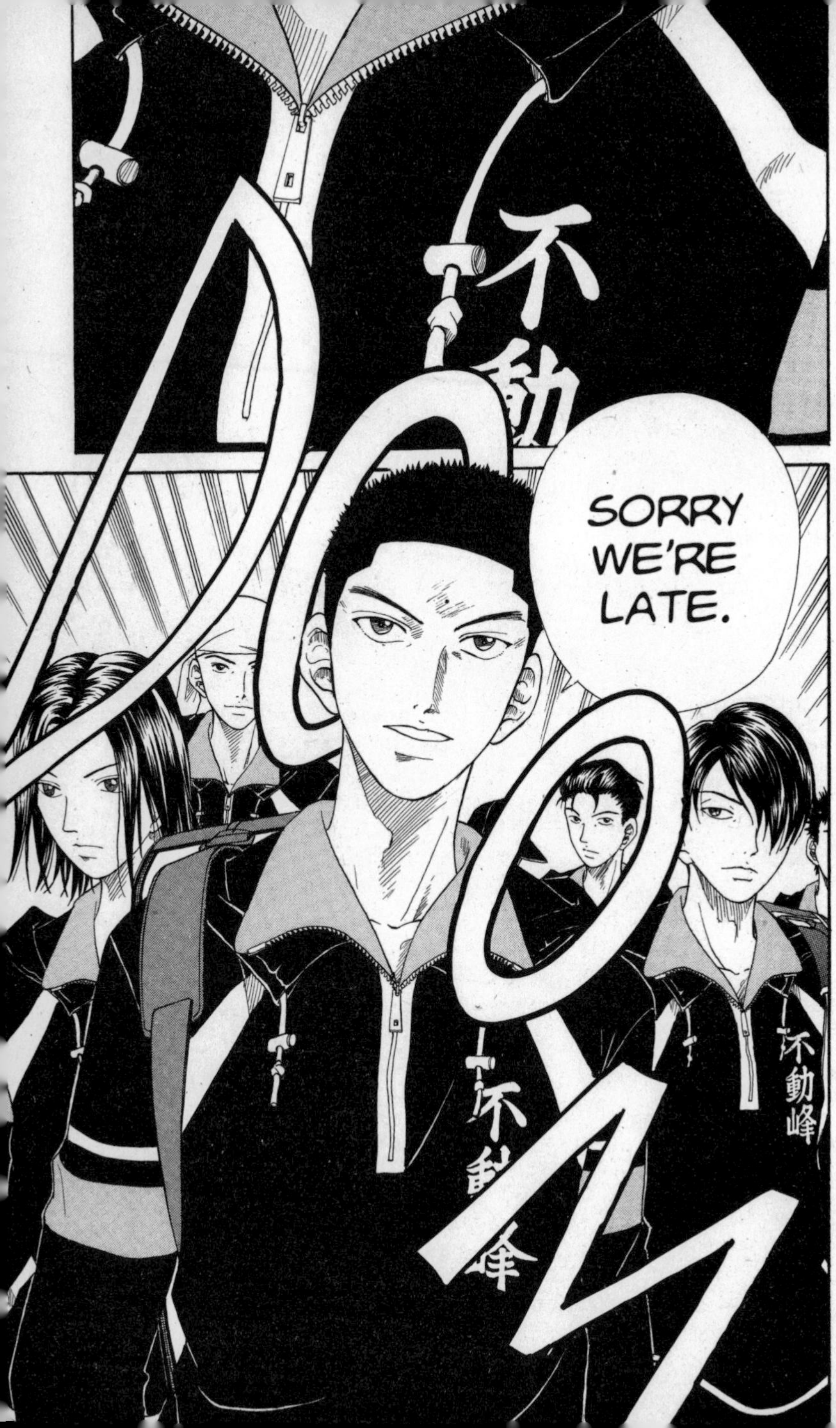
不動
SORRY WE'RE LATE.
不動峰

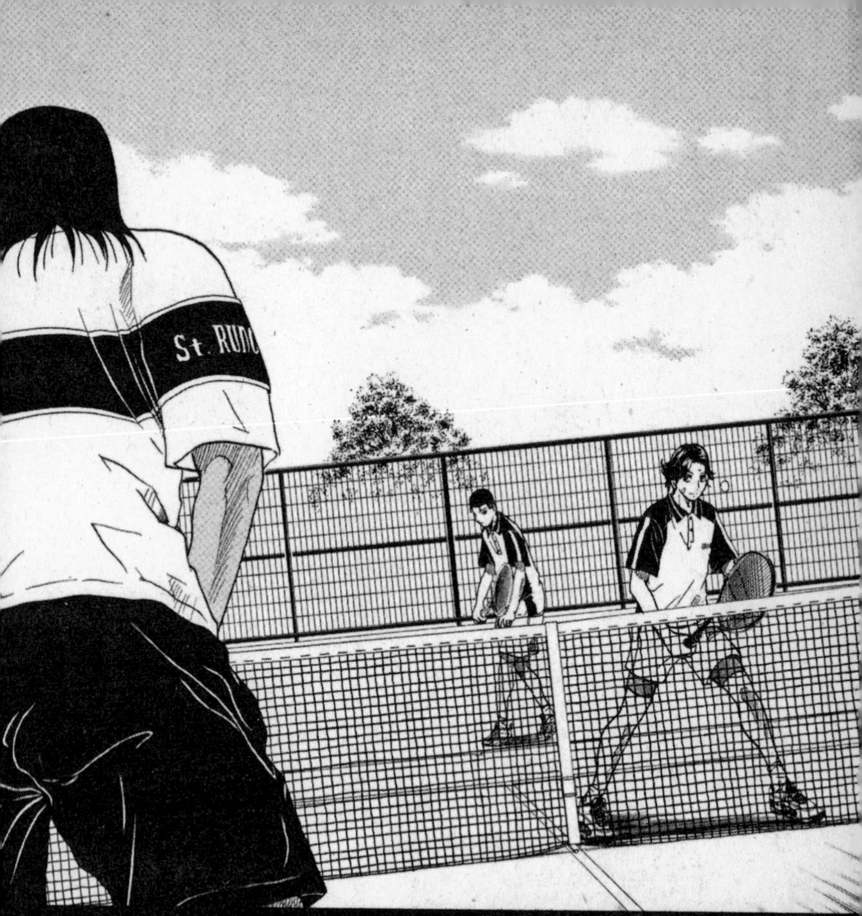

Seishun Academy's Ryoma Echizen tackles Saint Rudolph's "Lefty Killer" Yuta and finds out that it was all part of Hajime's—St. Rudolph's conniving team manager—malicious master plan. Meanwhile, the doubles pair of Eiji and Shuichiro get into the Australian Formation as part of their strategy, but there's no telling if this gutsy move will help them send St. Rudolph's Academy packing.

Available in May 2005

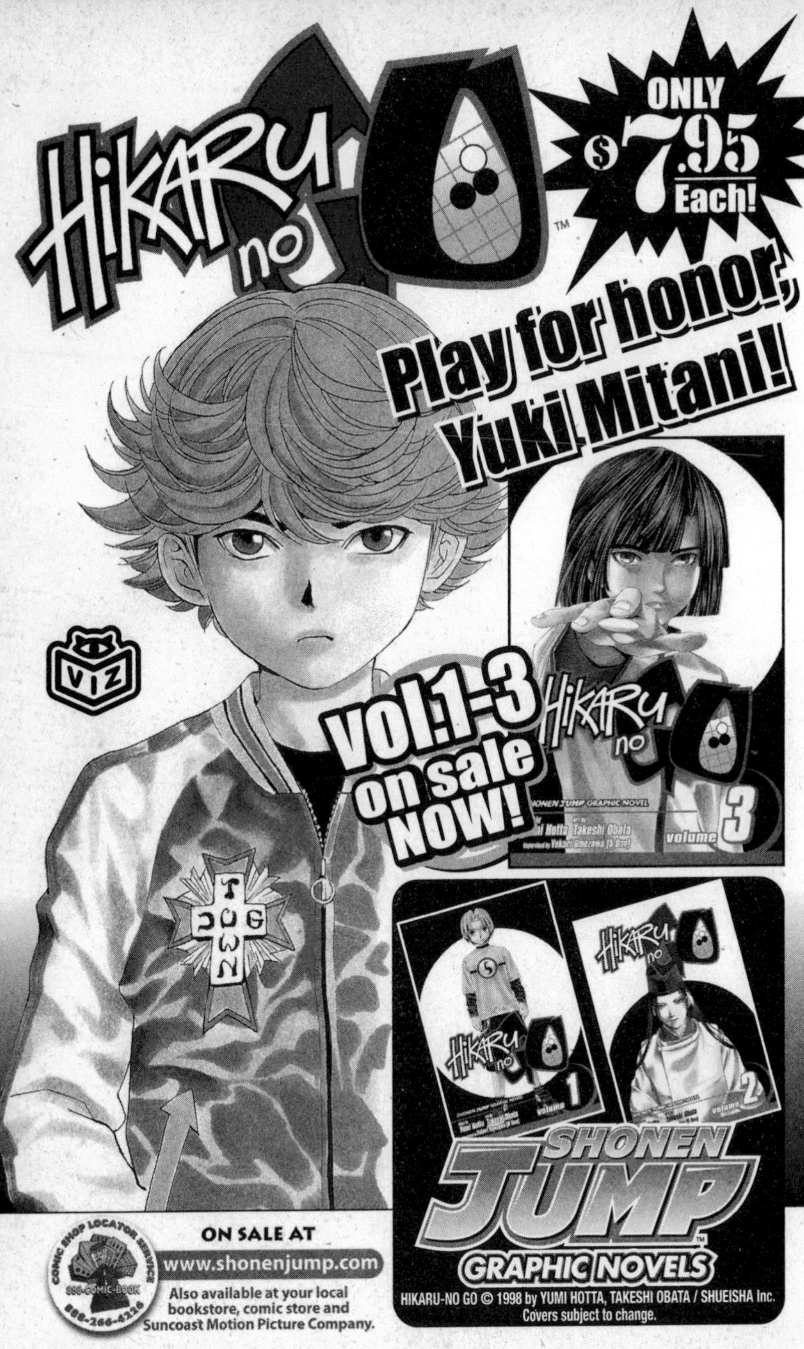
HIKARU no GO™
ONLY $7.95 Each!
Play for honor, Yuki Mitani!
vol.1-3 on sale NOW!
VIZ
SHONEN JUMP
GRAPHIC NOVELS
HIKARU-NO GO © 1998 by YUMI HOTTA, TAKESHI OBATA / SHUEISHA Inc.
Covers subject to change.
COMIC SHOP LOCATOR SERVICE
888-COMIC-BOOK
888-266-4226
ON SALE AT
www.shonenjump.com
Also available at your local bookstore, comic store and Suncoast Motion Picture Company.

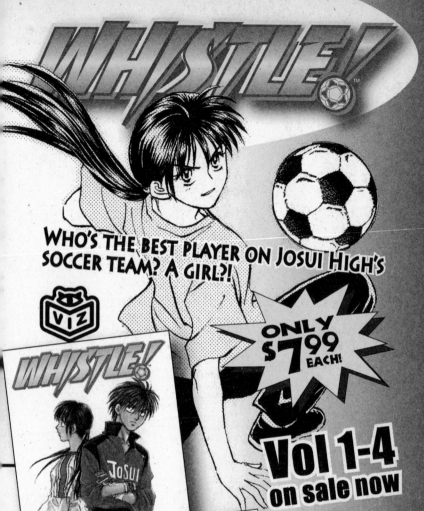

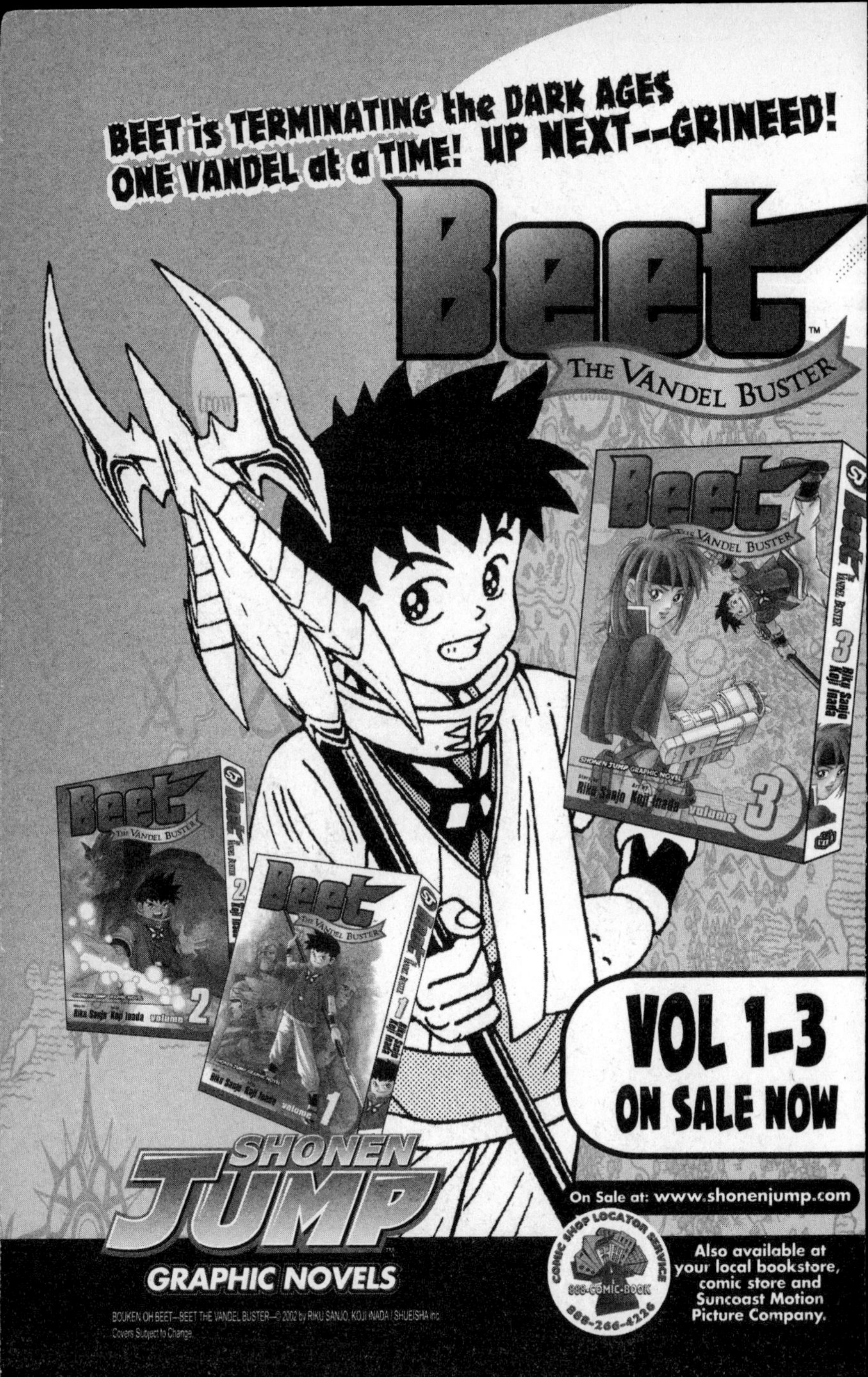
BEET is TERMINATING the DARK AGES ONE VANDEL at a TIME! UP NEXT--GRINEED!
Beet™
THE VANDEL BUSTER
VOL 1-3
ON SALE NOW
SHONEN JUMP
GRAPHIC NOVELS
On Sale at: www.shonenjump.com
COMIC SHOP LOCATOR SERVICE
888-COMIC-BOOK
888-266-4226
Also available at your local bookstore, comic store and Suncoast Motion Picture Company.
BOUKEN OH BEET—BEET THE VANDEL BUSTER—© 2002 by RIKU SANJO, KOJI INADA / SHUEISHA Inc.
Covers Subject to Change.

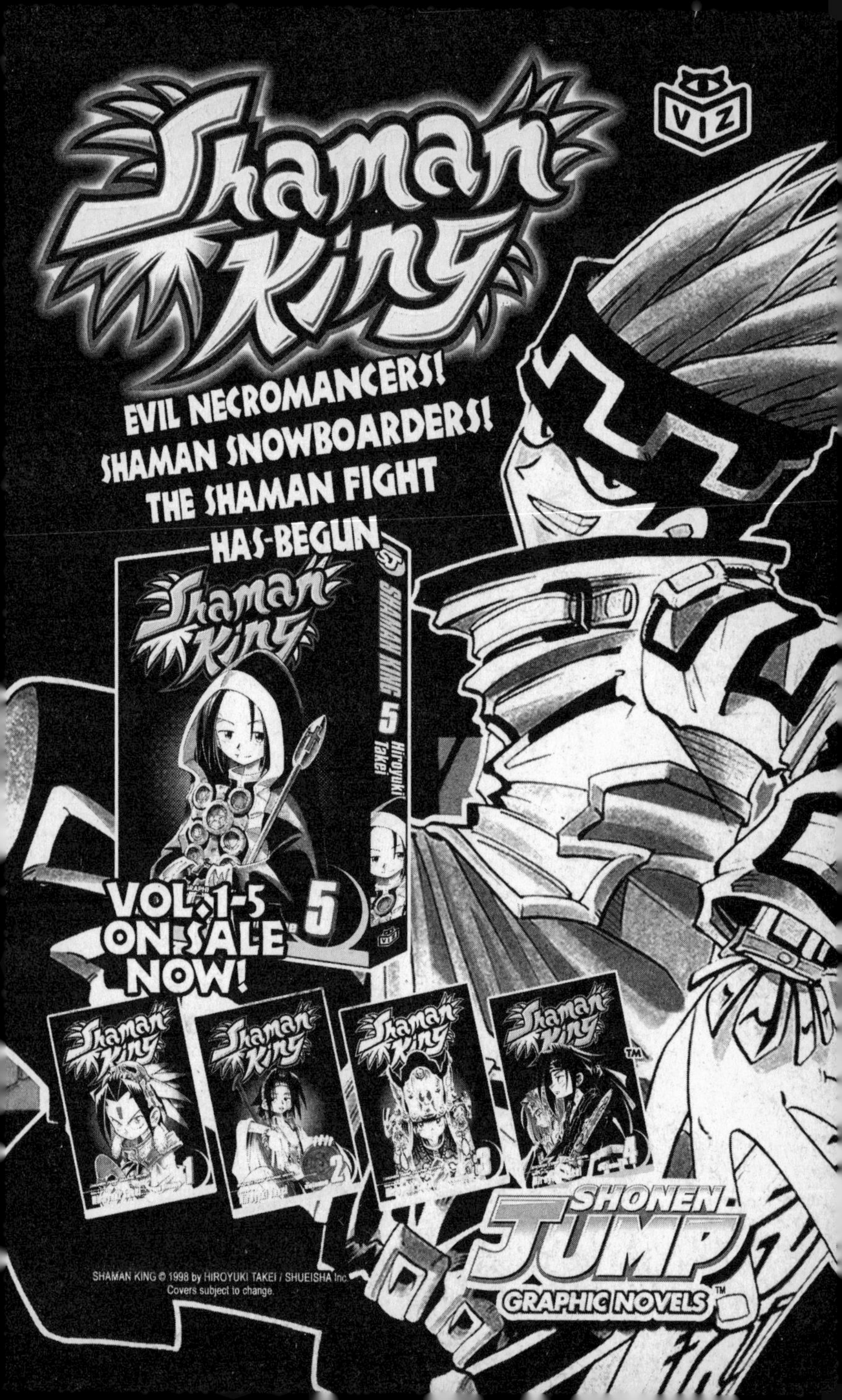
Shaman King
VIZ
EVIL NECROMANCERS!
SHAMAN SNOWBOARDERS!
THE SHAMAN FIGHT
HAS BEGUN
VOL. 1-5
ON SALE
NOW!
SHONEN JUMP
GRAPHIC NOVELS™
SHAMAN KING © 1998 by HIROYUKI TAKEI / SHUEISHA Inc.
Covers subject to change.

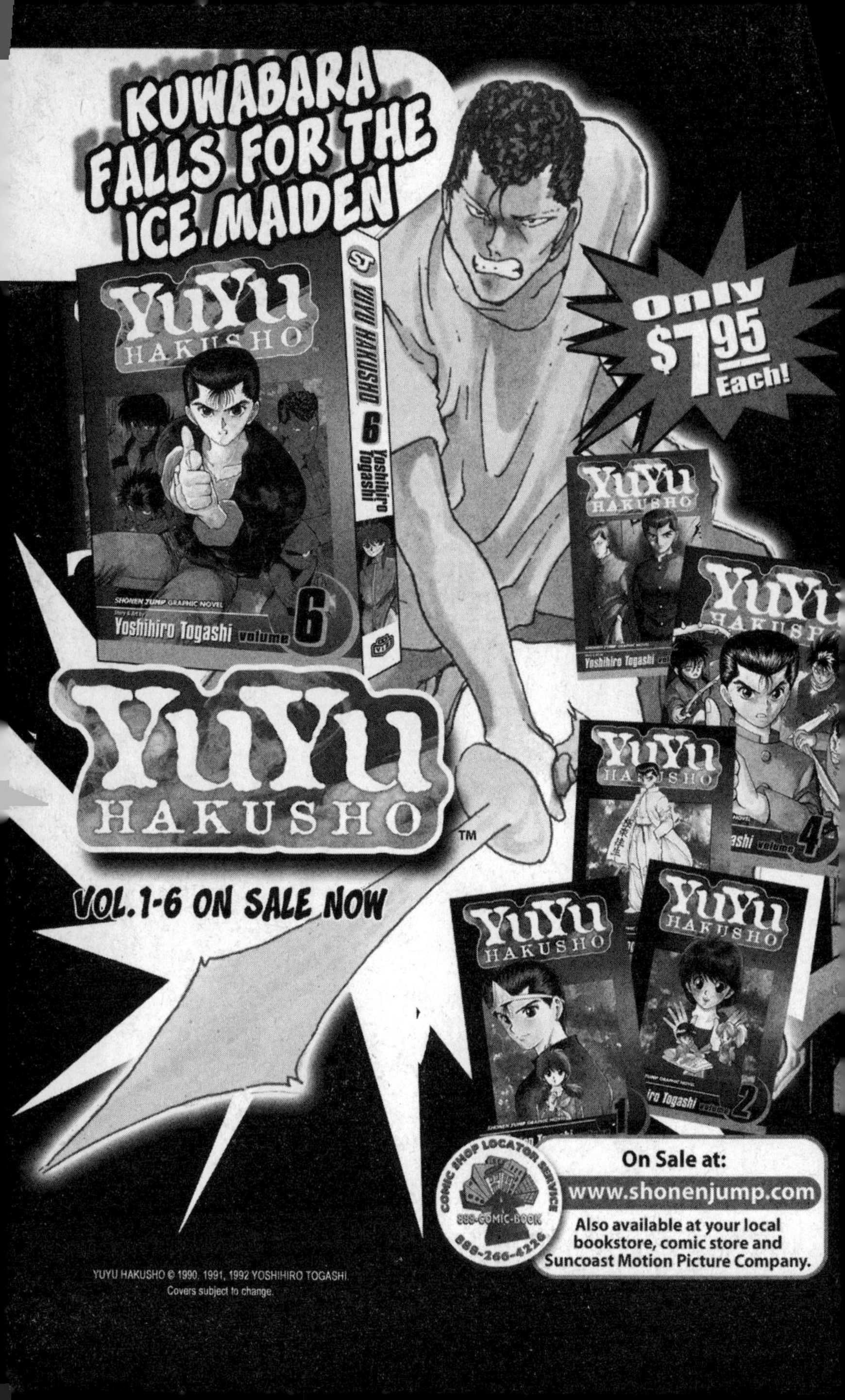
KUWABARA FALLS FOR THE ICE MAIDEN
YUYU HAKUSHO
Only $7.95 Each!
VOL.1-6 ON SALE NOW
On Sale at:
www.shonenjump.com
Also available at your local bookstore, comic store and Suncoast Motion Picture Company.
COMIC SHOP LOCATOR SERVICE
888-COMIC-BOOK
888-266-4226
YUYU HAKUSHO © 1990, 1991, 1992 YOSHIHIRO TOGASHI.
Covers subject to change.

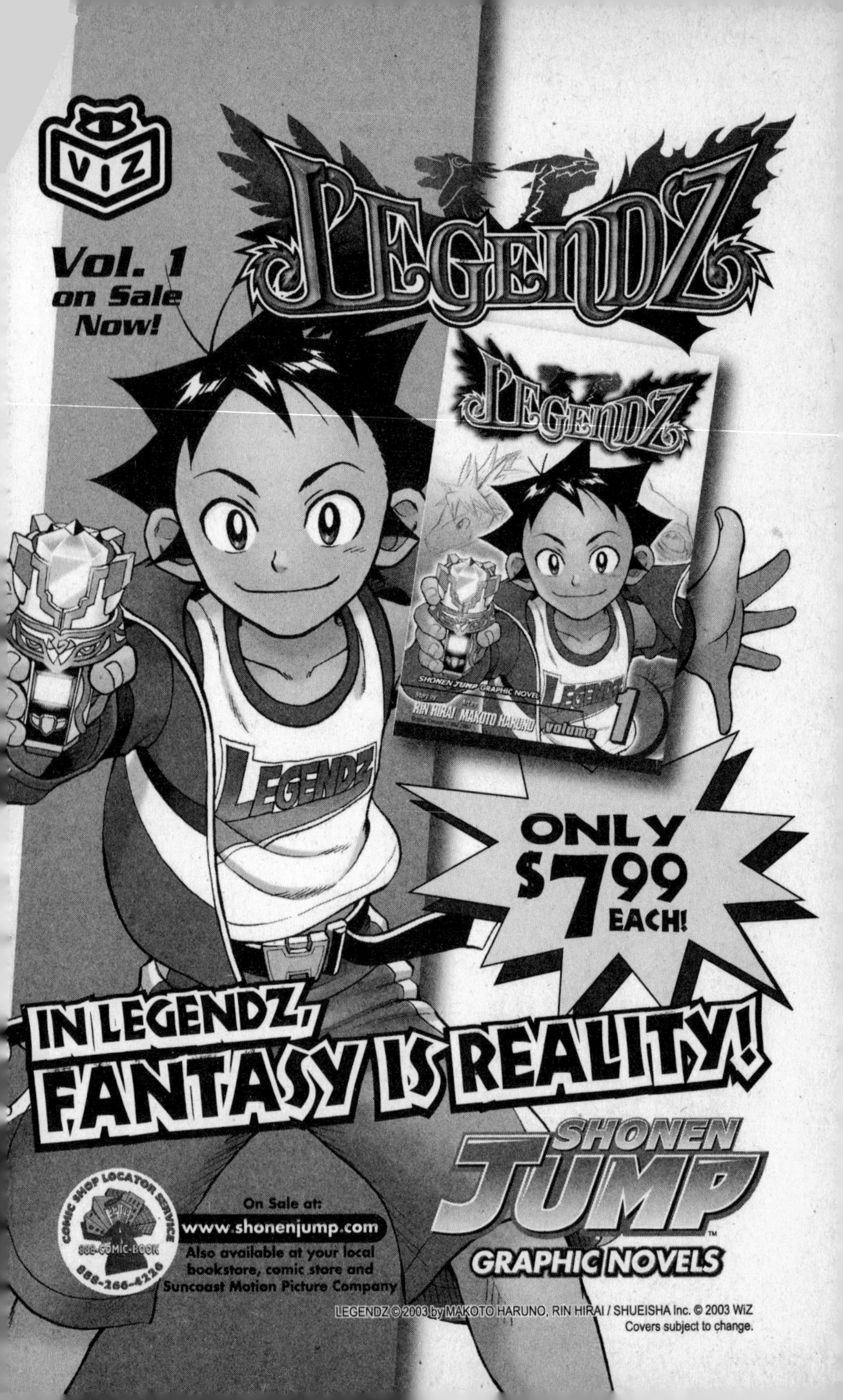
VIZ
Vol. 1 on Sale Now!
LEGENDZ
LEGENDZ
SHONEN JUMP GRAPHIC NOVEL
RIN HIRAI
MAKOTO HARUNO
LEGENDZ volume 1
LEGENDZ
ONLY $7.99 EACH!
IN LEGENDZ, FANTASY IS REALITY!
SHONEN JUMP™
GRAPHIC NOVELS
COMIC SHOP LOCATOR SERVICE
888-COMIC-BOOK
888-266-4226
On Sale at:
www.shonenjump.com
Also available at your local bookstore, comic store and Suncoast Motion Picture Company
LEGENDZ © 2003 by MAKOTO HARUNO, RIN HIRAI / SHUEISHA Inc. © 2003 WiZ
Covers subject to change.